Elderly Client Handbook

Third edition

Other handbooks by Law Society Publishing:

Conveyancing Handbook (10th edition)
General Editor: Frances Silverman
1 85328 847 0

Data Protection Handbook (June 2004)
General Editor: Peter Carey
1 85328 940 X

Employment Law Handbook (2nd edition)
Daniel Barnett and Henry Scrope
1 85328 970 1

Environmental Law Handbook (5th edition)
Trevor Hellawell
1 85328 891 8

Probate Practitioner's Handbook (4th edition)
General Editor: Lesley King
1 85328 831 4

Titles from Law Society Publishing can be ordered from all good bookshops or direct from our distributors, Marston Book Services (tel. 01235 465656 or email law.society@marston.co.uk).

For further information or a catalogue, email publishing@lawsociety.org.uk.

ELDERLY CLIENT HANDBOOK

Third edition

Consultant Editor:

Gordon R. Ashton

General Editors:

Caroline Bielanska and Martin Terrell

Published in association with Solicitors for the Elderly

The Law Society

© Gordon R. Ashton and the Law Society 2004

ISBN 1 85328 872 1

First edition published in 1994
Second edition published in 2000

This third edition published in 2004 by the Law Society
113 Chancery Lane, London WC2A 1PL

Crown copyright material is reproduced with the permission of the Controller of Her Majesty's Stationery Office

Typeset by J&L Composition, Filey, North Yorkshire
Printed by Antony Rowe Ltd, Chippenham, Wilts

Contents

3   The elderly client practice   **45**
Jennifer Margrave and Martin Terrell

4   Managing the affairs of the elderly   **81**
Martin Terrell

5   Legal proceedings   **121**
David Rees

APPENDICES

Foreword to the third edition

The seed for this Handbook was sown at the Law Society's National Conference in Birmingham on 22 October 1992, when I gave a lecture entitled 'Providing a service for elderly clients'. I then commented that the existence of elderly (or disabled) people as a client group was not recognised by our profession and that we talk of criminal or matrimonial practices so why not elderly practices? By way of encouragement to younger lawyers, I added that partners in criminal or matrimonial practices are not criminals or divorced, so you do not need to be elderly to run an elderly client practice. In retrospect my approach was deficient in that it concentrated upon mental incapacity and financial arrangements: there was no mention of personal welfare decision-making, or essential services such as community or health care.

Having commenced writing the Handbook soon after this conference, I was encouraged and assisted by colleagues on the Mental Health and Disability Committee of the Law Society. It would be remiss of me not to mention their contributions. Denzil Lush and Lydia Sinclair (both of the committee), Ann Edis (Palmer Wheeldon), Angela Donen (Bryan & Armstrong), Anthea Grainger (Darlington & Parkinson) and Sarah Hobbs (Tyndallwoods & Millichip) kindly took the trouble to read the text in draft form and made helpful suggestions. Nigel Hodkinson (Hodkinsons), Luke Clements (Thorpes) and Bryan Wordsworth (Eastleys) considered parts of the text and tried to ensure that my material bore a reasonable resemblance to the present state of the law. Penny Letts, secretary of the Committee and herself an author on this subject, co-ordinated these and other contributions and supported me from the inception to the conclusion of the work. Evelyn McEwen of Age Concern England (also a member of the committee) co-ordinated the support of Age Concern, whose practical experience in this field is unrivalled. Denzil is now Master of the Court of Protection, but sadly Lydia and Evelyn are no longer with us.

Anne Edis, who became Chair of Solicitors for the Elderly, collaborated with me on the second edition which I then stated must be my final contribution. My own energies are now devoted to encouraging judges to recognise and address the needs of litigants and witnesses who are vulnerable by reason of age or mental and physical disabilities.

In his foreword to the first edition in March 1994, David Keating, Chair of the Mental Health and Disability Committee, referred to the 'marked increase in the number of people who live well beyond normal retirement age' and identified older people as 'one large and conspicuous client group which so far has not been singled out by the legal profession as representing an area of special interest'. In the foreword to the second edition published some six years later, Michael Napier, a vice-president of the Law Society (and himself a former chairman of the committee), stated: 'By making their services more relevant to older people's needs, by using their "ingenuity" to help older people to protect their interests and solve their legal (sometimes social or health) problems, solicitors can develop a thriving elderly client practice to play a part in recognising and respecting the value of old age.'

Although I was seeking to identify older people in society as a discrete client group for whom the legal profession should provide a comprehensive service, little did I foresee the progress that would be achieved over the next decade. The elderly client practice is now recognised, more books have been written for practitioners (not merely my own) and university courses cover the subject. Solicitors for the Elderly has also been formed and takes over the updating of this Handbook for the third edition, hopefully ensuring that it continues into old age. The perceived unmet need has become a reality, the breadth of that need is increasing and this further edition of the Handbook should go some way towards assisting the legal profession to tackle its important role.

District Judge Gordon R. Ashton
Deputy Master of the Court of Protection
January 2004

Notes on contributors

Julia Abrey is a solicitor, a principal of Withers LLP in London and co-chair of Solicitors for the Elderly. She is a member of STEP, the editorial board of *Elderly Client Adviser*, consultant editor of *Tolley's Finance and Law for the Older Client*, and a contributor to *Practical Will Precedents* (Sweet & Maxwell) and *Encyclopaedia of Forms and Precedents* (LexisNexis).

Gordon R. Ashton is a district judge and Deputy Master of the Court of Protection. He is a former practising solicitor and author of *Elderly People and the Law* (LexisNexis) and general editor of *Butterworths Older Client Service*.

Caroline Bielanska is a solicitor, lecturer and freelance consultant, and co-chair of Solicitors for the Elderly. She is a regular contributor to the *Elderly Client Adviser* and a member of its editorial board, and technical editor of *Coldrick on Personal Injury Trusts* (ARK publishing, 2002).

Alison Callcott is a solicitor at Douglas & Partners. She has specialised in criminal and mental health law since 1987, for several years in London as a freelance solicitor advocate and in private practice since 1998. She sits as a president of the Mental Health Review Tribunal and has taught criminal advocacy to trainee solicitors at the University of Northumbria for many years.

Caroline Coats is a solicitor, lecturer and writer with over 15 years' experience in private client work. Specialising in the legal issues of most concern to the elderly and disabled, she set up her own practice in 2003 and is currently training to be a notary public. She is a member of STEP, a regional co-ordinator for Solicitors for the Elderly and a Public Guardianship Office panel receiver.

David Foster is a partner at Fisher Meredith in London where he was appointed head of the housing department in 1998. After graduating in Law from Exeter College, Oxford in 1974 he spent several years specialising in housing and social welfare law, before jointly setting up a private Legal Aid practice in Canning Town. David was a founder member of the Housing Law Practitioners Association, and was the first Law Society

Council Member for Housing Law and is now also a member of its Housing Law Committee.

Amanda King-Jones has been a partner of Thomas Eggar since 1987 specialising in wills, personal tax planning, probate, trusts and the affairs of the elderly. She is instructed as a professional witness for probate related matters and is co-author of the *Probate Practice Manual* (Sweet & Maxwell). She is a member of the Public Guardianship Office Panel, STEP and Solicitors for the Elderly.

Penny Letts is a freelance policy consultant and trainer, and from 1987–2001 was the Law Society's policy adviser on mental health and disability. She is a member of the Mental Health Act Commission and of the Council on Tribunals, and was recently Specialist Adviser to the Joint Select Committee on the Draft Mental Incapacity Bill. She is managing editor and co-author of the revised Law Society/BMA guidance for doctors and lawyers, *Assessment of Mental Capacity.*

Jennifer Margrave was a journalist before training as a solicitor. She was a partner in a private client firm before setting up her own practice in 1995 specifically to advise the elderly. She is a member of STEP and joint vice-chair of Solicitors for the Elderly. She regulars lectures and gives workshops on elderly client subjects as well as writing articles for legal journals.

David Rees is a barrister at 5 Stone Buildings, Lincoln's Inn. His practice covers a range of Chancery work with a particular emphasis on trusts, estates and capital tax planning. He frequently appears in the Court of Protection (including the leading case of *Re W* ([2000] Ch 343 and [2001] Ch 609 about registration of enduring powers of attorney) and is a contributor to *Heywood & Massey's Court of Protection Practice* (Sweet & Maxwell). He is regularly instructed by the Official Solicitor to represent patients and children in various types of litigation. In 2002–2003 he was a member of the Lord Chancellor's Department working group set up to review the operation of enduring powers of attorney.

Henry Scrope specialises in employment law. He worked for many years in the City both in practice and as an in-house lawyer. He is co-author of the Law Society's *Employment Law Handbook* and is mainly responsible for the leading employment website at www.emplaw.co.uk.

Joanna Sulek is qualified as a barrister and has worked as a member of Mind's Legal Unit since 1995, where she has contributed extensively to training and publications on mental health and related areas of law.

Martin Terrell is a partner in the firm of Rix & Kay and a joint vice-chair of Solicitors for the Elderly. He is author of *A Practitioner's Guide to the Court of Protection* (Lexis Nexis, 2002) and a regular contributor to *Heywood & Massey's Court of Protection Practice* (Sweet & Maxwell), *Tolley's Finance and Law for the Older Client, Butterworths Older Client Service* and *Elderly Client Adviser.*

Abbreviations

AA	attendance allowance
AP	authorised party
ASW	Approved Social Worker
ATP	authorised third party
AVC	additional voluntary contribution
CGT	capital gains tax
CPR	Civil Procedure Rules 1998, SI 1998/3132
CHAI	Commission for Healthcare Audit and Inspection
CSCI	Commission for Social Care Inspection
CSIW	Care Standards Inspectorate for Wales
DDA	Disability Discrimination Act 1995
DLA	disability living allowance
DPB	designated professional body
DWP	Department of Work and Pensions
EPA	Enduring Power of Attorney
EPAA	Enduring Powers of Attorney Act 1985
FSA	Financial Services Authority
ICA	invalid care allowance
IFA	independent financial adviser
IHT	inheritance tax
LHB	local health board
LPA	Lasting Power of Attorney
LQPM	legally qualified panel member
NCSC	National Care Standards Commission
PC	pension credit
PCT	Primary Care Trust
PGO	Public Guardianship Office
RAO	Financial Services and Markets Act (Regulated Activities) Order 2001, SI 2001/544
SDA	severe disablement allowance
SSD	social services department

Table of cases

Table of statutes

Table of statutory instruments

Introduction: the elderly client

Martin Terrell and Caroline Bielanska

There is no universal definition of 'the elderly client' and it may seem inappropriate to define clients according to their age. After all, elderly clients are in most respects no different from any other clients who have legal requirements which they expect their solicitor to deal with. They buy houses, make wills, get married or divorced and have accidents in the same way as people in their 30s. However, we all get older and cannot always avoid the particular problems that come with old age. Conventional legal issues may need to be dealt with in a slightly different way, taking account of our changing needs and circumstances. And then there is a whole new world of laws, regulations and benefits that most of us live in happy ignorance of for as long as possible, as no one willingly becomes a patient of the Court of Protection or claims attendance allowance.

What this books sets out to do is to bring together conventional and specialist areas of law which are relevant and particular to the elderly client so that the law centres on the client rather than the other way around. By placing the needs of the elderly client first, we appear to create a new area of client-based law, and 'elderly client law' has become an increasingly recognised specialism. Paradoxically, it is a specialism that is very broad and reflects a very traditional aspect of the solicitor's role, where the solicitor looks after the whole range of a client's needs.

It is the breadth of the subject that brings its own problems, especially in an area where we cannot be both generalists and specialists. Our own experience comes from the conventional area of wills and probate. With a large number of elderly clients, this has extended to dealing with Enduring Powers of Attorney and receiverships. As time has gone on, those elderly clients have needed advice on their welfare benefits, care needs, housing needs, litigation, contracts, employment, insurance and a host of other seemingly unconnected problems. This is not an uncommon experience, and it has therefore been a privilege to contribute to a book that attempts to bring all these aspects of a client's needs into one comprehensive work. However, no one can be both a specialist and a generalist and this work cannot likewise pretend to both characteristics. It aims to provide a general overview of the law and practice particular to the needs of the elderly client. Where their own areas of expertise are covered, a brief summary is always useful to hard-pressed practitioners, and for those working outside such areas, there needs to be an easy introduction. In both cases practical reminders, tips and signposts to more detailed support and knowledge are always valuable.

The danger of modern practice is that as we become more specialised we lose the language of other areas of law. In dealing with the elderly client, we often need the skill of the generalist, who is conversant but not necessarily fluent in languages other than his own. We often need to guide the client into other areas and need to know when we need translators and when we need to hand over to someone more fluent. Sometimes the client will move from one specialist to another but at other times the client still needs the same person to act as guide and advocate. As attorneys and receivers, solicitors become clients themselves, for instance when dealing with conveyancing and litigation. Other specialists need the same skills to look beyond their own territories. Conveyancers and litigators need to be conversant with Enduring Powers of Attorney and the Court of Protection, persons under disability, presumptions of capacity and undue influence, for they too are acting for the same clients.

That elderly client law has become a recognised area of law is due to the hard work over the last decade of four individuals: Gordon Ashton, Denzil Lush, Anne Edis and Margaret Richards. It was Gordon Ashton who wrote the first edition of this book and revised the second edition with Anne Edis and they have generously allowed the use of their material in this work. Gordon Ashton has gone on to write and edit numerous books and periodicals while working as a District Judge and more recently an Assistant Master of the Court of Protection. Denzil Lush has been solicitor, author, lecturer and now Master of the Court of Protection. They have all been instrumental in creating and supporting Solicitors for the Elderly, in conjunction with which this work is being published.

The work of Solicitors for the Elderly and the criteria for and advantages of membership are set out in more detail in Appendix D. That there is a need for this organisation is without doubt. To begin with there is a shortage of 'new blood' coming into what are perceived to be the more traditional areas of legal practice. It takes time to discover how interesting and rewarding it can be to deal with the vagaries of human nature when legal advice is at its most necessary. For most people, for the majority of their lives, going to a solicitor is a rare and involuntary experience. But as their needs increase, competent, professional and practical advice may be all that stands between protection and abuse. And there is no doubt that such needs are increasing.

In 2002 there were nearly 11 million people over the age of 65 years in the United Kingdom (some 18 per cent of the population) and both the numbers and proportion have steadily increased over the last 25 years. The change in the population structure is even more pronounced in those over 85 years of age, whose numbers had doubled to over 1.24 million (1.9 per cent of the population) in that period, with roughly 75 per cent being women. In 1996, there were over 5,000 people over 100. It is estimated that by 2036 that number will have increased to 39,000. It is estimated that one person in five will at some stage suffer from dementia or require nursing care. Approximately 10,000 applications are made each year to register Enduring Powers of Attorney and the Public Guardianship Office oversees over 20,000 receivership cases at any one time.

The same area of law also extends to younger disabled people whose needs may be different but to whom the same legal principles are applied. The Court of Protection has, for instance, noted a large increase in the number of younger patients, often the victims of road traffic accidents or medical negligence. In many such cases substantial sums of money are involved which need to be used carefully to maximise a person's quality of life over several decades.

There is therefore no shortage of clients or potential clients! But it is not just numbers, but the needs of those clients which are ever increasing. We live in a society which is increasingly complex, bureaucratic, litigious and demanding. New regulations and targets pour out of government departments ever anxious to please the electorate and restrain the pressures on public expenditure. Families meanwhile become smaller and more fragmented, with fewer elderly people being able to take the nearby assistance of their family for granted. Divorce and remarriage brings its own problems for elderly clients and their children. At the same time, many older clients have benefited from rising property prices over the last two decades. In many parts of the country, what the client sees as a modest retirement bungalow or a small terraced house is well over the inheritance tax threshold. This apparent wealth brings its own problems. How does the older client who wants to go on living in his own home utilise that wealth if the asset cannot be realised? How important is it to protect the asset against inheritance tax and care costs for the benefit of the next generation?

The problem for the elderly client adviser is to take account of a host of legal and practical issues in providing apparently simple advice. The client may only want a simple will and yet this alone involves looking at the value of the estate, the nature of the client's assets, the effects of care costs and inheritance tax, family relationships, lifetime gifts – and that is before addressing issues of capacity, undue influence, the client's life expectancy and arranging execution of the will. It is this that brings the greatest difficulty. In looking at developments in case law since the last edition of this work was published in March 2000, we have been struck by the number of high profile cases that involve issues of capacity, undue influence and the role of solicitors. In our own recent experience we came across the manager of a well-regarded nursing home who obtained Enduring Powers of Attorney from a local solicitor (who never saw the clients for himself) and as attorney for over a dozen elderly residents defrauded them of several hundred thousand pounds. Eventually he was convicted, but not on all counts, as the victims of his fraud were mentally incapable of understanding what had happened, let alone providing evidence.

In coming across such cases, it is easy to be wise with hindsight and assume that if we are the type of person who reads this book, it is very unlikely that these problems will arise in our own practices. Unfortunately, no one can afford to be complacent. Our professional obligations – as well as our moral responsibilities – to our elderly clients are increasing all the time. The simplest instruction needs to encompass so many different considerations. Can we do justice to all of them without making our lives intolerable and putting off our clients with endless questionnaires, interviews, detailed reports containing pages of disclaimers and enormous fees to pay for this? The aim of this book is to show that a conscientious and competent solicitor can serve our profession efficiently provided he or she works in the same spirit. Thus he or she will need a wide-ranging knowledge of the issues affecting the elderly client, an awareness of when more detailed information is required and where to find it, an understanding of professional and ethical guidance, an ability to apply up-to-date risk analysis with a traditional concern for the client's welfare and best interests, as well as a fair amount of common sense.

To achieve this end, we have tried to set this work out in a logical sequence. Part A looks at the elderly client and the law, starting with the fundamental issue of capacity and covering the legal framework for management of property and affairs, litigation, practical issues concerning the elderly client and running an elderly client practice. Part B looks at welfare and treatment including the very topical areas of hospital discharge and consent to treatment. Part C deals with financial affairs in more detail, covering issues such as welfare benefits, local authority funding, employment and housing. Part D then deals with inheritance and death. The work is not intended to be exhaustive and statutes, case digests and precedents are better served by specialist texts. The appendices do, however, provide a comprehensive list of contacts, websites and other resources. The draft Mental Incapacity Bill is set out in full not just because it is topical but because its definitions of best practice and capacity are already being used by lawyers as well as by the courts. We have also included the Law Society's two sets of guidelines on Enduring Powers of Attorney and Gifts. These are essential reading for any practitioner in this area of law and will be used in evidence against us if anything goes wrong. The Guidelines, as with the rest of this work, are designed to ensure that things do not go wrong for us, or for our clients.

In preparing this work we must record a profound debt to Gordon Ashton for creating the title and the concept. Some of his work, as well as Anne Edis' work on the second edition, has been used by contributors, especially in those few areas where there have been few changes in the law and it has proved difficult to improve an excellent text. The contributors, who are all busy practitioners themselves, have produced excellent material at short notice and all deserve praise for their efforts. For each of us and for each contributor there are spouses, children, partners and secretaries who have suffered while we disappeared to our computers and littered our surroundings with papers.

The law is as stated on 1 January 2004.

PART A

The legal framework

CHAPTER 1

Capacity

Penny Letts

1.1 THE IMPORTANCE OF DETERMINING CAPACITY

It is a key principle of the law that every adult has the right to make his or her own decisions and is assumed to have the capacity (ability) to do so unless it is proved otherwise. In relation to older clients, the client's legal capacity to make a particular decision or carry out a legal transaction may be questioned either at the time the decision needs to be made or retrospectively (e.g. after the client has died). It is therefore important that lawyers who act for older clients must be able to recognise and cope with the legal implications of incapacity.

When referring to a person lacking capacity, the words 'incapacitated', 'incapable' or 'incompetent' may be used to have the same meaning.

1.1.1 Capacity and human rights

Capacity is the pivotal issue in balancing the right to autonomy in decision-making and the right to protection from harm. In determining someone's capacity, anyone with authority over that individual can deprive the person of the civil rights and liberties enjoyed by most adults and now safeguarded by the Human Rights Act 1998. In particular, a judicial declaration that a person lacks a specific legal capacity may result in that person losing fundamental rights and freedoms (see *Winterwerp* v. *Netherlands* (1979) 2 EHRR 387). Alternatively, such a determination could permit the person lacking capacity to do something, or carry on doing something, whereby serious prejudice could result either to the person lacking capacity or to others. Practitioners should always bear in mind that, if they conclude that someone has or lacks capacity to enter into a transaction, they might have to account to a court for the reasons why they came to that conclusion.

In seeking to achieve an appropriate balance between autonomy and protection of incapacitated adults, the application of the law must be determined in compliance with the European Convention on Human Rights. Relevant Convention rights include:

- Article 2: the right to life. Medical intervention or non-intervention must be in accordance with common law, which is particularly important for those who lack capacity to express their wishes. See Chapter 11.
- Article 3: no one should be subjected to torture, inhuman or degrading treatment or punishment, which may extend to treatment received in care homes and hospitals.
- Article 5: the right to liberty and security. Any deprivation of liberty, including detention or compulsory treatment of 'persons of unsound mind', must be in accordance with a procedure prescribed by domestic law (currently the Mental Health Act 1983).
- Article 6: entitlement to a fair and public hearing by an independent and impartial tribunal established by law in the determination of civil rights and obligations.
- Article 8: the right to respect for private and family life, the individual's home and their correspondence.
- Article 14: the prohibition of discrimination. Differential treatment of people with a mental disability must be justified. Unnecessary denial of decision-making autonomy could be considered an infringement of equality rights.
- Article 1 of the First Protocol: every person is entitled to the peaceful enjoyment of his or her possessions and property. There must be a reasonable proportionality between any interference with this right and the aim being pursued, which must be in the public interest and subject to conditions provided for by law.

1.1.2   Proposals for law reform

It has long been recognised that the law relating to mental incapacity is fragmented, complex and out of date. Reform of the law in this area has taken a long time to achieve but at the time of writing, changes are expected in several areas of legislation affecting people with mental disabilities. Changes in the pipeline include reform of mental health law and the law on sex offences aimed at providing greater protection to vulnerable people.

More directly relevant is the draft Mental Incapacity Bill (see **www.dca. gov.uk/menincap/meninc.pdf**) published for consultation and pre-legislative scrutiny in June 2003. The draft Bill is based on proposals for law reform put forward by the Law Commission (Law Com. Report No. 231, *Mental Incapacity*, TSO (1995)) following a comprehensive investigation of this area of law and widespread consultation on proposals for reform. In the absence of law reform, both professionals and the courts have turned to the Law Commission's Report for guidance on the approach to adopt in defining and assessing mental capacity. In particular, the definitions proposed by the Law Commission to ascertain whether a person lacks capacity have found their way into case law and established practice.

The Bill proposes to create a statutory framework to improve and clarify the decision-making process for people aged 16 and over who are unable to make decisions for themselves. The principles on which the Bill is based and its main provisions are described at 1.7. The Bill is intended to cover all those 'substitute decision-making' situations which are presently covered by common law or come to the courts for determination. As the Bill is based on common law principles and existing best practice, it is unlikely to result in major changes for the majority of people lacking capacity and their families and carers. However, legal definitions and procedures will change and a new Code of Practice giving guidance on common standards for good practice will be issued. At the time of writing, no date has been set for the implementation of new legislation, but practitioners must be sure to inform themselves as changes in the law are introduced.

1.2 TERMINOLOGY

1.2.1 Labels

In relation to mental capacity, terms with distinct meanings are often applied as labels and may be used in a wrong context. A correct use of the common terms is as follows:

- an individual may have or suffer from an illness or disorder;
- this may result in a disability which imposes a limitation on the individual by reason of his or her physical, mental or sensory impairment as well as a handicap (social consequences and loss in freedom) on the individual in his or her environment;
- if the disability is of a sufficient degree the individual may be treated as legally incapable (or incompetent) – this may be due to mental incapacity or physical inability (e.g. to communicate) or both.

1.2.2 Definitions

Capacity is usually addressed in terms of mental capacity, but in practical terms an individual who cannot communicate or who is the object of undue influence may be just as incapable as a person who is suffering a serious mental impairment. To the extent that a wide range of physical and mental conditions can be defined, practitioners have two sets of definitions to refer to: the Mental Health Act 1983 and clause 1 of the draft Mental Incapacity Bill.

Mental Health Act 1983

The court has jurisdiction over the property and affairs of the person where it is satisfied that the person is 'incapable by reason of mental disorder of managing his property and affairs' (s.94(2)):

- *mental disorder* means 'mental illness, arrested or incomplete development of mind, psychopathic disorder and any other disorder or disability of mind' (s.1(2));
- *psychopathic disorder* means 'a persistent disorder or disability of mind (whether or not including significant impairment of intelligence) which results in abnormally aggressive or seriously irresponsible conduct on the part of the person concerned' (s.1(2)).

Clause 1 of the Mental Incapacity Bill

Clause 1 reads:

> A person lacks capacity in relation to a matter if at the material time he is unable to make a decision for himself in relation to the matter because of an impairment of or a disturbance in the functioning of the mind or brain.

1.2.3   Vulnerability

Particular difficulties arise in relation to individuals who require assistance or support from others in order to make decisions. Although they may be able to make the decision in question if the information relevant to it is explained to them in a simple and straightforward manner, they are reliant on the person providing the information to be both honest and balanced. They are therefore potentially vulnerable to the risks of undue influence, bad advice or even the malign intent of others. See *Finsbury Park Mortgage Funding Ltd* v. *Ronald Burrows and Pegram Heron* LTL 3.5.02, where it was held solicitors owed a duty of care to a vulnerable older man to ensure he knew what he was doing.

In determining capacity, a balance must be struck between empowering, assisting and enabling vulnerable people to make their own decisions, or alternatively, justifying the restrictions imposed on personal freedoms and autonomy which may result from actions intended to protect vulnerable people from harm.

Because this is a difficult and sensitive exercise, practitioners are advised to keep a detailed record or attendance note of the whole decision-making process involving clients whose capacity may be in doubt.

1.3 PRESUMPTIONS

1.3.1 Presumption of capacity

There is a presumption that an adult is capable until the contrary is proved, but this may be rebutted by a specific finding of incapacity:

- if an act and the manner in which it was carried out are rational, there is a strong presumption that the individual was mentally capable at the time;
- eccentricity of behaviour is not necessarily a sign of incapacity and care should be exercised before any assumption is made.

1.3.2 Presumption of continuance

Following a finding of incapacity:

- if a person is proved incapable of entering into contracts generally, the law presumes such condition to continue until it is proved to have ceased, although a lucid interval may still be proved;
- the longer the time that has elapsed since an act which it is sought to challenge or set aside on grounds of incapacity, the stronger the evidence required to do so will need to be.

1.3.3 Burden of proof

These presumptions are relevant to the burden of proof. In general, the person who alleges that an individual lacks capacity must prove this. However, in cases involving an objection to the registration of an Enduring Power of Attorney (EPA) the burden of proof is always on the objector (see *In re W (Enduring Power of Attorney)* [2001] 2 WLR 957).

The standard of proof is the usual standard in civil proceedings, the 'balance of probabilities', rather than the higher standard 'beyond reasonable doubt' which applies in criminal proceedings.

1.4 ASSESSMENT OF CAPACITY

It would be convenient if people could be legally categorised as either capable or incapable according to a simple test based upon a general assessment, but this would be inappropriate and discriminatory. The law adopts a functional approach – that capacity must be assessed in relation to the particular decision an individual purports to make at the time the decision needs to be made. The legal capacity required for each decision will depend on the complexity of the information relevant to the decision and the particular legal test of capacity (if one exists) to be applied.

Most individuals have some level of capacity and this should be identified and respected, so:

- legal definitions of mental capacity differ for different purposes;
- the severity of the test and means of assessment may depend upon the nature and implications of the particular decision.

Helpful guidance is given in *Assessment of Mental Capacity: Guidance for Doctors and Lawyers*, published jointly by the Law Society and BMA (1995) (second edition due in 2004).

1.4.1 Approaches

There are three possible approaches to the question of incapacity:

- *outcome*: determined by the content of the decision (e.g. if it is foolish the maker must be incompetent);
- *status*: judged according to the status of the individual such as age (e.g. over 90 years), a medical diagnosis (e.g. senile dementia) or place of residence (e.g. being in a mental hospital);
- *understanding*: the ability of the individual to understand the nature and effect of the particular decision is assessed.

A test based on understanding is generally appropriate when dealing with elderly people, but in certain circumstances the status test may apply, e.g. if a receiver has been appointed by the Court of Protection the individual is presumed to lack capacity in relation to financial affairs except to the extent that limited capacity may be retained, for example to manage small sums of money or over personal decisions). Conversely, detention under the Mental Health Act 1983 does not automatically deprive the patient of decision-making capacity.

The outcome of a decision may cause doubts to be raised about a person's capacity and result in a test of capacity being applied, e.g:

- an elderly spinster instructs you to sell her substantial house for £900;
- a widow decides to go and live with her 'husband'.

However, just the fact of being very old or in a nursing home, or even making decisions that others would regard as eccentric, do not necessarily imply a lack of capacity.

Appearances

Whilst the law is concerned with what is going on in the mind, society tends to be concerned with the outward manifestations. Note that:

- you must recognise the difference between ability and capacity as it is not unusual for communication difficulties to disguise mental capacity;
- conversely, a person may be capable but unable to understand something due to the complexity of the subject matter or the manner in which it is explained;
- appearance (perhaps the consequence of physical disabilities) can create an impression of mental incapacity which is not justified;
- conversely, the absence of physical characteristics may disguise an underlying mental disability;
- observance of the conventions of society can disguise lack of capacity when a person is demented, e.g. a learnt behaviour pattern.

1.4.2   When capacity may need to be assessed

Doubts as to the mental capacity of the client may arise for many reasons:

- the client's circumstances (e.g. in a nursing home);
- what you have been told in advance (e.g. by family, nurses or doctors);
- your own observations (e.g. how the client looks and behaves);
- what the client says (e.g. a widow insists that her husband is still alive or proposes an irrational gift);
- the outcome of the client's decisions (e.g. to do impossible things);
- previous knowledge of the client.

It is essential for practitioners to take the trouble to investigate any of these indications, to ensure that the correct test of capacity is applied and any advice takes account of the client's circumstances. Much of the guidance that follows may be seen as 'best practice' and what can actually be done may be limited by time factors and costs, but once a solicitor is involved, their professional duty to the client must be an overriding factor in all circumstances. Remember that:

- different tests apply for different purposes so apply the appropriate test (see 1.5);
- capacity is a question of fact and your opinion may be as good as that of others;
- the conclusion should be reached 'on the balance of probabilities' – you do not need to be satisfied beyond reasonable doubt;
- there is a presumption of capacity if the client has not previously been found to be incapable;
- carers (lay or professional) may have had more experience than you, so be wary if your conclusions are seriously at variance with theirs;
- capacity is a legal test, which may be informed by medical advice – your judgement will be very important;

- be alert to any conflict of interest when others are expressing their view; and
- if in doubt, obtain medical advice.

1.4.3   Who should assess capacity

Whether an individual has or lacks capacity to do something is ultimately a judicial question. It is not a decision that can be made conclusively by anyone else, including a solicitor or a doctor, although their opinions as to capacity may be of assistance in enabling a court to arrive at its own conclusions. Capacity is ultimately a question for the courts because people with an interest in the outcome may wish to challenge an assessment, either on their own behalf or on behalf of the person who is alleged to lack capacity. In practice, of course, very few decisions are challenged in court but anyone called on to assess capacity must be prepared to justify their actions.

The question of who should assess capacity will depend on the particular decision to be made. For most day-to-day decisions, the carer most directly involved with the person needing support at the time the decision has to be made should assess their capacity to make the decision in question. Where a legal transaction is involved, such as making a will or an EPA, the solicitor handling the transaction will need to be satisfied that the client has the required capacity, taking account of the views of carers or relatives where appropriate (bearing in mind the duty of confidentiality, see 2.4.2) and perhaps assisted by an opinion from a doctor. Where consent to medical treatment or examination is required, the doctor proposing the treatment should decide whether the patient has capacity to consent. Ultimately, if a person's capacity to do something is disputed, it is a question for a court to decide.

When making assessments, different professionals tend to apply different criteria:

- the medical profession is concerned with diagnosis, prognosis and medical treatment;
- care workers classify people according to their degree of independence which involves consideration of levels of competence in performing skills such as eating, dressing, communication and social skills;
- the lawyer is concerned with legal competence, namely whether the individual is capable of making a reasoned and informed decision (the test of capacity) and able to communicate that decision.

This should be borne in mind when seeking opinions about capacity. A multi-disciplinary approach is usually best when assessing capacity in difficult or disputed cases, and the assessment should not then be left entirely to a doctor. The role of the practitioner is crucial at the outset in ensuring that the doctor has the right information to make an informed assessment. The doctor needs to know the purpose for which capacity is required, the legal test involved and any relevant background information. It is no use asking the doctor if a particular client can make a will. The doctor needs to have some indication of the extent of the client's property and the claims he should give effect to (see 1.5.3). A consultant who has never met the client before may need more information than a GP who has known the client for many years.

Clear and concise letters of instruction to fellow professionals will help to set the requisite criteria needed by the lawyer (see *Assessment of Mental Capacity: Guidance for Doctors and Lawyers*, Law Society and BMA (1995)).

When medical evidence should be obtained: the 'golden rule'

The law tends to regard any registered medical practitioner as a *de facto* expert on mental capacity, and therefore entitled to express an opinion as to whether a person is or was capable of understanding the nature and effects of a particular transaction. The Court of Appeal has confirmed that in almost every case where a court is required to make a decision as to capacity, it will need medical evidence to guide it (*Masterman-Lister* v. *Brutton & Co and Jewell and Home Counties Dairies* [2003] All ER 162 at 181), although this will not necessarily be given greater weight than other relevant evidence (see *Richmond* v. *Richmond* (1914) 111 LT 273; *Birkin* v. *Wing* (1890) 63 LT 80).

Obtaining medical evidence about a person's capacity is sometimes required by the law (e.g. when an application is made to the Court of Protection – see Chapter 4), while in other cases, it is merely desirable or a matter of good practice. There are particular circumstances, however, where the law virtually demands that a doctor should witness a person's signature, thereby providing medical evidence as to the person's capacity. In *Kenward* v. *Adams* (*The Times*, 29 November 1975) Templeman J. set out what he called 'the golden if tactless rule' that, where a will has been drawn up for an elderly person or for someone who is seriously ill, it should be witnessed or approved by a medical practitioner, who should make a formal assessment of capacity and fully record the examination and findings. The need to observe this 'golden rule' was restated in *Re Simpson (Deceased), Schaniel* v. *Simpson* (1977) 121 SJ 224, in *Buckenham* v. *Dickinson* [1997] CLY 661, and more forcefully in *Great Ormond Street Hospital* v. *Pauline Rushie* (unreported, 19 April 2000) in which the solicitor was strongly criticised for failing to follow the 'golden rule'.

Dealings with the client's doctor are considered in more detail in Chapter 2.

1.4.4 Techniques for assessment of capacity

When trying to determine whether a client has capacity to make a particular decision, it is essential to see the client personally. How and when you see the client may be important. It is suggested that you first chat about matters other than the business that you intend to carry out. It is helpful to know from other sources something of the family background and client's career so that you can verify the client's recollection. Also ask a few questions about current affairs and past events.

See the client again if there remain doubts as to capacity because first impressions can be misleading (either way) and you may have called at a time when the client could not concentrate for some reason.

At any subsequent interview seek to discuss some of the same matters and see if there is consistency in what the client says. Also, seek detailed instructions again – if they are materially different there is a good chance that the client is not legally competent.

Do not rely upon the views of other persons without question. However well qualified they may seem they may have applied the wrong legal criteria or they may be influenced by a personal interest in the outcome. Where appropriate, always involve the client's GP, hospital staff or carers (but be aware of your duty of confidentiality, see 2.4.2).

Try to see the client at such time of the day as is best for the client and in the most favourable circumstances. Remember that you are testing the client's understanding of the decision to be made, not whether you agree with this or whether the client could make other decisions.

Optimising the conditions for assessing capacity

The following suggestions may be helpful in optimising the conditions for assessing a client's capacity at its highest level of functioning:

- Try to minimise anxiety or stress by making the person feel at ease. Choose the best location where the client feels most comfortable and the time of day when the client is most alert.
- If the person's capacity is likely to improve, wait until it has improved (unless the assessment is urgent). If the cause of the incapacity can be treated, a doctor should treat it before the assessment of capacity is made.
- If there are communication or language problems, consider using a speech therapist or interpreter, or consult family members on the best methods of communication.
- Be aware of any cultural, ethnic or religious factors which may have a bearing on the person's way of thinking, behaviour or communication.
- If more than one test of capacity has to be applied, try to do each assessment on a different day, if possible, or allow time for a break and relaxation between each test.
- Consider whether or not a friend or family member should be present to help reduce anxiety. But in some cases the presence of others may be intrusive.

Previous solicitor and assessment of capacity

When introduced to a new client who is elderly, ascertain if another solicitor has previously acted and seek the client's permission to enquire of that solicitor whether there is anything that you ought to know. Be cautious if such permission is not forthcoming without an adequate explanation, especially if a member of the family or carer discourages such contact. The former solicitor may have more information than you or may have declined, on grounds of capacity, to take the step that you are now being asked to take and, whilst you are not bound by his view, it is likely to be influential in your own assessment.

Another solicitor may have known and acted for the client for many years and the family may now be diverting the client to you in order to by-pass advice which is inconvenient to them but in the best interests of the client.

1.5   LEGAL TESTS OF CAPACITY

As described above, the law takes a functional approach to mental capacity and the courts have confirmed that capacity is usually 'function-specific' or 'issue-specific' (see *Masterman-Lister* v. *Brutton & Co and Jewell and Home Counties Dairies* [2003] All ER 162 at 173). There are some exceptions, the main one being the general capacity to manage and administer property and financial affairs, although it is the individual's particular circumstances and own financial affairs that are relevant. Different legal tests of capacity apply to different decisions or transactions and these tests are usually to be found in the common law.

The legal tests of capacity which are most relevant to elderly clients are described in the following sections, which cover personal, financial and medical decisions. More detailed guidance is given in *Assessment of Mental Capacity: Guidance for Doctors and Lawyers*, Law Society and BMA (1995)).

1.5.1   Capacity to make a decision

Capacity to make a decision was considered in two medical treatment cases (see 1.5.10), first in *Re C (Adult: Refusal of Treatment)* [1994] 1 All ER 819 and later refined in *Re MB* [1997] 2 FLR 426. The first case described a three-stage analysis of the decision-making process, of 'first, comprehending and retaining treatment information; second, believing it; and third, weighing it in the balance to arrive at a choice'. In the latter case, this was reduced to a two-stage test of capacity to make a decision, that the person must be able to:

- understand and retain the information relevant to the decision in question, especially as to the likely consequences, and

13

- use that information and weigh it in the balance as part of the process in arriving at a decision.

The test of capacity set out in *Re MB* was in the context of capacity to consent to or refuse medical treatment. However, in the Official Solicitor's view and endorsed by the court, the test can be used for a wide range of decisions (see Practice Note (Official Solicitor: Declaratory Proceedings) [2001] 2 FLR 158, para. 7(1)), including decisions relating to personal welfare, family and personal relationships.

1.5.2 Capacity to marry

The marriage ceremony requires both parties to enter into a contract. Capacity to do this was considered by the courts in a number of cases in the 1880s. In the case of *Hunter* v. *Edney* (1885) 10 PD 93, a distinction was made between marriage and the wedding ceremony itself: 'The question . . . is not whether she was aware that she was going through the ceremony of marriage, but whether she was capable of understanding the nature of the contract she was entering into'. In order to understand the marriage contract, the person must be free from the influence of any 'morbid delusions'.

The degree of understanding required in order to have capacity to enter into the marriage contract was considered in the case of *Durham* v. *Durham* (1885) 10 PD 80 in which it was held that: 'the contract of marriage is a very simple one which does not require a high degree of intelligence to understand. It is an engagement between a man and a woman to live together, and love one another as husband and wife, to the exclusion of all others'.

These considerations were upheld by the Court of Appeal in the more recent case of *In the Estate of Park Deceased* [1954] P 89, where the level of understanding was expressed as a broad understanding of 'the duties and responsibilities normally entailing to a marriage'.

Implications of marriage

The level of understanding required for marriage is less than that required for some other decisions or transactions. Since the status of marriage affects other matters, such as financial affairs and rights to property, subsequent arrangements may need to be made for a person who lacks capacity to manage these affairs. In particular, a valid marriage revokes any existing will made by either of the parties, including a statutory will. If one person lacks testamentary capacity (see 1.5.3), an application may need to be made to the Court of Protection for a statutory will to be made on the person's behalf (see Chapter 5).

Capacity to separate and divorce

The only reported court decision concerning the capacity required to separate or divorce occurred in the Ontario Court in the case of *Calvert (Litigation Guardian)* v. *Calvert* (1997) 32 OR (3d) 281 – such decisions are regarded as persuasive but not binding on UK courts. In this case, a distinction was drawn between the varying levels of capacity required to make different decisions and separate consideration was given to the three levels of capacity which were relevant: capacity to separate, capacity to divorce and capacity to instruct counsel in connection with the divorce.

It was held that:

> Separation is the simplest act requiring the lowest level of understanding. A person has to know with whom he or she does or does not want to live. Divorce, while still simple, requires a bit more understanding. It requires the desire to remain separate and to be no longer married to one's spouse. It is the undoing of the contract of marriage. . . . If marriage is simple, divorce must be equally simple . . . the mental capacity required for divorce is the same as required for entering into a marriage. . . . The capacity to instruct counsel involves the ability to understand financial and legal issues. This puts it significantly higher on the competence hierarchy.

1.5.3 Capacity to make a will

A person making a will should have testamentary capacity at two important stages:

- first, when giving instructions for the preparation of a will, or if it is prepared or typed by the will-maker personally, at the time of writing or typing it;
- secondly, when the will is executed.

If the person making the will becomes ill or deteriorates between giving instructions and executing the will, the will may still be valid if it has been prepared in strict accordance with the instructions and the will-maker recalls giving instructions to a solicitor and believes that the will complies with those instructions (*Parker* v. *Felgate and Tilley* (1883) 8 PD 171).

The most important case on testamentary capacity is *Banks* v. *Goodfellow* (1870) LR 5 QB 549, in which the Lord Chief Justice set out the following criteria for testamentary capacity:

> It is essential . . . that a testator shall understand the nature of the act and its effects; shall understand the extent of the property of which he is disposing; shall be able to comprehend and appreciate the claims to which he ought to give effect; and, with a view to the latter object, that no disorder of mind shall poison his affections, pervert his sense of right, or prevent the exercise of his natural faculties – that no insane delusion shall influence his will in disposing of his property and bring about a disposal of it which, if the mind had been sound, would not have been made.

The first three elements (understanding the nature of the act and its effects, and the extent of the property being disposed of) involve the will-maker's understanding, that is the ability to receive and evaluate information which may possibly be communicated or explained by others. The final test (being able to comprehend the claims to which he or she ought to give effect) goes beyond understanding and requires the person making the will to be able to distinguish and compare potential beneficiaries and make a choice. A person making a will can, if mentally capable, ignore the claims of relatives and other potential beneficiaries.

It is important to remember that, when someone's capacity is being assessed, it is the ability to make a decision (not necessarily a sensible or wise decision) that is under consideration. In the case of *Bird* v. *Luckie* (1850) 8 Hare 301, the judge specifically remarked that, although the law requires a person to be capable of understanding the nature and effect of an action, it does not insist that the person behave 'in such a manner as to deserve appro-bation from the prudent, the wise, or the good'.

Capacity to revoke a will

The capacity required to revoke a will was considered in the case of *Re Sabatini* (1970) 114 SJ 35, which established that a person who intends to revoke his or her will must have the same degree of understanding as when he or she made the will. The person must therefore be capable of:

- understanding the nature of the act of revoking a will;
- understanding the effect of revoking the will (this might even involve a greater understanding of the operation of the intestacy rules than is necessary for the purpose of making a will, although there is no direct authority on the point and it would be extremely difficult to prove retrospectively);
- understanding the extent of his or her property; and
- comprehending and appreciating the claims to which he or she ought to give effect.

1.5.4 Capacity to make a gift

People who are, or are becoming, incapable of looking after their own affairs are at particular risk of financial abuse and one of the easiest forms of abuse is the improper gifting of their money or other assets. The careful assessment of capacity to make a gift is therefore an important safeguard against financial abuse.

The most important case on capacity to make a gift is *Re Beaney (Deceased)* [1978] 1 WLR 770. The judge in the case set out the following criteria for capacity to make a lifetime gift:

The degree or extent of understanding required in respect of any instrument is relative to the particular transaction which it is to effect. . . . Thus, at one extreme, if the subject matter and value of a gift are trivial in relation to the donor's other assets, a low degree of understanding will suffice. But, at the other, if its effect is to dispose of the donor's only asset of value and thus, for practical purposes, to preempt the devolution of his estate under [the donor's] will or . . . intestacy, then the degree of understanding required is as high as that required for a will, and the donor must understand the claims of all potential donees and the extent of the property to be disposed of.

It has more recently been held that where a person makes a substantial gift, he should be capable of understanding the consequences during the remainder of his lifetime (*Hammond* v. *Osborn* [2002] EWCA Civ 885).

1.5.5 Capacity to make an Enduring Power of Attorney

Shortly after the Enduring Powers of Attorney Act 1985 came into force, the Court of Protection received a considerable number of applications to register enduring powers which had only just been created. This raised doubts as to whether the donors had been mentally capable when they created the powers. The problem was resolved in the test cases *Re K, Re F* [1988] Ch 310.

Having stated that the test of capacity to create an Enduring Power of Attorney was that the donor understood the nature and effect of the document, the judge in the case set out four pieces of information which any person creating an EPA should understand:

- if such be the terms of the power, that the attorney will be able to assume complete authority over the donor's affairs;
- if such be the terms of the power, that the attorney will be able to do anything with the donor's property which the donor could have done;
- that the authority will continue if the donor should be or should become mentally incapable; and
- that if he or she should be or should become mentally incapable, the power will be irrevocable without confirmation by the Court of Protection.

It is worth noting that the donor need not have the capacity to do all the things which the attorney will be able to do under the power. The donor need only have capacity to create the EPA.

The decision in *Re K, Re F* has been criticised for imposing too simple a test of capacity to create an EPA. But the rigour of the test depends largely on the way in which questions are asked by the person assessing the donor's capacity. It has been confirmed by the Court of Appeal in *Re W (Enduring Power of Attorney)* [2001] 1 FLR 832, at paras 23 and 25), that questions susceptible of the answers 'Yes' or 'No' may be inadequate for the purpose of assessing capacity.

Capacity to revoke an Enduring Power of Attorney

There have been no reported decisions on capacity to revoke an EPA. The Master of the Court of Protection has summarised the evidence which the Court of Protection requires to see in order to be satisfied that the donor has the necessary capacity to revoke the power. The donor should know:

- who the attorney(s) are;
- what authority the attorney(s) have;
- why it is necessary or expedient to revoke the EPA; and
- what are the foreseeable consequences of revoking the power.

In practice, where the donor of a registered EPA wishes to revoke it, the attorney often disclaims. The Court must then decide whether the donor has capacity to resume management of his or her own affairs, or whether a receivership order or some other order should be made in respect of the donor.

1.5.6   Capacity to manage property and affairs

The jurisdiction of the Court of Protection, both under the Mental Health Act 1983 and the Enduring Powers of Attorney Act 1985, is invoked in relation to any person who is 'incapable, by reason of mental disorder, of managing and administering his [or her] property and affairs'.

It is therefore necessary to prove three things:

- first, that the person is suffering from mental disorder; and
- secondly, that the person has property and affairs that need to be managed; and
- thirdly, that, because of the mental disorder, the person is incapable of managing and administering his or her property and affairs.

To become a patient under the jurisdiction of the Court of Protection, a person's inability to manage his or her property and affairs must be as a result of mental disorder. The definition of 'mental disorder' is set out at 1.2.2.

Property and affairs means 'business matters, legal transactions, and other dealings of a similar kind' (*F* v. *West Berkshire Health Authority* [1989] 2 All ER 545, at 554d). It does not include personal matters such as where to live or medical treatment decisions.

Assessing a patient's capacity to manage and administer his property and affairs is extremely subjective to the patient and their particular circumstances. It involves not just the carrying out of a single act such as making a gift or a will, but the carrying out of a series of actions which may or may not be connected to each other. It will depend on the value and complexity of the property and affairs as well as to the extent to which the patient may be vulnerable to exploitation.

Until 2002, there had been no reported decisions on the meaning of the term 'capacity to manage property and affairs'. It was generally accepted that the extent, importance and complexity of the individual's property and affairs must be taken into account (*Re CAF*, unreported, 1962). Another consideration is the extent to which the person may rely upon the advice or support of others (*White* v. *Fell*, unreported, 1987). In line with these decisions, *Assessment of Mental Capacity: Guidance for Doctors and Lawyers*, Law Society and BMA (1995) includes a checklist of factors to be taken into account when assessing capacity to administer property and affairs.

In *Masterman-Lister* v. *Jewell and Another* [2002] EWCA 417, the judge at first instance, Wright J., reviewed all of the existing authorities and guidance relating to capacity to manage property and affairs. He set out the following principles:

- legal capacity depends on understanding rather than wisdom – the quality of the decision is irrelevant so long as the person understands what he was deciding;
- capacity to manage property and affairs is a question of functional capacity and essentially a subjective matter; the nature and extent of the individual's property and affairs are therefore relevant;
- personal information must also be considered, including the condition in which the person lives, family background, family and social responsibilities and the degree of back-up and support available.

This decision was upheld by the Court of Appeal (*Masterman-Lister* v. *Brutton & Co and Jewell and Home Counties Dairies* [2003] All ER 162, which confirmed the 'issue-specific nature' of the test of capacity, which must be considered in relation to the particular transaction (its nature and complexity) under consideration. A distinction was drawn between capacity to manage day-to-day affairs, capacity to deal with the complexities of personal injury litigation; and capacity to manage a large award of damages.

1.5.7 Capacity to claim and manage social security benefits

If a person is entitled to social security benefits, but is considered to be incapable of claiming and managing them, another person (known as an *appointee*) can be appointed to act on the claimant's behalf. Appointeeship is governed by reg. 33 of the Social Security (Claims and Payments) Regulations 1987, SI 1987/1968, which provides that an appointee may be appointed by the Secretary of State where:

> a person is, or is alleged to be, entitled to benefit, whether or not a claim for benefit has been made by him or on his behalf; and that person is unable for the time being to act; and no receiver has been appointed by the Court of Protection with power to claim or, as the case may be, receive benefit on his behalf.

The test of capacity is therefore that the person is 'for the time being unable to act'. The regulation does not define this phrase, but internal guidance published by the Department for Work and Pensions (DWP) suggests that people may be unable to act 'for example, because of senility or mental illness' (*Decision Makers Guide*, para. 02308). There are no formal legal criteria which specify the capacity required. It has been suggested (see R. Lavery and L. Lundy, 'The Social Security Appointee System' (1994) *Journal of Social Welfare Law* 313, 316) that in order to have the capacity to claim, receive and deal with benefits, an individual should be able to:

- understand the basis of possible entitlement (presumably with advice where necessary);
- understand and complete the claim form;
- respond to correspondence relating to social security benefits;
- collect or receive the benefits;
- manage the benefits in the sense of knowing what the money is for;
- choose whether to use it for that purpose and if so, how.

1.5.8   Capacity to litigate

People who lack mental capacity may also become parties to proceedings in the High Court and the county courts, as well as in the Court of Protection. If they lack the capacity to give instructions to lawyers on the conduct of the litigation, a procedure is then needed to enable the proceedings to continue by appointing someone else (in civil proceedings, known as a 'litigation friend') to give instructions and otherwise act on their behalf. These procedures are to be found in the relevant Rules of Court for the type of proceedings, which are:

- Civil Procedure Rules 1998, SI 1998/3132 (CPR), Part 21;
- Family Proceedings Rules 1991, SI 1991/1247, Part IX;
- Insolvency Rules 1986, SI 1986/1925, Part 7, Chapter 7.

An adult litigant who lacks capacity is referred to as a 'patient', defined as 'a person who by reason of mental disorder within the meaning of the Mental Health Act 1983 is incapable of managing and administering his own affairs' (CPR, Part 21 r.1(2)(b)) (see 1.5.6). Although it is not specifically stated in the wording of the various Rules, the Court of Appeal has held in the case of *Masterman-Lister* that the test of capacity is 'issue-specific' and in the context of litigation, relates to capacity to manage the particular legal proceedings rather than the whole of the person's affairs (*Masterman-Lister* v. *Brutton & Co and Jewell and Home Counties Dairies* [2003] All ER 162 at 181).

This case established the test of capacity for legal proceedings to be:

whether the party is capable of understanding, with the assistance of such proper explanation from legal advisers and experts in other disciplines as the case may require, the issues on which his consent or decision is likely to be necessary in the course of those proceedings ([2003] All ER 162 at 188).

The Court of Appeal confirmed the approach adopted in the case of *White* v. *Fell*, that capacity to litigate requires the person:

- to have 'insight and understanding of the fact that [she] has a problem in respect of which [she] needs advice';
- to be able to instruct an appropriate adviser 'with sufficient clarity to enable [the adviser] to understand the problem and advise [her] appropriately';
- 'to understand and make decisions based upon, or otherwise give effect to, such advice as [she] may receive'.

However, the Court of Appeal in *Masterman-Lister* also stressed that the test of capacity includes the ability to weigh information (and advice) in the balance as part of the process of understanding and acting on that advice (at 172) but that it does not require a detailed understanding of how that advice is to be carried out (at 190).

1.5.9 Contractual capacity

There are four general rules which apply when trying to assess an individual's capacity to enter into a contract:

- *Specificity*: contractual capacity relates to a specific contract, rather than to contracts in general. For example, this means that a person could have capacity to buy a bus ticket but not the capacity required to enter into a credit agreement.
- *Understanding*: the person must be capable of understanding the nature and effects of the specific contract and of agreeing to it (*Boughton* v. *Knight* (1873) LR 3 PD 64). Obviously, the degree of understanding varies according to the kind of agreement involved.
- *Timing*: contractual capacity must be assessed at the time that the contract was to be entered into (i.e. not the day before or even the hour before). The capacity of an individual can fluctuate over a period of time. Evidence of capacity or lack of capacity at a different time is irrelevant, and would be inadmissible in any court proceedings about the validity of the contract, although evidence of a general lack of capacity may be significant.
- *Intention to create legal relations*: the parties must have intended to enter into a contract that is legally binding. In the case of social and domestic arrangements (e.g. financial arrangements within the family) there is a presumption that there is no such intention although this presumption may be rebutted by evidence to the contrary.

21

In dealing with contracts made by people whose mental capacity is in doubt, the courts have had to counterbalance two important policy consider-ations. One is a duty to protect those who are incapable of looking after themselves, and the other is to ensure that other people are not prejudiced by the actions of persons who appear to have full capacity. So, people without capacity will be bound by the terms of a contract they have entered into, even if it was unfair, unless it can be shown that the other party to the contract was aware of their mental incapacity or should have been aware of this (*Imperial Loan Company* v. *Stone* [1892] 1 QB 599). In addition, a person without mental capacity who agrees to pay for goods or services which are necessaries is legally obliged to pay a reasonable price for them (Sale of Goods Act 1979, s.3(3)).

1.5.10   Capacity to consent to medical treatment

The assessment of an adult patient's capacity to make a decision about his or her own medical treatment is a matter for clinical judgement guided by pro-fessional practice and subject to legal requirements. It is the personal respon-sibility of any doctor proposing to treat a patient to determine whether the patient has the capacity to give a valid consent. The doctor has a duty to give the patient an account in simple terms of the benefits and risks of the proposed treatment and explain possible alternatives to it.

Two cases have been particularly significant in setting out the test of capacity required to make a decision about medical treatment. In the first case of *Re C (Adult: Refusal of Treatment)* [1994] 1 All ER 819, it was held that an adult has capacity to consent (or refuse consent) to medical treatment if he or she can:

- understand and retain the information relevant to the decision in question;
- believe that information; and
- weigh that information in the balance to arrive at a choice.

The second case, *Re MB (Medical Treatment)* [1997] 2 FLR 426, con-cerned a pregnant woman's refusal to consent to the medical procedures necessary for a Caesarean section, because of her needle phobia. The Court of Appeal noted the presumption of capacity and confirmed that a compe-tent woman may, for religious or other reasons, for rational or irrational reasons or for no reason at all, choose not to have medical intervention, even though the consequences may be death or serious handicap of the child she bears or her own death. The court held that a person lacks capacity if some impairment or disturbance of mental functioning renders the person unable to make a decision whether to consent to or refuse treatment. The inability to make a decision occurs when:

- the patient is unable to comprehend and retain the information which is material to the decision, especially as to the consequences of having or not having the treatment in question;
- the patient is unable to use the information and weigh it in the balance as part of the process of arriving at a decision.

The principles that arise from these cases are that, in order to demonstrate capacity to consent to medical treatment, individuals should be able to:

- understand in simple language what the medical treatment is, its nature and purpose and why it is being proposed;
- understand its principal benefits, risks and alternatives;
- understand in broad terms what will be the consequences of not receiving the proposed treatment;
- retain the information for long enough to use it and weigh it in the balance in order to arrive at a decision.

The courts have also held, particularly in medical treatment cases, that a person's capacity must be commensurate with the gravity of the decision: the more serious the condition or complex the treatment proposed, the greater the capacity required (*Re T (Adult: Refusal of Treatment)* [1992] 4 All ER 649).

1.6 DECISION-MAKING FOR PEOPLE WHO LACK CAPACITY

Procedures are needed for decision-making on behalf of those whose capacity has been assessed and who are deemed to be legally incapacitated (i.e. incapable of making or communicating their own decisions).

1.6.1 Types of decision

There are various fields of decision-making:

Management	• financial matters (e.g. claiming benefits, managing money)
	• legal matters (e.g. buying property, making a will, court proceedings)
Personal	• day-to-day living (e.g. what to eat or wear, to have a haircut)
	• activities involving more risk (e.g. going out alone, holidays)
	• major decisions (e.g. where to live)
	• highly personal decisions (e.g. getting married)
Medical	• minor routine treatment (e.g. dentistry, vaccinations)
	• treatment with advantages and disadvantages (e.g. optional minor surgery)
	• controversial treatment (e.g. sterilisation, participation in medical research)
	• refusal of medical treatment (e.g. that would prolong life)

1.6.2 Procedures

Some decisions cannot be delegated, either because they are too personal or the law does not make any provision. The law only makes specific provision for decisions of a management nature (see Chapter 4), and medical treatment for certain mental disorders (see Chapter 12).

The courts have increasingly been called upon to enable significant medical and personal welfare decisions to be taken on behalf of mentally incapable people where previously such decisions could not lawfully be made because there was no procedure. The court's jurisdiction to grant declarations in the best interests of a mentally incapable person was comprehensively reviewed and confirmed in the case *Re F (Adult: Court's Jurisdiction)* [2000] 2 FLR 512. Other minor personal and medical decisions are taken by carers of necessity without any legal authority or are simply not taken at all. The absence of approved procedures causes problems and uncertainty through-out the whole range of personal decision-making. The draft Mental Incapacity Bill (see **www.dca.gov.uk/menincap/meninc.pdf**) proposes a statutory framework for decision-making in an attempt to address these problems.

1.6.3 Basis of decisions

There are two approaches to making a decision on behalf of an incapacitated person:

- best interests: that which the decision-maker considers is in the best interests of the individual;
- substituted judgement: that which the individual would have chosen if capable of making the decision.

Both present problems, the former because it denies individuality and poses the risk of the decision-maker imposing his or her view as to what is best, and the latter because in many cases it cannot be conjectured what the individual would have wished. In general, it has been established through common law that a decision-maker should act in the best interests of the incapacitated person.

The draft Mental Incapacity Bill follows both approaches in that a consideration of 'best interests' must take into account a person's actual and likely wishes. The Bill proposes that any determination of the best interests of an incapacitated person should take into account:

- the need to permit and encourage him to participate in any decision-making to the fullest extent to which he is capable;
- his ascertainable past and present wishes and feelings and the factors he would consider if able to;
- the views of other people whom it is appropriate and practical to consult about his wishes and feelings and what would be in his best interests; and

- the general principle that the course least restrictive of his freedom of decision and action is likely to be in his best interests.

1.7 PROPOSALS FOR LAW REFORM

The draft Mental Incapacity Bill published in June 2003 proposes a new statutory framework for decision-making on behalf of people who lack capacity to make their own decisions (see **www.dca.gov.uk/menincap/meninc.pdf**). The Bill is based on two key principles – capacity and best interests – aimed at defining who the legislation will apply to and the ways in which decisions can lawfully be taken on their behalf.

1.7.1 The definition of capacity

Clause 1 sets out the definition of 'persons who lacks capacity'. Capacity is decision-specific, focusing on the particular time when a particular decision has to be made. People should not be considered 'incapable' simply on the basis that they have a particular diagnosis, but the inability to decide must be 'because of an impairment of or a disturbance in the functioning of the mind or brain', whether permanent or temporary. There is therefore no specific diagnostic threshold, requiring a 'mental disability' to be established before someone is deemed to lack capacity. Instead, the draft Bill incorporates a diagnostic test within the definition of capacity, without specifying a requirement to establish a 'mental disability'.

Clause 2 sets out the test for assessing whether a person is unable to make a decision and therefore lacks capacity – a 'functional' test, looking at the decision-making process itself. One criteria which would indicate an inability to make a decision is the fact that the person is unable to communicate the decision by any possible means. Under clause 3, a person must be presumed to have capacity until it is proved otherwise. Where a person has 'an impairment of or a disturbance in the functioning of the mind or brain' and appears to lack capacity for any given decision, 'all practical steps', including efforts to assist communication, must be taken to help the person make the decision before he or she should be regarded as lacking the capacity to make that particular decision.

In setting out its proposals for law reform on which the Bill is based, the Law Commission stressed that it was not intended to replace any of the existing definitions and tests of capacity with the new statutory definition. After implementation of the new law, it is likely that judges would consider the new statutory definition and adopt it if they saw fit (Law Com. Report No. 231, *Mental Incapacity* (1995), para. 3.23). The new definition was intended to expand on, rather than contradict, the terms of the existing common law tests. The main difference will be the requirement that 'a person is not to be treated as unable to make the decision unless all practicable steps to help him to do so have been taken without success' (clause 2(3)), which will include an explanation of the information relevant to the decision.

1.7.2   Best interests

Clause 4 of the Bill establishes the concept of 'best interests' as the over-riding principle for making decisions on behalf of people who lack capacity to make their own decisions. As indicated above (see 1.6.3), this principle has already been established in common law. The Bill sets out a checklist of the factors that need to be considered when deciding what is in a person's best interests, based on those proposed by the Law Commission. It will therefore provide what is described as 'a common standard' which all relevant parties can discuss and agree upon when determining best interests in any given situation. It will apply to all decision-makers with authority under the Bill, ranging from informal decisions made under the 'general authority' provided by the Bill, to orders and judgments made by the proposed new Court of Protection.

1.7.3   Decision-making mechanisms

The Bill includes the following main provisions:

- People making decisions on behalf of someone who lacks capacity will have a 'general authority to act reasonably' so long as they are acting in the person's best interests. This brings into statute present common law practice for what are essentially day-to-day health care and welfare decisions.
- Lasting Powers of Attorney (LPAs) will enable a person whilst capable to appoint a person to act for him or her if he or she becomes incapacitated. The powers will go beyond the present Enduring Powers of Attorney and include not only decisions with respect to financial matters but also health and welfare decisions.
- A new Court of Protection will be established as a superior court of record able to establish precedent and build up a body of case law. It will have a regional presence with judges nominated to it from all levels of the judiciary. The new court will take over the work undertaken by the present Court of Protection on financial matters and will also deal with health and welfare matters that presently come before the High Court. Preference will be given to making a single order to resolve the matter, but the appointment of a deputy will be available in cases where there is a need for ongoing decision-making powers.
- Specific provision is made to bring into statute the common law require-ments relating to advance refusals of medical treatment, in order to clarify

the status of advance refusals within a comprehensive statutory framework for decision-making.

- The Bill also establishes a new criminal offence of ill-treatment or wilful neglect of a person who lacks capacity by an attorney or deputy or someone who has care of that person. It will also be an offence to ignore or destroy an advanced decision to refuse treatment.
- Statutory guidance will be given in supporting Code(s) of Practice which will apply to anyone with decision-making powers under the Bill or who acts in a professional capacity or for remuneration in relation to a person who lacks capacity.

At the time of writing, no date has been set for the introduction of the Bill into Parliament or for implementation of new legislation. Practitioners must be sure to inform themselves of the detail of the new legislation and the statutory guidance as changes in law and practice are introduced.

CHAPTER 2

Acting for the elderly client

Martin Terrell

2.1 THE CLIENT

Before any work is carried out, it is of crucial importance to:

- identify who the client is (this may not be the person who first approaches you, for example a relative or carer);
- take instructions from and advise that client; if information or instructions come from an intermediary then it is all the more important to see the client and obtain confirmation;
- ensure that the client can give instructions freely and is not under the influence of another person (and always ensure that you see the client alone on at least one occasion);
- ascertain that the client has the required capacity for the proposed course of action (see Chapter 1);
- identify potential conflicts of interest at an early stage, and if appropriate recommend independent legal advice either for the would-be elderly client or for the intermediary;
- continue to act in the best interests of the client, even if instructions are communicated by the client's attorney or receiver.

2.1.1 Communication

A client should not be prevented from giving his own instructions just because of communication difficulties. It is the responsibility of the solicitor to make every effort to overcome such difficulties, for instance by:

- using an interpreter when necessary, and not only when the client's first language is a foreign language – versions of English can be difficult for some to follow;
- using physical aids where these may assist – it is surprising how many elderly clients forget their hearing aids or glasses when seeing a solicitor;
- allowing a friend or carer to be present initially to reassure the client and explain the best methods of communication;

- arranging to see the client at a convenient time (many care homes start getting their residents ready for meals long before conventional meal times);
- accepting a simple 'yes' or 'no' response to questions or even particular signs such as the movement of a finger or a raised eyebrow.

Interview techniques

A different technique is required when interviewing clients who are mentally frail or otherwise vulnerable. In general:

- Speak slowly, using simple words and sentences.
- Try to avoid where possible 'yes' or 'no' answers to questions which suggest the answer or contain a choice of answers which may not include the correct one.
- Do not keep repeating questions as this may suggest that you do not believe the answers and encourages a change; but the same question may be asked at a later stage to check that consistent answers are being given.
- Do not move to new topics without explanation (e.g. 'can we now talk about . . .').
- Do not ask abstract questions (e.g. 'was it after 9 a.m.' – instead ask 'was it after breakfast').
- Allow the client to tell his or her story and do not simply ignore information which does not fit in with your assumptions.
- Be patient, allow time for pleasantries and to put the client at his ease; a discussion about the client's last holiday or grandchildren may provide useful background information and help with the assessment of capacity.
- If the client is required to read a document, try to avoid unnecessarily long or complicated precedents and use large print where necessary.
- Do not go on too long without a break.
- Be prepared to arrange a further meeting or an independent assessment and be tactful in explaining why this is required.

Avoiding pitfalls

When interviewing the client, keep an open mind and do not assume that everything you are told is accurate. You may have to justify your conduct in court and while there is a legal presumption of capacity, it is important to address whether the client is incapable on the basis of a potential challenge. You need to be assured of the client's capacity and therefore it is the client who needs to demonstrate to you that he or she is capable. Remember to:

- take great care with simple 'yes' and 'no' responses; the client must have received, retained and understood sufficient information to make an informed decision;

- make detailed attendance notes;
- always see the client alone or with an independent witness, even if you need to spend time initially with an intermediary;
- take care where you are seeing a husband and wife together: one may be more informative than the other either out of many years' custom or to compensate for the lack of capacity of the other;
- if in doubt, obtain medical evidence.

Assessing capacity is dealt with in more detail at 1.4, but it is not the only issue that is relevant when taking instructions from the elderly client. The client may, for instance, be subject to undue influence or pressure to do something that he is not inclined to do. Conversely, the client may want to do something which is not in his best interests. The client may have strong views of his own, and in the words of Chadwick L.J. in *Masterman-Lister* v. *Brutton & Co and Jewell and Home Counties Dairies* [2003] All ER 162 at 181:

> It is unnecessary to deny them [clients of borderline capacity] the opportunity to take their own decisions if they are not being exploited. It is not the task of the courts to prevent those who have mental capacity to make rational decisions from making decisions which others may regard as rash or irresponsible.

2.2   THE SOLICITOR

2.2.1   Importance of the solicitor's role

The elderly client is entitled to an independent solicitor prepared to listen to and communicate with the client for their needs however much patience this may require. The role of the solicitor providing independent advice and guidance is crucial. For the elderly client it may provide the means of carrying out a particular wish or the only safeguard against financial abuse. In many cases the solicitor is the judge of whether an action is possible or not. If he or she decides that the client is capable and goes ahead and completes the will or Enduring Power of Attorney or transfer deed, that document will be presumed to be valid and will be all the more difficult to overturn if it is subsequently apparent that an injustice has taken place.

2.2.2   Who is the client?

Instructions may come from an intermediary, who may be a spouse, a son or daughter, carer or concerned neighbour. In the majority of cases their contact is well-intentioned and they are communicating on behalf of the client. But conflict of interest situations do arise and the fundamental rule is to ask 'Who is my client?'.

A solicitor must act on the instructions of the client or, when these are given on behalf of a client who is incapable, in the best interests of that client. A balancing act will often be necessary, but the elderly client's views and wishes must be respected even if they cannot always be followed.

This overriding duty to the client applies even if the solicitor is taking instructions from an agent such as a receiver or attorney. The principal is still the client (*Re EG* [1914] 1 Ch 927) and if it becomes necessary, the solicitor must inform the agent that he may not be acting in the best interests of his principal. The solicitor should decline to act on the instructions of the agent if he or she believes that these are not in the best interests of the principal, and if necessary refer the circumstances to the Court of Protection (and the solicitor should not abandon the client at that stage).

In certain situations however, the solicitor is deemed to be acting for the agent rather than the principal:

- where the attorney instructs the solicitor to apply to the Court of Protection for registration of the Enduring Power of Attorney;
- where a prospective receiver instructs the solicitor to apply to the Court of Protection for the appointment of a receiver (Court of Protection Practice Direction, *Authority to Solicitors to Act for Patients or Donors* (9 August 1995));
- where the solicitor represents the receiver, attorney or other party to Court of Protection proceedings when there is a conflict of interest: in such a situation, the solicitor may act for the party to the proceedings and the Court of Protection will direct that the Official Solicitor represent the interests of the principal (Court of Protection Rules 2001, SI 2001/824, r.13 and see generally, Chapter 4);
- where the solicitor believes that there is a conflict of interest and that he or she must act for the agent rather than the principal (who should then be separately represented).

2.2.3 Termination of retainer

A solicitor must not terminate his or her retainer with an existing client except for good reason and upon reasonable notice. Generally a retainer terminates by operation of law at the onset of the incapacity of the client, but this is when the client most needs professional support. The solicitor should consult the client's relatives and, if appropriate, take steps to ensure that the client's affairs will continue to be dealt with in a proper manner.

If the client's relatives refuse to register the Enduring Power of Attorney or apply to the Court of Protection for the appointment of a receiver, the solicitor needs to record his or her advice to the relatives clearly and give them notice that any person may apply to the court for the appointment of a receiver. If there is no response to this or if there is a danger of financial abuse or neglect, it would not be inappropriate for the solicitor to apply in his or her own name for the appointment of him or herself or a panel receiver as receiver for the client. The Court of Protection would accept representations from the family and may well appoint someone else as receiver, but it is unlikely that the solicitor would not be awarded the costs of the application.

2.3 CARERS

2.3.1 Definition

A 'carer' has been defined as a person who 'provides a substantial amount of care on a regular basis for a disabled person living at home' (Disabled Persons (Services, Consultation and Representation) Act 1986, s.8).

In practice, the expression does not have so restricted a meaning and includes informal carers such as relatives or friends providing personal care or supervision full time or merely on a casual basis, as well as professional carers such as care workers, social workers and community nurses.

2.3.2 Status

Relatives and friends who fulfil the role of carer tend to find informal ways of dealing with situations as they arise, but situations may arise where they need to be aware of their rights to make decisions on behalf of the person cared for.

Family relationship by itself does not confer any legal rights. In practice 'next of kin' will be consulted although this may (wrongly) be in preference to a person who has (or had, prior to incapacity) a far closer relationship with the individual, such as a cohabitee or partner.

In so far as the carer has any legal status this can only be based upon agreement with the person cared for, either express or implied. Often the *de facto* relationship is the only evidence of this but the significant point is whether the relationship is recognised by others.

The role of carers is reinforced by the Carers (Recognition and Services) Act 1995 and the Carers and Disabled Children Act 2000 and related policy guidelines. This applies whether or not the carer is related to the individual.

2.3.3 Consulting carers

It is usually helpful, where the client is (or is becoming) mentally incapable, to develop a dialogue with those responsible for the day-to-day care or supervision of the client. It is also desirable to establish a link with the family or next of kin. Useful information can be obtained in this way, but be careful not to be unduly influenced by their views and to retain your professional independence.

The views of carers may alert you to problems and limitations, and will be of assistance if you need to consider the extent to which your client is dependent upon others because you will seldom receive a realistic assessment from the client.

You should still form your own view, taking into account all the available evidence, because carers in particular may be influenced by other factors and cannot be assumed always to be acting in the best interests of your client.

2.3.4   Caring for carers

It is important not to assume that informal carers have chosen this role. They are often involuntary carers needing encouragement and support because they:

- have a severely restricted lifestyle;
- face substantial costs of caring and loss of personal income;
- feel a mixture of emotions including inadequacy, frustration, resentment, embarrassment and guilt that they are not doing enough;
- need recognition, reassurance and information;
- need practical help in the form of services, financial support and respite care;
- may not always wish to take responsibility for the type of decisions that are often referred to them.

A duty is imposed on the local authority to assess the carer on their ability to provide or continue to provide care when deciding what services should be provided. For more information on community care and carers rights see Chapters 7 and 8.

2.4   OTHER PROFESSIONALS

When acting for elderly clients you must be prepared to develop relationships with other professionals in the interests of your clients. Often these pro- fessionals will already be involved with your client, but on occasions you will take the initiative by seeking their involvement. Wherever possible seek the consent and authority of your client to discuss matters with other pro- fessionals – some professionals will refuse to disclose information without such authority.

2.4.1 Medical practitioners

Assessing capacity

Capacity is a legal test (see 1.5) and it is for the solicitor (and ultimately for the courts) to decide whether a person is capable. This may seem harsh, but the solicitor needs to decide whether he can accept and act on the client's instructions. Obviously medical advice may be crucial in informing the solicitor and any solicitor who acted against clear medical advice to the contrary would be foolish at the very least.

Doctors may be reluctant to make decisions concerning capacity and may be wary of becoming a party to what may become a contentious act, especially if there is a dispute in the family. Paradoxically, doctors make decisions about capacity on a regular basis where they are deciding whether patients can give consent to treatment. Where you need to obtain medical evidence, remember to:

- provide the client's written consent if this can be given or confirm that the client has agreed to be assessed;
- explain clearly the purpose of the assessment and appropriate test of capacity (see 1.5);
- supply sufficient background information to enable the doctor to make an informed assessment. There is no point asking simply whether the patient can make a gift – the doctor may need to know in general terms the size of the proposed gift relative to the size of the estate, whether the gift affects the will, whether there is a history of making gifts or whether the gift is unusual in some way. The information the doctor receives may well affect his assessment, which places a burden on you to provide the right information;
- set out any concerns you may have about the patient, especially if you are concerned about the appropriateness of the proposed action and need the doctor to reinforce your opinion;
- provide a timescale for any response, especially if the matter is urgent;
- let the doctor know that he is to be paid for his assessment and if there is a recommended fee scale, the amount. Some doctors are more prepared to go out of their way to assist if they know they will be paid.

Importance of consulting doctor generally

A doctor's opinion is not only required to provide an assessment of capacity. A medical opinion may be extremely useful because the doctor may:

- have significant views and alert you to the possibility that the client may be confused;

35

- have records of past treatment or symptoms which support a particular view;
- provide a diagnosis of a condition which either produces odd behaviour without there being impairment of reason or affects reason without this being apparent;
- provide a prognosis as to whether any such condition is likely to be temporary or permanent, worsening or improving, changing rapidly or slowly.

Choosing the right doctor

Not all doctors will have a sufficient level of knowledge or expertise to determine issues of capacity. Many people can be assessed by their general practitioner (GP). A close and long-term acquaintance with the person being assessed may be helpful, particularly if the person feels more at ease with a familiar doctor. However, such familiarity and knowledge of the patient's family may make an objective assessment more difficult. In such cases, or where the client's medical condition is complex, it may then be more appropriate to request an assessment from a specialist practitioner, such as a psychiatrist or a geriatrician, who has expertise in the client's particular medical condition. It is worthwhile telephoning the doctor before instructing to prevent delays if the doctor feels he is not the appropriate person. This can occur where the GP is instructed and there is a consultant also involved with the patient's care.

See *Assessment of Mental Capacity: Guidance for Doctors and Lawyers*, Law Society and BMA (1995).

2.4.2 Confidentiality

Carrying out an assessment of capacity requires the sharing of information about the personal circumstances of the person being assessed. Yet doctors, lawyers and other professionals are bound by a duty of confidentiality towards their clients, imposed through their professional ethical codes and reinforced by law. As a general principle, personal information may only be disclosed with the client's consent, even to close relatives or 'next of kin'. However, there are circumstances when disclosure is necessary in the absence of consent, such as where it is in the interests of the patient, ordered by the court or where the patient has a notifiable disease.

In relation to people who lack capacity to consent (or refuse) disclosure, a balance must be struck between the public and private interests in maintaining confidentiality and the public and private interest in permitting, and occasionally requiring, disclosure for certain purposes. Some guidance has been offered in the case of *S* v. *Plymouth City Council and C* [2002] EWCA Civ 388, which established 'a clear distinction between disclosure to the media with a view to publication to all and sundry and disclosure in confidence to those with a proper interest in having the information in question' (at para. 49).

A similar balancing act must be carried out by professionals seeking or undertaking assessments of capacity. It is essential that information concerning the person being assessed which is directly relevant to the decision in question is made available to ensure that an accurate and focused assessment can take place. Every effort must first be made to obtain the person's consent to disclosure by providing a full explanation as to why this is necessary and the risks and consequences involved. If the person is unable to consent, relevant disclosure – that is the minimum necessary to achieve the objective of assessing capacity – may be permitted where this is in the person's interests. However, this does not mean that everyone has to know everything.

2.4.3 Nurses and professional carers

Do not overlook the fact that professional carers are the people who will be in closest day-to-day contact with your client and they may have considerable experience. They can provide valuable information and their views may be relevant although they may not be able to give expert evidence.

2.4.4 Social workers

Social workers are employed by local authority social services departments. They have clients whose welfare and interests they look after by providing support, guidance and advice, and an introduction to services. They also have a statutory role and may need to use their powers to protect the client. Some social workers have special knowledge, training and responsibilities and there are approved social workers under the Mental Health Act 1983 with certain statutory powers (see Chapter 12 at 12.6).

Social services departments now have the key role in the delivery of community care. If your client becomes unable to cope and does not have the necessary support within the family you should take the initiative by contacting the social services department for the area where the client lives and asking for an assessment of welfare and community care services (see Chapter 8). Consent of the client is advisable where possible if you are not the attorney or receiver (or acting on instructions from such person).

2.4.5 Accountants, stockbrokers, etc.

Your client may have used the services of various firms before becoming incapable of instructing them personally and you may now have taken on the role of co-ordinating the management of the client's affairs.

It would be inappropriate to disregard these firms unless there were good reason to do so in the client's best interests, not your own. It would not be sufficient that you could more conveniently deal with a firm that you usually employ or would receive more commission from such a firm. The client's own professional advisers may have considerable knowledge of the client's affairs and preferences, and this represents part of the resources that you can draw upon.

The reality may be that your client has never taken the professional advice that his circumstances require. Whether or not the client is capable, it may be appropriate for you to be involved in the choice of suitable firms to provide services, or provide them yourself if you have the resources and expertise to do so.

You may work with other professional firms as part of a team acting in the mutual client's best interests and should not see yourself as being in competition with these other firms, but should ensure that you obtain their advice when appropriate.

Remember that any action taken may at a later date be challenged by some interested person or by an actual or potential beneficiary after the client's death. Solicitors should therefore keep adequate records and notes of interviews, telephone attendances and deliberations. Where advice is given by other professionals which is to be acted upon, ensure that it is also confirmed by them in writing. Above all, ensure that any adviser is suitably qualified to give advice appropriate to the needs of the older client and receives all information necessary to do so.

Advise your client wherever possible and appropriate of the need to notify members of the family of your involvement and that of other firms. This may be done by a suitable letter retained with the client's copy of the will or Enduring Power of Attorney (EPA). The solicitor's role may be made known at the earliest possible stage, when the documents are prepared. Where a client makes a will, executors or beneficiaries need to know where the will is stored. Where a client makes an EPA it is appropriate for the solicitor to write to the attorneys to execute their part of the document.

2.5 OBTAINING INFORMATION ABOUT THE CLIENT

2.5.1 The client

Clearly the first source of information is the client from whom instructions are obtained, but be prepared to verify any such information if the client is mentally frail or there is doubt about mental capacity. You should try to inspect documents, when these are significant, rather than relying upon the client's interpretation. Where circumstances justify this, a visit to the client's home greatly assists in forming a view about memory and understanding. It is often the case that a client is vague about how much money he has or you are not sure the client can have as much or as little as he claims. A visit to the client and a quick look at the bank statements or portfolio valuations will soon clear up any such confusion.

If the client has a property, you should have some idea of what the property is worth. The client's own valuation may be several years out of date and it may be worth asking relatives, neighbours or a local estate agent to obtain an approximate idea of the value. It is also advisable to check the deeds, or if these cannot readily be obtained obtain office copy entries (assuming the property is registered). The client's wishes may well be inconsistent with the manner in which the property is held, as in the case of *Re Ernest Chittock (Deceased)* [2001] EWCA Civ 915, in which the matrimonial home was assumed to be in joint names and to have passed by survivorship to the widow. In fact it was in the late husband's sole name and subject to a partial intestacy.

Where the client lacks capacity

Obtaining information from a client who lacks capacity is much harder. Banks and other financial institutions should not divulge information. All you can do is to go through the client's papers and look at recent bank statements, passbooks, valuations, share certificates and correspondence. If an EPA is in place then certified copies can be sent out and up-to-date statements and valuations will be supplied to the attorney.

If there is no EPA in place then you need to provide the Court of Protection with as much information as is available. If your assessment of the client's estate is incomplete do not delay an application to the Court of Protection. Once a receiver has been appointed, information will be released to a receiver on production of a sealed copy of the First General Order. If even the minimum information to prepare a full application cannot be supplied, then the application should still be made and the Court will supply an interim authority to make enquiries on behalf of the client.

2.5.2 Couples

When acting for a couple it is essential to see them both at some stage, if only to confirm the extent to which one is authorised to give instructions on behalf of both.

Always take care when dealing with elderly couples if you do not know the family background. Ascertain whether they are actually married, whether it was a recent marriage and whether either party has previously been married with a family. Be particularly sensitive to long-term cohabitees whether in heterosexual or same sex partnerships.

Solicitors should also be cautious about allowing one partner to obtain the signature of the other on important documents – it is better to see both clients yourself. It may even be necessary for each party to be independently advised.

As mentioned at the beginning of this chapter, both husband and wife need to be assessed. Sometimes one may lack capacity and this is overlooked by the other dominating the discussion and whether deliberately or subconsciously, concealing the lack of capacity.

2.5.3 Carers and family

When the client is no longer living an independent life it can be helpful to talk to care workers, nurses, etc., as well as other members of the family, sometimes in the presence of the client. If doubts arise as to the extent that you have implied authority to do this you should clarify your intentions with the client at an early stage. It is desirable to explain the nature of your professional involvement to such persons and give them your name, address and telephone number. Do not omit to check whether anyone else in your practice has acted for the client and whether they have any insights that might help.

Background information and corroboration of essential information can be obtained from these sources; such contact also assists in ascertaining the level of dependence of the client upon other people and services and forming a preliminary view as to the capacity of the client.

2.5.4 Financial bodies

With the authority of the client when capable, or otherwise with an EPA or order of the Court of Protection, useful information or confirmation about the client's financial position can often be obtained from:

- the client's bank, as to balances and documents or valuables held in safe custody;
- the Inland Revenue, simply by requesting a copy of the last tax return or statement of account;
- the Department of Work and Pensions to ascertain what benefits are paid to the client;
- the client's accountant or tax adviser (if there is one);
- the client's stockbroker or insurance broker (if there is one);
- company registrars to obtain confirmation of shareholdings;
- any trustees making regular payments to the client from a trust;
- a care home to check who is paying, the level of fees payable, whether there are any arrears and the costs of additional extras which may be required for the client.

2.5.5 Care authorities

Good contacts at a personal level with those involved in the NHS, social services and housing departments for the area where you practise are invaluable:

- in ascertaining any involvement they have previously had with the client;
- if you need to assist in arranging services for the client;
- in avoiding or resolving disputes about service provision or charges.
- in building up your elderly client practice (they increasingly refer clients with resources to independent lawyers).

Although you may not normally deal with these matters, if you are acting for the client in respect of his general affairs, your brief could extend to seeing if you can improve the personal circumstances of the client or reduce the cost to the client. Your advice should be informed by knowledge of the range of services and care provision available in the private and public sectors and the criteria for obtaining those services. You should also be aware of the authority and department responsible for providing these services and the officials who actually make the decisions.

2.6 FREEDOM OF INFORMATION

2.6.1 Code of Practice

A Code of Practice on Access to Government Information was introduced in 1994 as part of the Citizen's Charter initiative. It covers bodies under the jurisdiction of the Parliamentary Commissioner for Administration to whom a complaint may be made if it is not observed, but other recognised government bodies are also expected to comply. This national Code will override any versions produced by individual organisations.

The Code is accompanied by guidance which provides that:

- there is an assumption that information should be released except where disclosure would not be in the public interest;
- reasons should be given for administrative decisions except when there is statutory authority or established convention to the contrary;
- internal procedures, guidance and manuals should be published except where this could prejudice any matter which should be kept confidential (a wide range of internal manuals has since been released by the Department of Work and Pensions).

Requests under the Code referring to it should be made by letter to the source of the information. There is a target response time of 20 days, and although fees can be charged for individual information it may not be reasonable to charge for documents that should be published.

2.6.2 Legislation

The Freedom of Information Act 2000 creates new rights of access to information. It is intended to supersede the Code of Practice on Access to

41

Government Information. The Act amends the Data Protection Act 1998 and the Public Records Act 1958. It is not yet fully in force until 30 November 2005 so until then it will be necessary to refer to the Code of Practice and other pieces of legislation.

Freedom of Information Act 2000

The Act creates a statutory right of access, provides for a more extensive scheme for making information publicly available and covers a much wider range of public authorities including: local government, NHS bodies, schools and colleges, the police and other public bodies and offices. The provisions in the Act will be regulated by the Information Commissioner (the same person who acts as Commissioner under the Data Protection Act 1998) to whom the public will have direct access, rather than access only through the intervention of their Member of Parliament as under the Code. The Act will permit people to apply for access to documents, or copies of documents, as well as to the information itself. The Public Records Act 1958 reorganised the arrangements for the preservation of public records. It places a duty on the Keeper of the Public Record Office to provide reasonable facilities for inspecting and obtaining copies of such records. The statutory rights under the Act and the Information Commissioner's regulatory powers will be extended to information contained in these records.

The Act:

- provides a right of access to recorded information held by public authorities and specifies the conditions which need to be fulfilled before an authority is obliged to comply with a request;
- creates exemptions from the duty to disclose information;
- establishes the arrangements for enforcement and appeal;
- allows public authorities to charge fees in accordance with regulations made by the Secretary of State;
- provides for time limits for complying with a request;
- requires public authorities to provide advice and assistance to applicants;
- requires public authorities to state the basis for refusal of a request;
- requires public authorities to adopt and maintain a publication scheme and to publish information in accordance with it.

Data Protection Act 1998

Individuals have the right to see most information stored about themselves on any relevant filing system. This includes information stored on a computer as well as manual data. There is a right to have incorrect or misleading information corrected or erased and provision for compensation, but certain types of data are exempt. The Information Commissioner keeps a register of data controllers who hold personal information, and fees for subject access are set by regulations.

Further provision must be made to comply with the EU Data Protection Directive (95/46/EC) which came into effect in the United Kingdom on 24 October 1998. The Commissioner publishes from time to time codes of practice.

See information on the Data Protection Act 1998 and the Freedom of Information Act available from the Data Protection Commissioner (at **www.dataprotection.gov.uk**) or request by post to the Information Commissioner, Wycliffe House, Water Lane, Wilmslow, Cheshire, SK9 5AF.

Access to Medical Reports Act 1988

People have a right, in respect of a medical report about them prepared after January 1989 for an employer or insurance company, to see the report before it is sent and for six months afterwards and to ask for corrections to be made. Before applying for a report the employer or insurer must obtain the individual's written consent and inform him of these rights. A doctor can withhold information about any third party or which is likely to cause serious harm to the individual.

Access to Health Records Act 1990 (as amended)

People are allowed to see and copy information which has been manually recorded on their health records (as defined) since November 1991. This includes health records in the private sector (e.g. private nursing homes) as well as the NHS. The Act provides that:

- information which in the record holder's opinion is likely to cause serious harm to the physical or mental health of the patient or someone else need not be disclosed;
- a person who believes that part of a record is incorrect, misleading or incomplete can apply for it to be corrected;
- where the patient is incapable of managing his or her own affairs, any person appointed by a court to manage those affairs may apply;
- there is an internal complaints procedure but if still dissatisfied an application may be made to the court to order compliance.

2.6.3 Local government

A member of the public has the right to attend any meeting of the council or a committee (or sub-committee) unless the council has exercised its power to exclude the public from all or part of the meeting, which it may only do for certain reasons.

Local Government (Access to Information) Act 1985

This Act extends the right of members of the public to information from and about local government. See the Local Government Act 1972, Part VA, ss.100A–100K, as inserted by the 1985 Act. However, certain categories of information are exempt from disclosure: see the 1985 Act and Part I of Sched. 12A to the 1972 Act.

You can inspect the registers of councillors, committees and delegated decision-making powers, and should be able to obtain copies of agendas, minutes, reports discussed at meetings, background papers, etc.

2.6.4   Mentally incapacitated persons

The right to apply for information is given to the individual about whom the information is held, and there is no provision for another person to apply on the individual's behalf. This causes problems when the individual lacks mental capacity, yet it is precisely in that situation that information is likely to exist and be needed by those seeking to make arrangements for care or support. The difficulty lies in identifying those who have a legitimate interest in obtaining the information – the right to confidentiality does not lapse by reason of lack of competence and family or carers might have an ulterior motive for seeking information.

The Access to Health Records Act 1990 allows access to the medical records of a patient by other persons, including 'any person appointed by a court to manage [the] affairs [of the patient]' (s.3(1)). This means a receiver appointed by the Court of Protection (not an attorney under a registered EPA), yet a receiver will only be appointed where the financial affairs justify this. Accordingly this provision is not adequate to deal with most normal situations.

A solution has yet to be found, and it is probably better to approach this on the basis of when confidential information should be disclosed rather than who has a right to receive it. Carers or next of kin can always ask for information from the NHS body or social services authority and, although there may be no statutory obligation to provide this, the authority may recognise that it is in the best interests of the individual to do so. Policies on disclosure of information should cover this. A climate of mutual co-operation is usually preferable to undue reliance upon legal rights. But there remain situations where information is withheld with no effective remedy in the case of mentally incapacitated persons.

CHAPTER 3

The elderly client practice

Jennifer Margrave and Martin Terrell

3.1 RULES AND GUIDANCE

3.1.1 Rules for all practitioners

All solicitors in whatever area of practice are subject to the general law and a myriad of professional rules, including the Solicitors Act 1974 (as amended), the Solicitors' Practice Rules 1990, and the Solicitors' Accounts Rules 1998.

The relevant law, rules and guidance is set out in *The Guide to the Professional Conduct of Solicitors*, Law Society (8th edn, 1999). An updated version is available at **www.guide-on-line.lawsociety.org.uk**.

3.1.2 Rules relevant to elderly client practice

The rules that are most relevant to an elderly client practice include:

- Solicitors' Practice Rules 1990;
- Solicitors' Introduction and Referral Code 1990;
- Solicitors' Accounts Rules 1998;
- Solicitors' Publicity Code 2001;
- Solicitors' Costs Information and Client Care Code 1999;
- Solicitors' Anti-Discrimination Rule 1995;
- Solicitors' (Non-Contentious Business) Remuneration Order 1994, SI 1994/2616;
- Solicitors' Financial Services (Scope) Rules 2001;
- Solicitors' Financial Services (Amendment) Rules 2001;
- Solicitors' Financial Services (Conduct of Business) Rules 2001.

3.1.3 Mental health and disability committee

The Law Society's Mental Health and Disability Committee has issued guidance for solicitors on topics of particular relevance to the elderly client practice. This guidance is all available on **www.lawsociety.org.uk** (from the home page, click 'View all specialisms' then 'Mental Health and Disability'):

- *The Disability Discrimination Act 1995: An Essential Guide for solicitors*, Law Society (2001);
- *Enduring Powers of Attorney: Guidelines for Solicitors* (1999) (see Appendix A);
- *Gifts of Property: Implications for Future Liability to Pay for Long-Term Care* (2000) (see Appendix B).

3.1.4   Money laundering

Solicitors acting for elderly clients must also comply with the relevant provisions of the Proceeds of Crime Act 2002 and the Money Laundering Regulations 2003, which apply to private clients and elderly clients as they do to other areas of legal practice.

At the time of writing (October 2003) the 2003 Regulations have yet to be made in their final form. After this date, solicitors will have three months to ensure their practices comply.

The Law Society has produced the following guidance (**www.lawsociety. org.uk**) and is updating it to reflect the new Regulations:

- 'Proceeds of Crime Act 2002: It's Here and Now!' ([2003] *Gazette*, April);
- Money Laundering Warning Card (September 2002);
- Money Laundering Legislation Guidance Pack (February 2002);
- 'Solicitors as Gatekeepers' (letter, February 2002);
- 'Solicitors as Gatekeepers' (letter, September 2002).

3.1.5   Disability discrimination

The Disability Discrimination Act (DDA) 1995 imposes duties on, among others, employers and service providers (including solicitors) not to discriminate against disabled people. Discrimination is defined in s.20 for the purposes of the provision of goods and services:

a provider of services discriminates against a disabled person if:

(a)   for a reason which relates to the disabled person's disability, he treats him less favourably than he treats or would treat others to whom that reason does not or would not apply; and

(b)   he cannot show that the treatment in question is justified.

This discrimination may manifest itself in a variety of ways, including a refusal of service, providing a service on different terms, or providing a service of a different standard or manner.

Code of Practice

The full Code of Practice (as revised) *Rights of Access, Goods, Facilities, Services and Premises* can be viewed at **www.drc.gov.uk**. The following extract explains the implementation dates:

> The duties on service providers are being introduced in three stages:
>
> - since 2 December 1996 it has been unlawful for service providers to treat disabled people less favourably for a reason related to their disability;
> - since 1 October 1999 service providers have had to make 'reasonable adjustments' for disabled people, such as providing extra help or making changes to the way they provide their services; and
> - from 1 October 2004 service providers may have to make other 'reasonable adjustments' in relation to the physical features of their premises to overcome physical barriers to access.
>
> This Code ... takes account of the further duties on service providers to make adjustments when the physical features of their premises make it impossible or unreasonably difficult for disabled people to use their services.

See *The Disability Discrimination Act 1995: An Essential Guide for Solicitors*, the Solicitors' Anti-Discrimination Rule 1995, Chapter 6 at 6.5.1 and Chapter 16 at 16.1.5.

Solicitors as employers

Part II of the Disability Discrimination Act 1995 sets out employers' duties. These provisions are supplemented by regulations relating to employment and small businesses, and the Code of Practice for the elimination of discrimination in the field of employment against disabled persons or persons who have had a disability.

Firms should comply with the Law Society's Anti-Discrimination Rule 1995 and ensure that they have an anti-discrimination policy which is reviewed in light of the provisions of the Disability Discrimination Act 1995 and supporting regulations.

See *The Disability Discrimination Act 1995: An Essential Guide for Solicitors* (2001).

There are several organisations, including Employers' Forum for Disability, Royal Association for Disability and Rehabilitation (RADAR), the Disability Rights Commission (see Appendix E for contact details) that provide information for employers to help them to comply with the Disability Discrimination Act 1995.

3.1.6 Practice management guidance

The Law Society publishes a wide range of books on practice management topics that will be useful to solicitors managing an elderly client practice or in the process of setting up a new practice. These management topics include accounts, client care, e-business and technology. Solicitors may benefit from two in particular:

- Law Society, *Lexcel Practice Excellence Kit* (3rd edn, 2004);
- Martin Smith, *Setting Up and Managing a Small Practice* (2nd edn, 2002).

3.2 OFFICE MANAGEMENT

Running an efficient office combines management skills, interpersonal skills and common sense. The aim of this chapter is to highlight those skills generally relevant to the elderly client practice as well as those which are essential. You cannot assume that simply because some of your clients are old, you have the makings of a professional and profitable elderly client practice.

To begin with, the practice must have the relevant knowledge and expertise to handle the many problems that arise and have efficient office systems to cope with administration. Clients or those assisting with their affairs will soon become dissatisfied if there is delay and uncertainty or they are not kept advised. Elderly clients come to a solicitor because they have a problem, often in distressing circumstances. They may be asked to confront their own failing health and mental faculties or cope with the dementia, disability or even violence of a loved husband or wife. They need reassurance followed by clear, courteous and practical advice. A solicitor has a very valuable role in such situations, especially in providing personal contact. Elderly clients more than most appreciate knowing where to turn for advice in an increasingly impersonal society. So many institutions – banks, government departments, hospitals, insurance companies – are prone to treat their customers as numbers, statistics or targets: customers can never get hold of a person or have to negotiate a telephone obstacle course to speak to a person. The aim of the solicitor must be to use the benefits of modern technology and management practice to provide that client with a personal and professional service.

3.2.1 Staff

All staff working with elderly clients and their families must be aware of the basic standards of good practice which they are expected to follow. It is important to value their contribution and recognise the particular stresses working with the elderly client can cause. You should ensure that:

- fee earners and support staff receive proper training and are continually updated on changes in the law, regulations and procedures;
- all staff can recognise particular problems which may arise in working with older clients, e.g. questions of capacity, inter-generational conflicts, long-term care issues;

- there are opportunities for obtaining specialist qualifications (e.g. Society of Trust and Estate Practitioners) or joining specialist groups (e.g. Solicitors for the Elderly and the Law Society's Probate Section).

3.2.2 Delegation

An efficient and profitable office aims to delegate case work to staff, leaving the supervising partner or senior solicitor to cope with problems and develop a relationship with the client. However, this can cause its own problems with the client not knowing whom to contact and the solicitor and his or her staff working at cross purposes.

For any delegation to be effective, the client needs to be informed from the outset who will be dealing with the case. This is not just a professional requirement under Practice Rule 15, but a reflection of common sense and professional courtesy. The solicitor cannot work effectively and be available for every client at all times of day all year round. The client must therefore be informed in writing of:

- who will be responsible for their matter;
- who to contact if the solicitor is unavailable;
- who to contact if there is a problem or complaint.

It is far more personal, especially in long running cases, to explain to clients how the office works and introduce the staff who will be the other points of contact. Many clients end up feeling more comfortable dealing with a junior fee earner or a secretary.

Delegation cannot be an excuse for avoiding responsibility. Staff must not be allowed to do work beyond their capabilities or to overlook matters through neglect, embarrassment or because the solicitor is too busy. Neither should the possibility of financial mismanagement and even fraud be ignored. Adequate, regular and continuing supervision of staff in accordance with clear office protocols and guidance is essential. The responsibility of the solicitor is all the greater where he holds the trust of the vulnerable or incapable client.

The solicitor should therefore:

- set up regular file audits and client reviews;
- discuss the case and any unusual or interesting aspects;
- encourage staff to talk about cases and any queries or difficulties they have;
- use modern practice management systems such as Lexcel or ISO 9002 to ensure consistent working practices, file management, document production etc.;
- ensure that discussions are clearly recorded on the file as contemporaneously as possible;

- remember the overall common law duty of care to the client and be aware that the client may be unaware that the matter has not been properly dealt with;
- review the contracts of unqualified staff to ensure that they are not appointed to act as attorneys or executors;
- regularly audit accounts for which the solicitor is responsible as attorney or receiver;
- make staff aware of any professional implications of their role and ensure that any gifts from clients are disclosed and recorded.

3.2.3   Departments

As should be clear from the areas of law covered by this work, the needs of the elderly client do not sit neatly with the conventional departmental structure used by most firms. Often work falls between two or more departments or involves more than one department. A seemingly simple case of appointing a receiver may involve conveyancing on the sale of the property, litigation on an Inheritance (Provision for Family and Dependants) Act 1975 claim or civil debt, contract law in respect of the nursing home, community care law and welfare benefit law, investment advice, employment law as regards the carers, company law in respect of the family business and issues of capacity concerning residence and treatment.

Some firms have set up specialist departments or found a single fee earner who has become the firm's expert and main point of reference, usually within an existing private client or probate department. Generally such expertise grows out of the traditional private client areas of practice, largely due to those areas having the most elderly clients. However, as the above example illustrates, the work may involve more than one department and if the client needs to use more than one department, the client may still wish to have a single contact within the firm. It is often the case that what the client values most in his solicitor is a single contact, and a relationship with the client coupled with access to specific expertise is generally more valuable than expertise in a particular field of law but no knowledge of the client.

Links between departments

Where work is done by more than one department for the same client, departments must inform each other, and the principal client contact, of all major developments. Modern technology facilitates this so that correspondence and e-mails can be copied very easily from one file to another across two or more departments within a firm.

The role of the practice is as much in giving support to the client as in giving legal advice and this needs to be conveyed to colleagues who may be unfamiliar with the character and history of the client.

3.2.4 Branch offices

Every office where the firm practises must conform with Rule 13 of the Solicitors' Practice Rules 1990 and must be properly and clearly supervised in accordance with certain minimum standards:

- It must be attended on each day when open to the public by a solicitor who holds a practising certificate and has been admitted for at least three years. The solicitor may be a principal, employee or consultant of your firm and must spend sufficient time at the office to ensure adequate control of the staff employed there and afford requisite facilities for consultation with clients.
- It must be managed by a practising solicitor or suitably qualified legal executive (or licensed conveyancer if solely dealing with conveyancing). The person must normally be in attendance at that office during all the hours when it is open to the public (including for telephone calls).
- In cases of absence due to illness, accident, etc. for a prolonged period, suitable alternative arrangements should be made.

3.2.5 Monitoring

Clients will not always know when they need further legal assistance especially as their circumstances and needs can change quite radically in a relatively short period of time. A couple with a young family may not change their wills for 20 years, while an older client may unexpectedly find that he is intestate or that a carefully planned gift in a will has adeemed due to a disposal of the asset. You need to take a more pro-active role with elderly clients who will often be unaware of the problems inherent in their situations. It is better to be forward and risk your client ignoring your advice than not to have proffered the advice at all.

As the client's circumstances change:

- Do not overlook the need for a will to be updated or a statutory will to be considered.
- Check whether an Enduring Power of Attorney (EPA) is still operable or whether it should be registered. Is it properly executed?
- Check that all current state benefits are being claimed in the light of benefit changes or the qualifying conditions of the client.
- Should the client be advised on community care services and how to obtain best delivery of services?
- Is assistance needed in negotiating any contract with social services or a residential care or nursing home?
- Do the present housing arrangements still meet the client's needs?

The client's financial affairs require particular attention to ensure they are still being handled properly and have been reviewed in the light of changes in circumstances:

- Is it time for a change of investment policy?
- Is the client living on capital and if so how long will this last? Can/should changes be made?
- Can the client afford the level of care to which he or she is committed?
- Should the client consider some tax planning measures?
- Should assistance be offered to cope with self-assessment?
- Is there any reason to suspect that the client is vulnerable to financial exploitation or any other form of abuse?

Lastly, make sure that your retainer and terms of business are up to date. Do they cover the additional work being carried out? Have you undertaken to do more than your client has asked you to do?

It is a matter of judgement and practice as to how best to monitor clients' needs. Some firms have systems for regular contacts and reminders, although these cannot address all clients at the right time. It is worth bearing in mind that you cannot monitor your clients all the time and there is always a danger of creating hostages to fortune in offering to do more than is practicable.

The aim of the elderly client solicitor should be to think pro-actively, anticipating the needs and future needs of the client, putting out markers for further action being required. If you cannot monitor the client yourself, make sure those who are in regular contact will monitor the client and know when to contact you. Also ensure that an attorney knows when they need to register an EPA so that they contact you when the need arises. The solicitor who can achieve this is not only acting in the client's best interests but also marketing his or her business and securing future work for the firm (see also 3.7).

3.2.6 Systems

Systems introduced in the office make monitoring clients' affairs and safe custody of papers and documents more effective. The use of computerised systems will assist with:

- access to current files;
- archiving of old files;
- storage of documents, including deeds, wills, ordinary powers of attorney and EPAs, securities, and birth, death or marriage certificates;
- maintenance of accounting records;
- upkeep of diaries;
- reminders of significant dates (not just deadlines but also to review the client's needs or simply to send a birthday card);

- effective use of client database to target or review for new work;
- reviewing files and work in progress.

3.2.7 Computers

Computers are now ubiquitous in almost every office but they are not always used to their full potential. Often they are used simply for word processing and checking ledgers, but there are many ways in which computers can help to provide a more effective and efficient service. For example, they can be used for:

- standard form letters;
- precedents of regularly used documents;
- storage of clients' previous wills for easy amendment;
- amending documents to make them more accessible, e.g. using larger fonts or heavier type;
- databases of clients with whom regular contact should be maintained, of current and old files, of deeds and documents in safe custody, of clients falling into specific work areas or age groups;
- spreadsheets of schedules of investments, tax returns and interest schedules for reproducing annually;
- keeping receivers' and attorneys' accounts up to date;
- accounting software for clients' accounts and trust accounts with facilities to calculate interest;
- time recording to ensure that work is properly costed and the client is kept informed of costs arising;
- diaries to manage appointments and reminders of action to take;
- Internet access for up-to-date information from countless websites run by government departments, the court service, charities, publishers and lobby groups (see e.g. the website information in Appendix E).

Client database

You may have a database containing information about individual clients from which all other storage records are derived. All relevant information can then be seen in respect of a client at a glance, whilst lists of deeds, wills, securities, etc. can still be produced (according to categories of client, date, name or otherwise as desired).

Advice about purchasing suitable systems from approved suppliers is given in the Law Society's *Software Solutions* guide. This booklet and further guidance can be found at **www.it.lawsociety.org.uk**.

Data protection issues

If you send, receive, process or store material containing personal data you must ensure that you comply with the provisions of the Data Protection Act 1998 and subsequent codes of conduct or regulations relating to it, including the Data Protection Directive 95/46/EC, which must be implemented by 31 October 2003. Visit **www.dataprotection.gov.uk** for more information and guidance.

3.3   DUTIES TO THE CLIENT

The solicitor's first duty is to identify the client, as this is not always as obvious as it may appear (see Chapter 2 at 2.2.2). Professional duties are owed to the client throughout and not, where the client lacks capacity, to the person through whom instructions are given, even though communications may well be with that person. Do not be too easily persuaded by third parties as to the client's best interests, because however well intentioned they may seem, they may have a personal interest. Also be alert to the potential for financial abuse with EPAs.

3.3.1   Client care

Client care is at the heart of any solicitor's professional duties towards his or her client. Before even considering the quality of the legal advice, a solicitor should always aim to:

- reply to correspondence within three working days;
- keep the client informed of progress and advise of any delays with reasons;
- send copies of significant letters;
- explain the effect of any important documents;
- explain promptly to the client any changes to the costs forecast or basis of assessment and of staff affecting the client or of law affecting the matter.

At the outset you should confirm to the client in writing:

- the person responsible for day-to-day conduct of the matter and their status or qualification, and also the partner responsible for overall supervision;
- the instructions that you have received and any advice you have given;
- what action you will be taking and what action you need the client to take;
- any further information you need from the client;
- the approximate time the matter will take and when the client is next likely to hear from you;
- the basis for charging for your work and the likely costs of your acting for the client (see below);

- the likely effect of the client's action or lack of action, giving any relevant warnings;
- the complaints procedures for use if the client is not satisfied.

See Rule 15 of the Solicitors' Practice Rules 1990 and Heather Stewart, *Excellent Client Service*, Law Society (2003).

At the end of the matter you should:

- confirm to the client, in writing, how the matter has been concluded;
- explain any continuing consequences and risks from their action or inaction;
- render your bill as promptly as possible and account to the client for all money due;
- consider with the client whether any papers and property are to be handed over or retained by your firm.

It is often useful to send out a simple questionnaire on the service rendered. This allows the client to evaluate the solicitor's work which will either provide welcome reassurance or identify improvements which may be necessary. A questionnaire can also be a useful marketing tool in reminding the client of their importance to the firm and also introducing the client to other areas of work.

3.3.2 Costs

There are detailed professional rules and guidance on the issue of costs and these can be found at **www.guide-on-line.lawsociety.org.uk**. Their extent illustrates the seriousness of the subject and reflect the problems that disputes over costs can cause in practice. You may do an excellent job for your client but all the credit for this and future goodwill can be destroyed by costs being dealt with inappropriately.

It is essential to inform clients and potential clients in advance what costs and expenses they may expect to incur and to consider with the client whether the likely outcome will justify the expense or risk involved.

Send a statement of Terms and Conditions of Business to the client at the outset together with a duplicate to sign and return confirming agreement.

It is good practice to be open about costs at the earliest stage. This avoids acrimony later on when the cost of the work exceeds what the client expected to pay. A client may be equally satisfied by being informed of the costs of a particular course of action and deciding that he does not want to incur those costs. If the client does not want to pay for the advice he genuinely needs then be prepared to recommend another firm which may be more willing to take on such work or else inform the client where they can find voluntary help or a useful website. Some sources of help and websites are set out in Appendix E.

The following issues need to be addressed.

The basis of charging

Consider the following:

- hourly rates;
- prospects of a free initial interview or fixed fee interviews or work;
- best estimate of the likely costs involved and placing a limit on total costs;
- choice and cost of fee earners;
- interim estimates of costs incurred and any options on billing e.g. quarterly, monthly, etc.;
- the authority for charging if the client cannot consent, especially if this depends on the provisions of an EPA or the terms of the appointment of the receiver (see 4.5.5 and 4.11);
- implications of VAT.

The means of payment and when costs may be deducted

Relevant matters are:

- eligibility for legal aid (and the effect of the statutory charge);
- whether a payment in advance is required and why;
- nature and frequency of interim bills and the treatment of disbursements;
- charges for interest on unpaid bills and any credit facilities available.

Prospects of recovering all or any part of the cost

The options are recovery:

- from the Legal Aid fund (ensure you have the relevant leaflets from the Legal Services Commission);
- from the other party;
- from insurance or some other source.

Procedure for complaints about costs

Make the client aware of:

- their right to an itemised bill, remuneration certificate or assessment by the court;
- the complaints procedure to the firm;
- the possibility of reference to the local Law Society, the Office for the Supervision of Solicitors or the Legal Services Ombudsman.

Remember that a dissatisfied client will nullify all your best marketing efforts to develop your practice.

Incapable clients

A solicitor owes a higher duty of care to a client for whom he or she is acting in a fiduciary role and who may not be able to comprehend the legal issues being dealt with, let alone the contract between himself and his solicitor. Where the solicitor is an attorney the instrument may well provide authority to charge in the same way as a 'charging clause' in a will. But although the solicitor has a legal right to charge, there may be little *de facto* oversight of the charges. There have regrettably been cases of solicitors abusing their roles as attorneys and charging excessively for their work to the point of committing a fraud against the client.

It is therefore essential that solicitors acting in a fiduciary role, especially as attorneys, keep careful accounts which can be audited by the Public Guardianship Office or a beneficiary on the death of the client. Time ledgers and detailed fee accounts should also be retained with the file.

Where a receiver has been appointed by the Court of Protection then the costs of the solicitor acting are in the discretion of the Court and generally payable from the patient's estate. Costs are therefore either fixed at a predetermined level or subject to assessment by the court (see 4.11).

Contentious cases

Although there are different rules in contentious cases, similar considerations apply. In addition, the client must be informed at the outset and at appropriate stages of the matter:

- that he will be personally responsible for payment of your bill unless entitled to legal aid regardless of any order for costs made against his opponent;
- that if he loses he will probably have to pay his opponent's costs as well as his own;
- that even if he wins his opponent may not be ordered to pay the full amount of his costs and may not be capable of paying what he is ordered to pay;
- that if his opponent is legally aided he may not recover costs even if successful;
- if the firm operates a 'no win no fee' scheme or uses contingency fee agreements.

Legal aid

If the client is legally aided in civil proceedings he should be informed:

- of his obligation to pay any contribution assessed, the consequences of any failure to do so and the effect of the statutory charge;

- that if he loses he may still be ordered to contribute to his opponent's costs even though his own costs are covered by legal aid;
- that even if he wins his opponent may not be ordered to pay the full amount of his costs and may not be capable of paying what he is ordered to pay.

The following books may be helpful to practitioners:

- V. Ling and S. Pugh *Understanding Legal Aid: A Practical Guide to Public Funding*, Law Society (2003);
- P. Owston and S. McCall *Making a Success of Legal Aid*, Law Society (2003).

3.4 FINANCIAL SERVICES

3.4.1 Financial Services and Markets Act 2000

The Financial Services and Markets Act 2000 (FSMA), which came into force on 1 December 2001, has made major changes to the regulation of the financial services industry. It is a criminal offence to carry on 'regulated activities', as defined in the Financial Services and Markets Act (Regulated Activities) Order 2001 (RAO), SI 2001/544, without authorisation. From 1 December 2001 authorisation must be obtained from the Financial Services Authority. The Law Society has ceased to be a Recognised Professional Body and solicitors can no longer obtain authorisation for the purposes of the Act in this way. However, large numbers of firms of solicitors will fall outside the requirements to be authorised providing they undertake regulated activities strictly in accordance with statutory exclusions or exemptions.

The following activities may involve a solicitor who is acting for the elderly in regulated activities:

- advice on or arrangements made for the purchase or sale of investment bonds or other specified investments;
- advice on or arrangements made for the purchase of a funeral plan contract;
- advice on or arrangements made for the purchase of an annuity;
- acting as trustee or executor or acting on the administration of a trust fund or estate on behalf of an outside trustee or executor.

3.4.2 Regulated activities

'Regulated activities' are defined in the Financial Services and Markets Act (Regulated Activities) Order 2001.

A regulated activity is potentially undertaken when a solicitor is involved in any one of the activities referred to in articles 5–61 RAO and relating to any one of the specified investments listed in articles 74–89. The most common activities will be:

- advice on the merits of buying or selling a specified investment;
- arranging on behalf of a client the sale or purchase of a specified investment;
- discretionary management of specified investments (this will arise where the trustees or executors are all partners or employees in the firm, or where a solicitor is a donee under a power of attorney which allows discretion in relation to the purchase/sale of specified investments);
- safeguarding and administration of specified investments.

Shares, bonds, unit trusts, annuities, funeral plan contracts and ISAs constitute common specified investments.

Advising the client on or arranging the purchase or sale of the following investments does not constitute a regulated activity since these activities in relation to the investments are not caught by the definition of regulated activities:

- a normal bank or building society current or deposit account;
- buildings or contents insurance;
- National Savings and Investments products.

Generic investment advice is not within the definition of regulated activities in the RAO. Generic advice is advice about general categories of investment, as opposed to specific investments. Recommendations to the client that 'it would be wise to invest capital in equity shares/unit trusts' or 'you should take out an annuity' are both examples of generic advice.

3.4.3 Exclusions

Solicitors can avoid the need for authorisation by showing that certain exclusions contained in the RAO apply. The most important are as follows:

- Arrangements made with or through an authorised person (i.e. an independent financial adviser (IFA)) are excluded where the transaction is entered into on advice given to the client by an authorised person. However, this exclusion does not apply if the solicitor receives from any person other than the client any pecuniary award or advantage, for which he does not account to the client, arising out of his entering into the transaction. The Law Society has taken the view that retaining commission with the informed consent of the client in accordance with Rule 10 of the Solicitors' Practice Rules 1990 does represent 'accounting to the client' and the benefit of the exception will still apply in these circumstances.
- Introductions are excluded where a solicitor introduces a client to an authorised person and the introduction is made with a view to the provision of independent advice (i.e. an introduction to an IFA).

- Discretionary management through the appointment of a solicitor as a donee under a power of attorney is excluded if all routine or day-to-day decisions are taken by an authorised person (i.e. an IFA).
- Arranging deals, discretionary management, safeguarding and administration and investment advice are all excluded if undertaken by a solicitor who is a trustee or executor (but not if a solicitor is merely acting for outside trustees or executors). Note that for this exclusion to apply, the solicitor must not be remunerated for these activities in addition to any remuneration received for acting as a trustee or executor. Furthermore, for the exclusion to apply to discretionary management or safeguarding and administration activities, the solicitor must not hold himself out as providing such services.

3.4.4 Exempt regulated activities

Where an exclusion is not available for any reason, an alternative means of avoiding the need for authorisation is to use Part XX FSMA which contains provisions relating to 'exempt regulated activities' carried on by members of a profession which is supervised and regulated by a designated professional body (DPB). The Law Society is a DPB.

Section 327 FSMA provides that the prohibition against carrying on regulated activities contained in the Act does not apply to the carrying on of a regulated activity by a member of a profession if certain conditions apply:

(a) the person must be a member of a profession or controlled or managed by one or more such members;

(b) the person must not receive from anyone other than his client any pecuniary reward or other advantage, for which he does not account to his client, arising out of his carrying on of any of the activities;

(c) the manner of the provision of any service in the course of carrying on the activities must be incidental to the provision by him of professional services;

(d) only regulated activities permitted by the DPB's rules may be carried out.

The Law Society has issued rules (Solicitors' Financial Services (Scope) Rules 2001), covering the requirements of (d) above. These rules will limit the scope of solicitors benefiting from Part XX. The prohibited activities include:

- market making;
- buying, selling, subscribing or underwriting as principal where the firm holds itself out as engaging in the business of buying investments with a view to selling them;
- acting as a trustee or operator of a regulated CIS;
- acting as a stakeholder pension scheme manger;
- entering as provider into a funeral plan contract.

There are further restrictions in the use of Part XX contained in the Scope Rules.

Packaged products

These are defined as long term insurance contracts (including annuities), units or shares in regulated Collective Investment Schemes (e.g. unit trusts or shares in Open Ended Investment Companies) or an investment trust savings scheme, in each case whether or not held within an ISA or PEP or a stakeholder pension scheme. Where such investments are involved, firms cannot use the 'incidental' exception in Part XX in relation to recommendations or arrangements to purchase a packaged product but should use an authorised person (i.e. an IFA). However, firms may, within Part XX:

- pass on and endorse the advice of an authorised person;
- recommend or arrange the disposal of a packaged product;
- recommend or arrange the acquisition of a packaged product by means of an assignfment;
- recommend that a client should not buy a packaged product (i.e. give negative advice).

Other investments

Recommending an individual to buy an investment is not permitted if the transaction is with a person whose business it is to deal in those investments (e.g. a stockbroker), or the transaction is on an investment exchange or in response to an invitation to subscribe for an investment admitted or to be admitted on an investment exchange. However, firms may, within Part XX:

- pass on and endorse the advice of an authorised person;
- recommend or arrange the disposal of such investments;
- arrange the acquisition of such investments;
- recommend that a client should not buy such investments (i.e. give negative advice).

Managing investments

Discretionary management of investments can only fall within Part XX if the management is undertaken by a solicitor who is a trustee, personal representative, donee under a power of attorney, or a receiver appointed by the Court of Protection. Further, to benefit from Part XX, it must be shown that all routine or day-to-day decisions are taken by an authorised person, or that any decision taken to buy or subscribe for an investment is taken in accordance with the advice of an authorised person.

3.4.5   Conduct of Business Rules

The Law Society has also issued the Solicitors' Financial Services (Conduct of Business) Rules 2001, applicable to solicitors seeking exemption under Part XX. These include rules relating to:

- *status disclosure* requiring firms to indicate in writing that they are not authorised by the FSA but are regulated by the Law Society;
- *execution of transactions* requiring firms to carry out transactions as soon as possible;
- *records of transactions* requiring firms to keep records of instructions received and instructions given;
- *record of commissions* requiring firms to keep records of commissions received and records of how such commission has been accounted to clients;
- *execution only – packaged products* requiring firms to give written confirmation of execution only transactions involving packaged products.

3.4.6   Commissions

Life assurance companies and the providers of some other types of investment product pay commissions to intermediaries on the sale of their products. A solicitor who introduces a client to an authorised person will usually receive a commission for the introduction.

Any commission received by the solicitor is subject to Rule 10 Solicitors' Practice Rules 1990. As noted above, the exclusions and exemption from the need for authorisation require solicitors to account for any commission. If a solicitor retains commission without the client's consent (even if the commission is not more than the £20 *de minimis* allowed for in Practice Rule 10) the exclusions and the exemption will not apply. Solicitors risk committing a criminal offence if they undertake regulated activities without being authorised and without the benefit of an appropriate exclusion or exemption.

3.4.7   The marketplace for financial services

Research and the experience of many practitioners indicate that elderly people are very receptive to the idea of seeking financial advice through their solicitor. Having encountered the constant marketing of financial services and products through advertisements and mail-shots, a client may believe that he will not be sold something or indeed rushed into anything against his interests by his solicitor. It is far safer to introduce your elderly client to an independent financial adviser, whom you know and trust. If you ignore the client's financial requirements all your good work in other areas could be rendered ineffective by someone selling the client an inappropriate or unwise investment.

In addition it may be easier to manage a client's tax and other affairs if you are fully aware of the financial products being sold to them. You should also be aware of the need to 'know your client' and therefore to have some knowledge of their investments and assets the ownership of which may otherwise be inconsistent with other advice you have given in connection with tax or welfare benefits. Few solicitors are themselves authorised to provide financial advice. Yet whether advice is provided by your firm in-house or with an authorised party (AP), you will need to understand in broad terms the advice being given to the client. You may act as an intermediary and be responsible for providing the AP with sufficient details about your client to enable sound advice to be given. You may otherwise be asked to interpret, comment upon, endorse or provide 'negative advice' on the AP's recommendations.

3.4.8 General advice

You should not be deterred from providing any financial advice to your client simply by reason of the Financial Services and Markets Act 2000, because much of the advice that a typical elderly client needs will not come within the scope of that legislation. Such advice may be general or strategic and often the client's affairs may be neglected and simply need to be tidied up and simplified.

You should therefore consider whether:

- money is safely invested and at the very least providing a good rate of interest. The client may have large sums of cash in the house which should be banked or a large balance on current account could be put on deposit. The client may have a number of small building society accounts which could be amalgamated or on which a better rate of interest obtained in a different class of account. Matured savings certificates should be encashed.
- income is being paid net of tax if the client would benefit from gross income, and recoverable tax deducted is being recovered;
- any increase or decrease in income would affect welfare benefits;
- permitted expenditure such as the purchase of a funeral plan would reduce the client's assets below the Pension Credit levels;
- the client might be better advised to reduce the value of his taxable estate through capital expenditure or lifetime gifts rather than necessarily generate a larger income;
- capital could be preserved by purchasing an annuity or long-term care plan to fund residential or nursing care, so enabling the client to be self-funding with the consequent beneficial effects on state benefits and in preserving assets.

Advice such as this, provided it is generic, does not constitute a 'regulated activity' but you must be able to recognise the need to obtain expert and regulated financial advice when it is needed and, if possible, know where to obtain it.

3.5 THE MARKET FOR THE ELDERLY CLIENT ADVISER

It should be clear from the very nature of this work just how extensive is the need for specialist advice for the elderly client, and as the number of elderly clients grows, so does the market for their business. For more information and statistics on the elderly population see Age Concern's annually updated fact card *Older People in the United Kingdom: Some Basic Facts* (on **www.ace. org.uk**).

Marketing is often seen as promoting your practice or particular specialist services which you can offer to potential clients. Advertising is one aspect and may not appeal to you; other possibilities can and should be considered. The best and simplest marketing involves making existing clients and people you deal with aware of the services you provide. You can easily spend a small fortune on clever brochures and adverts and overlook the large number of elderly clients and potential referrers of elderly clients you already have!

Although marketing is often seen as a complex and separate area, involving large resources and the recruitment of specialist staff or consultants, we can at least seek to identify matters of particular significance to elderly clients which you should consider in developing your practice.

Practitioners may find the following books helpful:

- Dianne Bown-Wilson and Gail Courtney *Marketing, Management and Motivation*, Law Society (2002);
- Lucy Adam, *Marketing Your Law Firm*, Law Society (2001);
- Nicola Webb, *Internet Marketing: Strategies for Law Firms*, Law Society (2003).

3.5.1 Trends

Solicitors do not have a monopoly in providing for the legal needs of elderly people, but there are many areas of this work that the profession should seek to retain and develop in the face of growing competition from others in the marketplace. The solicitor in general practice is uniquely qualified to respond to the legal needs of older members of the local community, and the consequence of doing so may be a wide range of new work and an introduction to new clients (not only elderly ones, as many satisfied clients will have families, friends or other professional connections).

Financial and legal problems of older people are increasing because they are living longer and demographics and lifestyle mean that families do not live so close and cannot always provide support. Older people tend (and wish) to be cared for in the community rather than in hospitals or institutions and have more money (from home ownership, pensions and state benefits).

The need for delegation arises more often in the case of women because men generally die younger and are more reluctant to give up management of their affairs. Also, many widows have been wholly dependent on their husbands for managing routine financial matters.

3.5.2 Areas of work

The law relating to the elderly client is unlike other areas of law which are subject-based. Instead of identifying an area of law such as divorce or crime and then finding the clients to service, elderly client law is client focused. The focus is the client and the solicitor needs to apply different areas of law to meet the needs of the client. To develop an elderly client practice a solicitor or a firm of solicitors needs to provide expertise in many different areas of work.

Financial

See:

- social security benefits, Chapter 13;
- local authority benefits, Chapters 13 and 14;
- financial planning, Chapter 17;
- tax and tax planning, Chapter 17;
- providing for infirm or disabled relatives, Chapter 20;
- wills and gifts, Chapters 19 and 20;
- loans to relatives and guarantees for their liabilities, Chapter 17;
- long-term care planning, Chapters 8, 9 and 10.

Management

See:

- coping with mental and/or physical frailty, Chapters 1 and 4;
- issues as to capacity, Chapter 1;
- handling financial affairs and dealing with problems, Chapters 1, 4 and 17;
- EPAs, Chapter 4;
- Court of Protection applications and receivership, Chapter 4;
- negotiating service delivery for domiciliary, residential or nursing care, Chapters 7 and 9.

Personal

See:

- continuing employment or involvement in business, Chapter 16;
- involvement with the police, Chapter 6;

- issues of civil status, Chapter 6;
- planning for the future (e.g. residential care, funeral), Chapters 8, 9 and 21;
- community care provision and funding and advocacy services for service delivery, Chapters 7 and 8;
- accidents (e.g. tripping on pavement), Chapter 5;
- consumer problems, Chapter 6.

Relationships

See:

- supporting carers and dealing with professionals, Chapters 2 and 8;
- marriage and cohabitation difficulties, Chapter 6;
- problems with family, Chapter 6;
- abuse and domestic violence, Chapter 6;
- disputes with others, Chapters 5 and 6.

Housing

See:

- moving house, Chapter 18;
- sharing the home or moving in with relatives, Chapter 18;
- exercising the 'right to buy' council accommodation, Chapter 18;
- disabled facilities and grants, Chapter 15;
- home income plans, Chapters 17 and 18;
- sheltered housing schemes, Chapter 18;
- moving into residential care, Chapter 9.

Health

See:

- coping with the NHS, Chapters 10 and 15;
- private medical schemes, Chapter 10;
- medical negligence claims, Chapter 5;
- implications of mental incapacity, Chapter 1;
- implications of mental illness, Chapter 12;
- living wills and other forms of advance directives, Chapter 11;
- arrangements immediately following death, Chapter 21.

3.6 TARGETING ELDERLY CLIENTS

The areas of law covered by this work as outlined above encompass almost all areas of legal practice. However, this is far more than a summary of the general law applicable to private clients. Making a will or a personal injury claim may involve similar legal issues whether the client is 30 years old or 80 years old. However, for the elderly client the issues may be very different and the elderly client practitioner needs to be aware of this. In these two examples, the will of a parent with a young family will be different to that of an elderly spinster with no dependants; and a personal injury claim will involve very different consequences in terms of life expectancy, lost prospects, dependants and long-term care. Moreover, these general areas of law very often do interact with legal principles applicable to the elderly client especially in areas of capacity and financial management. Taking these two examples again, an elderly client's will may involve issues of capacity or substituted decision-making through the Court of Protection, issues which would not apply to the youthful parent; while the elderly litigant may need to be represented by a litigation friend.

Running an elderly client practice therefore involves having elderly clients and knowing the law that is relevant to their needs. Developing a successful elderly client practice also requires other qualities that may appear mundane but can make all the difference. These may well involve changes to and within your office and your attitude to clients. The qualities described below are of general application but some relate specifically to the elderly client.

Before you think that no one can acquire all these qualities, bear in mind that you cannot offer or change everything instantly but can continue to update and improve what you can offer. You must comply with the Disability Discrimination Act 1995 to facilitate access to services for all, irrespective of their limitations. This covers not only the premises but also communication (see 3.1.5).

3.6.1 A user-friendly office: checklist

Examine the facilities your firm has and the services that are offered from the point of view of the elderly client.

Access

❏   Is the location of your office easily accessible by road (one way systems are not user friendly for anybody, least of all the elderly)?

❏   Is there provision for parking close by?

❏   Is there convenient access to public transport?

❏   Is the street easy to cross near your office?

❏   Can you provide a map or written travel instructions?

❏   Does your office have aids to improve physical accessibility (signs, steps, staircases, stair rails, ramps, door widths, etc.). Are these enough to comply with the provisions of the Disability Discrimination Act 1995?

❏   Is your office free of obstructions?

❏   Are there clear signs to the reception area?

❏   Is the lighting in and outside your office sufficient?

❏   Do you offer home visits when the client wishes this and is advised of the extra cost? The client may ask for this even if able to visit your office (remember that the client is paying the fee and if they would feel more comfortable at home then it is for the adviser to accommodate this).

Waiting area

❏   Is there room to leave bags, shopping trolleys, umbrellas, etc.?

❏   Is your waiting area warm and draught free (and cool in summer)?

❏   Is there a choice of seating in your waiting area (e.g. higher/upright chairs with arms)?

❏   Do you have accessible toilet facilities (a disabled toilet may not always be feasible, but a toilet should be available on the same level as the waiting room)?

Interview room

❏   Is your interview room situated on the ground floor?

❏   Does your interview room offer a choice of seating (e.g. higher/upright chairs with arms)?

❏   Is it private (especially if having to speak loudly)?

❏   Is the lighting sufficient (also consider that a window behind the solicitor will create a silhouette effect making it difficult for the client to see)?

❏   Do you offer any adaptations to assist those with disabilities? Consider a hearing loop for example. The Royal National Institute for the Deaf and the Royal National Institute for the Blind will be able to assist you with information.

Impressions

❏   Do you have ground floor premises?

❏   Do your premises appear well cared for?

❏   Is your office furniture, carpets, and decorations in good condition?

❏   Can the impression your office creates be improved with pictures and flowers?

❏   Are your staff cheerful, polite and presentable?

❏   Are your staff well trained and able to be helpful and efficient?

❏   Do your support staff have any special training for working with elderly clients?

Communication

❏   Does your receptionist project the image of your firm that you would like to elderly clients?

❏   Does your receptionist communicate clearly with elderly clients in person and on the telephone?

❏   Do you provide elderly clients with information on the legal services available; the people in your office; costs; common legal issues (such as wills, long-term care, and EPAs)?

❏   Are clients kept informed about the progress of their case and the reasons for any delays?

❏   Have you considered suitable methods of communication such as large print in letters and documents; plain English in letters, documents and speech; installing an induction loop or minicom (for more information contact: RNID Sound Advantage, 1 Metro Way, Welbeck Way, Peterborough, PE2 7UH).

Convenience

❏   Do you offer appointments that suit the client?

❏   Do you always make appointments and never keep clients waiting?

❏   Do your staff offer assistance to clients with their travel arrangements (e.g. offering to ring for a taxi or escorting clients across the road, etc.)?

❏   Are there clinics or surgeries close by?

❏   Do you always offer clients the opportunity of home appointments?

❏   Have you considered the problems caused by limited mobility, use of wheelchairs, visual and hearing impairments and communication difficulties? Have you complied with the Disability Discrimination Act 1995?

3.6.2   Relationship with elderly clients

Dealing with older people is often based upon a one-to-one relationship working at the client's pace and level of understanding:

- Do not see working with elderly clients to be as competitive as when dealing with other solicitors or commercial clients.

- Ensure that the client knows who you are and that you are dealing personally with his or her matter.
- Explain how you may be contacted when the need arises.
- Introduce an alternative contact for occasions when you are not available.
- Make sure the client has the option of private discussion with you and thus is alerted to any potential problems or conflicts which may arise.
- If the client wishes to bring a friend to interviews, see the client on their own at first to assess mental capacity and special needs. Do not discourage the client from bringing a friend, however, because that friend will discuss the matter with the client when you are not there and may be able to provide valuable assistance as advocate for the client.
- Always be aware of undue influence but do not see this as a spectre in every situation.
- Avoid being patronising and do not assume that older people are less legally competent merely because they are mentally or physically infirm.
- Take care when raising painful subjects such as mental incapacity or death.
- Treat the client professionally at all times, but also consider how you would wish your elderly parent (or grandparent) to be treated in this situation or indeed how you will want to be treated when you become an elderly client yourself.

3.6.3 Addressing the client

Establish a policy throughout the firm as to the manner in which clients are addressed, particularly in letters. Do not assume that a first name approach should be encouraged as many elderly clients prefer a more formal approach.

Although partners and senior staff may wish to be on first name terms with clients, would you wish employees to follow suit and to address them in that manner in letters?

Make sure that clients are addressed correctly. A long-standing client may be on first name terms with the senior partner, but may not expect to be addressed in the same way by a trainee. Often it is a case of finding out how the client wishes to be addressed and letting the client dictate the style of the relationship. Check that you and your staff are consistent in their dealings and use the right form of address:

- 'Dear Madam';
- 'Dear Mrs Smith';
- 'Dear Ms Smith';
- 'Dear Ethel'.

Take care with titles, decorations, religious offices and military ranks. If such designations are used then they should be used correctly.

How does the client view you?

Do you:

- dress outrageously (nose rings, short skirts, loud ties)? The older client may expect professionals to look professional;
- appear too busy to discuss the client's problem or not easily available?
- talk down to the client?
- explain matters clearly to the client and appear to enjoy doing so?
- offer the client alternatives or impose your own viewpoint?
- give the client time to decide and consider matters with a follow-up letter?
- greet the client in reception or expect him or her to find your room and enter whilst you are working?
- take care how you address the client and invite the client to address you?

How can the client help you (and indirectly himself)?

Ensure the client can (if able):

- prepare for the meeting by drawing up a statement of facts and questions;
- give you clear instructions;
- explain if there are any important time constraints;
- make sure that you have understood each other;
- ask if not sure or worried about anything;
- keep in regular touch with you;
- deal promptly with any important or urgent questions that arise;
- ask for a progress report if the client has not heard from you when expecting to do so;
- talk about his or her family and history so that the client feels you are interested in what he or she has to say – this will help the client to feel at ease and you can gather valuable background information to assist with your advice or in assessing capacity;
- write rather than telephone unless it is urgent;
- make an appointment if wanting to see you;
- avoid unnecessary calls (which may increase the cost);
- speak to someone else whose time may be less expensive to the client, especially if the call is not urgent.

How can you help older clients?

Consider the following (as a matter of course):

- Have information packs to send in advance of an appointment to help prepare for any meeting relating to wills, tax planning, EPAs, living wills and long-term care.

- Visit elderly clients at their homes if it is difficult for them to get out or if your office premises are not suitable for visits by them and cannot be adapted.
- Visit just for a chat when they have not asked to see you and you have no specific business but feel concerned about their welfare.
- Consider paying a social call if you are passing or visiting another client in the same nursing home.
- Remember to send birthday or Christmas cards especially when the client has few other relatives or friends.
- Tell clients in advance that you are willing to visit them (without adding substantially to the bill).
- Make appointments at a time that suits them or in a residential care home or hospital at a convenient time (check with the nurse in charge) and keep these appointments (and conduct them in a cheerful manner).

3.6.4   Office brochures

Each firm will have its own style and the use of a 'logo' may create continuity between documents and give the firm an identity. Different brochures may be produced for different purposes, and it may be relevant to ask clients what their needs are. The following general brochures may be helpful to the older client.

An introduction to the firm

A marketing brochure or leaflet can inform potential clients about your firm and create the appropriate image. However, the brochure or leaflet needs to be appropriate to the client for whom it is designed. A glossy brochure promoting the firm's corporate business with bright pictures of glamorous lawyers in designer offices may deter some elderly clients. A brochure or leaflet should at the very least provide reassurance that your firm is reputable and can provide expertise in different areas of law as well as basic information (with photographs) about the firm's:

- name, address and telephone numbers;
- history (formation, growth, previous partners, names and locations);
- premises (history, location, access and facilities);
- partners (qualifications, expertise, interests and backgrounds);
- staff (number, nature and any special experience);
- availability during and outside normal office hours;
- areas of work, particular expertise and philosophy;
- other relevant information used in marketing.

A guide for clients

You may provide separate client brochures to provide a range of information to persons who are or become clients of the firm. These may include:

- basic information relating to the firm (name, full contact details, list of partners, list of department managers or fee earners, office hours, emergency telephone numbers);
- specific details, added to the printed brochure, of persons with whom the client may become involved (the person dealing with the client's matter, another person in the event that this person is unavailable, the supervising partner);
- guidance to the client on dealing effectively with the firm (e.g. standards that the firm seeks to maintain, the basis of charging, and complaints procedures);
- an overview of legal services provided by the firm (e.g. details of the general range of work undertaken, specialist services which are unique to the firm, a list of any newsletters promoting different services and issues).

3.7   PROMOTING LEGAL SERVICES

3.7.1   Establishing a reputation

Some firms will already have a sound reputation for specialising in elderly client work built up over several generations, but positive steps can be taken either to ensure that the firm is known locally as being willing and able to undertake this area of work, or to maintain the reputation. Remember that existing clients will bring your firm the most work.

Some suggestions for positive steps to improve your firm's reputation in the area are:

- join specialist legal groups, e.g. Society for Trust and Estate Practitioners, Solicitors for the Elderly, the Law Society's Probate Section (see 3.11);
- offer a free initial interview for retired people;
- join a hobby group in which you are interested;
- give public talks to the Women's Institute, Rotary or other groups (if you are a trained and confident speaker and can provide talks at the right level for the group);
- provide support for suitable organisations (e.g. staff associations, pensioners' groups, charities working with the elderly);
- use the media to provide guidance about legal matters concerning the elderly (e.g. articles in local newspapers, writing letters on relevant subjects to local and national newspapers, making appearances on local radio and television);

- sponsor suitable local events, or activities provided by voluntary services and organisations;
- place advertisements targeted at older people and their needs (in magazines for older people, nursing home guides, local papers, etc.);
- distribute information leaflets of interest to elderly clients (through CABs, health centres, day centres or by inserts into local magazines, newspapers, etc.);
- use mailshots to existing clients (to advise on the extent of your services) or potential new clients about particular services.

But beware the scattergun approach. This is less effective than specially focused campaigns to become known. It is also worth assessing, prior to launching a campaign, whether the firm has the relevant expertise and can service the work. Marketing without the necessary back-up is a waste of skills and energies. Bringing in work and not being able to service it is a pointless exercise.

Ensure that your firm complies with the Solicitors' Publicity Code 1990 and other relevant professional guidance as set out in this chapter. Also be aware of the provisions of the Data Protection Act 1998 and any subsequent codes and regulations associated with it. If in doubt contact the Law Society's Practice Advice Service (0870 606 2522) or Professional Ethics (0870 606 2577).

3.7.2 Contacts

Developing personal contacts in the community reaps its own rewards, and willingness to offer your services without charge on occasions can be valuable:

- Give talks to local groups or societies e.g. Rotary, pensioners, Age Concern (if possible, keep material for talks in stock on subjects such as EPAs, wills, state benefits, community care and the role of a solicitor, and tie these in with information packs).
- Attend national conferences and seminars on issues relevant to older people (these may involve other professionals working with the elderly, e.g. specialist financial advisers, local and health authorities, accountants and charities).
- Attend business meetings (Rotary, Institute of Directors) and talk to other attendees.
- Work with other professionals to inform them of the services you can provide (e.g. accountants may know all about your tax planning expertise but they also have older clients who may benefit from your expertise).
- Attend local charity-run fetes and open days at nursing homes and other places relevant to the elderly (try not to refuse an invitation to a residential home's Christmas party).

- Volunteer for work for local societies and join any relevant committees providing services to elderly people (e.g. Age Concern, Help the Aged).
- Cultivate contacts with retirement and nursing homes and sheltered housing complexes (make it known that you are prepared to visit residents).
- Cultivate contacts with officers of the NHS and local authority (they need to know who specialises so ask if they keep a register of solicitors for their clients – not all will be without assets).
- Organise a firm's seminar on matters of concern to older people. Consider whether to advertise or to make it invitation only. Also consider whether or not to make a charge to attend.

3.7.3 Suitable topics for seminars

These include:

- providing for long-term care;
- financial management for those who become incapable;
- employment issues for residential care and nursing homes;
- EPAs and how they work (and how they do not work);
- asset protection for the family;
- inheritance tax planning;
- provision for disabled dependants;
- wills;
- housing options for older people.

3.7.4 Image

The current use of advertising and publicity by solicitors is something which many older clients do not associate with the professions. However, it is part of modern practice and is significant in this particular marketplace when so many people are competing for other clients' business. Thus, although the more formal approach may be appropriate, in today's competitive market-place this needs to be linked with the use of information technology and systems as well as well trained, informed staff.

A conservative approach

Consider the term you use: is it 'old' or 'elderly'? Fashions change and some consider 'old' to be a derogatory term. It is advisable to ask your clients. Those who are over 85 generally are quite proud of being old. Remember that in some eastern cultures to be old is to be venerable and respected! Think about it very carefully before ordering expensive brochures.

Your brochure should also reflect this approach:

- avoid garish colours, fussy designs and youth-orientated pictures;
- avoid negative pictures of elderly persons, i.e. lolling in an orthopaedic chair in a crowded nursing home sitting room;
- use a clear font for text (preferably a sans serif variety such as Arial);
- ensure the size of the text is as high as is practical (at least font size 12, but preferably 14);
- use background colour and text colour sensibly (black text on a white background or black on bright yellow);
- ensure you comply with the Solicitors' Publicity Code 2001 (**www.guide-on-line.lawsociety.org.uk**).

A professional image

It is important to become known not only as having expertise in working with and for older clients but also:

- being able to understand and communicate with them;
- being flexible and allowing them to develop their own wishes;
- not promoting a level of expertise which your firm does not have!

It may also be helpful to market your image and professionalism as a member of the solicitors' profession and the benefits that membership gives to your clients:

- independence;
- all round advice;
- adherence to strict standards of professional conduct;
- professional indemnity insurance.

Elderly clients will in general be resistant to an over-aggressive commercial approach to marketing and promotion, but beware of taking a patronising tone as well. Remember that elderly clients also have the sophistication and experience to be discerning.

3.7.5   Websites

Do not reject the idea of a firm's website because you believe it will not be accessed by your target market. Elderly people have the time to learn and are quite often willing to learn, usually with the help of grandchildren.

It is not just the elderly, however, who would access a website, but their children and relatives who may live in other countries or in other parts of the United Kingdom. They will be looking for solicitors who may be able to help them to sort out the problems arising when they discover their relatives are becoming frail or forgetful and they cannot reach their elderly relatives quickly.

Keep the website clear and simple unless you wish to go down the full route of an interactive site with clients accessing their own files etc. Use it as a 'window box' to tell visitors about your services.

Before getting started in this relatively new area it is vital to research it carefully. There are two books that may help you:

- A. Terrett, *The Internet: Business Strategies for Law Firms*, Law Society (2000);
- N. Webb, *Internet Marketing: Strategies for Law Firms*. Law Society (2003).

3.7.6 Quality of service

However much trouble you take to develop your reputation and to cultivate the right image, it will be wasted if your firm does not have the knowledge and expertise to do the work and the staff and facilities to do it efficiently.

3.7.7 Providing information

Clients need information as well as advice. It can be time-consuming to provide this information so consider the following:

- Keep a supply of leaflets on relevant topics for handing to clients (Inland Revenue leaflets, Department of Work and Pensions leaflets, Court of Protection booklets, Age Concern leaflets etc.). See Appendix F.
- Create your own in-house information packs and make them available to your clients.
- Print and distribute your own elderly client newsletter.
- Create and print your own booklets on particular topics and make them available to your clients (including an introduction to the services you offer).
- Buy in inexpensive booklets and leaflets and provide them to your clients (e.g. publications from Age Concern, see Appendix F).

3.7.8 Packages of services

A fixed fee regime could be implemented for wills, EPAs and related matters such as advance directives, severance of joint tenancy, financial planning.

Simple packages may be appropriate in providing your services to older clients:

- offer an EPA when you make a will, but advise as to the dangers as well as the potential advantages (see Chapter 4);
- discuss a living will when making an ordinary will, but be tactful as many people have no wish to address this issue (see Chapter 11);

- provide a stockbroker's valuation with recommendations when completing annual tax returns or repayment claims.

You may wish to market special packages in conjunction with other professionals for older clients, such as:

- an annual 'wealth check' (e.g. an investment review, tax planning assessment, and state benefit survey);
- a 'plan ahead' programme (e.g. consideration of appropriate options for housing and care based upon client's wealth and needs);
- a 're-housing' package (e.g. support and legal services on finding and moving to a more suitable home);
- a 'balance the family' package (e.g. advice and preparation of wills and EPAs for cohabitees or second marriages);
- a 'family support' programme (e.g. support for children looking after parents);
- a 'residential care' package (e.g. legal assistance in respect of a move into residential care and disposal of the home);
- a 'financial management' package (e.g. legal services in respect of the registration of an EPA or application for receivership followed by first year support for the attorney or receiver).

3.8   SUPPORT GROUPS

3.8.1   Solicitors for the Elderly

Solicitors for the Elderly are a group that provides appropriate training and assistance to solicitors wishing to specialise in elderly client practice. New members must have some detailed knowledge in the field to be a full member but those who do not have sufficient experience but are working towards it can become associate members. Solicitors for the Elderly was set up specifically to enable solicitors, barristers and legal executives to exchange ideas, information on practice development and legal issues affecting older people as well as being part of an organisation that charities and voluntary bodies would feel confident referring clients to. It organises an annual conference but also provides specialist training at local level. It provides e-news, resource information on its website and discounts on some books and journals. It is organised by way of local county branches.

See the website **www.solicitorsfortheelderly.com** and Appendix D for more information.

3.8.2   Law Society's Probate Section

The Law Society's Probate Section is dedicated to the interests of the solicitors' profession, and offers a number of benefits, including:

- practice development (news and data on the competition and client needs; research on market trends);
- opportunities for contact, communication, and information sharing with other members;
- media and PR campaigns to focus attention on the value of using a solicitor;
- discounts on conferences and publications;
- regular newsletters providing succinct authoritative legal updates;
- free regional seminars;
- specialist software buyers' guides;
- a website (**www.probatesection.org.uk**) for updates and sharing information;
- a guide to marketing to your existing clients.

All enquiries to: Sonia Purser, The Probate Section, The Law Society, 113 Chancery Lane, London WC2A 1PL, DX 56 London/Chancery Lane.

3.8.3   Society for Trust and Estate Practitioners

The Society for Trust and Estate Practitioners (STEP) is a worldwide organisation that deals with trust issues including the taxation and law relating to trusts. It has a large membership of lawyers and accountants throughout the world. Contact STEP, 26 Dover Street, London W14 4LY, Tel. 020 7763 7152.

CHAPTER 4

Managing the affairs of the elderly

Martin Terrell

4.1 INTRODUCTION

Everyone hopes to go on managing his or her own affairs for as long as possible and no elderly person should be prevented from so doing where possible. Tact and sensitivity are often required where an elderly person may simply need help writing out cheques and paying bills or is capable of running a bank account but unable to deal with a share portfolio or tax return. In many cases, practical help and professional advice may be all that is required.

As the elderly client's needs increase, so does the extent to which someone else needs to intervene to manage a part, or the whole, of the client's estate. The manner in which this is done then depends on a wide range of factors according to the nature of the client's estate and whether the client has planned for these eventualities. Some assets can be dealt with individually with minimal formality. In other cases a person is able to give an authority to deal with the full extent of his or her assets and if this is inadequate or no such authority is in place, the involvement of the Court of Protection may be required.

4.2 STATE BENEFITS

Benefits may be paid to another person when the claimant is unable to claim personally; see the Social Security (Claims and Payments) Regulations 1987, SI 1987/1968.

4.2.1 Agency

A claimant who is capable may nominate someone to collect state benefits by signing the form of authority on the allowance order slip. An agency card may be obtained where this is to be done long term and residents in local authority accommodation can nominate an official of the authority to act as signing agent and collect payments.

It is not, however, appropriate to appoint a residential care or nursing home owner or employee who would be subject to special Department of Work and Pensions (DWP) requirements.

4.2.2 Appointee

If the claimant is 'unable for the time being to act' and a receiver has not been appointed, the Secretary of State can appoint someone (known as an 'appointee') to claim any benefits on his behalf (SI 1987/1968, reg. 33). The appointee can collect, and must deal with and spend, the money for the benefit of the claimant but his powers do not extend beyond handling the social security benefit.

Application is in writing and staff at the DWP satisfy themselves as to the claimant's inability to manage his affairs and the suitability of the appointee. A close relative who lives with or someone else who cares for the claimant is usually the most suitable person to be the appointee. The appointee is under a duty to disclose relevant information to the DWP when claiming benefits (and may be personally liable in the event of non-disclosure) and if the appointee is not acting properly or in the best interests of the claimant, the appointment may be revoked. Where a receiver has been appointed then benefits cannot be paid to an appointee (see also 4.8.4).

4.2.3 Other powers

The Secretary of State may also direct that benefit be paid to another person acting on behalf of the claimant if this appears necessary for protecting the interests of the claimant or a dependant (SI 1987/1968, reg. 34).

The costs of housing, accommodation and fuel and water services may be deducted from certain benefits and paid direct to third parties on behalf of the claimant in accordance with detailed procedures (reg. 35 and Sched. 9).

4.3   OTHER ASSETS

4.3.1   Bank or building society accounts

There are five possibilities in respect of accounts for elderly individuals:

- A third party mandate can be completed allowing another person to manage the account. This arrangement may be convenient in cases of physical disability. The mandate would be revoked by the subsequent mental incapacity of the account-holder.
- The account can for convenience be held in the joint names of the individual and another person on the basis of either to sign. Such authority may be revoked if either account-holder loses mental capacity. It should

be recorded (when appropriate) that this is not intended to be a joint account that passes to the survivor on death but that the money belongs to the elderly individual.

- The account can be in the name of another as express nominee for the elderly individual.
- The account can simply be in the name of another although it belongs to the elderly individual. This can result in tax problems and it is vulnerable to misappropriation, so not suitable for larger sums. There may be confusion over whom the money belongs to, especially if the account-holder himself became incapable, was made bankrupt or died.
- In some situations deposits and withdrawals may be allowed on a National Savings Bank account in the name of a person who lacks mental capacity (National Savings Bank Act 1971, s.8(1)(f); and National Savings Bank Regulations 1972, SI 1972/764, regs. 6 and 7).

4.3.2   Government payments

Any pay, pensions or other periodical payments due from the government to a person who is, by reason of mental disorder, unable to manage his or her affairs may be paid to the person having care of the patient for his or her benefit: Mental Health Act 1983, s.142. Similar arrangements apply to local authority pensions.

4.3.3   Income tax

Tax returns must generally be signed by the taxpayer in person but under the Taxes Management Act 1970, s.8, may be signed by:

- a receiver appointed by the Court of Protection;
- an attorney under a registered Enduring Power of Attorney (EPA) in cases of mental incapacity;
- an attorney in cases of physical inability to sign.

4.3.4   Deduction of tax

A parent, guardian, spouse, son or daughter of a person suffering from mental disorder may register on the person's behalf for interest to be paid without deduction of tax on bank and building society accounts. See Income Tax (Deposit-takers) (Interest Payments) (Amendment) Regulations 1992, SI 1992/13 and Income Tax (Building Societies) (Dividends and Interest) (Amendment) Regulations 1992, SI 1992/2915.

4.3.5 Trusts

Where it is desired to make provision for a person who may be or become incapable of dealing with his own affairs, problems may be avoided by appointing trustees and transferring property to them on suitably worded trusts. A trust may also be appropriate where a person receives an award for a personal injury and this is excluded from assessment to means tested benefits (Income Support (General) Regulations 1987, SI 1987/1967, reg. 51(1)(a) and Sched. 10 para. 12) and National Assistance (Assessment of Resources) Regulations 1992 (as amended).

Where a trust is in existence, the trustees may hold and manage the trust property with power to apply it for the benefit of the beneficiary. For example, care home fees can be paid directly to the home for the beneficiary's benefit and therefore without involving the beneficiary.

Informal trusts

Money may be held in the name of another person who acknowledges (formally or informally) the true ownership. In some family situations a trust is not even created, but money or assets are simply given to children or other relatives in the expectation that it will be made available in case of need. This arrangement is, however, only suitable for relatively small sums because tax and other complications can arise especially if the understanding goes wrong.

4.3.6 Hospitals

A hospital does not provide for all personal needs and some spending money in the hands of the patient is desirable. If relatives are attending to the patient's financial affairs they may hand over regular sums in cash when they visit, but if these visits are not regular or the patient cannot cope with cash the following procedures may be of assistance.

Monies could be held in the hospital bank. An initial sum may be deposited by the patient and relatives may also deposit money. Further money may well come from continuing state benefits. The hospital must keep an account of all money held for a patient and produce this to the patient on request. The money belongs to the patient and not to the hospital which is merely providing a facility for it to be looked after. Upon leaving hospital any balance must be accounted for to the patient or to the patient's representative or estate.

Where there is no one available to handle the patient's money, a welfare officer will assist with benefit claims and in making money available for the patient's benefit.

Where the patient is able to cope with small sums of cash, a form can be obtained and taken either by the patient or a member of staff to the hospital bank or cash office to effect withdrawals.

4.4 POWERS OF ATTORNEY

A power of attorney is a document whereby a person (the donor) gives another person (an attorney) power to act on his behalf in his name in regard to his property and financial affairs. Note that the power:

- must be executed as a deed: see the Law of Property (Miscellaneous Provisions) Act 1989 as to execution;
- may be in general terms or limited to specific acts or circumstances, for instance a general power under Powers of Attorney Act 1971;
- can only be granted by a competent adult person;
- subject to any express limitation in the power, subsists until revoked by an act of the donor, the death of the donor or the attorney or the bankruptcy of the attorney.

A power of attorney is also revoked by the donor becoming mentally incapable of managing his own property and affairs, as he is unable to continue to delegate powers to the attorney. An EPA is therefore an exception to this principle (see 4.5).

4.4.1 Evidence of power

A photocopy which bears a certificate signed by a solicitor at the end (of each page) that it is a true and complete copy of the original must be accepted as proof of the contents of the original. A certified copy must be accepted if satisfying these requirements (this also applies to EPA) (Powers of Attorney Act 1971, s.3).

4.5 ENDURING POWERS OF ATTORNEY

4.5.1 Introduction

The Enduring Powers of Attorney Act 1985 created the Enduring Power of Attorney, a statutory form of power of attorney which remains valid notwithstanding the donor's subsequent incapacity to manage his or her own property and affairs. An EPA has the same application as an ordinary power of attorney and can be used as an ordinary power, but contains a number of important differences.

- An EPA must be executed in the prescribed form (see 4.5.2).
- An EPA survives the incapacity of the donor provided it is registered with the Court of Protection (see 4.5.6).
- The attorney has certain powers to provide for the needs of persons other than the donor and make gifts on behalf of the donor.
- When an application is made to register an EPA and until it is registered, the attorney's powers are limited to maintaining the donor and preventing loss to the donor's estate.
- On the incapacity of the donor, the EPA is subject to the jurisdiction of the Court of Protection which may intervene to supervise, restrict, revoke or supplement the powers of the attorney contained within the EPA.

Relevant legislation:

- Powers of Attorney Act 1971;
- Enduring Powers of Attorney Act (EPAA) 1985;
- Enduring Powers of Attorney (Prescribed Form) Regulations 1990, SI 1990/1376;
- Enduring Power of Attorney (Welsh Language Prescribed Form) Regulations 2000, SI 2000/289;
- Court of Protection (Enduring Powers of Attorney) Rules 2001, SI 2001/825.

4.5.2 Formal requirements

For an EPA to be valid, it must be executed in the manner and form prescribed in the 1990 Regulations. This is because the prescribed form contains explanatory information informing the donor of the effect of executing the power and must be read by or to the donor and understood by the donor. The form also ensures the donor is aware of important choices and provides space for additional wording so the form may be adapted to the wishes of the donor.

The form prescribed by the 1990 Regulations must be used, or the Welsh language version of the same form permitted by the 2000 Regulations. Forms prescribed by the previous 1986 and 1987 Regulations could only be used for EPAs executed prior to June 1988 and July 1991 respectively.

For the form to take effect as a valid Enduring Power of Attorney, it must be executed by the donor as well as by the attorney(s). Execution is required from the attorney to signify acceptance and to acknowledge the duty to register in certain circumstances. Although the parties need not all sign at the same time, the donor must sign first and the attorney(s) must have signed before the donor loses mental capacity. Signatures of donor and attorney(s) must be witnessed by an independent person or persons. The donor and attorney(s) cannot witness each other's signatures and a spouse should not act as a witness.

A donor who is unable to sign may make a mark and the attestation clause should be amended to explain this. Where the donor cannot sign or make a mark, a person may sign on behalf of the donor but two witnesses are then needed and the signatory person should not witness any other signature.

Any deletions or additions to the prescribed form need not be initialled as they are presumed to have been made before execution.

An individual may complete more than one EPA and a new EPA will not revoke an earlier one unless express provision is made.

4.5.3 Validity

Completion of a valid EPA presupposes that the donor has sufficient capacity to grant the power. Although the legislation does not define the degree of capacity required, as a matter of law a person's capacity to perform a particular legal act is specific to the act in question (see also Chapter 1). A person may be 'becoming incapable' of managing his property and affairs so that if he had an EPA it should be registered and if he had not, an application could be made for a receiver to be appointed. Paradoxically, that same person may be capable of carrying out a single legal act such as making a will or an EPA. The degree of understanding specific to an EPA was considered by Hoffman J. in the case of *Re K, Re F* [1988] 1 All ER 358 where an EPA had been made very shortly before being registered. The judge upheld the validity of the EPA so long as the donor understood:

> first, if such be the terms of the power, that the attorney will be able to assume complete authority over the donor's affairs; second, if such be the terms of the power, that the attorney will in general be able to do anything with the donor's property which the donor could have done; third, that the authority will continue if the donor should be or become mentally incapable; fourth, that if he should be or become mentally incapable, the power will be irrevocable without confirmation by the court. (at 363)

An EPA which has been properly executed is presumed to be valid. In the case of *Re W* [2001] 1 FLR 832 it was held that the burden of proof when challenging the validity of an EPA rested on the objectors. Unless the objectors could satisfy the court that the instrument was invalid, the court had to register the EPA.

4.5.4 Restrictions

An EPA may be general in its terms or for specific purposes only, and the donor may place restrictions or conditions on the power. For example, a donor may limit the scope of the EPA to certain property or exclude certain property from its scope. It is also common for a donor to restrict the power to operate when he ceases to have mental capacity (so that the power does not operate as a general power immediately). This can, however, impose limitations if the donor remains mentally capable but becomes physically incapable.

There are also statutory restrictions (EPAA 1985, s.3) on what an attorney under an EPA can do, so that the attorney cannot:

- benefit himself or persons other than the donor except to the extent that the donor might have been expected to provide for his or their needs;
- make gifts except for presents of reasonable value at Christmas, birthdays, weddings and such like to persons related to or connected with the donor or charitable gifts which the donor might have been expected to make.

The donor can, if he wishes, further restrict these powers.

4.5.5 Professional attorneys

Professional attorneys need to be aware of their personal liability for actions taken whilst acting for the donor. It is recommended that protocols are adopted within the practice over the conduct of clients' affairs when a member of the firm is acting under an EPA. See generally Chapter 3.

It is good practice where a solicitor, accountant or other professional is appointed as attorney to include a charging clause in the EPA so that it is clear to the donor (and others) that professional costs will be incurred. This should avoid any later queries (although not necessarily as to the amount of the charges). The fact that the conduct of attorneys is rarely scrutinised by a third party imposes a greater professional and moral responsibility on the attorney.

A professional attorney also has a long-term responsibility to the client and should consider in advance the consequences of the donor's assets not being able to support the costs involved. If it is likely that the attorney might renounce in such circumstances, the donor should be advised before the EPA is granted.

4.5.6 Registration

In the event that the donor becomes mentally incapable, the EPA must be registered with the Court of Protection. If it is not so registered, the power is voided by the supervening incapacity of the donor. Registration also provides some safeguards against misuse, because certain relatives must be given notice, and although the court does have supervisory powers it has to rely on problems being brought to its attention. Note that:

- An attorney is under a duty to apply to the court for registration of the EPA as soon as practicable once he has reason to believe that the donor is or is becoming mentally incapable (EPAA 1985, s.4).

- This means 'incapable by reason of mental disorder of managing and administering his property and affairs'.
- Once this situation arises the EPA is suspended, although the court may exercise its powers if satisfied that the donor is incapable (EPAA 1985, s.5).
- Once an application is made, then until the EPA is registered, the attorney's powers are limited to maintaining the donor and preventing loss to his estate (EPAA 1985, s.1(2)).

Notice

Notice must first be given to the donor and to the donor's closest relatives in the prescribed form (EP1), which states that the attorney proposes to apply for registration of the EPA and that the recipient may object to this within four weeks on any ground therein specified. Notice must be handed to the donor personally but other relatives may be served by first class post and all notices must be served within 14 days of each other.

Application can be made to dispense with giving notice to a person for special reasons, although the court is generally unwilling to remove the donor's statutory safeguards. Application is made in form EP3 and must be supported by medical evidence to show that it would be undesirable or impracticable for the attorney to give notice or some other clear evidence to show that no useful purpose is served by the giving of notice.

Notice need not, in any event, be given to anyone who has not attained 18 years, is mentally incapable or cannot be traced.

Subject to these exceptions, the relatives who must be notified must be taken in order of priority from the statutory list, class by class:

(a) the donor's husband or wife;
(b) the donor's children (no distinction is made between legitimate or illegitimate children);
(c) the donor's parents;
(d) the donor's brothers and sisters, whether of the whole or half blood;
(e) the widow or widower of a child of the donor;
(f) the donor's grandchildren;
(g) the children of the donor's brothers and sisters of the whole blood;
(h) the children of the donor's brothers and sisters of the half blood;
(i) the donor's uncles and aunts of the whole blood; and
(j) the children of the donor's uncles and aunts of the whole blood.

At least three relatives must be served but if anyone from a class has to be served then all members of that class must be served, even if more than four persons are notified. If the attorney is a relative, then he counts as one of the persons who must be notified and if there are fewer than three relatives, then only those relatives need to be notified.

Application

The attorney(s) must send the application in form EP2 together with the original EPA and registration fee of £220 to the Public Guardianship Office within 10 days of service of the last relevant notice. If no objections are received after 35 days of the last notice being served, the court must register the power. The original EPA is returned to the attorney or his solicitor, duly stamped and sealed.

Objections

The persons to whom notice is given may object to registration on one or more of the grounds contained in EPAA 1985, s.6(5):

(a) the power was not validly created;
(b) the power no longer subsists;
(c) the application is premature because the donor is not yet becoming mentally incapable;
(d) fraud or undue pressure was used to induce the donor to create the power;
(e) having regard to all the circumstances and in particular the attorney's relationship to or connection with the donor he is unsuitable to be the donor's attorney.

Implications of registration

Once an EPA is registered the attorney(s) can again operate under its authority, and the EPA cannot be revoked by the donor without the confirmation of the court. The court has jurisdiction to supervise, restrict, revoke or supplement the powers of the attorney contained within the EPA, and in the event that the EPA is revoked, direct that a receiver be appointed. The attorney may also apply to the court for a substantial gift to be made and has standing to apply for a statutory will or for the court to exercise any other powers available to it under the Mental Health Act 1983, s.97.

The register is open to the public. Applications to inspect are on form EP4 on payment of the prescribed fee of £20.

4.5.7   The attorney

Anyone over 18 and not bankrupt or mentally incapable may be appointed as an attorney, and two or more people may be appointed to act jointly or jointly and severally. Statutory protection is available for attorneys in specific circumstances.

Duties

An attorney is expected to manage the donor's affairs in accordance with the EPA, and may seek the guidance of the court which only has supervisory powers in the case of a power which has been registered or which has become registerable. Note that an attorney:

- has a fiduciary duty towards the donor and must use such skill as he possesses and show such care as he would in conducting his own affairs;
- if being paid must exercise the care, skill and diligence of a reasonable person, and if acting in the course of a profession must exercise proper professional competence;
- may not appoint a substitute or otherwise delegate his general authority, but may employ persons to do specific tasks;
- has no power over the donor so cannot dictate where he or she shall live (although may have influence over such matters);
- should keep accounts, although he need only produce these to the Court if so directed; an attorney must in any event retain any money or other assets of the donor in the name of the donor;
- where an EPA has been registered, notify the Public Guardianship Office of the death of the donor.

4.5.8 Solicitor's duty

Although instructions to prepare an EPA may come from the intended attorney, a solicitor is acting for the donor so should see him or her personally and alone so that independent advice may be given and confirmation of instructions obtained. When acting on the instructions of an attorney (whether or not the EPA is registered) a solicitor should remember that his or her client is the donor whose best interests should be safeguarded even if this results in conflict with the attorney.

These issues are comprehensively addressed in the Law Society's Enduring Power of Attorney Guidelines which are set out in full at Appendix A.

4.5.9 Trustees

The Trustee Delegation Act 1999 makes changes to the use of enduring powers by trustees with effect from 1 January 2000. Prior to this, the Enduring Powers of Attorney Act 1985, s.3(3) allowed trustees to delegate their trustee functions under an EPA. The general rule now is that any trustee functions delegated to an attorney (whether under an ordinary power or an enduring power) must comply with the provisions of the Trustee Act 1925, s.25 (as amended by the 1999 Act).

There are, however, limited but practical exceptions to the general rule to cover the most common situation where trustee powers need to be delegated.

The attorney can exercise a trustee function of the donor if it relates to land, or the capital proceeds or income from land, in which the donor has a beneficial interest. However, where there are two trustees, a sale of land must be made by two persons (whether jointly in the same capacity or in different capacities). Thus an attorney cannot sell as attorney and trustee, and if both trustees are incapable, the same attorney cannot sell as attorney for each trustee. For example, if a husband and wife own a property and the husband is incapable, his attorney (not being his wife) can join the wife in selling the property and overreaching the husband's beneficial interests. If the wife is sole attorney under a registered EPA, she must appoint a second trustee to act with her in selling the property (Trustee Delegation Act 1999, ss.8 and 9).

4.5.10 Pitfalls

According to the Master of the Court of Protection:

> financial abuse probably occurs in about 10–15% of cases. Expressed as a percentage this may seem to be a relatively minor problem, and maybe even an acceptable price to pay for the 85–90% of cases where attorneys act lawfully. (*Cretney & Lush on Enduring Powers of Attorney*, 5th edn, Jordans (2001), para.12.1)

EPAs are intended for use in cases where the attorney is absolutely trustworthy and can fulfil his role without conflict. The fact that the donor has chosen the person he or she wants to administer his or her affairs imposes a less rigorous framework on the parties than where the court imposes a receiver. The benefit to the majority is, however, at the expense of those whose affairs are administered fraudulently or negligently.

Because incapacity is a distant and hypothetical state, and no one wishes to spend too much time and money in dealing with the subject, too many EPAs are created without sufficient thought being given to the practical aspects of the donor's affairs which might need to be administered. There is no easy way of reconciling the interests of the honest and competent with the need to protect against the conduct of the dishonest and incompetent. The best that can be done is for solicitors to be aware of these problems and address a few simple questions such as:

- Is there any conflict in the family?
- Do the assets require any particular attention or professional skills?
- Are there any practical difficulties, for instance in where the attorneys live?
- If attorneys are appointed jointly and severally, is it obvious how they would allocate tasks between them?
- If any close relatives are not appointed as attorneys, to what extent should they be kept informed of the attorneys' activities?
- What would happen if the attorney (e.g. a spouse) died or became incapable?

It is also important that donors are given clear information about their rights and choices and attorneys about their obligations. If all else fails, solicitors need to know what procedural remedies are available so they can join the ever-increasing number of EPA cases being dealt with by the Court of Protection.

4.6   THE COURT OF PROTECTION

4.6.1   Introduction

The Court of Protection has jurisdiction over the property and affairs, within England and Wales, of any person who is incapable, by reason of mental disorder, of managing his or her property and affairs. Such a person is defined by the legislation as a 'patient'. The court's jurisdiction is therefore only relevant in clearly defined circumstances:

- The court's jurisdiction relates to property and affairs only. The expression 'property and affairs' refers to 'only business matters, legal transactions and other dealings of a similar kind' (*F* v. *West Berkshire Health Authority* [1989] 2 All ER 545). Although the proper management of the patient's property and affairs is closely linked with the welfare of the patient, the Court has no direct jurisdiction over where and how the patient is treated.
- The patient has property and affairs which need to be administered. A person with negligible assets and income derived from state benefits may not require the involvement of the Court of Protection.
- The patient must be incapable of managing his particular property and affairs, the test of capacity being specific to its function. An elderly client may be able to manage a small bank account but unable shortly afterwards to manage a substantial sum of money arising from an inheritance or the sale of a property. That person might have been able to manage with assistance from a relative or professional adviser, while a person in similar circumstances may be at risk of financial abuse from grasping relatives.
- There is no other way of dealing with the patient's affairs, for instance by the appointment of an appointee to receive state benefits (see 4.2.2) or through the appointment of an attorney under an EPA (see 4.5). A person may not be incapable if he is capable of giving instructions and acting on advice received (*Masterman-Lister* v. *Jewell* [2003] 1 WLR 1511). Any person should be presumed capable and a person's most basic rights are compromised by the jurisdiction of the Court.
- The patient is incapable as a result of mental disorder. A patient who is physically incapable may be mentally capable of managing his property and affairs. This can cause problems with, for instance, someone who has

suffered a stroke and has lost the ability to communicate but retains a degree of understanding.

Relevance of Court of Protection

The involvement of the Court of Protection is therefore a matter of necessity rather than choice for most people who come within its jurisdiction. Occasionally there is an element of choice, where for instance a person may be incapable of managing his property and affairs but might be capable of making an EPA and appointing an attorney. As seen above, the EPA jurisdiction is simple and cost-effective but comes with its own problems (see 4.5.10). In most cases, therefore, it is self-evident that formal legal authority is required to replace or supplement the client's lack of legal capacity. The role of the Court of Protection is, however, to go beyond simply providing that authority, by providing a framework for the management and supervision – and the protection – of the client's property and affairs.

Where the Court of Protection is directly involved, its jurisdiction is often perceived as being impersonal, bureaucratic and expensive. However, these perceptions have to be weighed against the importance of protecting the client's property and affairs and managing such property and affairs for the benefit of the patient and any dependants of the patient. The cost of a receivership may therefore appear expensive, but this can be minimal if the estate would otherwise be mismanaged or exploited.

4.6.2   Jurisdiction

Although the Court of Protection exercises the inherent prerogative of the Crown to manage the affairs of incapable persons, its current status and jurisdiction are relatively recent statutory creations. Although the Lord Chancellor and the nominated judges (judges of the Chancery and Family Divisions of the High Court) exercise the statutory power of the court, the body known as the Court of Protection is an office of the Supreme Court, headed by a Master.

The court may exercise its jurisdiction through the making of orders or directions to deal with a specific matter or through delegating general management powers to a receiver. Applications to appoint a receiver and the business of supervising and supporting individuals exercising the court's authority are dealt with by the Public Guardianship Office.

Relevant legislation

- Mental Health Act 1983, Part VII;
- Public Trustee and Administration of Funds Act 1986;
- Court of Protection Rules 2001, SI 2001/824.

4.6.3 The Court's officers

The body known as the Court of Protection consists of only a small number of individuals:

- the Master, Denzil Lush;
- a Deputy Master, Gordon Ashton;
- two senior nominated officers (the Assistant Masters), Norman Prime and Jill Martin;
- a number of other nominated officers; and
- the Judicial Support Unit.

The Master has overall responsibility for the work of the court and determining the scope of the nominated officers' authority. The Assistant Masters, for instance, deal with complex applications or contested cases requiring attended hearings. Other nominated officers deal with specific areas of work such as appointments of receivers or cases involving trusts.

The Deputy Master is a full time county court judge who exercises the Court's jurisdiction under a pilot project which began on 1 October 2001. With only one location in London, the court was perceived as being inaccessible. As a result of this project, Court of Protection cases requiring attended hearings can, with the agreement of the parties, be heard at the Preston County Court. While this is helpful in a limited number of cases, the majority of cases are either dealt with through correspondence or at attended hearings in London where the presence of the Official Solicitor is also required (see 4.6.5).

4.6.4 Public Guardianship Office

The Public Guardianship Office (PGO) came into existence on 1 April 2001 to replace the much maligned Public Trust Office. The PGO continues to have responsibility for the administrative (as distinct from judicial) functions of the Court of Protection and is based in the same offices at Archway Tower. Although the PGO is an executive agency within the Department for Constitutional Affairs and is the main point of contact between the public and the Court of Protection, it has no statutory basis.

The difference between administrative and judicial decisions is easy to explain in practice. An application to appoint a receiver is sent to the PGO, which checks the papers are in order, requests further information if required, corresponds over notices and security and drafts the order. The order itself is made by an officer of the court, either one of the Masters or one of the nominated officers. To assist with routine orders, nominated officers work within the PGO dealing with matters such as short orders, orders for sale and authorising the lodgement or payment of monies.

Despite being created to improve on the performance of the Public Trust Office, the performance of the PGO deteriorated steadily in its first two years of existence. After several reorganisations, it has only recently begun to provide a reasonable level of service. This has been achieved through the court giving receivers greater autonomy where possible and creating a number of groups and teams dealing with different types of work. Most work is currently handled within the following groups:

- Group A: cases involving lay receivers where client's surname begins A–K;
- Group B: cases involving panel receivers, local authority receivers and other professional receivers;
- Group C: cases involving lay receivers where client's surname begins L–Z;
- First Applications Group: dealing with all new applications for the appointment of a receiver except applications made for the appointment of a panel receiver, local authority receiver or professional receiver which are dealt with by the relevant teams in Group B.

Other teams provide specialist support services principally in investments, accounts, short orders, winding up cases, EPAs and in-house receiverships where the Chief Executive of the Public Guardianship Office acts as receiver.

4.6.5 Official Solicitor

The Official Solicitor is a confidential adviser and assistant to the Supreme Court whose principal function is to ensure, by intervention in proceedings or otherwise, that the legal rights and duties of persons under a disability are recognised and enforced (Supreme Court Act 1981, s.90).

In Court of Protection proceedings the Official Solicitor is frequently directed to act as the solicitor of the patient (Court of Protection Rules r.13), in the same way as a litigation friend may represent a person under disability in civil proceedings. In practice, an applicant in a case where the interests of the patient are affected, such as an application for a statutory will or lifetime gift, will be directed to serve the proceedings on the Official Solicitor. The role of the Official Solicitor is to give priority to the interests of the patient and advise the court on the merits of the application. The Official Solicitor serves a vital function in terms of the patient's interests but is often very helpful to the other parties to proceedings, for example by establishing any common ground between the parties and putting forward a consensus for approval by the court, thereby avoiding the expense and delay of an attended hearing. The costs of the Official Solicitor are payable from the patient's estate.

4.6.6 Lord Chancellor's Visitors

Visitors work within the PGO but are appointed by the Lord Chancellor to visit people who are, or are believed to be, patients or donors of EPAs which are registerable and to report to the Court of Protection. The work of the court and PGO is often hampered by an incomplete picture of the patient's situation, being dependent largely on written reports and submissions.

The Visitors provide the court and PGO with direct access to patients and they have therefore been described 'as the eyes and ears of the Public [Guardianship] Office, gathering information essential to the patient's welfare and the effective running of their estates' (National Audit Office, *Protecting the Financial Welfare of People with Mental Incapacity* (1999)). Although the court is primarily concerned with the patient's property and affairs, the Visitors are also concerned with the patient's welfare and ensuring that the receivership is working to the benefit of the actual patient.

There are in practice two types of Visitors.

Medical Visitors

There are currently six registered medical practitioners with special knowledge and experience of mental disorder and each covers a particular Circuit. They visit patients for the purpose of assessing their mental capacity, generally in relation to a specific issue which concerns the court, for example to determine whether a person is incapable of managing his or her property and affairs or has recovered capacity.

General Visitors

There are currently 16 General Visitors who report on whether a patient's property and affairs are being handled in his best interests. Each of the General Visitors aims to see around 300 patients each year, so that each patient is seen at least once during the course of the receivership. Where problems are identified or the patient is vulnerable, perhaps where there are no relatives or there has been suspected abuse or disputed proceedings, then more frequent visits can be arranged.

4.7 POWERS OF THE COURT OF PROTECTION

4.7.1 General

Section 95(1) of the Mental Health Act 1983 gives the court very general powers, with respect to the property and affairs of a patient, to do or secure the doing of all such things as appear necessary or expedient for the following purposes:

97

(a) the maintenance or other benefit of the patient;
(b) the maintenance or other benefit of members of the patient's family;
(c) making provision for other persons or purposes for whom or which the patient might be expected to provide if he were not mentally disordered; or
(d) otherwise for administering the patient's affairs.

The court has power to make such orders and give such directions and authorities as it thinks fit for these purposes. Without prejudice to these general powers, the court may make orders and give directions to:

(a) control and manage property;
(b) sell, exchange or charge any property;
(c) buy property;
(d) make a settlement or gift;
(e) make a will;
(f) carry out a profession, trade or business;
(g) dissolve a partnership;
(h) carry out a contract;
(i) conduct legal proceedings;
(j) reimburse money paid out for the maintenance of the patient; and
(k) exercise any powers vested in the patient as a trustee.

4.7.2 Exercise of powers

In authorising the exercise of such powers, the court must first have regard to the requirements of the patient, but must also take into account the interests of creditors and the desirability of making provision for obligations of the patient even if these are not legally enforceable.

Where gifts are made on behalf of the patient, these must be for the persons or purposes set out in s.95(1). Thus gifts must be for the maintenance or other benefit of members of the patient's family, or the making of provision for other persons or purposes for whom or which the patient might be expected to provide if he were not mentally disordered. The words 'which the patient might be expected to provide' impose on the court an obligation to look at the actual or presumed wishes of the patient before conferring any benefit on another party.

The court may exercise all or any of these powers in one or more of the following ways:

• directly, of its own motion.
• by delegating a range of powers (as well as a general power to receive income and apply it for the patient's benefit) to a receiver;
• by giving specific authority to an individual; specific authority may be appropriate where no receiver has been appointed, a registered EPA is in

place, or a person (whether a receiver or not) is authorised to carry out an act such as the making of a gift or the execution of a will.

Medical evidence required

The court's powers may only be exercised after medical evidence has been considered and on the basis of such evidence, the court is satisfied that the patient is incapable of managing his property and affairs (Mental Health Act 1983, s.94(2)). If the court is approving a statutory will for a patient, then the Court must also be satisfied that the patient lacks testamentary capacity.

4.7.3 Urgent cases

Because the court's powers may be exercised immediately it has satisfactory evidence, an order or direction can be given relatively quickly to deal with a particular asset or aspect of the patient's estate. This might be necessary if there are urgent bills to be paid or there is a risk of financial abuse. If a wider range of powers is required to supervise the patient's affairs at short notice, the court may appoint an interim receiver.

Under the Mental Health Act 1983, s.98, the court can give directions before medical evidence is available, provided the court has reason to believe the person concerned may be incapable and is of the opinion that it is necessary to make immediate provision. It is extremely rare for the court to rely on this section of the Act because of the risk of violating the basic rights of the individual.

4.8 RECEIVERSHIP

4.8.1 When necessary

In most cases involving the jurisdiction of the Court of Protection, the court will delegate powers to a receiver to conduct the day-to-day administration of the patient's property and affairs. The appointment of a receiver presupposes that there is no other way of dealing with the patient's assets which cannot be dealt with by:

- an appointee responsible for receiving state benefits (see 4.2.2);
- a person authorised to receive a government or local authority pension (see 4.3.2);
- an attorney acting under a registered EPA (see 4.5);
- a person authorised to act under a short order (see 4.9.1).

4.8.2   Procedure on first application

Any person may apply for the appointment of a receiver. Forms for making an application can be obtained free of charge from the PGO Customer Services Unit, or from the PGO website (www.guardianship.gov.uk).

The following should then be lodged with the Public Guardianship Office:

- the receiver's declaration;
- medical certificate (form CP3);
- statement of patient assets and income (form CP5);
- a cheque for the commencement fee of £70, payable to the PGO;
- a copy of the patient's current will;
- a covering letter drawing attention to any matters requiring urgent attention.

The medical certificate is confidential to the Court and may, if required by the patient's doctor, be sent directly to the PGO.

Notice to relatives and others

Before applying, the applicant must give notice of his intention to all the patient's relatives of a degree of relationship equal to or nearer than the applicant or proposed receiver. The applicant is also expected to notify any other person who ought to be informed on account of his or her close connection with the patient, for example a partner or carer who is not a relative.

Notice to any such person is given in the prescribed notification letter.

Notice to the patient

The PGO also sends the applicant or his solicitor a letter addressed personally to the patient notifying the date on which the application will be considered and explaining how representations and observations can be made. This letter must be served on the patient even if the patient is incapable of understanding the letter or might be distressed by it. Service must be effected at least 10 clear days before the date on which the application is heard by the court and no order will be issued until that notice period has expired (Court of Protection Rules r.46).

The person who serves the letter on the patient must complete a certificate of service (form CP7) and return this to the Public Guardianship Office.

Security

An important safeguard for the patient is in the provision of security by the receiver. Although an order appointing a receiver refers to a substantial sum of money (equivalent to two years' income) being paid into court as security, security is actually provided by the receiver entering into an insurance bond.

The PGO offers prospective receivers the opportunity of being added to the court's master bond and payment of the first year's premium and completion of the documentation must ocur before the receiver can be appointed.

The premiums of such a policy are payable from the patient's estate.

Hearing

Although correspondence from the PGO will refer to a date on which an application is considered, almost all applications are dealt with on the papers and without an attended hearing. An attended hearing would only be required if the application is particularly complex or is contested.

Order appointing the receiver

If everything is in order, the court will draw up and seal an order appointing the receiver. On a first application, the terms of the appointment are embodied in the First General Order.

The order confirms the appointment of the receiver, and sets out the receiver's right to collect or 'receive' 'all social security benefits, pensions, rents, annuities, dividends and interest (being so far as holdings on the Bank of England Register are concerned the interest on any securities standing in the sole name of the Patient) and any other income (including arrears) of whatever nature and from whatever source to which the Patient is entitled'.

The receiver is therefore authorised to recover all the income of the patient and apply this for the patient's maintenance. Capital assets can only be dealt with as provided by the order. If the order makes no reference to a particular asset such as a bank account or a shareholding, the receiver is still entitled to recover the interest or dividends from such assets.

Office copies of the order should be registered with the DWP, pension providers, banks and building societies with which the patient has accounts and all companies in which he holds shares or other investments.

The order is valid until the death of the patient, or the court cancels the order on the recovery of the patient or the appointment of a new receiver.

Further orders

The order appointing the receiver does not preclude other orders being made beforehand or subsequently. For instance, an interim order may be required to conduct proceedings, sell a property or access a bank account to maintain the patient. An interim order can be issued before the receiver is appointed (Court of Protection Rules r.42).

After the receiver has been appointed orders may be made as and when required, dealing with one-off matters which come to light or require action subsequently. Examples include the sale or purchase of property, the making of gifts or the authorisation of costs. Matters that need to be dealt with by way of a formal application are considered in more detail at 4.9.5 and 4.10.

4.8.3 Choice of receiver

The receiver will usually be a relative or friend of the patient, who has an active involvement in the welfare of the patient. However, the duties of a receiver are onerous (see 4.8.6) and many relatives feel obliged to take on this role out of loyalty to the patient and at the expense of time and effort which could be better devoted to the care of the patient. There are also cases where the patient has no relatives who are available and willing to take on this role. In such cases the court may appoint as receiver:

- a local authority (the appointment is by reference to the holder of an office such as the Chief Executive);
- a solicitor who is a member of the PGO Panel of External Receivers;
- a solicitor or accountant who has some connection with the patient or expertise relevant to the particular requirements of the case;
- in the last resort, the Chief Executive of the Public Guardianship Office.

4.8.4 Status

When the court makes an order appointing a receiver, the patient ceases to have any power over his financial affairs, such power being transferred to the court which then delegates certain powers to the receiver. Some confusion (and inconvenience) is caused where the patient retains capacity to deal with particular matters. To those involved with the patient, it may be quite clear what the patient can do and what the patient cannot do. The problem is that to the rest of the world the patient is incapable and unable to perform any act personally. A receiver may need to take a pragmatic approach and allow the patient, so long as he is capable, to deal with his own assets. For example a patient may operate a bank account or savings account or collect a pension. However, once a body such as a bank or the DWP has notice of the appointment of a receiver then it will only release funds to the receiver or in accordance with the order of the court.

The receiver is the statutory agent of the patient, so that property of the patient does not legally vest in the receiver personally. The patient's property remains in his legal ownership. Assets such as bank accounts may show the name of the receiver but always 'as receiver for' the patient.

4.8.5 Powers of the receiver

A receiver's powers are clearly defined in the order appointing the receiver. A receiver's powers do not extend to deciding where or with whom the patient shall live, consenting to medical treatment or other personal decisions, although in practice personal and financial decisions are often linked. A receiver must be concerned for the welfare of the patient and may be involved in formal decisions such as the sale of a property or paying for nursing home fees, which have a bearing on the welfare of the patient. Often the receiver acts as an advocate for the patient in dealings with social services and nursing homes.

A receiver has the authority delegated to him by the court, generally to receive the patient's income and any assets specified in the order. The receiver's role is also fiduciary in nature and a receiver is not entitled to any remuneration save that:

- a solicitor may be entitled to costs (see 4.11);
- other professional receivers (such as accountants or a local authority) may be allowed remuneration as specified in the order appointing the receiver;
- reasonable out-of-pocket expenses are reimbursed and fees for professional advice will be covered (though approval must be obtained in advance).

4.8.6 Duties of the receiver

A receiver is generally responsible for collecting the patient's income, paying the bills and administering the patient's affairs in his best interests. The receiver does, however, have a general role in safeguarding the patient's estate and to be aware of the patient's wishes and requirements.

The receiver's duties are summarised by the PGO in its book *The Receiver's Handbook* (2003), confirming that receivers are expected to:

- act at all times in the best interests of the patient;
- safeguard the patient's assets;
- open a receivership account at a local bank or building society;
- claim from the Pension Service and Disability and Carers Directorate all social security benefits to which the patient is entitled;
- take out security and pay any bond premiums as and when required;
- prepare accounts annually or as and when required;
- ensure that the patient's funds are being used to provide him with the best possible quality of life;
- ensure that all income is collected and bills are paid on time;
- arrange safe-keeping of all deeds, documents of title, testamentary documents and other valuable items;
- keep any property in a reasonable state of repair and adequately insured;
- deal with the patient's income tax and other tax matters;
- notify the PGO of any changes in the patient's financial situation, for example, if the client inherits property or money;

- inform the Driver and Vehicle Licensing Authority if the patient holds or applies for a driving licence;
- advise the PGO if there is any likelihood of the patient getting married, divorced or involved in legal proceedings;
- advise the PGO if the preparation of a will is being considered;
- co-operate with any Lord Chancellor's Visitors;
- obtain the permission of the PGO before dealing with any capital monies;
- inform the PGO of the patient's recovery or death;
- pay the fees of the PGO out of the patient's monies as and when requested;
- inform the PGO of any change in the patient's address;
- comply with all directions and orders from the Court of Protection.

4.9   OTHER ORDERS

4.9.1   Short orders

If the patient's estate is simple and straightforward, or is less than about £16,000, the court can issue an order authorising an individual to deal with one or more assets of the patient in a specified way for the patient's benefit rather than appointing a receiver (Court of Protection Rules r.8).

A short order may be relevant where the estate is small and an authority is needed to close a small bank account and collect a pension, or to deal with a particular problem (e.g. signing a tenancy agreement or residential care home contract, giving a receipt for a legacy or disposing of money accumulated whilst in hospital).

Application is made in the same way as for the appointment of a receiver (see 4.8.2) but the applicant should make clear that a short order is being sought. The same application fee of £70 is also payable and while it may be inconvenient for the applicant to complete the same number of detailed forms, once the short order is issued no further fees are charged by the court, which generally has no further involvement in the matter.

4.9.2   Order determining proceedings

Where the patient's mental capacity has improved sufficiently for him to be restored to the management of his own affairs an application should be made for an order determining proceedings under the Mental Health Act 1983, s.99(3). Application is made in form A (the general form of application specified in the Court of Protection Rules 2001) supported by medical evidence of the patient's recovery.

4.9.3 Order appointing a new receiver

An application to replace an existing receiver must be made formally, using form A and supported by evidence in support. Strong evidence must be supplied to justify the expense and inconvenience of changing a pre-existing arrangement.

The court will decide any such case on its own merits and while there is no formal precedent to determine precisely when a receiver should be replaced, the Australian case *Holt* v. *Protective Commissioner* (1993) 31 NSWLR 227 lays down some very helpful guidelines for use in such cases:

(a) An application for the removal of a receiver may be made by any interested person, including the patient.

(b) The burden of proof is on the person seeking the change in the status quo.

(c) It is normally necessary for the person seeking the change to show some reason why the court should remove the existing receiver and appoint someone else in his place.

(d) Where it is shown that the existing receiver is unsuitable to be the receiver for the particular patient (perhaps because he is incompetent, or has acted unlawfully or improperly, or is not acting in the patient's best interests), the court will terminate the appointment and appoint some other suitable person as receiver.

(e) If, however, the unsuitability of the existing receiver is not an issue, or if the applicant fails to prove that the existing receiver is unsuitable, it must be shown forensically that the best interests of the patient will in some way be advanced or promoted by discharging the existing receiver and appointing another receiver in his place.

(f) The standard of proof is the usual civil standard, namely the 'balance of probabilities'. It does not have to be 'clear and convincing' or 'compelling'.

(g) In deciding what is in the patient's best interests the court will have regard to all the circumstances.

4.9.4 Sale of the patient's property

Where the patient is the legal owner of a residential property and is already living in alternative accommodation without there being any prospect of his returning to his own home, an order for sale will usually be issued. This can be incorporated in the First General Order, but if the sale needs to take place before the receiver is appointed or after the receiver has been appointed then a separate order for sale will be issued.

Application for a sale is usually made in form CP5 (see 4.8.2) as part of the application for the appointment of a receiver. If a receiver has already been appointed, then application should be made by letter with evidence of the patient's alternative accommodation arrangements and confirming that there is no prospect of the patient returning to live in his own home. An order for sale will be subject to the court approving the sale price and the receiver's solicitor filing an undertaking to hold the proceeds of sale to the order of the court.

The procedures involved in the sale (or purchase) of a property are set out in more detail in the Court's Procedure Note PN4.

Property the subject of a specific bequest

If the property is the subject of a specific legacy in the patient's will, the net proceeds of sale will be set aside in the patient's name and preserve the nature of the specific legacy (Mental Health Act 1983, s.101). This prevents the sale of a property from causing a legacy to lapse, with the proceeds falling into residue and overturning the provisions of the patient's will.

Where the proceeds of sale are set aside in this way, they are held in a separate account in the name of the patient. Money from that account can be released for the maintenance of the patient. Care needs to be taken whenever the proceeds of sale are set aside in this way, as s.101 merely reverses the presumption that a specific gift in a will lapses where the asset is disposed of. This may itself be inappropriate to the patient's circumstances and likely wishes and in all such cases the patient's will should be checked and a statutory will considered if necessary (see 4.10).

4.9.5 Replacing the patient as a trustee

A patient who is a trustee cannot exercise his functions as a trustee and needs to be replaced. This is a problem not just with conventional trusts but increasingly in cases where a couple own a property which needs to be sold and the husband or wife is incapable.

The procedure for replacing a trustee depends on whether the patient is a trustee with a beneficial interest in land, on whether there are other assets in which the patient has a beneficial interest and on whether or not there is a competent trustee:

- If the patient has a beneficial interest in the land then the other competent trustee (if there is one) needs to apply to the Court of Protection for leave to appoint a new trustee under the Trustee Act 1925, s.36(9). If an application to appoint a receiver has already been made then an application for leave may be made in writing by the competent trustee. If no application is before the court then the competent trustee must apply in form A and supply suitable medical evidence. In either case the competent trustee executes a deed of appointment.

- If the patient has a beneficial interest in a trust which consists of other assets or there is no continuing trustee of a trust of land, then the court may replace that trustee under the Trustee Act 1925, ss.41, 54. The court will direct the vesting of assets in the new trustees and application for such an order is made in form A with supporting evidence.

A more detailed account of the procedures involved and the requirements of the court is set out in the Court's Procedure Notes PN8 and PN8A.

4.10   GIFTS AND DISPOSITIONS OF PROPERTY

4.10.1   General

Where an application relates to the disposal of the patient's property by life-time gift, then if a receiver has already been appointed and the proposed gift is small in itself or in relation to the estate, the procedure is straightforward. Application may be made by letter setting out the reasons for the gift and providing evidence for the gift being affordable. Gifts of the inheritance tax allowance (£3,000 per year) may be dealt with in this way.

4.10.2   Formal application required

Where larger gifts are involved or the gift involves the creation of a settlement or the execution of a will then a formal application is required. Application is made in form A supported by detailed sworn evidence and in the case of an application for a will, medical evidence detailing specifically the lack of testamentary capacity (Mental Health Act 1983, s.96(4)). Where the application is for a will or settlement, the applicant is also responsible for providing a suitable draft will or settlement deed.

The evidence in support of the application needs to explain the proposed dispositions in sufficient detail for the court to make an informed decision on the merits of the case and for the Official Solicitor and any other interested parties to be able to respond. The onus is on the applicant to prove that the proposed disposition is within the competence of the court (see 4.7.2) and reflects the actual or presumed wishes of the patient. The affidavit in support of the application therefore needs to deal with the following matters:

- the status of the applicant and his entitlement to make the application;
- the recent history of the patient, providing a 'character sketch' of his interests and family relationships, how he is cared for and who looks after or visits the patient;
- a history of gifts made or anticipated in any will; copies of earlier wills should be exhibited;

- the consequences of not making the proposed gift (in terms of how it will pass on death and any tax which might be payable) or proposed will;
- the patient's health and prospects of life;
- the value and composition of the patient's estate both before and after any proposed gifts;
- the costs and likely costs of the patient's maintenance and the effects of this on the estate;
- the patient's family and any dependants, including anyone who may have a financial claim on the estate; family relationships should be shown in the form of a family tree;
- whether anyone is adversely affected by the application (any proposed gift must be to the detriment of some other person, whether entitled under an earlier will or intestacy);
- the means of any proposed beneficiary and why such beneficiary should benefit, addressing two simple questions: does the beneficiary deserve the gift and would the patient wish to make the gift?;
- the tax consequences of the gift or will;
- the patient's domicile;
- whether there is any property outside England and Wales (which may be outside the scope of the statutory will).

4.10.3 General considerations

In determining whether a will or any other proposed gift is suitable, the court must make assumptions about the patient's wishes and interfere with decisions made by the patient (whether deliberately or by omission) before losing capacity. The five propositions laid down by Sir Robert Megarry in the 1982 case of *Re D(J)* are still relevant and frequently relied on by the court for guidance. The Vice Chancellor's five principles, factors or propositions should be considered carefully before any application is made ([1982] Ch 237 at 243, [1982] 2 All ER 37 at 43):

> The first of the principles or factors which I think it is possible to discern is that it is to be assumed that the patient is having a brief lucid interval at the time the will is made.
>
> The second is that during the lucid interval the patient has a full knowledge of the past, and a full realisation that as soon as the will is executed he or she will relapse into the actual mental state that previously existed, with the prognosis as it actually is.
>
> The third proposition is that it is the actual patient who has to be considered and not a hypothetical patient on the Clapham omnibus. I say that because the will is being made by the court, and so by an impartial entity skilled in the law, rather than the actual patient, whose views while still of a sound disposing mind might be idiosyncratic and far from impartial. In *Re Davey (decd)* [1980] 3 All ER 342 at 348, [1981] 1 WLR 164 at 171 Fox J. is reported as saying, in relation to a will made by the Court of Protection, that the essential question was 'what if anything

108

would be reasonable provision in all the circumstances for the various contestants', and it could be said that this indicates an objective approach made with the wisdom of the court rather than the approach likely to be made by the patient if restored to full mental capacity. I very much doubt if the judge meant to indicate thus, and in any case I do not think it is right. The whole approach of Cross J. in *Re WJGL* [1965] 3 All ER 865, [1966] Ch 135 was that of considering the particular patient, momentarily restored to full mental capacity, as being the settlor. Further, in s.102(1)(c) [now s.95(1)(c)], the question is one of making provision for persons or purposes 'for whom or for which the patient might be expected to provide if he were not mentally disordered'; and I think that this provision governs the making of a will for the patient, and contemplated the particular patient: and see Re *CMG* [1970] 2 All ER 740 at 741, [1970] Ch 574 at 575.

Before losing testamentary capacity the patient may have been a person with strong antipathies or deep affections for particular persons or causes, or with vigorous religious or political views; and of course the patient was then able to give effect to those views when making a will. I think that the court must take the patient as he or she was before losing testamentary capacity. No doubt allowance may be made for the passage of years since the patient was of full capacity, for sometimes strong feelings mellow into indifference, and even family feuds evaporate. Furthermore, I do not think that the court should give effect to antipathies or affections of the patient which are beyond reason. But subject to all due allowances, I think the court must seek to make the will which the actual patient, acting reasonably, would have made if notionally restored to full mental capacity, memory and foresight. If I may adopt Dr Johnson's words, used for another purpose, the court is to do for the patient what the patient would fairly do for himself, if he could.

Fourth, I think that during the hypothetical lucid interval the patient is to be envisaged as being advised by competent solicitors. The court will in fact be making the will, of course, and the court should not make a will on the assumption that the terms of the will are to be framed by someone who, for instance, knows nothing about lapse and ademption. Furthermore, as the court will be surveying the past and the future, the hypothetically lucid patient should be assumed to have a skilled solicitor to draw his or her attention to matters which a testator should bear in mind. In *Re DML* [1965] 2 All ER 129 at 133, [1965] Ch 1133 at 1139, a case on a proposed purchase of an annuity in order to save estate duty, Cross J. put a lucid explanation of the proposal into the mouth of a hypothetical legal adviser to the hypothetically lucid patient. In any case, I cannot imagine Parliament intended the court to match the sort of home made will that some testators make. I do not, of course, say that one must treat the patient as being bound to accept the imaginary legal advice that is given to him: but the patient is to be treated as doing what he does either because of the advice or in spite of it, and not without having had it.

Fifth, in all normal cases the patient is to be envisaged as taking a broad brush to the claims on his bounty, rather than an accountant's pen. There will be nothing like a balance sheet or profit and loss account. There may be many to whom the patient feels morally indebted; and some of the moral indebtedness may be readily expressible in terms of money, and some of it may not. But when giving legacies or shares of residue few testators are likely to reckon up in terms of cash the value of the hospitality and gifts that he has received from his friends and relations, and then seek to make some form of testamentary repayment, even if his estate is large enough for this. Instead, there is likely to be some general recognition of outstanding kindness by some gift which in quantum may bear very little relation to the cost or value of those kindnesses.

4.10.4 Considerations when making a statutory will

Where a statutory will is proposed, its provisions need to be considered very carefully, not least because it will deal with the totality of the patient's estate rather than a small part of it and because its provisions cannot be changed after the death of the patient (*Re Davey (Deceased)* [1980] 3 All ER 342).

An application also requires a great deal of evidence and therefore effort in its preparation and even a straightforward application may cost several thousand pounds. There is also a court fee, the costs of the Official Solicitor and the costs of any other party to the proceedings to consider. Statutory wills are therefore quite rare and between 200 and 300 are approved by the court each year. However, they are extremely useful in certain situations, for example:

- an executor or principal beneficiary has predeceased the patient;
- the patient has remarried with the effect of revoking an existing will (*Re Davey (Deceased)* [1980] 3 All ER 342, [1981] 1 WLR 164);
- an asset which is the subject matter of a legacy has been sold by the receiver, and it may not be appropriate for the proceeds of sale to be preserved under the Mental Health Act 1983, s.101, for instance where the value of the asset is no longer proportionate to the value of the estate when the gift was made; s.101 furthermore does not apply to assets disposed of by an attorney acting under an EPA;
- a legacy in an existing will has adeemed prior to the patient becoming incapable (*Re D(J)* [1982] 2 All ER 37, [1982] Ch 237);
- there has been a significant change in the patient's circumstances or in his relationship with the beneficiaries in an existing will or the existing will fails to make adequate provision for persons or objects who have acquired a moral or legal claim on the patient's estate;
- a saving in inheritance tax, for example by passing a benefit to younger beneficiaries or using the nil rate band on the first death.

4.10.5 Who may make an application

Court of Protection Rules r.18 specifies who may apply to the court for a gift, settlement or will. An application may only be made by one of the following:

- the receiver for the patient;
- any person who has made an application for the appointment of a receiver which has not yet been determined;
- any person who, under any known will of the patient or under his intestacy, may become entitled to any property of the patient or any interest in it;

- any person for whom the patient might be expected to provide if he were not mentally disordered;
- an attorney under a registered EPA;
- any other person whom the court may authorise to make it.

4.10.6 Procedure

The applicant is required to lodge the application with the Judicial Support Unit. The Judicial Support Unit will check the papers are in order, that the applicant is authorised to make the application, that suitable medical evidence has been filed and direct who should be notified of the application. Form A is then endorsed with a hearing date and the names of the parties to be notified and returned to the applicant or his solicitor.

The hearing date is usually around three months after the application has been filed. This gives adequate time for other parties to be notified and the Official Solicitor to review the papers. Where possible the parties should agree the application and failing agreement, identify the differences between them. If the application can be agreed then the Official Solicitor will confirm this to the court and the court will issue the order authorising the gift, settlement or will. Where a settlement or will needs to be executed, the court will also approve the form of the document and return this to the applicant together with the sealed order.

If the issues set out in the application cannot be agreed, or an attended hearing is desirable, then the application will proceed to an attended hearing. The hearing is in chambers at the Court of Protection and is heard before the Master or one of the Assistant Masters. A hearing is relatively informal, in that it is inquisitorial rather than adversarial in nature, and once submissions have been made the Master will make his own enquiries of the parties. The parties may appear in person or by their solicitors. In complex or contentious cases counsel may also appear on behalf of the party. Where possible, the order will be made during the course of the hearing and is effective immediately. A sealed order is merely evidence of this, so that in an emergency, the order can be carried into effect immediately.

Once the approved document has been executed, two certified copies must be returned to the Judicial Support Unit together with any fee payable.

Notices

The court is obliged to apply the basic principles set out in *Re B (Court of Protection) (Notice of Proceedings)* [1987] 2 All ER 475, that any person adversely affected by the application must be notified. For instance, where a statutory will is proposed, any beneficiary under an existing will or intestacy who might receive less under the statutory will must be notified.

Where the person adversely affected is a patient then his receiver must be notified and he should be represented by his receiver (Court of Protection Rules r.12). Where the person is a minor or patient for whom no receiver has been appointed, then he must be represented by a guardian ad litem (Court of Protection Rules r.14).

In most cases the court will direct that the patient is represented by the Official Solicitor (Court of Protection Rules r.13). This must be done where the receiver brings the application and there is a potential conflict of interest between the receiver and the patient.

Where possible, a person who should be notified should be given as much notice as possible. Too short a notice period may not allow sufficient time to respond and so breach principles of natural justice. Court of Protection Rules r.19 does, however, allow two clear days' notice to be given.

Notice may be given by personal service, sending the papers by first class post or document exchange to the last known address or transmitting them to the last known address 'by fax or other electronic means' (Court of Protection Rules r.20).

Emergency applications

In an emergency, for example where the patient is in imminent danger of dying before the application can usually be heard, the court will try to assist provided there is unequivocal medical evidence showing that the patient is terminally ill and giving an indication of his life expectancy. The court does not generally favour emergency applications as they are by their nature biased towards the applicant. The onus is on the applicant to demonstrate why the application has been brought at such a late stage and if the application could have been made sooner then the risk of the application not being dealt with in time falls on the applicant.

The application must be lodged immediately and served on the Official Solicitor as well as other persons whom the court would normally expect to be notified so as to save time. The application can, if it is essential, be heard within a matter of days. Where a will is authorised, this can be executed immediately the order is made.

Execution and custody of statutory will

Once the will has been approved by the court, the applicant is responsible for engrossing a fair copy and certifying that this is a true copy of the draft approved by the court. The will may then be executed by the person authorised by the court ('the authorised person') who must execute the will in accordance with the Mental Health Act 1983, s.97(1). The statutory will must be:

(a) signed by the authorised person with the name of the patient, and with his own name, in the presence of two or more witnesses present at the same time;
(b) attested and subscribed by those witnesses in the presence of the authorised person; and
(c) sealed with the official seal of the Court of Protection.

To ensure that the will complies with these requirements, the form of the will and the attestation clause need to be adapted. The form of wording to be used is set out in the Court's Procedure Note PN9 and most precedent books use the same formula.

For the will to be effective it needs to be signed twice by the authorised person, first with the patient's name and then with his own name. The authorised person is not a witness, and as such may be a beneficiary under the will. In all other respects the will is the same as any other will, so that no other beneficiary or spouse of a beneficiary may act as a witness.

Once the will has been executed, the original is sent to the Judicial Support Unit with two certified copies, the draft will approved by the court and a cheque for the transaction fee of £505. The Judicial Support Unit checks the will has been correctly executed and then seals the will with the seal of the Court of Protection. The applicant's solicitor is usually authorised to retain the will in his or her safe custody and must supply a standard form of undertaking not to part with the original during the lifetime of the patient without the approval of the court.

4.10.7 Complaints, reviews and appeals

The PGO has its own internal complaints and reviews procedure and where complaints cannot be resolved internally they may be reviewed by an independent examiner.

Where a decision is made by the court other than on a hearing, the applicant may apply within 14 days for a review of the matter at a hearing. There is, however, no review of a decision about fee remission, postponement or exemption.

A person dissatisfied with a decision made on an attended hearing may appeal within 14 days to a nominated judge (Court of Protection Rules r.55).

4.11 COSTS

4.11.1 Fees

Fees are payable out of the patient's estate at various stages to cover the cost of applications to the court and administration by the PGO. They comprise a commencement fee, administration fees and transaction fees. A request may be made to postpone or waive the fees in case of hardship.

The principal fees charged (Court of Protection Rules rr.76 to 81) are:

- a commencement fee of £70: fee payable on the first application for the appointment of a receiver or an originating application (e.g., a short order or direction);
- a receivership appointment fee of £515: fee payable when the order appointing the receiver is made (thus no fee is payable if a short order is issued and no receiver appointed);
- An Annual administration fee of £220.

Transaction fees are also payable in respect of individual transactions as follows:

- on any order or approval under an order for the settlement or gift of property or carrying out of a contract under the Mental Health Act 1983, s.96(1)(d) and (h) or approval of the variation of a trust under the Variation of Trusts Act 1958, s.1(3): 0.25 per cent of the pecuniary consideration but no fee will be taken if the property is worth less than £50 and no fee will exceed £500;
- on the vesting of stock held in England and Wales in a foreign curator appointed for a foreign patient: £50;
- on an application for an order or the giving of approval in relation to the exercise of powers as guardian or trustee: £120;
- on an application for an order for the appointment of trustees under, the Trustee Act 1925, s.36(9) or the Trustee Act 1925, s.54: £120;
- on an application for authorisation of a person under the Trusts of Land and Appointment of Trustees Act 1996, s.20: £120;
- on the making of an application for an order authorising the execution of a statutory will: £505;
- on an application for the appointment of a new receiver: £185;
- on an application for an order or direction ordering or authorising the sale or purchase of land: £155;
- on the death of the patient: £360;
- on the filing of a request for a detailed assessment of costs: £165;
- on an appeal against a decision made in a detailed assessment of costs a further fee of £50 is payable.

4.11.2 Costs

Costs are normally ordered to be paid from the patient's estate (legal aid is not available), although the court is looking more carefully at costs in applications which should not have been made as well as excessive receivership fees which are occasionally charged.

There are three ways of dealing with costs:

- fixed costs: annually reviewed fixed maximum amounts for different classes of work which the solicitor can claim, with VAT and disbursements, without any further authorisation (see 4.11.3);
- detailed assessment: where fixed costs are not appropriate, the court will authorise the solicitor to submit his or her costs for assessment (see 4.11.4);
- agreed costs: where costs (excluding VAT and disbursements) incurred by the Official Solicitor do not exceed a specified sum (currently £2,500), then the Official Solicitor may submit a bill directly to the court providing a description of the work carried out, the time spent and the rates charged and the amount which would be acceptable by way of costs. The court may authorise directly the payment of such costs from a patient's estate. This facility (see Practice Note of 16 November 2000) is currently available to solicitors although it is likely to be replaced by a procedure for short form assessment.

4.11.3 Fixed costs

In respect of orders made in 2004, on an application to the court and for further work, fixed costs are as follows (note: Categories II and III may be claimed together):

- Category I: work up to and including the date upon which the First General Order is entered (the commencement and disbursements are payable in addition): £665;
- Category II: preparation and lodgement of a receivership account: £175;
- Category II: preparation and lodgement of a receivership account which has been certified by a solicitor: £190;
- Category III: general management work in the second and subsequent years where there are lay receivers: £520;
- Category III: general management work in the second and subsequent years where there are solicitor-receivers: £590;
- Category V: in respect of conveyancing, a sum of £125 in every case to cover correspondence with the Public Guardianship Office, the preparation of the certificate or affidavit of value and all other work solely attributable to the Court of Protection or the Public Guardianship Office, together with a value element of 0.5 per cent of the consideration up to £400,000 and 0.25 per cent thereafter, with a minimum sum for this element of £330.

VAT and disbursements are payable in addition to the above and the costs are reviewed each year, with new costs applying in respect of orders made from the beginning of the new year.

4.11.4 Assessed costs

In all cases where fixed costs are inappropriate, the costs of a receiver or his solicitor must be assessed by the court. Costs can only be assessed with the authority of the court, which may be provided by:

- the order appointing the receiver;
- the order issued in proceedings before the Court of Protection;
- a direction of the court;
- where the work relates to general management, by letter from the Public Guardianship Office.

An authority for assessment of costs will generally provide for costs to be assessed on a standard basis, so that the costs officer is entitled to take account of costs being proportionate to the matters in issue.

Procedure

Solicitors must lodge the following with the Supreme Court Costs Office (Court of Protection Section) at Cliffords Inn, Fetter Lane, London EC4A 1DQ:

- the authority for assessment;
- a request for detailed assessment in form N258B if the costs are payable by the patient or form N258 if payable by a party to proceedings;
- a detailed narrative bill in the form shown in the Schedules to the Civil Procedure Rules 1998, setting out the title of the matter, the names of the parties, the details of the authority for assessment, the period covered by any general management work, a brief narrative of the work covered by the bill, the charging rates of the fee earners involved and each chargeable item of work in chronological order and any disbursements incurred;
- all supporting papers including the correspondence file, exhibits and documents;
- a cheque for £165 payable to HM Paymaster General.

The assessment is usually dealt with on a provisional basis by post. The draft bill is returned with directions for service on any other party to proceedings if required. If the solicitor is not satisfied with the provisionally assessed bill, he or she may within 14 days of receipt request a hearing. If the bill is acceptable, the solicitor must complete the cost summary, certify the castings as correct and return the provisionally assessed bill to the Costs Office so that the costs certificate can be issued.

Short form assessment

It has been proposed by the Public Guardianship Office that where the amount to be charged in a bill (including VAT and disbursements) is less than £3,000, a short form assessment may be used. The procedure is the same as for a detailed assessment except that costs may be summarised using a simplified standard form.

General management

A solicitor must have authority to charge for general management work which is distinct from an application to appoint a receiver or a formal application which is covered by an order for assessment. General management relates only to a person's financial affairs and property although for a professional receiver it is often difficult to separate this role from the wider personal duties of a receiver (see 4.8.6). For example, personal visits or attendance at case conferences should be delegated where possible to relatives or friends and if this cannot be done for whatever reason, the receiver must explain the reason why the costs of such attendance should be recovered.

General management costs can be high, especially where a solicitor is appointed receiver in complex cases where there are no relatives to take on this role. Costs should also be assessed annually, to coincide with a receiver's accounting period. Because the receiver would otherwise have to carry out a year's work before he can even begin the assessment process, let alone receive payment, the Public Guardianship Office has proposed that costs be paid on account. If annual costs may exceed £3,000 the receiver should notify the Public Guardianship Office in advance to enable him to take quarterly payments on account. The quarterly payments should cumulatively not exceed £3,000 (or part thereof) but a higher threshold can be agreed in advance with the Public Guardianship Office. Once the year's costs have been assessed, a final bill can be entered showing the deduction of payments on account and the balance due. Copies of all bills (including interim bills) must be sent to the Public Guardianship Office.

4.12 ADMINISTRATION OF THE PATIENT'S AFFAIRS

4.12.1 Investment management

The receiver is responsible for overseeing the patient's investments and is expected to provide the PGO with details of any investments already in the patient's name. Where these require disposal, consolidation or management, the receiver must work with the PGO to protect the patient's assets in determining how these should be administered. A number of choices arise:

- Investments may be left undisturbed. Often small investments not required for the patient's maintenance can be left for the time being.
- Cash should be consolidated in the Court Special Account which provides security as well as a competitive rate of interest, which is paid without deduction of tax. Other investments can be sold and the proceeds invested in the Special Account.
- The receiver can invest in the Lord Chancellor's Equity Index Tracker Fund, a low cost tracker fund managed by Legal & General.
- Investments can be held in court and professionally managed by one of the two firms of panel brokers, Gerrard and Carr Sheppards Crosthwaite.
- Investments can be managed out of court and held by fund manager or stockbroker provided the firm's custody agreements and terms of service are agreed in advance with the PGO.

4.12.2 Investment policy

An investment policy is set for each patient, usually when the First General Order is made. The court considers the patient's age and prospects of life as well as the patient's risk profile. There are four sets of policy guidelines which may be applied:

- COP 1: 100 per cent investment in the Special Account;
- COP 2: 70 per cent cash and 30 per cent equities; the equity content may be split with 24 per cent held in the FTSE All Share Index and the remaining 6 per cent in the FTSE All-World (i.e. ex-UK) Index;
- COP 3: 50 per cent cash and 50 per cent equities; the equity content may be split with 40 per cent held in the FTSE All Share Index and 10 per cent in the FTSE All-World Index;
- COP 4: 30 per cent cash and 70 per cent equities; the equity content may be split with 56 per cent held in the FTSE All Share Index and the remaining 14 per cent in the FTSE All-World index.

These guidelines are reviewed regularly by the Lord Chancellor's Strategic Investment Board. The policy of the PGO is not to force the receiver to adopt a particular strategy or invest the patient's funds in a particular way. Provided the patient's funds are secure and can be shown to be properly managed, the PGO will endeavour to work with receivers and assist them in looking after the patient's assets.

4.12.3 General administration

The following points are not exhaustive but are intended to assist the receiver who should:

- retain all original orders but obtain office copies and produce these to third parties as required;
- notify persons dealing with the patient (e.g. the staff at a residential care home) of the receiver's appointment so that they do not inadvertently seek to enter into transactions with the patient directly;
- open a bank account in the receiver's name as receiver for the purpose of receiving all income due to the patient, discharging liabilities and providing such funding as the patient requires; all financial dealings entered into by the receiver should be conducted through this account so that there is a clear audit trail and to assist in preparing the receiver's account;
- sign any authorised document in his own name adding: 'as receiver of (patient)';
- where the receiver is authorised to execute a deed then to sign this twice, once with the patient's name and then with his own name (for execution of a statutory will see 4.10.5).
- remember that the patient's money is there to be used for the patient's benefit rather than preserved for those who would inherit on the patient's death; financial arrangements should reflect the needs of the patient and be structured so as to be as supportive and provide as much freedom to the patient as circumstances permit;
- take into account the terms of the patient's will and any disposals of property and changes in the value of the estate in the light of that will; if the patient is capable of making a new will then the receiver should liaise with the patient's doctor and the Public Guardianship Office; if not, a statutory will should be considered;
- in cases where guidance is needed on the patient's capacity consult the patient's doctor;
- whenever issues arise concerning the patient's welfare and residence, consult with family members, the patient's doctor and the social services department for the area in which the patient resides and ensure that there is a consensus as to what is in the patient's best interests; the receiver cannot determine these for himself, although he may have an opinion and an influence in terms of the patient's available resources; however, the receiver's main role is to apply the patient's resources for the patient's needs, in the most appropriate manner;
- take account of the patient's longer term needs, especially as continuity of care is desirable so elderly patients should not be moved to a private nursing home where the costs would be likely to exhaust resources;
- disclose assets to the DWP and social services department where means assessment applies and ensure that all benefits to which the patient is entitled are claimed;
- obtain specialist advice where necessary.

A professional receiver should never treat receivership work as being of low priority or importance. It is of vital importance to the elderly client and if dealt with efficiently, it can also be properly remunerated, therefore achieving the rare combination in most professional lives of doing a worthwhile job and being properly paid for it.

4.12.4 Further resources

Court of Protection work is a relatively specialist area of legal practice and there is only a limited range of information available. The Public Guardianship Office and Official Solicitor websites contain all the application forms, Procedure Notes, details of fees and other useful information (see Appendix E). The Official Solicitor website also contains some very helpful advice on statutory will applications.

CHAPTER 5

Legal proceedings

David Rees

5.1 INTRODUCTION

It would be impossible to categorise all of the circumstances in which an older person may become involved in proceedings before civil courts or tribunals. This chapter sets out a general introduction to proceedings before the civil courts and then looks in greater detail at some of the causes of action and remedies that may be of particular significance to the affairs of older people.

5.2 CIVIL PROCEEDINGS

An older person may have difficulty coping as a party to proceedings, or as a witness at a hearing, because of some physical or mental impairment. Whilst the court staff should be helpful and judges are being trained so as to become 'disability aware', a litigant is only treated in a different manner by the rules in the case of serious mental disability.

Advisers should, whenever necessary, draw to the attention of the court any situation where disabled facilities or special directions are needed.

5.2.1 Discrimination

The civil courts are not exempted from the provisions of the Disability Discrimination Act 1995 which extends to legal services, and could find themselves in breach of this legislation if they do not take into account the needs of disabled people. There are civil remedies for doing an act made unlawful by the Act, but most non-employment claims will be dealt with as small claims because of the level of damages. To the disabled individual it does not matter whether the problem is physical access to the court, hearing and understanding the proceedings or being heard and understood by the judge – each would be seen as discrimination.

The Human Rights Act 1998 may also provide some support for disabled litigants.

5.2.2 Court Rules

There are several sets of rules that apply to different types of proceedings:

- Civil Procedure Rules 1998, SI 1998/3132 (CPR) for all civil proceedings in the High Court or county courts. The CPR replaced both the Rules of the Supreme Court 1965 (RSC) and County Court Rules 1981 (CCR), but many of those old rules have been retained in modified form in Schedules to the new rules. The CPR are supplemented by Practice Directions (PDs) that indicate how the rules should be applied. These are made by the Head of Civil Justice and should always be referred to when considering a rule. Local practice directions are forbidden.
- Family Proceedings Rules 1991, SI 1991/1247 (FPR) for all family proceedings: the former RSC and CCR (in their final form) fill most gaps (FPR r.1.3) although certain provisions of the CPR also apply (in particular in relation to costs).
- Insolvency Rules 1986, SI 1986/1925 for insolvency proceedings: the CPR will fill any gaps.
- Non-Contentious Probate Rules 1987, SI 1987/2024 for non-contentious probate proceedings: the RSC in its final form fills any gaps.
- Court of Protection Rules 2001, SI 2001/824 and Court of Protection (Enduring Powers of Attorney) Rules 2001, SI 2001/825 for matters dealt with by the Court of Protection. Again the CPR fills certain gaps.

5.2.3 Civil Procedure Rules 1998

The rules governing family proceedings were already more interventionist, but the introduction of a new procedural code from 26 April 1999 by the Civil Procedure Rules 1998 represented a change of culture in the civil justice system. The problems of the old system were identified as delay, cost and inequality of the parties, and the aim of the reforms was to achieve access to justice for all with procedures that are easier to understand. Proceedings are now governed by the overriding objective of enabling the court to deal with cases justly, which means:

- ensuring that the parties are on an equal footing;
- saving expense;
- dealing with cases in ways which are proportionate to the money involved, importance of the case, complexity of the issues and financial position of each party;
- ensuring that cases are dealt with expeditiously and fairly;
- allotting to cases an appropriate share of the court's resources.

The court must seek to give effect to the overriding objective and the parties are required to help:

- instead of leaving the parties to progress litigation, the judge henceforth should act as 'case manager' and adopt an interventionist role;
- this includes encouraging the parties to co-operate, identifying the real issues at an early stage and deciding how they can best be resolved, and fixing timetables;
- a 'cost-benefit' approach is adopted and hearings will be dealt with without the need for the parties to attend at court if possible;
- alternative dispute resolution is encouraged and attempts should be made to settle proceedings at an early stage.

Cases are allocated to one of three 'tracks' according to the amount in issue, complexity and other factors:

- the small claims track for most cases up to £5,000 (£1,000 for personal injuries or housing disrepair) or by consent;
- the 'fast track' for most cases up to £15,000 which can be tried within a day;
- the 'multi-track', being a flexible procedure for all other cases.

The Civil Justice Reforms are sometimes referred to as the 'Woolf Reforms' after Lord Woolf, M.R., whose report *Access to Justice* (July 1996) formed the basis for the reforms.

5.2.4 Pre-action protocols

Since the CPR came into force, various pre-action protocols have been published relating to certain types of proceedings such as professional negligence cases, personal injury claims and judicial review. Underlying these protocols is a hope that they may assist the parties to resolve their dispute without having to resort to litigation. Even where proceedings need to be issued, the protocol may have assisted the parties in identifying the issues genuinely in dispute.

If a claim is of a type for which a protocol has been published, the protocol should be followed before proceedings are issued. The court has power under the CPR, in determining liability for costs at the conclusion of a claim, to take into account the extent to which the parties followed any relevant pre-action protocol.

5.2.5 Bringing a claim

Proceedings to which the Civil Procedure Rules apply are brought by the issue of a claim form. Two types of claim form exist: the Part 7 Claim Form (form N1) which should be used where there is a factual dispute between the parties and the Part 8 Claim Form (form N208) which is generally used where the claim is unlikely to involve a substantial dispute of fact. Some types of claim are required by the rules to be brought by a specific procedure (e.g. claims under the Inheritance (Provision for Family and Dependants) Act 1975 must be brought under CPR Part 8).

5.2.6 Choice of court

For most types of proceedings, the county courts and the High Court have concurrent jurisdiction. However, some types of claim can only be issued in certain courts.

- Proceedings claiming less than £15,000 may not be started in the High Court (£50,000 in the case of damages for personal injury) (CPR Part 7 PD para. 2);
- Probate actions and proceedings relating to trusts can only be commenced in the county court if the estate or trust property is less than £30,000, although the parties can agree to confer jurisdiction on the court to hear the claim (see High Court and County Courts Jurisdiction Order 1991, SI 1991/724 and County Courts Act 1984 Part II).

Both the High Court and county courts have wide powers to transfer proceedings from one court to another (CPR Part 30).

5.2.7 Part 7 claims

Where a claim is brought on a Part 7 Claim Form, the claimant must serve Particulars of Claim either with the Claim Form or within 14 days of its service on the defendant (but in any event within four months of the issue of the Claim Form). The defendant must acknowledge service no later than 14 days after the Particulars of Claim were served upon him. A Defence must then be served within 28 days of the service of the Particulars of Claim.

Once the statements of case have been exchanged, the court will list the case for a case management conference before the district judge or Master. The first such conference will provide an opportunity for the court to consider whether all relevant parties have been joined or whether the proceedings should be transferred to another court. The claim will be allocated to a track and directions will also be given for disclosure, inspection and exchange of witness statements. Depending on the nature and complexity of the case, several case management conferences may be necessary.

5.2.8 Part 8 claims

Where the claim is brought by way of Part 8, the claimant must serve the evidence on which he wishes to rely with the claim form. The defendant must acknowledge service within 14 days of the service upon him of the Claim Form and is required by the rules to file his evidence at the same time. In practice the time for the service of the defendant's evidence is frequently extended by agreement. The claimant has a further 14 days from the date of service of the defendant's evidence to file any evidence he wishes to adduce in reply.

The court will then list the matter for a hearing. The nature of the hearing will depend upon the case. Some cases will be suitable to be listed for disposal at the initial hearing. In other cases, the court may give directions for the future conduct of the case, and this may include a direction that it should continue as if it had been commenced under Part 7. Part 8 claims are treated as having been allocated to the multi-track.

5.2.9 Allocation

As mentioned above, the court will need to decide to which of the three 'tracks' a Part 7 claim should be allocated.

Claims where the sum in dispute is less than £5,000 (£1,000 for a personal injury or housing disrepair claim) will usually be allocated to the small claims track.

- There are standard sets of directions available for various common types of claim (e.g. road traffic, wedding or holiday claims).
- Any hearing will usually be relatively informal and take place before a district judge.
- Lay representatives are permitted.
- There is generally no award of legal costs (so no risk of costs) although the court fees and reasonable expenses of attending the hearing may be recovered (see CPR Part 27).

Claims which are not suitable for the small claims track but which have a financial value of less than £15,000, and where the trial is unlikely to last for more than one day, will usually be allocated to the fast track.

- Standard directions are usually given in fast track cases.
- The trial takes place in open court.
- The normal rules regarding rights of audience apply.
- There are limitations on the amount of costs usually recoverable (see CPR Part 28).

Other claims will be allocated to the multi-track. In practice it is highly unlikely that a claim in the High Court would be allocated to any other track (see CPR Part 29).

5.2.10 Applications

The general rules for applications for court orders are set out in CPR Part 23. Where a party wishes to make an application he should file form N244 together with any evidence he wishes to rely upon in support with the court and serve copies on the other parties. In general the minimum time for the service of an application is three clear days before the hearing. The court may deal with certain applications without a hearing.

Where injunctions are being sought it may be necessary to make an application without notice being given to the other party. This may be because the application is urgent, or because to give notice would destroy the purpose of the application (for example where the court is being asked to make a freezing order). Where the court makes an order on a 'without notice' basis, it will direct that a further hearing should take place with the other party being put on notice.

5.2.11 Appeals

Appeals are governed by CPR Part 52, Part IV of the Access to Justice Act 1999 and the Access to Justice Act 1999 (Destination of Appeals) Order 2000, SI 2000/1071. In general, permission is required to appeal from any decision of any judge or Master in the High Court or county courts (the most important exception to the requirement for permission being appeals against committal orders). Permission may be given either by the judge who made the decision under appeal or by the court that will hear the appeal. However, where the decision under appeal was itself made on an appeal, permission can only be given by the Court of Appeal.

Appeals lie as follows:

- from a county court district judge to a county court circuit judge;
- from a county court circuit judge, where the decision under appeal is a final decision made in multi-track or specialist proceedings, to the Court of Appeal;
- from a county court circuit judge, where the decision under appeal was itself made on appeal, to the Court of Appeal;
- in all other cases from a county court circuit judge to a High Court Judge;
- from a district judge or Master of the High Court to a High Court Judge;
- from a High Court Judge to the Court of Appeal.

Where a party wishes to appeal a decision he must file an Appellant's Notice (form N161) within 14 days of the decision. This must then be served on other parties within seven days of being filed with the court. Where the party requires permission to appeal, this is sought on the same form. The court has power in an appropriate case to extend the time for filing form N161.

5.3   LITIGANTS WITH PHYSICAL DISABILITIES

5.3.1   Implications and solutions

Many forms of physical disability (or mental impairment falling short of incapacity) may affect the ability of an older person to participate in litigation, but when the problem is drawn to the attention of the court steps may be taken to cope with the impairment:

- Impaired mobility may render it impossible to gain access to the court or cope in a particular courtroom – transfer the case to a court in the area where the disabled party resides or with disabled access.
- Impaired hearing or vision may make it difficult to follow what is going on – move the hearing to a courtroom or chambers with facilities for the hard of hearing or produce all documents in large print.
- Communication limitations may prevent others from understanding the individual, or vice versa – arrange for an interpreter to be present and allow a longer time estimate.
- Limited concentration spans or the need for regular medication may make it impossible to remain in court for more than a limited period – arrange regular adjournments or shorter hearings.
- Some ailment may make it impossible to attend court at all – arrange for the evidence of the disabled person to be taken away from the court prior to the hearing or for the hearing to take place other than in a courtroom.

5.3.2   Evidence

Need to attend court

The court now controls the issues on which it requires evidence and the way that evidence is given. It will only be necessary for a party or witness to attend a hearing (other than the trial) to give evidence if cross-examination is required. A statement or pleading verified by a 'statement of truth' may be treated as evidence of the facts stated if it has been duly served on the other parties.

At the trial itself oral evidence is generally required. Witness statements will have been served in advance and will generally stand as evidence in chief, being amplified only with the permission of the court. The court may take into account the age or infirmity of a potential witness when deciding whether evidence is required from that source.

For evidence see CPR Part 32 and the Practice Direction. For the need to attend court see CPR Part 34 and the Practice Direction.

Taking evidence away from court

When an elderly person is too infirm to attend the hearing, arrangements may be made for that person's evidence to be taken in advance in a manner that suits the circumstances (the procedure is known as taking depositions). This could be in a local court before the district judge, or in the individual's own home or a nursing home before an independent solicitor appointed for the purpose. The power is discretionary but an order will usually be made (and is often made by consent) where the witness:

- is too old and frail to attend the trial;
- is so ill or infirm that there is no prospect of being able to attend the trial;
- might die before the trial;
- intends to leave the country before the trial.

The procedure for taking depositions is to be found in CPR Part 34, rr. 34.8–34.12. For family proceedings see RSC Order 39 r. 1; CCR Order 20 r. 13.

Hearings other than in a courtroom

Where the circumstances render it expedient in the interests of justice the court may arrange the trial at, or adjourn it to, the place where a party or witness is, so as to allow for the participation and oral examination of that person at the trial itself. This could be the individual's own home or a nursing home. See CPR r. 2.7 which provides that a court may sit anywhere (family proceedings can be adjourned to such place as the judge thinks fit).

Interpreters

Regulations under the Disability Discrimination Act 1995 may require the court to take such steps as are reasonable, in all the circumstances, to provide auxiliary aids or services that assist disabled people, and sign language interpreters are specifically mentioned. The court when required may now provide these.

An interpreter in court should swear an oath in the following terms which would appear to apply whether the communication difficulty was due to language or some other cause:

> I will well and faithfully interpret and true explanation make of all such matters and things as shall be required of me according to the best of my skill and understanding.

5.3.3 Representation

Rights of audience in court are strictly controlled. A party to proceedings has a right of audience in his capacity as such but in general only a barrister, solicitor or Fellow of the Institute of Legal Executives may represent a party (Courts and Legal Services Act 1990, Part II (ss.27 and 28)). A person employed or engaged to assist in the conduct of litigation under instructions given by a solicitor may have a right of audience in chambers.

The judge may refuse to hear a person who would otherwise have a right of audience in a specific instance, but reasons must be given.

An attorney under an Enduring Power of Attorney (EPA) does not have a right of audience on behalf of the donor (*Gregory* v. *Turner* [2003] 2 All ER 1114).

In exceptional circumstances the court may grant a lay person a right of audience for particular proceedings (*Clarkson* v. *Gilbert*, *The Times*, 4 July 2000, CA).

'McKenzie friend'

During a hearing in open court (and generally also in chambers) a litigant in person has the right to be accompanied by a 'friend' to take notes, quietly make suggestions and give advice. The judge has a discretion to refuse this if the friend is not acting in the best interests of the litigant (e.g. pursuing a personal agenda). This is not the same as allowing such person to act as a representative although where a litigant in person is elderly, disabled or inarticulate the judge may seek assistance from any such person present in court who clearly has the confidence of the litigant.

Lay representatives

At a 'small claims' hearing any person (known as a lay representative) may speak on behalf of a party. This is a right of audience only and does not extend to the conduct of the litigation generally. The permission of the court is required if the party is not present (CPR Part 27 PD para. 3.2(3)) and permission is unlikely to be refused in the case of a responsible representative where the party is unable to attend due to infirmity or disability. The judge may refuse to hear an unsuitable lay representative but the reasons should be stated and the court is entitled to expect the representative to behave honestly, reasonably and responsibly.

5.4   LITIGANTS WITH MENTAL DISABILITIES

Special procedures apply in respect of proceedings by and against a mentally incapacitated litigant. These ensure that a representative is appointed, the court approves compromises and settlements of claims, and there is supervision of any money recovered.

5.4.1   Rules

The procedures are to be found in the following rules (see 5.2.2):

- CPR Part 21;
- FPR Part IX supplemented by RSC Order 80 and CCR Order 10 in their final form;
- Insolvency Rules 1986, Part 7, ch. 7;
- Court of Protection Rules 2001, r. 14.

Definitions

In proceedings by and against a person under disability, the rules refer to a child where the person is under 18, or to a patient. 'Patient' is defined as:

> a person who, by reason of mental disorder within the meaning of the Mental Health Act 1983, is incapable of managing and administering his property and affairs' (see CPR Part 21 r. 21(2)(b), FPR r. 9.1; RSC Order 80 r. 1; CCR Order 1 r. 3).

The same definition is also used to establish the jurisdiction of the Court of Protection to administer the property and affairs of patients (see generally 4.6). The test is issue-specific and will therefore depend upon the particular issues raised in each individual case (see *Masterman-Lister* v. *Brutton & Co and Jewell and Home Counties Dairies* [2003] 3 All ER 162 and 1.5.8).

In the context of legal proceedings, it should be noted that the definition used by the CPR concludes with the words 'his affairs' so that capacity is defined by reference to the patient's ability to manage his (own specific) property and affairs rather than his capacity to manage the proceedings. However, the proceedings themselves may constitute an integral part of the person's property and affairs, although this need not necessarily be the case. A person may be capable of pursuing a claim for compensation but incapable of managing the money recovered as a result of such claim. However, if a receiver has been appointed for that person, the court is entitled to assume (in the absence of clear evidence to the contrary) that that person is a patient.

5.4.2   Assessing capacity

The rules assume that you know whether a party is a patient. In case of doubt the proceedings should be stayed whilst the court deals with this as a preliminary issue.

Unlike the Court of Protection, other courts do not have specific facilities to investigate (e.g. to obtain medical evidence):

- The Official Solicitor may be referred to where assistance is required.
- Under the CPR (but not the FPR) the court can give permission for steps

to be taken before the finding has been made and a representative appointed (CPR Part 21 r. 21.3(2)).

- A medical report is likely to be necessary (see *Masterman-Lister* v. *Brutton & Co* [2003] 3 All ER 162).

If the Court of Protection has already assumed jurisdiction over the property and affairs of the patient and authorised a person to conduct proceedings, then that person will be entitled to conduct proceedings.

The judge may be prepared to find that a party is incapable of managing his affairs by reason of conduct in or giving rise to the proceedings, and the question is then whether this is by reason of mental disorder. There is no difficulty in the case of a claimant because the proceedings may be stayed until that party submits to a medical examination. A defendant who will not submit to a medical examination does, however, present a problem.

5.4.3 Procedure

Need for a representative

A patient must have a representative to conduct proceedings, whether bringing or defending them. In civil proceedings this representative is a litigation friend, the patient is referred to as AB (by CD his litigation friend). In family proceedings it is a next friend if bringing the proceedings or a guardian ad litem if responding. Any step which might normally have been taken in the proceedings may be taken by the representative, but steps otherwise taken on behalf of a patient may not be effective. His solicitor may be personally liable for the costs wasted even though ignorant of the incapacity: see *Yonge* v. *Toynbee* [1910] 1 KB 215.

In the absence of a person being authorised to conduct proceedings by the Court of Protection, a representative may nominate himself and provided he gives the required notice to the other party and to the court, he may act as such without a court order. In default, the court may appoint a representative. If a party becomes a patient during the course of proceedings an application must be made for such an appointment to be made.

The procedure for appointing, removing or changing the representative is to be found in the relevant court rules.

Who is appointed

A person within the jurisdiction not being under an incapacity and not having an interest adverse to the patient or being connected to an opposing party may be a litigation friend. For instance, a person authorised by the Court of Protection to conduct proceedings on behalf of a patient (usually the receiver, unless there is a clear conflict of interest) is entitled to become the representative. Otherwise it should be a substantial person and a relation of or person connected with the patient, or friend of the family, and not a mere volunteer. If no suitable person can be found the Official Solicitor may be appointed but should first be consulted and give his consent.

The duty of the representative is:

> fairly and competently to conduct proceedings on behalf of [the] patient. He must have no interest in the proceedings adverse to that of the . . . patient and all steps and decisions he takes in the proceedings must be taken for the benefit of the . . . patient (CPR Part 21 PD, para. 2.1).

Unless also a receiver appointed by the Court of Protection or an attorney under a registered EPA, the representative will have no status in regard to the affairs of the patient outside the proceedings.

Service of proceedings

If a party is a patient proceedings must be served upon, initially, the person authorised by the Court of Protection (if any) or 'the person with whom the patient resides or in whose care he is', and thereafter the duly authorised representative of the patient (or solicitor on the record).

The court may make an order for deemed service or dispensing with service in appropriate circumstances.

Compromises and settlements

No compromise or settlement of a claim for a patient is valid without the approval of the court but an action may be brought solely for that purpose:

- this extends to costs and applies even if the representative is the receiver or attorney of the patient;
- the overriding consideration is the interest of the patient, having regard to all the circumstances of the case;
- approval of the Court of Protection will be sought first (if involved);
- it would be an abuse of process to proceed without the court's approval in any subsisting proceedings;
- in view of the cost of obtaining approval small claims are often settled on indemnities being given by the person to whom the money is paid.

See CPR Part 21 r. 21.10(2) (or for family proceedings RSC Order 80 rr. 10 and 11; CCR Order 10 r. 10).

5.4.4 General matters

Evidence

In civil and family proceedings evidence may only be given by an individual who is considered by the judge to be competent to give evidence. Evidence may be admitted as to the capacity of the witness in general terms but not as to the likelihood of being able to give a truthful account.

A different technique is required when examining vulnerable witnesses and the judge should control this where necessary. The aim is to elicit true and accurate information and not to break the already vulnerable witness. You should take account of the general considerations relevant to communicating with any elderly or potentially incapable client which are set out at 2.1.1.

Limitation of actions

The limitation periods are 12 years for action on a deed, six years for action on a contract and three years for personal injury claims. Special rules apply if the person was under a disability when the right of action accrued:

- the action may be brought within six (or three) years of the date when the disability ceased or the person died;
- where a disability arises after the cause of action has accrued, time will continue to run;
- the court has a discretion to extend the time for bringing personal injury claims;
- a person is treated as under a disability while he or she is of unsound mind.

'Unsound mind' means incapable by reason of mental disorder (within the Mental Health Act 1983) of managing and administering his or her property and affairs. It is a question of fact to be decided in each individual case (see Chapter 1 and 5.4.1). It is also conclusively presumed for a person who is liable to be detained or subject to guardianship under the Mental Health Act 1983 (or receiving in-patient treatment in any hospital within the meaning of that Act immediately thereafter).

See the Limitation Act 1980, ss. 28(1), 33(3)(d), 38(2) and 38(3) as amended by Mental Health Act 1983.

Stay of execution

If proceedings are taken to enforce a judgment against a patient a court would stay execution to enable steps to be taken on the patient's behalf, e.g.

- an application to the Court of Protection for the appointment of a receiver.
- registration of an EPA.

Injunctions

Being a patient is not itself a bar to the granting of an injunction and the question is whether the person understood the particular proceedings and the nature and requirements of the injunction. If he intended to do what he did and did it consciously, the necessary mens rea existed (*In re de Court, The Times*, 27 November 1997). An injunction ought not to be granted against a person who is incapable of understanding what he is doing or that it is wrong since he would not be capable of complying with it:

- any breach would not be subject to effective enforcement since he would have a defence to an application for committal for contempt (*Wookey* v. *Wookey*, *Re S.* (a minor) [1991] 3 All ER 365);
- the use of Mental Health Act powers of compulsory admission to hospital might be considered but if the patient's mental state does not justify this no effective remedy is available.

The court could make a hospital order under the Contempt of Court Act 1981, s.14(4) where the party was suffering from serious mental incapacity at the time of the contempt proceedings but if that incapacity had existed earlier it would have precluded any contempt (*Wookey* v. *Wookey*).

5.4.5 Costs

Solicitor and client

Unless the court otherwise directs, the costs payable in most proceedings by a patient to his own solicitor must be assessed by the court and no costs are payable to that solicitor except the amount so allowed. Solicitors should be aware that CPR Part 48 r. 48.5 applies also to family proceedings and that the rule extends to costs payable to a patient by another party. If those costs can be agreed and the patient's solicitor waives any claim to further costs, the district judge may waive detailed assessment if satisfied with the amount notified (see CPR Part 48 PD para. 51).

Conditional fees

There is an increasing trend for conditional or contingency fees to be available to cover the costs of the claimant's own solicitor in claims for damages, particularly in cases where funding from the Legal Services Commission is not available: see the Access to Justice Act 1999. This may be a 'no win, no fee' arrangement whereby the solicitor receives an enhanced fee if the claim succeeds and no fee at all if it fails. If so, there are restrictions upon the percentage uplift in the fees with a cap on the proportion of the damages that can be taken by the uplift.

The agreement must be concluded before the fees are incurred but where the claimant is a patient no one has authority to enter into it:

- the litigation friend's authority is restricted to the conduct of the proceedings and does not extend to advance fee arrangements with the lawyers;
- the rules do not permit a judge to approve a conditional fee arrangement upon issue of proceedings;
- the Court of Protection may have power to authorise such an agreement being entered into on behalf of a patient.

Costs of another party

The representative may be ordered to pay the costs of the proceedings (and will on commencing them have had to give an undertaking to pay any costs which the patient may be ordered to pay). In the absence of misconduct on his part, the representative is entitled to recover any costs awarded against him from the property of the patient (if any). The representative responding to a claim will not be personally liable for costs unless these were occasioned by his personal negligence or misconduct.

Liability of solicitor

A solicitor may be ordered to pay the wasted costs incurred where he or she brings or continues an action for a claimant, or defends an action for a defendant, who is or has become a patient, without a litigation friend acting for him (*Yonge* v. *Toynbee* [1910] 1 KB 215, CA).

Public funding

The availability of funding from the Legal Services Commission does not depend upon age or mental capacity. It may be sought on behalf of a patient based upon the merits of the case and his financial circumstances. The application will be submitted by the person acting (or proposing to act) for the patient but the financial circumstances of this representative will not be taken into account.

5.4.6 Disposal of damages

The court must decide how damages awarded to a patient are to be handled. The award itself should allow for the additional cost of administering the damages.

Procedure

Damages awarded to a patient must be paid into court (known as a fund) and not paid out except in accordance with directions which may be specific or general. The directions should be sought when the court enters judgment or gives approval to any settlement or compromise. Funds up to £20,000 can be administered by the court in which recovered, or transferred to the patient's local county court (CPR Part 21 PD para. 11.2):

- this will not be appropriate where there are other assets and the Court of Protection should be involved;
- an order will be made stating the manner in which the fund is to be invested, though the range of investments is restricted;
- authority can be given for regular interest payments and requests can be made at intervals for other sums to be released for the patient's benefit.

Where the fund is between £20,000 and £30,000 advice should be sought from the Court of Protection. Otherwise an order directs the litigation friend to apply to the Court of Protection for the appointment of a receiver and that the fund be then transferred to the credit of the receiver's account. If a receiver has already been appointed the order will provide for transfer of the fund forthwith. Where substantial damages are likely to be recovered consult the Court of Protection at the outset and follow its directions.

See generally:

- CPR Part 21 r. 21.11 and PD para. 11.2;
- Practice Note: Transfer of Damages to Court of Protection, 7 September 1990, [1991] 1 All ER 436;
- Court of Protection Practice Note: Procedure for the Settlement of Personal Injury Awards to Patients, 15 November 1996.

5.5   CHALLENGING DECISIONS

5.5.1   General

There are many situations in which you may need to help an older client challenge a decision made by the authorities, or even a failure to make a decision. The emphasis in this chapter is upon the provision of services by the local authority, but the following are examples of other situations in which older clients may seek your assistance:

- appeals against decisions on claims for state benefits (see Chapter 13);
- appeals against decisions of local authorities on claims for housing benefit or council tax rebate (see Chapter 14);
- appeals against decisions of Valuation Officers on council tax banding (see Chapter 6);

- refusals of planning permission (see generally the appeal procedures under the Town and Country Planning Acts);
- compulsory purchase and compensation relating to highway development;
- decisions relating to registration of residential care homes or private nursing homes (see Chapter 9);
- decisions on health care or medical treatment (see Chapters 10, 11 and 12; for the provision of community care services see Chapter 8).

When acting for a client in dealings with the authorities, do not be too quick to use your letter heading as this can be counter-productive. It may result in a premature reference to the legal department! Assist the client to write a well reasoned letter and then monitor progress. Advising the client in the background is not a sign of weakness and may be effective in clarifying the approach of the authority before seeking to challenge this when necessary.

5.5.2 Entitlement to services

Assessments and case conferences are part of the procedure for the provision of services. Delay and indecision by the authority may be used to avoid provision when shortage of funds or lack of facilities make it difficult to fulfil a request.

Before embarking on a course of action against an authority, consider using the following checklist:

5.5.3 Checklist when dissatisfied with local authority

❏ Has a decision been made by the relevant authority?

❏ Is it a request which the authority is obliged to consider? The statutory duties of the authority may be general in nature and not enforceable in respect of an individual.

❏ Identify the authority, department and officer responsible for providing the services required and complain to this officer.

❏ Ask for a review of a decision and be prepared to compromise.

❏ Follow any complaints or appeal procedure.

❏ Check the time limits for taking any other available legal action.

❏ Should the Minister be asked to use his default powers?

❏ Is it a case for judicial review?

❏ Is it maladministration which can be referred to an Ombudsman?

❏ Reference to the European Court of Human Rights?

5.5.4   Structure of local authorities

There are three tiers of local government:

- county councils, generally responsible for provision of services to elderly persons through their social services departments;
- district (or borough) councils, responsible for housing and environmental health;
- parish (or town) councils, responsible for local issues.

In some areas, i.e. metropolitan districts, Greater London boroughs and unitary authorities, the responsibilities of the county level and the district level are combined in a single local authority.

The powers of councils are generally delegated: elected councillors are collectively responsible for policy decisions, officers are appointed to carry out policy decisions but have delegated powers, and administration is divided into departments each headed by a senior officer:

- housing: deals with provision of housing (including homeless persons);
- environmental health: covers public health and the environment;
- social services: responsibilities include welfare of the elderly.

Local authorities must establish a Social Services Committee which appoints a Director of Social Services and employs social workers (see the Local Authority Social Services Act 1970, s.2, and see the Local Government Act 1972, s.101(8) and (9)).

5.5.5   Complaints procedures

In many instances internal complaints procedures are available and you should be given information about these on enquiry. Any complaint must be in the appropriate form to the right person, but whether or not there is a formal procedure you may make representations to elected councillors, the chief executive or head of department. Most local authorities now have service charters advising of their standards and complaints procedures.

Local authorities must establish and publicise the existence of a procedure for considering any representations or complaints with respect to the discharge of their social services functions or the failure to discharge those functions. This must provide:

- a definition of a complaint and identify who can bring a complaint;
- for the role of the independent person;
- support for persons who need assistance in bringing a complaint.

See Chapter 8 for further details of social services complaints procedures and Chapter 10 for the complaints procedures available in respect of health care.

5.5.6 Appeal procedures

If not satisfied with a decision always enquire if there is a formal appeal procedure and if so the time limits for invoking this. The decision-making
authority will be under an obligation to tell you if there is a procedure. There
is no 'appeal' against a financial assessment for community care, although it
is possible to evoke the complaints procedure if guidance has not been
followed, complain to the Ombudsman or seek judicial review

5.6 OMBUDSMEN

Ombudsmen are independent people who investigate and report on complaints
by UK residents about treatment by particular public bodies. The complainant
must have suffered injustice and the matters complained of must amount to
maladministration. Maladministration includes delay, inattention, incompetence, ineptitude and neglect, discourtesy and harassment, bias, arbitrariness
and unfair discrimination.

5.6.1 Key points

There is generally a 12-month time limit before a complaint can be investigated. All existing means of seeking redress must first be exhausted and
matters before the courts cannot be investigated.

The complaint is normally made by the person who claims to have suffered injustice. Where he or she is for any reason unable to act for him or
herself it may usually be made by a member of his or her family or some
body or individual suitable to represent him or her. Legal representation is
not usually necessary but a solicitor may be able to assist in presenting the
complaint.

The procedure is usually private but the resulting report may be published.
Findings are not legally enforceable but the report may result in redress where
there is no legal remedy, e.g. compensation or apology and an attempt to
discourage similar administrative action in the future.

5.6.2 Parliamentary Commissioner for Administration

The Commissioner is someone completely independent of the government
who can investigate complaints by members of the public about the way they
have been treated by government departments and agencies.

These departments and agencies include the Departments of Work and
Pensions, Transport, Education and Skills, Constitutional Affairs and the
Office of the Deputy Prime Minister. Also certain non-departmental public
bodies such as Inland Revenue, Legal Services Commission, Information

Commissioner and the Commission for Racial Equality – the list was extended in March 1999 and is frequently updated.

Complaints about government policy or the content of legislation are not included but are matters for Parliament. Complaints must be channelled through an MP who will usually seek to sort the matter out with the department concerned first. The Commissioner decides whether to carry out a full investigation and he may inspect government files and papers and can summon anyone to give evidence in an investigation.

5.6.3 Commissioners for Local Administration

These Local Ombudsmen deal with complaints by anyone who considers that he or she has suffered injustice because of maladministration by a local authority. Their remit does not include parish councils or certain other authorities (e.g. police authorities). If the complaint passes initial screening it will be taken up in correspondence but there is power to examine the authority's internal papers and to take written and oral evidence from anyone who can provide relevant information. See the Local Government Act 1974, ss.25–27.

5.6.4 Health Service Commissioner

The Health Service Commissioner is an independent person who investigates certain types of complaint about the NHS which cannot otherwise be resolved. He cannot investigate complaints about independent practitioners or matters of clinical judgement. The complaint may relate to failure to provide or the provision of a service, or maladministration, and may be about attitude as well as actions of staff.

5.7 LEGAL CHALLENGES

When negotiation and persuasion, and the use of complaints procedures when available, do not result in the needs of the client being met it becomes necessary to consider the legal remedies that are available. There may be a choice of remedies but equally none may offer the certainty of positive results within an acceptable timescale. Nevertheless the threat to use one of these remedies or the taking of the initial steps may be sufficient to draw a response and create a further climate for negotiation.

5.7.1 Complaint to the Minister

Many statutes vest supervisory powers in government ministers and Codes of Guidance are issued by government departments. Some statutes giving powers to or imposing duties on local authorities authorise the Minister to make regulations prescribing how they shall exercise or perform these. A complaint may be made direct to a Minister if the authority does not comply with his directions and he may exercise default powers, although these are appropriate to deal with a general breakdown in some service provision rather than individual cases.

The Minister may call the authority to account for failure to exercise its functions, direct the authority to comply and take over the authority's functions, e.g. the National Health Service Act 1977, s.85.

There is a power for the Secretary of State to declare local authorities in default if they fail to comply with their social services duties, to direct compliance within time limits and to enforce this by judicial review (mandatory order): Local Authority Social Services Act 1970, s.7D (inserted by National Health Service and Community Care Act 1990, s.50).

5.7.2 Small claims procedure

Do not overlook the possibility of assisting the client with a claim in the county court where operational failings by a service provider (including a local authority) have resulted in financial loss to an elderly client or carer. An example is repeated failure to provide agreed transport to a day care centre resulting in expenditure on taxis so that the carer can meet other commitments. Under the above principles there remains some prospect of success, and the threat of a claim or the issue of proceedings may in itself be sufficient to persuade the service provider to be more careful in the future. Repeat claims could be brought if there was a continuing failure.

If the claim is under £5,000 (£1,000 for a personal injury or housing disrepair claim) it may be allocated to the small claims track thus providing many advantages to the claimant (see 5.2.3).

Also, whilst you may assist with the preparation of the case your client should be able to cope at the hearing itself if funds are limited as:

- the hearing is relatively informal and before a district judge;
- the district judge without 'entering the arena' must seek to make good the deficiencies of an unrepresented party;
- a lay representative (e.g. a relative or friend) will be permitted.

If funding from the Legal Services Commission is not available resist any application that the case should not be allocated to the small claims track by arguing that:

- there is no difficult issue of law or exceptional complexity in the facts;
- the client cannot afford legal representation whereas the local authority has the resources of its legal department;

- the client could not pursue the claim if faced with an open court trial and the risk of costs.

See CPR Part 27 and the Practice Direction.

5.7.3   Judicial review

The High Court may review the legality of a course of action by a public body and provide one or more of the following remedies in a final order:

- a mandatory order (formerly mandamus), to require the performance of a specific public law duty;
- a quashing order (formerly certiorari), to quash a decision which is invalid;
- a prohibiting order (formerly prohibition), to prohibit the body from acting in an unlawful manner;
- a declaration, to declare what the law is.

A typical order might include a quashing order to quash an unlawful decision and a mandatory order to require a new decision according to the law. As an interim measure the court may grant an injunction (which may be of a mandatory nature).

Claims for judicial review are heard by the Administrative Court (formerly the Crown Office List).

Relief is available where the decisions of public bodies (and also inferior courts and tribunals) are unlawful, which includes:

- *ultra vires* (i.e. outside the powers of the body making it);
- contrary to the rules of natural justice;
- made in a way that is procedurally incorrect;
- based on a misinterpretation of the law;
- unreasonable or irrational, e.g. a material consideration was not taken into account, or matters have been taken into account which ought not to have been.

The potential for judicial review has increased by reason of the obligation of authorities to assess the needs of individuals for community care services (see the Supreme Court Act 1981, s.31 and CPR Part 54.

The claim must be made promptly and in any event within three months of the grounds arising unless time is extended by the court (e.g. because of the need to get public funding).

The applicant should normally first comply with the pre-action protocol for judicial review. This requires the applicant to send a letter before action to the potential defendant identifying the decision or act that is being challenged and explaining the reasons for the challenge. A standard letter form is annexed to the protocol.

Before he can pursue the claim the applicant must obtain permission to proceed from a High Court judge. The claim is commenced by issuing a Part 8 Claim Form. This should be filed with the court accompanied by:

- a detailed statement of the grounds for bringing the claim;
- a statement of the facts relied upon;
- any applications for extending time for bringing the claim or directions;
- any written evidence in support of the claim;
- a copy of any order that the applicant wishes to have quashed;
- an approved copy of the decision of any court or tribunal that is being challenged;
- copies of any documents upon which the applicant relies;
- copies of any relevant statutory material;
- a reading list.

The claim form must be served on the defendant and any interested party within seven days of issue.

In the first instance the court will usually determine whether permission to proceed should be granted on the papers alone. If permission is refused at this stage, the applicant can request the matter to be reconsidered at an oral hearing. If permission is refused after an oral hearing an appeal lies to the Court of Appeal.

Where permission is given the court may give directions. The defendant and any other person served with the Claim Form has 35 days from the date of the grant of permission to serve a response and any written evidence. Disclosure is not usually required. Hearings normally take place before a single judge in open court and are often short (an expedited hearing may be sought) usually consisting of oral argument on legal matters based on the written evidence. The court may hear oral evidence, although it is rare for this to occur.

The remedy is discretionary and rules have developed to define the circumstances in which the court will intervene:

- An applicant must have sufficient interest in the matter (*locus standi*); this may include action groups in appropriate circumstances (see *R.* v. *Secretary of State for Social Services, ex parte CPAG* [1989] 1 All ER 1047).
- Any alternative remedy should usually have been pursued first, e.g. a complaints procedure, though the need for interim relief could be relevant; and the Minister's default powers are not usually an alternative to judicial review.
- The courts concern themselves with the decision-making process rather than the merits of the decision: note the *Wednesbury* principle in *Associated Provincial Picture Houses Ltd* v. *Wednesbury Corporation* [1948] 1 KB 223.

- The court will not grant relief if it considers that there is no need or it would be administratively inconvenient or the applicant's conduct does not merit it; lack of resources may prove an effective defence for a local authority in regard to its obligations to provide services (but will not necessarily be so).
- Relief may be refused if, by reason of delay, there may be either substantial hardship or prejudice to another person or detriment to good administration.

5.7.4 Breach of statutory duty

In certain limited situations an action may be brought for breach of statutory duty. It should be noted that this area of the law has been in a state of flux, with a significant number of cases being considered by the House of Lords in recent years. In *X (Minors)* v. *Bedfordshire County Council* [1995] 2 AC 633, the House of Lords considered the requirements to bring a claim for breach of statutory duty in the strict sense (which is where the cause of action depends neither on proof of any damage to the claimant's common law rights nor on any allegation of carelessness by the defendant).

In each case the question is one of statutory construction and will therefore depend on the provisions of the relevant statute. Such a cause of action will arise only if it can be shown that as a matter of construction of the statute, such a duty was imposed for the protection of a limited class of the public and that Parliament intended to confer on members of that class a private right of action for breach of the duty. If the legislation provides no other remedy for its breach and it is shown that Parliament intended to protect a limited class of the public, this indicates that there may be a private right of action. However, the existence of some other statutory remedy may not be fatal to a claim. The cases where a private law action for breach of statutory duty have been held to arise are cases where the statutory duty has been limited in its scope.

Where no direct action for breach of statutory duty lies, the authority will not be liable for careless performance of its duties unless the circumstances are such as to raise a duty of care at common law so as to enable a claim to be made in tort.

5.7.5 Tort

In the absence of express statutory authority a local authority is liable for torts in the same way as an individual. Damages may be claimed in negligence on the basis that a statutory duty itself gives rise to a common law duty of care or that the manner in which a statutory duty has been implemented has caused a duty of care to arise.

The circumstances where a statutory duty itself gives rise to a common law duty of care will be unusual. If the policy of a statute is not to create a statutory liability to pay compensation, the same policy will usually exclude the existence of a common law duty of care. For such a duty of care to arise there must be a public law duty to act (rather than merely a discretion or power) and exceptional circumstances for holding that the policy of the statute requires compensation to be paid to persons who suffer because the power was not exercised: *Stovin* v. *Wise* [1996] 3 All ER 801, HL (failure by highway authority to modify a dangerous junction where the claimant had an accident).

Even if there is no duty to provide a service (e.g. where there is merely a general duty or a power) there may be a common law duty of care in the manner in which it is carried out. This may possibly extend to administrative or operational failure to provide or in the provision of an agreed service: see *Barrett* v. *Enfield London Borough Council* [2001] 2 AC 550, HL and *Phelps* v. *Hillingdon London Borough Council* [2001] 2 AC 619, HL. The negligent manner in which a public authority carried out its statutory duty could give rise to liability where it created the danger which caused the injury: *Capital and Counties Plc* v. *Hampshire County Council* [1997] QB 1004, CA (negligence by fire brigade which owed a duty of care when it turned off a sprinkler system).

The fact that the acts which are claimed to be negligent are carried out within the ambit of a statutory discretion is not of itself a reason to prevent a claim in negligence arising (*Barrett* v. *Enfield*). However, where what has been done has involved the weighing of competing public interests or has been dictated by considerations on which Parliament could not have intended that the courts would substitute their views for the views of Ministers or officials, the court should decide that the issue is non-justiciable on the basis that the decision was made in the exercise of a statutory discretion (*Phelps* v. *Hillingdon*).

In practice where a claim is brought in negligence, a claim for breach of a statutory duty in the strict sense is often pleaded in the alternative (see above).

An authority may also be vicariously liable for the torts of its employees. There is no public policy reason why an authority may not be vicariously liable for the acts of a social worker who fails to provide significant information to foster parents: *W* v. *Essex County Council and Goulden* [1997] 2 FLR 535, FD; [1999] Fam 90, CA (and see [2001] 2 AC 592, HL) (they were not told that the foster child was an active sexual abuser and their own children were abused). An authority will not be vicariously liable for an independent act by an employee outside the course of employment. However, a range of acts may be connected with the employment: *Lister* v. *Hesley Hall Ltd* [2002] 1 AC 215, HL (employer vicariously liable for sexual abuse of children by warden of school boarding house).

5.7.6 Breach of contract

If a promise has been made it may be enforceable as such against the authority. This may possibly extend to the provision of agreed services for which a payment is made by the recipient (see the Supply of Goods and Services Act 1982).

5.7.7 Human Rights Act 1998

European Convention on Human Rights

The following substantive rights guaranteed by the European Convention on Human Rights may be of direct relevance to the older citizen, although these are subject to qualifications not mentioned here.

- Article 2: 'Everyone's right to life shall be protected by law'. This creates a positive obligation to safeguard life and can be relevant to the provision of medical treatment.
- Article 3: 'No one shall be subjected to ... inhuman or degrading treatment'. This may be relevant to standards of care provision.
- Article 5: 'Everyone has the right to liberty and security of person'. The 'lawful detention of ... persons of unsound mind' is allowed for but everyone who is deprived of his or her liberty by detention is entitled to have the lawfulness tested by a court and to compensation if it was unlawful. This may be relevant in the fields of mental health and other care provision.
- Article 6: 'In the determination of his civil rights and obligations ... everyone is entitled to a fair and public hearing within a reasonable time by an independent and impartial tribunal established by law'. This is relevant to access to justice for people with disabilities.
- Article 8: 'Everyone has the right to respect for his private and family life, his home and his correspondence'. This may prove relevant to standards in residential care and nursing homes as well as sheltered housing, but has far wider potential.
- Article 9: 'Everyone has the right to freedom of thought, conscience and religion'. This right has to date received little scrutiny but may be infringed by procedures to protect an elderly person who is perceived to be vulnerable.
- Article 12: the right to marry and found a family. Only the first part of this right is likely to be relevant to the older person but procedures for assessing capacity for marriage could be questioned.
- Article 1 First Protocol: 'Every ... person is entitled to the peaceful enjoyment of his possessions'. It may be that the absence of accessible legal procedures for decision-making on behalf of those who lack capacity could lead to a breach of this right.

146

- Article 14: 'The enjoyment of the rights and freedoms set forth in this Convention shall be secured without discrimination on any grounds such as sex, race . . . religion . . . property, birth or other status'. It has yet to be seen whether this opens the door to the requirement for legislation against age discrimination.

Human Rights Act 1998

The Convention is incorporated into UK domestic law by the Human Rights Act 1998, though with some limitations. The Act came into effect on 1 October 2000. It is unlawful for a public authority to act in a way which is incompatible with a Convention right:

- Individuals are able to rely upon the provisions of the Convention in any legal proceedings although claims brought expressly under it will only be permitted in certain courts.
- A party who wishes to rely on the provisions of the 1998 Act must give full details of his contentions in his statement of case (CPR Part 16 PD para. 16).
- All legislation must be read so far as is possible to give effect to the Convention in a way that is compatible with the rights that it lays down.
- When a court seeks to determine a question arising in connection with a Convention right it must take into account the case law of the European Court of Human Rights.
- Only a victim of an action by a public authority which is incompatible with a Convention right may complain under the Act and the law cannot be challenged in the abstract.
- There is a one-year time limit for bringing proceedings under the Act with a discretion to extend this.

If primary legislation proves to be incompatible with the Convention, despite the duty not to so interpret it if possible, all the higher courts can do is make a 'declaration of incompatibility' which may result in the legislation being amended. Courts may, however, within the limit of their general powers, give relief against subordinate legislation. If relief is not granted in our courts it may still be sought in the ECHR.

The 1998 Act may be of assistance in various types of claim. However, it must first be established that the body whose decision is being challenged is a public authority. A housing association may be a public authority in relation to certain actions (*Poplar Housing Association* v. *Donoghue* [2002] QB 48, CA) but a charity with whom a local authority had arrangements for the provision of accommodation was considered not to be a public authority (*R. (on the application of Heather)* v. *Leonard Cheshire Foundation* [2002] 2 All ER 936, CA).

Courts which have the power to award damages or order the payment of compensation in civil proceedings have limited powers to award damages in respect of a breach of a person's human rights (see the Human Rights Act 1998, s.8).

5.8 THE EUROPEAN DIMENSION

5.8.1 European Court of Justice

This European Court of Justice (ECJ) is based in Luxembourg and is the ultimate appeal court on matters relating to the Treaty of the European Community. Its decisions are binding upon our courts. It has 15 judges and eight Advocates-General, each appointed for a term of six years and all chosen by Member States 'by common accord' based upon qualification for the highest judicial office. An Advocate-General provides a written opinion with a recommendation at the end of the oral procedure and this is not binding but assists the judges who hand down a single judgment which may be a compromise because there is no provision for dissenting judgments.

The Court of First Instance handles certain cases including those brought against Community institutions by natural or legal persons. It is an inferior court with 15 judges and there is a right of appeal to the full court. There are no Advocates-General but one of the judges may adopt this role.

Where an issue of Community law arises before a national court, questions of interpretation or validity can be referred to the ECJ for a preliminary ruling:

- The procedure is available to the national court rather than to the parties.
- It is the court which decides the question to be referred although a party may make the initial request for a reference.
- Legal Services Commission funding may be available to cover the reference, but the ECJ may grant legal aid in special circumstances for 'the purpose of facilitating the representation or attendance of a party'.

The European Commission or another Member State may bring an action against a Member State for failure to fulfil its obligations under the EC Treaty and national governments are treated as responsible for the acts of local authorities and other public bodies. So instead of bringing a case in the local court an individual whose rights have been infringed by non-implementation of an EC Directive can complain to the Commission which can investigate and bring a case before the ECJ which can award damages to the individual.

5.8.2 European Court of Human Rights

An aggrieved person is able to make a direct complaint to the European Commission of Human Rights based in Strasbourg which is part of the

Council of Europe and acts as the screening and investigative chamber for complaints to the European Court of Human Rights (ECHR). The applicant must satisfy the Commission that:

- the complaint relates to a violation of one or more of the Articles of the European Convention on Human Rights or the First Protocol;
- he or she is a victim of that violation;
- efforts have been made to resolve the violation using the domestic legal system and all possible domestic remedies (if any) have been exhausted;
- the complaint to the Commission has been lodged within six months of the exhaustion of the last attempted domestic remedy.

If satisfied that the complaint complies with the admissibility criteria, the Commission will investigate the matter and ask the government for its observations. At this stage limited legal aid, subject to a means test, may be available from the Council of Europe. The procedure is slow, although many cases are settled by the government at a relatively early stage.

If a complaint survives scrutiny it is generally passed to the ECHR for a final decision. Substantial compensation and legal costs can be awarded to successful complainants under binding judgments, and there are no court fees or costs awards against unsuccessful complainants.

CHAPTER 6

The elderly client, society and the law

David Rees and Alison Callcott

6.1 INTRODUCTION

This chapter looks at the civil rights of the elderly client and the way in which these may be affected by increasing age and disability. While Chapter 4 considered the legal framework for the management of the client's property and affairs, not every aspect of the client's life can at every stage be dealt with in this way. For any client, we should begin with a presumption of capacity and provide practical assistance to the client to preserve his or her independence and autonomy as long as possible. And there are also personal decisions and circumstances which affect the elderly client and the way he or she conducts life in society.

6.2 CAPACITY

6.2.1 Overview

In order to exercise legal rights and powers a person must have the necessary mental capacity to do so. No one is legally incapable in the total sense but capacity may be taken away by law (e.g. minors, Court of Protection patients). Although capacity is considered in more detail in Chapter 1, it is worth remembering that in assessing a person's capacity to perform any action, capacity is a question of fact, and that the correct test of capacity must be applied in each case.

The test varies according to the circumstances and is determined by statute or common law. Although capacity depends upon understanding rather than wisdom, it is the state of mind at the time that is material (but do not ignore windows of opportunity). Evidence of conduct at other times is admissible, e.g. general pattern of life and inability to communicate does not necessarily mean lack of capacity.

There is a presumption of capacity. This presumption may be rebutted by evidence to the contrary. Medical evidence may be admitted but it is for the court to decide whether such evidence is adequate and apply the correct legal test in the particular circumstances. Unusual or eccentric behaviour does not give rise to a presumption of incapacity but may cause capacity to be questioned.

It is also necessary to consider in the case of agreements whether there was an intention to create legal relations, and for social and domestic arrangements it is presumed that there is no such intention. This may also be the case in regard to financial arrangements within the family so it may be advisable for these to be put on a legal footing, although any presumption may be rebutted by evidence to the contrary.

6.2.2 General contracts

A contract may be set aside at the option of a party if it can be shown that he did not understand its nature due to mental disorder and that the other party knew (or should have been aware) of this. The fact that the contract is unfair will not by itself be sufficient, see *Hart* v. *O'Connor* [1985] 2 All ER 880.

For the contract to be valid, the individual must understand the nature and effect of what he is doing and be capable of agreeing to it. The extent of that understanding depends upon the implications of the contract (in the case of an elderly person it may need to extend to the effect upon state benefits and local authority support). Capacity is judged in respect of each transaction at that moment and a lucid interval is sufficient.

Where the Court of Protection has appointed a receiver for a patient, the patient can in general no longer enter into a contract as this would interfere with the powers of control and management vested in the court (*Re Walker* [1905] 1 Ch 160; *Re Marshall* [1920] 1 Ch 284). However, a contract validly created before the onset of incapacity remains binding on the patient and while a contract entered into subsequently with another party acting in good faith without knowledge of the lack of capacity is voidable, the Court of Protection may give authority for the contract to be carried out.

Necessaries

A person who lacks capacity to contract may be required to pay a reasonable price for the purchase of items that are deemed to be 'necessaries'. The Sale of Goods Act 1979, s. 3(3) defines 'necessaries' as 'goods suitable to the [person's] condition in life and his actual requirements at the time of sale and delivery'. This legislation protects both the shopkeeper who may obtain payment for goods as well as the incapable person, who is obliged to pay a 'reasonable price'. Although the legislation applies to 'goods' the same principle applies to the provision of essential services such as care costs. Clearly a care home or nursing agency must be able to expect payment for essential services provided before a receiver has been appointed.

152

6.2.3   Specific contracts

Bank accounts

In regard to bank and building society accounts (as well as credit or charge cards):

- The duty and authority to pay a customer's cheque is determined by notice of mental disorder of a sufficient degree to prevent an understanding of the transaction. The size and nature of the cheque or payment is relevant (see *Drew* v. *Nunn* [1979] 4 QB 661).
- By custom a bank is entitled to charge simple interest at a reasonable rate upon overdrafts but a loan is a matter for specific agreement.
- A guarantor may not be liable if the fact of mental incapacity on the part of the debtor was known to all parties but a separate contract of indemnity could be enforced.
- National Savings Bank accounts may be opened on behalf and in the name of persons of unsound mind (National Savings Bank Act 1971, s.8(1)(f); National Savings Bank Regulations 1972, SI 1972/764, regs. 6 and 7).
- Accounts may be opened by a receiver or registered attorney for a person without capacity.

Until such time as a bank receives actual notice of a person's incapacity, it tends to look for the ability to provide a consistent signature rather than applying more sophisticated tests. However, once a bank has notice of incapacity, especially formal notice such as a First General Order or registered Enduring Power of Attorney (EPA) it will generally prevent any use of the account by the customer, even if technically the customer has capacity to manage such an account.

Insurance policies

Any relevant disability must be disclosed on the proposal form and also on renewal, and a policy may be void for non-disclosure. Attorneys and receivers need to take great care when taking out policies or renewing policies where the disability might be relevant, such as health policies. An express declaration as to medical condition or disability may be required.

If the policyholder is incapable when money is payable the insurers will only make payment to an attorney under a registered EPA or pursuant to an order of the Court of Protection. Where money is payable under a life insurance policy, this can be avoided (with sufficient foresight) if the policy is written in trust so that the proceeds are payable to trustees rather than to the incapable proposer.

Agency

The authority of an agent depends on the mental capacity of the principal at the time of appointment and throughout the period of the agency, so that this terminates once there is a loss of capacity.

A power of attorney involves the appointment of an agent, which is terminated by incapacity unless the power is an EPA created under the Enduring Powers of Attorney Act 1985 and duly registered with the Court of Protection (see 4.5).

Partnership and directorships are considered in Chapter 16.

6.2.4   Trustees

There is no upper age limit for a trustee but a trustee who is incapable is thereby unable to act in that capacity and should be replaced at the earliest opportunity. Problems most commonly arise where a husband and wife own a property together and therefore hold the legal title as trustees of land. A trustee of land who also has a beneficial interest in the land can delegate his trusteeship under the Trustee Delegation Act 1999 using an EPA and this delegation can continue even if he loses capacity.

Where the trust involves assets other than land in which the trustee has a beneficial interest, the situation is more complicated, unless the trustee is the donor of an EPA which was made before 1 March 2000 and registered with the Court of Protection before 1 March 2001. In all other cases application must be made to the Court of Protection either for a new trustee to be appointed (with an order vesting trust assets in the new trustee) or for leave to be given to the capable trustee to appoint a new trustee. These situations are considered in more detail in Chapter 4 at 4.9.5.

6.3   CIVIL STATUS

6.3.1   Driving licences

It is an offence to drive a motor vehicle on a road unless the driver holds a licence authorising him or her to drive a vehicle of the class being driven. An applicant for a licence must state whether he is suffering from a 'relevant disability':

- This means either a disability prescribed by the Secretary of State or any other disability which is or may become likely to cause the driving of a vehicle by the applicant to be a source of danger to the public (being under a guardianship order under the Mental Health Act 1983 is a prescribed disability).

- The holder of a licence must also report any subsequent disability that arises unless it is not expected to last for more than three months.
- The Driver and Vehicle Licensing Agency (DVLA) (Swansea SA6 7JL) may revoke the licence of a person who suffers from such a disability.
- A doctor is required to inform the DVLA if he or she believes a patient is unfit to drive. If the patient does not agree to disclosure, the doctor must notify the patient that the DVLA will be advised, and then write to the DVLA in confidence. The patient must also be informed.
- A receiver needs to notify the DVLA of a patient's incapacity (this can be done by sending the DVLA the licence together with a copy of form CP3, with the doctor's consent or the Court of Protection's approval as of course the medical certificate is for court purposes only); an attorney acting under a registered EPA should likewise inform the DVLA of the donor's incapacity.
- DVLA medical officers tend to adhere to rigid guidelines so it is difficult to persuade DVLA to reverse a decision.
- A right of appeal against a refusal to grant or revocation of a driving licence lies to the magistrates' court for the petty sessional area in which the aggrieved person resides and few applications are successful. The DVLA usually instruct lawyers and call medical evidence and costs may be awarded against the appellant (Road Traffic Act 1988, ss.87–94 and 100).

6.3.2 Passports

Where a person is unable to sign a passport application form through mental disability a declaration signed by a person responsible for the applicant's welfare may be accepted. This could be a son or daughter, doctor, social worker or officer-in-charge of a residential care home, or a receiver or attorney. The signatory should explain in the 'Other Information' section of the form, or in a separate letter if preferred, that the applicant is incapacitated and that the signatory (in whatever relevant capacity) has signed on his or her behalf.

6.3.3 Privileges

Certain privileges or concessions may be available to older people:

- parking schemes (the 'orange badge scheme' allows parking concessions to be made to assist people with mobility problems);
- disabled persons' rail travel may apply to older people and enables an escort to travel with them at a discounted rate;
- for concessionary payments see Chapter 15.

6.3.4 Voting

There is no upper age bar to voting but legal capacity to vote is unclear. The presiding officer may challenge a person who requests a ballot paper if lack of mental capacity is suspected and the test is then ability to answer statutory questions in an intelligible manner (Parliamentary Election Rules, r. 35(1)). There are procedures for postal and proxy voting and no test of capacity may then apply in practice.

6.3.5 Jury service

An individual is eligible for jury service up to the age of 70 years. The individual must also be registered as a parliamentary or local government elector and have been ordinarily resident in the United Kingdom (or the Isle of Man or the Channel Islands) for at least five years since the age of 13 years.

Various categories of person are ineligible, disqualified or excused, including:

- anyone in a hospital or similar institution, or regularly attending for treatment by a medical practitioner, due to mental illness;
- a person in guardianship or under the jurisdiction of the Court of Protection.

A judge may discharge a juror who is considered unable to understand the nature of the oath or the evidence. If a person called for jury service is not thought fit to sit the jury officer or court clerk should be informed and the summons may be withdrawn. When a person with a disability is called for jury service it is for the judge to determine whether or not that person should act as a juror:

- The presumption is that they should unless the judge is of the opinion that the person will not, on account of disability, be capable of acting effectively.
- There have been many cases in which blind persons have served on juries.
- No evidence has ever been presented that a deaf juror is less able to assess the demeanour of a witness but the need for a communicator in the jury room would be a fundamental obstacle.
- The Disability Discrimination Act 1995 does not apply because jury service is not deemed to be a 'service to the public'.

See the Juries Act 1974, ss.1, 9B and Schedule (as amended by Mental Health Act 1983 and Criminal Justice Act 1988).

6.4   CIVIL RESPONSIBILITY

6.4.1   Council tax

Council tax is a property tax with a personal element charged on an adult resident in a dwelling which is his or her sole or main residence. Joint and several liability can arise but not every individual will be liable. The tax assumes that two people live in a dwelling and assesses properties in valuation bands.

There is a 25 per cent discount for a sole resident and this also applies where a person in a disregarded category is living in the house with a person who is liable for the tax. Disregarded categories include people who are 'severely mentally impaired', some carers and those living in residential care or nursing homes. The maximum discount when all residents are disregarded is 50 per cent. Special band reductions apply to houses adapted for people witn disabilities. Appeals are to a tribunal, e.g. in respect of the band in which a property is placed (the time limit for appeals against initial assessments has passed).

See the Local Government Finance Act 1992 and for further information see Age Concern Fact Sheet 21, *The Council Tax and Older People.*

6.4.2   National insurance contributions

National insurance contributions are not payable by those over pensionable age but an adequate contributions record of the individual (or spouse) is required if the normal state retirement pension is to be paid. A contributions record may be checked by completing form BR19 and sending this to: Pension Forecasting Team, The Pension Service, Room TB001, Tyneview Park, Whitley Road, Newcastle-upon-Tyne, NE98 1BA.

In response a comprehensive pensions forecast is received. The record may also be made up by:

- credits, e.g. whilst unemployed and signing on or off work sick;
- home responsibilities protection for periods when unable to work whilst caring for a child or an elderly or disabled person (since 1978 only).

Voluntary or late contributions can in some circumstances be made to protect a pension record. A series of leaflets is available from the Pensions Service about contributions and see www.thepensionservice.gov.uk. For pensions generally see Chapter 17.

6.4.3   Income and capital taxes

For income and capital taxes see Chapter 17.

6.5 DISCRIMINATION

There is no law to prevent discrimination on grounds of age but other forms of discrimination may be relevant to an older person. Everyone has a right not to be discriminated against on the grounds of sex, race or disability. At present anti-discrimination legislation comprises:

- Sex Discrimination Act 1975;
- Race Relations Act 1976 (as amended by the Race Relations (Amendment) Act 2000): 'race' covers colour, race, ethnic or national origins and nationality (s.3);
- Disability Discrimination Act 1995;
- Disability Rights Commission Act 1999;
- Special Educational Needs and Disability Act 2001.

6.5.1 Disability discrimination

The Disability Discrimination Act 1995 is likely to prove of significance to older people although parts will not be brought into force until 2004 (e.g. the duty to make physical alterations to premises). The Act is divided into several distinct parts:

- Part I provides a definition of 'disability' and for guidance to be issued;
- Part II deals with discrimination by employers;
- Part III deals with discrimination in relation to goods, facilities and services and also in relation to premises;
- Part IV deals with education (including further and higher education);
- Part V deals with public transport.

Regulations and guidance

There has been a proliferation of secondary legislation and other sources of guidance including:

- Disability Discrimination (Meaning of Disability) Regulations 1996, SI 1996/1455;
- Disability Discrimination (Services and Premises) Regulations 1996, SI 1996/1836;
- Disability Discrimination (Sub-leases and Sub-tenancies) Regulations 1996, SI 1996/1333;
- Code of Practice on rights of access: goods, facilities, services and premises (revised 2002);
- Code of Practice on duties of trade organisations to their disabled members and applicants.

Definitions

A person has a 'disability' if he or she has 'a physical or mental impairment which has a substantial and long-term adverse effect on his ability to carry out normal day-to-day activities' and a 'disabled person' means 'a person who has a disability'. Note also:

- the concepts of 'impairment', 'long-term effects', 'normal day-to-day activities' and 'substantial adverse effects' are interpreted in Sched. 1 to the 1995 Act;
- the Secretary of State issues guidance about such matters, and the courts must take this into account; see s.3(3) and Guidance on Matters to be Taken into Account in Determining Questions Relating to the Definition of Disability.

Goods, facilities and services (s.19)

It is unlawful for a provider of services to discriminate against a disabled person in:

- refusing to provide, or deliberately not providing, to the disabled person any service which he provides, or is prepared to provide, to members of the public;
- the standard of service which he provides to the disabled person or the manner in which he provides it to him or her.
- the terms on which he provides a service to the disabled person.

The provision of services includes the provision of any goods or facilities. A person is 'a provider of services' if he is concerned with the provision of services to the public or to a section of the public; it is irrelevant whether a service is provided on payment or without payment.

Discrimination in employment is covered in Chapter 16.

Meaning of 'discrimination' (s.20)

A provider of services discriminates against a disabled person if, for a reason which relates to the disabled person's disability, he treats him or her less favourably than he treats or would treat others to whom that reason does not or would not apply; and if he cannot show that the treatment in question is justified.

Enforcement, remedies and procedure (s.25)

A claim by any person that another person has discriminated against him or her in a way which is unlawful may be made the subject of civil proceedings in the same way as any other claim in tort for breach of statutory duty:

- proceedings must be in the county court and brought within six months although the court may extend time if it considers that it is just and equitable to do so;
- damages may include compensation for injury to feelings whether or not they include compensation under any other head (this may be limited to a prescribed sum, see Sched. 3 para. 7);
- the remedies are those which are available in the High Court so include the granting of a declaration that there has been discrimination.

Disability Rights Commission

The Disability Rights Commission was set up under the Disability Rights Commission Act 1999 and replaced the National Disability Council set up under the 1995 Act. In addition to promoting equal opportunities and encouraging good practice the Commission will provide information and advice and may provide legal help to disabled people.

6.6   MARRIAGE

6.6.1   Competence

Marriage is 'a simple contract which it does not require a high degree of intelligence to understand'. For capacity to contract a valid marriage see Chapter 1 at 1.5.2.

6.6.2   Formalities

A caveat can be entered at the relevant register office, church or place registered for the celebration of marriage if it is believed that a party to a proposed marriage does not have the necessary capacity. This puts the registrar or clergyman on notice and creates a requirement to investigate the matter: see the Marriage Act 1949, s.29. The reading of banns in church may give an opportunity to concerned persons to record an objection to a proposed marriage, in which event an enquiry is made as to the capacity of the parties to enter into the ceremony.

It is now possible for a marriage ceremony to take place in a mental hospital for a detained patient: see the Marriage Act 1983, s.1.

6.6.3   Implications

Despite the relative ease with which a person can marry, there is a change of status with long-term financial implications and no warning is given to the parties of this:

- assets/chattels owned and used jointly need to be clearly defined and proper transfer on death ensured (this avoids potential litigation and post-death claims);
- assets may be redistributed in the event of a divorce;
- entitlement to state benefits and community care services may be affected (a widow's pension may be lost and a joint means test may apply);
- remarriage may lead to loss of a surviving spouse pension under an occupational pensions scheme;
- marriage revokes an existing will unless made in contemplation of the marriage; this can cause problems because of the low capacity threshold for marriage and the high threshold for testamentary capacity; a statutory will may be considered, see Chapter 4 at 4.10;
- claims can arise under the Inheritance (Provision for Family and Dependants) Act 1975, see Chapter 20.

Cohabitation (or sharing a home) may be an alternative to marriage and does not have all the above implications (see Chapter 6 at 6.9). Proper legal and financial advice is still needed.

6.6.4   Ante-nuptial agreements

Ante-nuptial agreements are particularly appropriate for second, or subsequent, marriages usually between an older couple, when either or both have children and wish to keep their own property separate in order to protect the children's inheritance. For the circumstances in which such agreements will be binding on a subsequent divorce see *K* v. *K* [2003] 1 FLR 120.

6.7   MARRIAGE BREAKDOWN

For the law relating to the breakdown of marriage see the Matrimonial Causes Act 1973 (MCA) as amended by the Matrimonial and Family Proceedings Act 1984. For the procedures adopted by the court see the Family Proceedings Rules 1991, SI 1991/1247. Note also:

- most proceedings are now brought in a county court with divorce jurisdiction;
- proceedings are generally commenced by a 'petition' and a defence is known as an 'answer';
- the 'petitioner' brings the proceedings and the 'respondent' responds to them. Refer to Part IX, rr. 9.1–9.5 when a party to proceedings is incapable by reason of mental disorder of managing and administering his or her property and affairs (i.e. a 'patient'). See generally Chapter 4.

Reform of the whole basis of divorce law and procedure was to have been brought about by Parts II and III of the Family Law Act 1996. However, the majority of these provisions were never brought into force and in January 2001 the government announced that they did not intend to implement them.

6.7.1 Nullity

Marriages may be void or voidable (MCA, ss.11–13). Check whether the marriage was before or after 31 July 1971 because the Nullity of Marriage Act 1971 changed the common law from that date (previously the grounds were restricted but may have made the marriage void).

A marriage is now void if inter alia:

- Certain of the necessary formalities have not been complied with.
- The parties are within the prohibited degrees of relationship.

A marriage is now voidable at the instance of one party (*inter alia*) on proof:

- of incapacity by either party to consummate the marriage;
- of wilful refusal by the respondent to consummate the marriage;
- that either party did not validly consent to the marriage (this may be due to duress, mistake, unsoundness of mind or otherwise);
- that at the time of the marriage either party, though capable of consenting, was suffering from mental disorder within the meaning of the Mental Health Act 1983, of such a kind or to such an extent as to be unfitted for marriage;
- that at the time of the marriage the respondent was suffering from VD or pregnant by another.

Bars to the granting of a decree in respect of a voidable marriage now include:

- for lack of consent, disease or pregnancy by another, proceedings were not commenced within three years;
- the petitioner, knowing that the marriage could be avoided, so conducted him or herself in relation to the respondent as to lead him or her reasonably to believe that he or she would not seek to do so, and it would be unjust to grant a decree (this may be relevant to a marriage for companionship only).

6.7.2 Divorce

Divorce is based on irretrievable breakdown of the marriage but no petition may be presented before the expiration of one year from the marriage, and one of five facts must also be established (MCA, ss.1–3):

1. respondent has committed adultery and petitioner finds it intolerable to live with respondent;

2. respondent has behaved in such a way that petitioner cannot reasonably be expected to live with respondent;

3. respondent has deserted petitioner for a continuous period of at least two years immediately preceding the presentation of the petition;

4. parties to the marriage have lived apart for a continuous period of at least two years immediately preceding the presentation of the petition and respondent consents to a decree being granted;

5. parties to the marriage have lived apart for a continuous period of at least five years immediately preceding the presentation of the petition.

The respondent may oppose dissolution on grounds of hardship when the petition is based upon 'living apart', see MCA, ss.5 and 10. This will usually mean financial hardship though loss of pension rights may be relevant.

Orders may be made in the divorce proceedings dealing with:

- arrangements for any relevant children;
- molestation and occupation of the home;
- temporary maintenance;
- a final financial settlement.

Judicial separation

A decree of judicial separation is obtained on the same basis as a divorce and orders relating to financial matters and children may be made but:

- a petition may be presented in the first year;
- the parties are not free to remarry;
- pension rights should not be affected;
- intestacy rights (but not the right to inherit under a will) are affected.

6.7.3 Financial provision

Orders made

The court can make all or any of the following ancillary relief orders for the benefit of a spouse:

- on or after filing of the petition: maintenance pending suit;
- on or after granting a decree (but with effect in the case of divorce or nullity from decree absolute): periodical payments (including secured periodical payments); lump sum; property adjustment (transfer/settlement of property, variation of settlement); pension adjustment; avoidance of disposition; release of future inheritance claims against the estate of the other spouse;
- variation of periodical payments orders following a change of circumstances.

Most cases are resolved by consent orders but these must be approved by the district judge after full disclosure of the financial position of each party. For orders that may be made see MCA, ss.21–24.

Matters taken into account

When making financial orders the court must 'have regard to all the circumstances of the case', first consideration being given to the welfare of any relevant minor child. The court (which generally means the district judge) will in particular have regard to the following matters:

- the income, earning capacity, property and other financial resources which each of the parties to the marriage has or is likely to have in the foreseeable future, including in the case of earning capacity any increase in that capacity which it would in the opinion of the court be reasonable to expect a party to the marriage to take steps to acquire;
- the financial needs, obligations and responsibilities which each of the parties to the marriage has or is likely to have in the foreseeable future;
- the standard of living enjoyed by the family before the breakdown of the marriage;
- the age of each party to the marriage and the duration of the marriage;
- any physical or mental disability of either of the parties to the marriage;
- contributions made by each of the parties to the welfare of the family, including any contribution made by looking after the home or caring for family;
- the conduct of each of the parties, if that conduct is such that it would in the opinion of the court be inequitable to disregard it.

For the basis of financial provision see MCA, s.25.

Outcome

The court seeks to achieve a clean break wherever possible, i.e. no continuing financial provision between the parties (see MCA, s.25A). This may not be possible following a long marriage where pension rights are involved and there is little further employment potential unless there is adequate capital to provide for the security of both parties or both parties are likely to depend on state benefits. The court also now has powers to make provision involving pension schemes (see MCA, ss.25B, 25C and 25D).

Ownership and continued occupation of the former matrimonial home is usually of paramount importance and this may be:

- ordered to be sold and the net proceeds divided in specified proportions with a view to each party making their own provision;

- transferred to one party outright or with a deferred charge to the other for a fixed sum or share of the value;
- settled on one spouse for their life or until their remarriage.

6.8 GRANDCHILDREN

Grandparents may become involved in disputes relating to their grand-children following the breakdown of the marriage of the parents. They may find themselves looking after these grandchildren on a full-time basis or wish to seek regular contact with them when this is denied.

6.8.1 Children Act 1989

The Children Act 1989 governs:

- private law disputes (involving the family) about the upbringing of children;
- public law applications (involving local authorities) relating to their welfare.

Key principles

The emphasis is on parental responsibility and agreement being reached as to the future upbringing of children. The court will not make an order unless it considers that doing so is better for the child than making no order at all (s.1(5)). The welfare of the child is the paramount consideration and when considering whether to make most orders, the court must have particular regard to the matters stated in s.1(3):

- the ascertainable wishes and feelings of the child;
- the physical, emotional and educational needs of the child;
- the likely effect on the child of a change of circumstances;
- the age, sex, background and any characteristics of the child which the court considers relevant;
- any harm which the child has suffered or is at risk of suffering;
- how capable each of the child's parents (and any other person) is of meeting the child's needs;
- the range of powers available to the court.

Although the wishes and feelings of the child, if of sufficient age and maturity, are ascertained and taken into account, a child should not be expected to choose. For key principles in regard to the welfare of a child see the Children Act 1989, s.1.

165

Parental responsibility

Parental responsibility means the authority, along with others similarly entitled, to make normal decisions relating to education, medical treatment and other such matters normally dealt with by parents. Married parents automatically each have parental responsibility as do single mothers, but unmarried fathers may acquire it by registered agreement or court order. A residence order confers parental responsibility but the court may also award it in appropriate circumstances. When the Adoption and Children Act 2002, s.111 is brought into force, unmarried fathers who are named on the birth certificates will automatically have parental responsibility.

For parental responsibility in respect of a child, see the Children Act 1989, ss.2–4.

6.8.2 Private law applications

A wide range of orders can be made (known as section 8 orders):

- contact: requires the person with whom a child lives, or is to live, to allow the child to visit or stay with the person named in the order, or provides for that person and the child otherwise to have contact with each other;
- prohibited steps: an order that no step which could be taken by a parent in meeting his parental responsibility for a child, and which is of a kind specified in the order, shall be taken by any person without the consent of the court;
- residence: settles the arrangements as to the person with whom a child is to live;
- specific issue: gives directions for the purpose of determining a specific question which has arisen, or which may arise, in connection with any aspect of parental responsibility for a child.

Interim orders can be made (e.g. to deal with an emergency) and the court has power to make a desired order even if no application has been made. No order is ever final although the court may be reluctant to disturb the status quo unless there are compelling reasons to do so.

The emphasis is now on the responsibility of the parents rather than their rights in regard to the child, hence the change of terminology from 'custody' and 'access' to 'residence' and 'contact'. The courts tend to concentrate upon the needs of the child but, all things being equal, it is thought best that the child should grow up knowing both parents (and both their families).

Role of grandparents

Grandparents may initiate or become involved in applications to the court for orders governing their relationship with grandchildren.

When appropriate in the best interests of the child, a grandparent may be joined as a party in proceedings between the parents. In these cases it should be shown that there is a need for such intervention, as usually the grandparent will co-operate with and support the case of a parent. This may be appropriate when the grandparent is at odds with both parents.

A grandparent can apply, with leave of the court (which must be justified), for a residence or contact order in respect of a grandchild. Such an application will not be appropriate when the same result can be achieved through a parent (e.g. contact may take place when that parent has contact). An order may be made requiring the person with whom a child lives, or is to live, to allow the child to visit or stay with a grandparent, or for that grandparent and the child otherwise to have contact with each other. Although it is generally in the best interests of a child to remain with the parents or one of them, a grandmother supported by a grandfather may be able to make out a stronger case especially if the parents are not stable. Where a child is living with grandparents with the agreement of parents, it may be necessary to apply for a residence order to achieve stability.

If grandparents are able to see both sides of the problem and avoid taking sides, they can be particularly helpful in facilitating contact in the best interests of the child or children when the relationship between the parents is hostile.

6.8.3 Public law applications

When a child is suffering, or likely to suffer, significant harm and this is attributable to inadequate care by the parent(s) the local authority in whose area the child is ordinarily resident may apply for a care order or a supervision order. In this instance the grandparents may apply for leave to be made parties and to be heard and an order for reasonable contact may be made in favour of grandparents.

Where a care order is made in favour of the local authority, the child may be accommodated with grandparents. The court cannot order this but failure by the authority to carry out its care plan might justify subsequent revocation of the care order on an application by the grandparents for a residence order. The grandparents may be paid an allowance if the child is placed with them by the authority but may not receive financial support under a residence order unless the parents are able to provide this or the authority makes payments under its discretionary powers.

For local authority applications see the Children Act 1989, Part IV, ss.31–42.

6.8.4   Adoption

Grandparents are unlikely to be permitted to adopt a grandchild because of their age and the confusion of roles that would result. An adoption order will only be made if it is in the best interests of the child but if a grandchild is placed for adoption all legal ties with the grandparents are severed:

- the grandparents may apply for leave to intervene and oppose this step;
- there can be post-adoption contact with parents or grandparents but this is unusual and likely to be restricted in its nature;
- adoption is a last resort so grandparents may wish to consider an application for a residence order.

See the Adoption Act 1976 and the Adoption and Children Act 2002 (not yet in force) which will replace it.

6.9   COHABITATION

An elderly couple may contemplate living together and it may be convenient, economical and mutually supportive for them to do so. In that event a formal agreement may be prepared.

6.9.1   Checklist of legal and practical implications to be discussed in advance of cohabitation

Where they are to live

- ❑   Who is to own the home or hold the tenancy?
- ❑   Is the non-owning party to make a capital contribution and on what basis?
- ❑   If the home is to be owned jointly, on what basis will it be held beneficially?

The shares and manner in which they are to meet household expenses

- ❑   Will there be a pooling of expenses?
- ❑   Is a joint bank account appropriate?
- ❑   Is one party to be merely a lodger at home and if so on what terms?

The basis on which they are to live together

- ❑   Is an intimate relationship intended or merely companionship?
- ❑   Will they take holidays together and share leisure activities?
- ❑   What will be the attitude of their respective families?

The effect on any benefit claims or services provided

❏ Will they be 'living together as man and wife' for benefits purposes?

❏ Will any services be withdrawn or restricted?

❏ Will increased charges be made for services?

Whether the relationship is intended to be mutually supportive for life

❏ Does this mean financially or on a caring basis, or both?

❏ What will be the effect upon any pension entitlement of the parties?

❏ Should any home and furnishings be owned jointly?

❏ Should an EPA be completed?

❏ If financially supportive, is this until the first death or the second death?

❏ If until death of survivor, what steps are to be taken to secure the intention?

❏ Should the home be held as joint tenants or on a tenancy in common?

❏ Are new wills required to ensure that the needs of the survivor are protected and dependency claims avoided?

6.9.2 Marriage

Advice may be sought as to whether it is in their best interests to marry, but if there is a possible conflict of interest each party should be separately advised. The parties must carefully consider:

- the effect on any benefits claims or liabilities, e.g. funding for community care services (what happens if one of them goes into a residential care home?);
- the implications for income tax and capital taxes;
- the consequences of any existing will being revoked by marriage so that they are effectively intestate.

6.10 ABUSE AND DOMESTIC VIOLENCE

6.10.1 Nature of abuse

Abuse of older people is more prevalent than previously recognised and may:

- take place in a family or domestic environment, in the community, or in a residential care or nursing home;
- be by a relative, a friend or neighbour (or even a stranger), or be by an informal carer or a professional carer or trustee;

- take the form of physical assault or threatening behaviour; sexual abuse; verbal or emotional pressure; neglect, abandonment or isolation; misuse of money or property;
- amount to a criminal offence; the tort of trespass to the person (assault, battery or false imprisonment); the tort of negligence; or theft.

The abused individual may not be in a position to complain or to seek a remedy so lawyers must be vigilant. Failure to recognise the personal and civil rights of an elderly person is a form of abuse, and this includes:

- undue influence and denial of access to independent legal advice;
- medical paternalism whereby the doctor administers treatment on the basis that he knows best without troubling to obtain the informed consent of the patient or ascertain what the patient would have wished.

Lawyers should not make the same mistake by advising relatives or carers without seeking to communicate with their elderly client. For more information contact: Action on Elder Abuse, Astral House, 1268 London Road, London SW16 4ER.

6.10.2   The right to intervene

Unless the abuse amounts to a serious criminal offence the victim is expected to initiate his or her own remedies or at least complain. We can counsel and advise, but cannot initiate action without the consent of the individual involved if he or she is competent. Older people are entitled to put themselves at risk and no one can legally interfere in their lives simply because it is considered that they are vulnerable to abuse. Any form of intervention against their wishes can only be justified when they lack the mental capacity to take the particular decision involved. It will then be lawful if it is in the best interests of the incapacitated person, but any intervention should be the least restrictive possible.

Seeking remedies without consulting the victim may amount to further abuse.

6.10.3   Remedies

Recourse to the law, whether civil or criminal, may not be the only way of achieving a remedy. Unless the abuse is particularly serious the victim will not be seeking compensation or retribution but merely wish to ensure that the abuse does not continue or is not repeated. Remedies that may be available include:

- Civil court proceedings (the standard of proof is the balance of probabilities). A claim may be made for damages or an injunction (see below). For the ability to initiate proceedings when the individual is mentally incapacitated see Chapter 4.

- Criminal proceedings (the standard of proof is beyond reasonable doubt). The police may prosecute on information given by a third party. A compensation order may be made (if the offender can pay). A claim may be made to the Criminal Injuries Compensation Authority under the statutory scheme.
- Non-legal remedies: the victim may be moved away from the abusive situation; the abuser may be a carer who simply cannot cope without additional help; a professional carer may be dismissed.
- Use of complaints procedures. If the abuse is by a care professional this may be appropriate and sufficient. For the regulation of residential care or nursing homes see Chapter 9.
- Report the situation to the appropriate authority. The social services department of the local authority should investigate all alleged incidents of abuse where a vulnerable older person is involved.
- Put financial affairs on a proper footing (see Chapter 4).

Failure to intervene may allow abuse to continue, but too much intervention may be a greater abuse than that which it is intended to prevent.

6.10.4   Injunctions

Enhanced protection for people who suffer from violence or harassment is now available through the courts. The victim may be given protection under one of the three recent statutes mentioned below in addition (or as an alternative) to bringing an action in tort.

Local courts provide effective remedies in a wide range of abusive situations.

Effect of mental disorder

An elderly person may become an abuser. Where persistent inappropriate behaviour is due to mental disorder an injunction may not be available to control this.

An injunction ought not to be granted against a person who is incapable of understanding what he is doing and that it is wrong, because a breach could not then be the subject of effective enforcement proceedings: *Wookey* v. *Wookey* [1991] 3 All ER 365, CA. However, it is possible for an injunction to be granted against a person who is or may be a patient because the tests of capacity are different. See *In re de Court, The Times,* 27 November 1997, clarified in *P* v. *P (Contempt of Court: Mental Capacity), The Times,* 21 July 1999, CA.

There may be a 'gap' with an elderly mentally disordered individual causing disruption to the lives of others which is not restrained by the health or social services authorities yet cannot be controlled by the courts.

Family Law Act 1996, Part IV

Proceedings may be brought against an abuser in the magistrates' court, county court or High Court by an associated person which includes:

- existing and former spouses and cohabitants;
- those who live or have lived in the same household, other than merely by reason of one of them being the other's employee, tenant, lodger or boarder;
- 'relatives' as widely defined;
- persons who have agreed to marry one another.

Various orders may be made or provisions included in the order. Urgent relief can even be obtained without giving notice to the other party (known as an *ex parte* or 'without notice' order) although notice is then given of a later hearing when the need for continuing orders will be considered.

Non-molestation order

Under a non-molestation order, the respondent is forbidden to use or threaten violence against the applicant or to intimidate, harass or pester the applicant. The respondent may also be ordered not to instruct, encourage or in any way suggest that any other person should do these things. The court must have regard to all the circumstances including the need to secure the health, safety and well-being of the applicant. What behaviour amounts to molestation will depend of the facts of the particular case, but implies some quite deliberate conduct which is aimed at a high degree of harassment of the other party, so as to justify the intervention of the court (see *C* v. *C* [1998] Fam 70).

Occupation order

An occupation order controls occupation of the home (see 6.10.5).

Undertaking

Instead of an injunction the respondent may undertake (i.e. promise the court) not to behave in a particular way in future. The alleged behaviour is not admitted and the court makes no findings but a contested hearing is avoided and there is usually no costs order. Breach is contempt of court so committal proceedings can be brought, but a power of arrest cannot be attached to the undertaking so the court should not accept it if this protection is needed.

Power of arrest

A power of arrest is attached to the order if violence has been used or threatened against the applicant unless the applicant will be adequately protected without it. A constable may then arrest without warrant a person whom he has reasonable cause for suspecting to be in breach. An arrested person must be brought before a court within 24 hours but the court can remand the arrested person in custody or on bail pending a hearing. The court has power to remand to enable a medical report to be obtained.

Warrant for arrest

Where breach of an injunction is alleged (and there is no power of arrest) an application may be made for the issue of a warrant.

Committal proceedings

An application can still be made on notice for a committal order under the 'show cause' procedure.

A power to make rules providing for a representative to act on behalf of another person in applying for or enforcing an occupation order or a non-molestation order has not yet been implemented. Such power could be used to assist a vulnerable elderly person.

Protection from Harassment Act 1997

The wording of the Protection from Harassment Act 1997 is broad enough to encompass a wide range of activities which may include 'elder abuse'. A person must not pursue a course of conduct (i.e. conduct on at least two occasions) which amounts to harassment of another and which he knows or ought to know amounts to harassment of the other. Harassment of a person includes alarming the person or causing the person distress, and 'conduct' includes speech where 'if a reasonable person would know that the course of conduct would amount to harassment then the person whose conduct is in question ought to know' (there is an exception if in the circumstances the course of conduct was 'reasonable').

Harassment is made a criminal offence as well as a tort, and breach of a civil injunction is a specific offence in addition to civil enforcement procedures:

- civil proceedings are brought in a county court (or the High Court);
- criminal proceedings are dealt with in the magistrates' court or (for the more serious offences) the Crown Court.

An actual or apprehended breach of the prohibition on harassment may be the subject of a claim in civil proceedings by the victim of the course of conduct:

- The court may grant an injunction to restrain such conduct and damages may be awarded for any anxiety caused or financial loss resulting from the harassment.
- If the claimant thereafter considers that the defendant has done anything which is prohibited by the injunction he may apply to the court *ex parte* (i.e. without notice to the other party) for a warrant of arrest against the defendant.
- If after considering all the evidence the defendant is found to have been in breach of the injunction he may be fined or committed to prison for contempt, or be tried for a separate statutory offence.

This legislation was hastily enacted to control 'stalking' but is not restricted to this and may assist in a wide range of other situations.

Housing Act 1996, Part V, ss.152–157

Local authorities (and to some extent public sector landlords) are given enhanced powers to control anti-social behaviour on housing estates. They may evict tenants who are responsible for the suffering of other tenants and may also apply for free-standing injunctions to prohibit anyone, whether or not a tenant from:

- engaging in or threatening to engage in conduct causing or likely to cause a nuisance or annoyance to anyone residing in, visiting or otherwise engaging in lawful activity in residential premises or in the locality of such premises;
- using or threatening to use residential premises for immoral or illegal purposes;
- entering residential premises or being found in the locality of such premises.

More effective control of anti-social behaviour on housing estates may assist vulnerable elderly residents.

6.10.5   Occupation of the home

Under the Family Law Act 1996, Part IV (see 6.10.4) a wide range of orders can also be made to regulate the occupation of a dwelling-house as between spouses and cohabitants. The terms and duration of the order depend upon whether or not the applicant has an estate or interest in the home:

- this could include matrimonial home rights, i.e. the right by virtue of a subsisting marriage to live in the home of the spouse;
- where the parties are not existing or former spouses or cohabitants but are within some other category of 'associated person' (see above) the applicant must have some pre-existing right to occupy before an order can be made.

Where a party is to be excluded from the home a 'balance of harm' test is applied. 'Harm' means ill-treatment or impairment of health, and 'ill-treatment' includes non-physical forms. The court must have regard to all relevant circumstances including:

- the housing needs and resources of the parties;
- the financial resources of the parties;
- the nature and length of their relationship (and otherwise);
- their conduct in relation to each other;
- the effect of an order upon the health, safety or well-being of the parties or a child.

These orders relate to 'dwelling-houses' but this includes a part of a building occupied as a dwelling-house, a caravan, houseboat or structure occupied as a dwelling-house, and any yard, garden, garage or outhouse occupied with the dwelling-house. Mortgagees or landlords are given a chance to make representations, but an order may include provision that in respect of the home or a part of the home:

- the applicant is entitled to occupy it and the respondent shall allow this;
- the respondent shall not obstruct, harass or interfere with peaceful occupation;
- the respondent shall not occupy it at all or between specified times or dates;
- the respondent shall leave it by a specified time and not return to, enter or attempt to enter it or go within a specified distance of it;
- a party maintains and repairs the home or furnishings and contents, and pays the rent or mortgage.

Where e.g. a drunken grandson or drug-using granddaughter is abusing an infirm grandmother in her own home whilst posing as a carer, it may be more effective to exclude this person from the home and arrange alternative support (if required) rather than to move the grandmother to a care home.

It is unfortunate that in many cases, the victim suffers twice, once from the abuse and then again from the remedy. Often the victim is incapable of providing clear evidence of abuse or does not want to exclude a close relative. Such painful cases are all too common notwithstanding a wide range of legal remedies which are technically available.

6.11 VICTIMS OF CRIME

6.11.1 Procedure

When it is alleged that an offence has been committed there must be an early decision about involving the police. Any serious offence should be reported promptly. If the victim wishes to press charges or the police decide to proceed anyway, an investigation begins:

- in cases of physical or sexual abuse, immediate police involvement is important to enable them to examine the victim and collect corroborative forensic evidence;
- the victim may be asked to take part in identification of suspects either informally or by means of a formal identification parade, and to identify photographs.

The victim may go to the police direct or with help from a third party, but should be consulted and where possible consent to a referral to the police.

6.11.2 Prosecution

There is a discretion whether to prosecute. The victim will not be involved in this but the effect of a prosecution on the victim's physical or mental health is taken into consideration. There may be no prosecution in the case of a victim who would make a poor witness because of lack of reliable evidence or corroboration.

The Code for Crown Prosecutors states that there should only be a prosecution if there is a 'realistic prospect of conviction'.

6.11.3 Information

Policy varies as to how much information is given to victims. The general practice is to tell victims of an arrest, a decision to prosecute or not and the outcome of a trial. Victims may feel excluded from the process and require advice and support to clarify their role as a prosecution witness and not as a party to proceedings.

Legal Services Commission funding is not available for a vulnerable witness in connection with a prosecution because the person is not a party to the proceedings.

Reports of the offence in the press can cause distress and the victim may suffer media attention during or after the trial. Vulnerable victims may request the police to withhold their name and address. Rape victims must not be identified: Sexual Offences (Amendment) Act 1976.

Many police forces have 'vulnerable persons officers' experienced in interviewing mentally vulnerable victims and investigating reports of crimes involving them.

6.11.4 Evidence

The victim's capacity to give clear evidence and cope with cross-examination and the trauma of a public appearance in the witness box may be crucial to the trial:

- Screens to prevent eye-contact with a defendant will only be used in exceptional circumstances and age or infirmity by themselves will not be sufficient.
- The judge decides if a potential witness has the necessary understanding of the concepts of truth and duty. The burden of proving this rests with the party calling the witness. If not satisfied beyond reasonable doubt, the person will not be allowed to give evidence.
- Once the decision has been made to admit the evidence it is for the jury to decide what weight to attach to it. The prosecution cannot call medical evidence to support the reliability of one of its witnesses unless this is to rebut a challenge by the defence.

Part II of the Youth Justice and Criminal Evidence Act 1999 provides that the court may make a 'special measures direction' in respect of the evidence of certain eligible witnesses. A witness may be eligible for such protection if:

- they suffer from a mental disorder within the meaning of the Mental Health Act 1983;
- they have a significant impairment of intelligence and social functioning;
- they have a physical disability or are suffering from a physical disorder;
- the court is satisfied that the quality of their evidence is likely to be diminished by reason of fear or distress on the part of the witness.

The special measures which the court may direct include:

- screening the witness from the accused;
- allowing the witness to give evidence by a live video link;
- excluding persons (other than the accused and the legal representatives) from court whilst the witness is giving evidence;
- the judge and counsel removing wigs and gowns.

6.12 CRIMINAL RESPONSIBILITY

Special consideration has to be given to people suffering from mental disorder who become caught up in the criminal justice system and this may include confused elderly people more often than is generally realised.

It is important to identify any mental disorder at an early stage so that:

- the safeguards of the PACE Codes of Practice are observed by the police in conducting their interrogation;

- prosecution may be avoided;
- issues such as fitness to plead and the insanity defence are addressed;
- Mental Health Act disposals and other sentencing options are considered;
- where appropriate, treatment is given rather than punishment.

The legal representative should advise the client and the court on these matters when relevant and obtain expert medical and social work reports as soon as possible.

Mentally ill people accused of criminal offences should be prosecuted only if this is in the public interest and those convicted should be cared for in the hospital system whenever this is appropriate.

Mental disorder is defined as mental illness, arrested or incomplete development of mind, psychopathic disorder and any other disorder or disability of mind (Mental Health Act 1983 s.1(2))

6.12.1   Police investigation

The Police and Criminal Evidence Act Codes of Practice contain detailed guidance in relation to treatment and questioning of those detained and interviewed by the police. Failure by the police to observe these Codes could lead to the exclusion of evidence at a subsequent trial if the breach is significant and substantial.

6.12.2   General rights

A detained person has the general rights:

- to be given information about and a notice of rights under PACE;
- to have someone informed of arrest;
- to be told that free and independent legal advice is available;
- to consult privately with a solicitor;
- to consult the Codes of Practice.

6.12.3   Additional safeguards

Appearance of disability

If the person in detention appears to be suffering from physical illness or mental disorder or otherwise appears to need medical attention, the custody officer must call the police surgeon (or an ambulance if the need appears urgent). This applies even if the detainee has not requested medical treatment.

The police surgeon can assess the detainee's fitness for detention and interview and advise on any particular safeguards that are necessary.

Mental illness, vulnerability

There are special provisions in the Codes of Practice that apply to the mentally disordered (see above) or mentally vulnerable. Mentally vulnerable is defined in broad terms and applies to any detainee who, because of their mental state or capacity, may not understand the significance of what is said, of questions or of their replies.

The most important right is to have an appropriate adult to safeguard their welfare. This will be:

- a relative, guardian or other person responsible for their care or custody;
- someone who is experienced in dealing with mentally disordered or mentally vulnerable people;
- failing these, some other responsible adult.

The appropriate adult must not be the solicitor, a police officer or an employee of the police.

The appropriate adult's duties include facilitating communication, being present at interview and observing whether it is being conducted fairly and making representations about the need for detention.

A solicitor should not take instructions from the detainee in the presence of the appropriate adult, as privilege will not apply.

6.12.4   The decision to prosecute

The initial decision to charge is taken by the police. If the detainee is elderly, frail and/or suffering from a mental disorder and has no recent involvement with the criminal justice system, and the allegation is not serious, the solicitor should make representations at this stage that the detainee should not be charged. See Home Office Circular 12/95, para. 12

After charge, the Crown Prosecution Service (CPS) will review the case in accordance with the Code for Crown Prosecutors. The solicitor can make representations at this stage, providing medical evidence where appropriate.

There are two tests:

1. evidential: is there a realistic prospect of conviction?
2. public interest: is it in the public interest to continue with this prosecution? Relevant factors would be the existence of a mental or physical disorder and the effect of a prosecution on the person's health.

Consideration should be given to alternatives such as cautioning and diversion to the health and social services systems – see below. The individual may, however, wish to be given the opportunity to answer any charges in court.

6.12.5 Alternatives to prosecution

Solicitors representing mentally disordered clients need to be aware of services in their area and make referrals and request reports wherever appropriate. The Home Office has produced guidance in relation to diverting mentally disordered offenders from the criminal justice system:

- Home Office Circular 66/90: *Provision for Mentally Disordered Offenders*;
- Home Office Circular 12/95: *Mentally Disordered Offenders: Inter-Agency Working*;
- Home Office Circular 59/90: *Cautioning of Offenders*: this gives guidance on the use of cautions and refers specifically to the special considerations that apply to older people.

Many courts have diversion schemes: a defendant's mental state can be assessed at court and he or she can be referred to local mental health services or detained in hospital under the Mental Health Act 1983, ss.2 and 3 as an alternative to prosecution.

6.12.6 Prosecution

There is now a very short period between charge and the first appearance in court, usually two or three days. It may well therefore be necessary for the solicitor to apply to have the case adjourned in order to advise an elderly client in detail, make representations to the CPS and obtain medical evidence where appropriate.

Representation

The court will grant legal aid in cases where there is a risk of a custodial sentence being imposed or where the defendant suffers from a disability. This legal aid is not means tested.

The duty solicitor is available to represent defendants at their first appearance at the magistrates' court.

Remand status

A defendant may be remanded in custody or on bail. The age, physical and mental health of the defendant are all matters that the court can take into account when considering bail.

Conditions of bail can be imposed where necessary. If the defendant requires medical treatment a condition to reside at a hospital could be imposed, although the hospital would have no power to prevent the defendant leaving.

If the defendant appears to be mentally disordered but bail is not appropriate the court has powers under the Mental Health Act 1983 to remand to hospital rather than prison:

- to remand for psychiatric reports (Mental Health Act 1983, s.35), this can be for periods of 28 days at a time to a maximum of 12 weeks;
- to remand for treatment (Mental Health Act 1983, s.36).

Both sections require medical evidence and confirmation that arrangements have been made for the defendant's admission to hospital within seven days.

The Home Secretary has the power to transfer a mentally disordered remand prisoner from prison to hospital when there is an urgent need for treatment (Mental Health Act 1983, s. 48).

6.12.7 Pleas and defences

There are a number of issues that need to be considered when a defendant is mentally disordered. The disorder may be so serious that the defendant is unfit to plead. Alternatively, the disorder may mean that the defendant lacked the required *mens rea* (mental state) for him to be convicted of the offence.

Fitness to plead

The test is whether the defendant is able to instruct his legal advisers, to plead to the indictment, to challenge jurors, to understand the evidence and to give evidence.

If the defendant is found to be unfit to plead, a jury may then decide whether he did the act or made the omission charged against him. If they make such a finding, the court now has a range of sentencing options including an absolute discharge or a hospital order (Criminal Procedure (Insanity and Unfitness to Plead) Act 1991).

Insanity

A jury may return a 'special verdict' of not guilty by reason of insanity. The defence would normally raise this issue and medical evidence would be called. The test is whether the defendant, at the time of committing the act, was labouring under such a defect of reason, from disease of the mind, as not to know the nature and quality of the act he was doing, or if he did know it, that he did not know that what he was doing was wrong (*E. M'Naghten's Case* (1843) 10 Cl & F 200).

The jury have to be satisfied that the defendant did the act charged.

If the special verdict is returned, the court can make a hospital or guardianship order, supervision and treatment order or an absolute discharge

(Criminal Procedure (Insanity) Act 1964, ss.4, 4A as amended by the Criminal Procedure (Insanity and Unfitness to Plead) Act 1991).

Both this provision and the fitness to plead provisions are rarely used in practice, as in most cases it is would be possible for the court to make a hospital order under the more straightforward provisions of the Mental Health Act 1983, s.37.

6.12.8 Sentences

If there is reason to believe that a defendant is mentally disordered the court must obtain a medical report before sentencing. There is a wide range of sentencing options open to the court when dealing with a defendant with a mental disorder, including:

- community rehabilitation order (probation);
- community rehabilitation with a condition of psychiatric treatment;
- hospital order (Mental Health Act 1983, s. 37);
- guardianship order (Mental Health Act 1983, s. 37).

If the court is considering a custodial sentence, it must consider the effect this will have on the mental condition of the defendant and his need for treatment (Criminal Justice Act 1991, s.4).

The Home Secretary has the power to direct the transfer of a serving prisoner to hospital under the Mental Health Act 1983, s.47.

PART B

Welfare and medical treatment

CHAPTER 7

Community care policies

Caroline Bielanska

7.1 SOURCES

7.1.1 Reports

The formal policy of community care grew out of a series of reports, in particular:

- Audit Commission Report, *Making a Reality of Community Care* (1986);
- Social Services Committee of the House of Commons, Reports 1989–90;
- Report to the Secretary of State for Social Services by Sir Roy Griffiths, *Community Care: Agenda for Action* (1988);
- White Paper, *Caring for People: Community Care in the Next Decade and Beyond*, HMSO (1989).

More recent policy has been implemented as a result of the 1998 White Paper, *Modernising Social Services*, the Royal Commission's Report, *With Respect to Old Age: Long Term Care: Rights and Responsibilities* (March 1999), and the Department of Health Report, *Modernising Mental Health Services* (December 1998). The relevant policies are contained in particular in:

- *The NHS Plan* (July 2000);
- *Shifting the Balance of Power within the NHS: Securing Delivery and Involving Patients and the Public in Healthcare* (July 2001);
- *Improving Health in Wales*, National Assembly of Wales (February 2001);
- *Delivering the NHS Plan* (July 2002).

7.1.2 Legislation

Community care provision is contained within numerous statutes:

- National Health Service and Community Care Act 1990, Part III;
- National Assistance Act 1948, Part III;
- Health Services and Public Health Act 1968, s.45;
- Chronically Sick and Disabled Persons Act 1970, s.2;
- National Health Service Act 1977, s.21 and Sched. 8;

- Mental Health Act 1983, s.117;
- Health and Social Services and Social Security Adjudications Act 1983, Part VII;
- Disabled Persons (Services, Consultation and Representation) Act 1986;
- Carers (Recognition and Services) Act 1995;
- Housing Act 1996, Part VII (replacing Housing Act 1985, Part III);
- Health Act 1999;
- Carers and Disabled Children Act 2000;
- Care Standards Act 2000;
- Health and Social Care Act 2001, Part 4;
- National Health Service Reform and Health Care Professions Act 2002, Part 1;
- Community Care (Delayed Discharge etc.) Act 2003.

The following statutes should also be considered:

- Local Government Act 1970;
- Pensions Act 1995;
- Disability Discrimination Act 1995;
- Human Rights Act 1998;
- Data Protection Act 1998;
- Welfare Reform and Pensions Act 1999;
- Freedom of Information Act 2000.

7.1.3   Directions and guidance

Many aspects of an authority's powers and duties are subject to directions issued by the Secretary of State and guidance issued by departments, and good policies are also identified by other sources. Some are issued jointly as health and local authority circulars with alternative references, and earlier ones may have been issued by the former DHSS. In Wales since 1999, the National Assembly of Wales has the power to issue directions and guidance in respect of the NHS and social services. They are constantly being updated (i.e. cancelled or superseded) but old guidance may remain relevant as to what could be expected at the time.

An authority is only obliged to take account of advice contained in circulars but is under a positive duty to comply if the circular is issued under the Local Authority Social Services Act 1970, s. 7(1), and can only depart from it if there is very good reason. (See *R* v. *Islington LBC, ex parte Rixon* [1998] 1 CCLR 119.)

Guidance and mandatory circulars are likely to be quoted in court proceedings and could form the basis for a legal challenge of an authority's action or inaction. Practice guidance is advice which an authority should have regard to when reaching a decision but need not follow. The policy documents of a local authority should take account of any directions and guidance contained in circulars.

Where an appeal to the Secretary of State is provided for, it may be expected that he will follow his own advice, and he may issue directions, which must be observed by local authorities in carrying out their social services functions, the sanction being the use of default powers in s.7A of the 1970 Act.

Examples of special significance are mentioned in Appendix F but this should not be assumed to be up to date as it is ever-changing and can be little more than an illustration of the extent to which policy and procedure is covered by the range of directions, circulars and general guidance from government departments or officials. They are easily accessible from the Department of Health website (www.doh.gov.uk) and searching in the publications' section.

7.2   ROLE OF LOCAL AUTHORITIES

7.2.1   Responsibilities

The 1990 Act does not create new rights to new services, although local authorities have a duty to assess anyone who appears to them to be in need of a community care service which they may provide and then decide what services (if any) are to be provided (s.47). It does not, however, create a duty to provide. The 1990 Act is to be understood by referring to other legislation and supplemented by regulations, government guidance, circulars and policy documents.

In an emergency situation the authority can provide services without having carried out an assessment (s.47(5)). If during the assessment it is apparent the person is disabled the authority must assess under the Disabled Persons (Services, Consultation and Representation) Act 1986, s.4. If the authority is satisfied that a service is required to meet the need of the disabled person it will have a duty under the Chronically Sick and Disabled Persons Act 1970, s.2 to make such provision.

Sections 44 and 45 of the 1990 Act created a change where charges for residential accommodation are made on the basis that it is more in line with that for income support. Income support case law has moulded government guidance on charging for residential accommodation.

The duty in s.46 to consult with health and housing authorities, and voluntary organisations so as to have and publish annual Community Care Plans has been removed from 9 July 2003. This duty became superfluous, as there are a range of joint plans and planning mechanisms, which achieved the same thing, such as Joint Investment Plans, Local Strategic Partnerships and Health and Modernisation Plans.

Authorities must provide access to information and establish a complaints procedure (s.50). The Better Care, Higher Standards Charter has built on this.

7.2.2   Social services department

The lead role in the arrangements is given to the social services department (SSD), which should disseminate information about statutory and voluntary services in its area, which would be of assistance to carers and their dependants. Where required, the SSD must assess the needs of the person cared for and see how these may best be met. There is a statutory duty to take into account the needs of the carer to continue to care (Disabled Persons (Services, Consultation and Representation) Act 1986) or to assess the unpaid carer if the carer is providing or intends to provide a substantial amount of care on a regular basis for the cared-for person. If the cared-for person is to be or has been assessed for services, this is under the Carers (Recognition and Services) Act 1995, but where the cared-for person does not want to be assessed the carer can have an independent assessment under the Carers and Disabled Children Act 2000.

The SSD makes a decision about what, if any, services to provide for the needs, which are determined by reference to eligibility criteria. When services are provided the SSD should review within three months and then annually unless circumstances alter.

The authority is allowed to use eligibility criteria as a way of managing its budget but once it has assessed someone in line with its criteria as requiring a service, it must provide services to meet the need assessed.

7.2.3   Other authorities

The local authority has a duty to notify the health or housing authority where the person assessed has apparent health or housing needs (s.47(3) of the 1990 Act). NHS bodies and the authority have a general duty to co-operate in order to secure and advance the health and welfare of people in England and Wales (NHS Act 1977, s.22). However, neither the local authority nor its SSD can oblige the NHS body or the housing authority to provide any services to an individual and this effectively limits the SSD's control over community care provision to that which it can itself provide. For many people the failure in community care may relate to health or housing provision, with disputes arising as to which authority is responsible for a particular type of care provision. Policies have evolved with improved discharge procedures formulated with NHS bodies. Increasingly health, housing and social services departments are expected to work together.

7.2.4 Powers and duties

Although it may appear that a local authority is obliged to provide a service this may not be enforceable in law by an individual. A distinction must be drawn between a power to provide a service and a duty to do so, and between a general duty to provide services and a duty to a particular individual.

Where an authority is not under a duty to a specific individual, action may only be taken if there is discrimination on grounds of sex, race or disability, the authority blindly follows a particular policy without considering the individual circumstances, or the authority makes an unreasonable decision (the *Wednesbury* principle).

Where an authority has a discretion it must be dealt with on its merits and an authority cannot fetter its discretion by imposing a blanket policy.

7.2.5 Ordinary residence

The responsibility for arranging and funding care has become increasingly complicated where clients move area, particularly where nursing care is also being provided. The current guidance within LAC (93) 7: *Ordinary Residence* is out of date and draft guidance has been issued entitled *Establishing the Responsible Commissioner* in November 2002.

The duties of a local authority apply in respect of an individual who is ordinarily resident in its area. In determining ordinary residence the place of residence must have been voluntarily adopted and there must have been a degree of settled purpose in relation to that decision (*R* v. *Barnet LBC, ex parte Shah* [1983] 1 All ER 226 and *Wiltshire County Council* v. *Cornwall County Council*, unreported, 1999. The term 'ordinarily resident' should be given its ordinary and natural meaning, subject to any interpretation in the courts (consider the National Assistance Act 1948 in this respect).

In respect of domiciliary care the receiving council will be responsible for assessing and arranging care. This may result in a change in services, as there is no obligation to provide the same services as the outgoing council. (See LAC (93) 7 and LAC (2002) 13.) With residential care the original authority remains responsible for the care in the new area. Where care is being arranged independently of the local authority the receiving authority will be responsible.

Residents in nursing homes are entitled to a contribution for their nursing care provided by a registered nurse. The authority responsible is the Primary Care Trust (PCT) where the resident is registered with a GP. It means that local authorities will have to liaise with PCTs where they previously had no partnership arrangements.

If the full cost of care is being met as the resident qualifies for NHS continuing health care the authority responsible is the NHS body that originally clinically assessed the resident. This is usually around the time of discharge from hospital.

7.3 ROLE OF THE PRIVATE SECTOR

The 1990 Act also enables the authority to adopt an enabling role and stimulate the provision of services by the private and not-for-profit sectors (a 'mixed economy of care'):

> It will be the responsibility of social services departments to make maximum possible use of private and voluntary providers and so increase the available range of options and widen consumer choice. (Circular LAC (93) 10)

With SSDs being bulk purchasers of care they have been able to negotiate better rates than the self-funding client. As a consequence, there has been a big shift towards service provision being made by the independent sector and this has seen the closure of many council-run facilities. In the last few years there has been a big increase in the number of private care homes closing, as they cannot afford to keep running on the amount the local authority pays for means-tested residents. Recently such homes began refusing to enter into contracts or maintain contracts with local authorities, as a result some council-funded residents may find it difficult to find a suitable home or be asked to move.

CHAPTER 8

Services in the community

Caroline Bielanska

8.1 ASSESSMENT FOR SERVICES

Care services may be for the benefit of a disabled or ill person or to assist a carer to provide care. They may include domiciliary services provided in the home, comprising domestic help (cleaning, shopping, cooking, laundry, etc.) and personal care (bathing, washing, dressing, eating, etc.); day services provided outside the home; and residential services (short or long-term including both residential care and nursing homes). There may also be assistance for the physically disabled with aids and appliances (continence pads, walking aids, wheelchairs, etc.) and the home (adaptations or provision of a suitable home).

The duty to assess is independent of provision, so exists even if the authority does not provide or have the resources to provide the services likely to be needed, and is a continuing duty, so extends to a regular review of the assessment when changes of circumstances must be taken into account.

8.1.1 Duty to assess under the NHS and Community Care Act 1990, s.47

The NHS and Community Care Act 1990 ('the 1990 Act'), s.47(1) creates a statutory duty on a local authority to assess the needs of a person where it appears to it that a person for whom it may provide or arrange community care services appears to need such services. It does not create a duty to provide, only a duty to assess.

The term 'community care services' is defined by reference to service provision under numerous other statutes namely:

- National Assistance Act 1948, Part III;
- Health Services and Public Health Act 1968, s.45;
- National Health Service Act 1977, s.21, Sched. 8; and
- Mental Health Act 1983, s.117.

No authority can refuse an assessment even if no service need is identified but a person cannot be required to co-operate. The threshold for appearing to need community care services is a low one. The practice of sifting out assessments where there is no hope of meeting any need is unlawful (*R* v. *Bristol City Council, ex parte Alice Penfold* [1998] 1 CCLR 315).

Where services are required as a matter of urgency they may be temporarily provided prior to an assessment (s.47(5) of the 1990 Act) but as soon as possible thereafter an assessment of need must be made (s.47(6)). If during the assessment it is apparent the assessed person has housing or health care needs the assessor should invite the appropriate body to the assessment, but there is nothing to compel them to act (s.47(3)). The NHS body must be involved where a place in a nursing home is sought, as the NHS will be responsible for funding the nursing care provided by a registered nurse.

It must be established that the person is one for whom the authority may provide and this is based on ordinary residence (see Chapter 7 at 7.2.5) though the requirement can be dispensed with in regard to certain services.

8.1.2   Duty to assess under the Disabled Persons (Services, Consultation and Representation) Act 1986, s.4

Section 47(2) of the 1990 Act provides that, if whilst carrying out the assessment under s.47(1), it appears to the authority that the person being assessed is a disabled person it must proceed to assess the need for services under the Disabled Persons (Services, Consultation and Representation) Act 1986, s.4, without being asked, and inform the person of his or her rights in that respect.

Under s.4 there is a duty to assess the need for services under the Chronically Sick and Disabled Persons Act 1970, s.2, when requested by the disabled person, his authorised representative, or any person who provides care for him (but not employed to care). The local authority must provide a written statement, which sets out the needs of the disabled person which the local authority should provide, and its proposals as to how it will meet those needs. See 8.4 on the 1970 Act.

8.1.3   Assessment of the carer

Help for carers may be provided and there is ear-marked funding paid by central government to local authorities to enable carers to continue providing care. The government has their own website for carers (www.carers.gov.uk).

The Disabled Persons (Services, Consultation and Representation) Act 1986

Under s.8 of the 1986 Act, when assessing the needs of a disabled person living at home, the authority must have regard to a carer's ability to continue to provide care on a regular basis. It is not an assessment of the carer and will only apply where the carer is already providing a substantial amount of care on a regular basis and is not employed to do so by a statutory body or private agency.

The authority should not use the presence of a carer as an excuse for not looking critically at the needs of the disabled person and for failing to provide the services that are needed (many are doing so by giving priority to those with greatest need).

Carers (Recognition and Services) Act 1995

Section 1 of the Carers (Recognition and Services) Act 1995 provides for an assessment of the carer, which is linked to an assessment for the cared-for person under s.47 of the 1990 Act.

The carer should ask the local authority to carry out an assessment of his or her ability to provide or to continue to provide a substantial amount of care on a regular basis. This should happen before the local authority makes its decision as to whether the needs of the cared-for person call for the provision of any services.

The local authority has a statutory duty to assess the carer and must take into account the results of that assessment in making its decision. It does not, however, create a duty to provide services. The service is provided to the cared-for person who may be means-tested for those that are provided.

Carers and Disabled Children Act 2000

The Carers and Disabled Children Act 2000 establishes an independent assessment of the carer where he or she asks a local authority to carry out an assessment of his or her ability to provide and to continue to provide care on a regular basis for the cared-for person.

The local authority must carry out such an assessment if it is satisfied that the person cared for is someone for whom it may provide or arrange the provision of community care services. Unlike services provided under the 1995 Act, the carer can be means-tested for the services they receive under the 2000 Act. This Act also contains provisions for the local authority to provide vouchers to be used to purchase care to allow the carer to have a break. Regulations and policy and practice guidance has now been issued as to how the scheme should work. It is to be found on the government carer's website (www.carers.gov.uk).

8.1.4 Form of assessment

A social services department (SSD) is required by the Chronically Sick and Disabled Persons Act 1970, s.1 (as amended) to publish general information as to the services available in its area and to inform disabled persons receiving any service from it of relevant services provided by the local authority or by any other authority or organisation of which the department has particulars. Under the Department of Health's Better Care, Higher Standards Charter, local authorities must publish information as to how a person can get an assessment and what services are available. The Secretary of State may give directions as to the manner in which an assessment is to be carried out or the form that it shall take. This has been done as part of the National Service Framework for Older People who can expect to have a single assessment for their health and social care needs with protocols agreed locally between health and social services to identify individual vulnerable needs. See LAC (2002) 1 and also *Care Management and Assessment: Practitioners' Guide*, Department of Health (1991).

The local assessment process is to be streamlined by April 2002 and fully operational by April 2004. Joint eligibility criteria for continuing health and social care should be agreed which cover the full range of health and social care services, without any gaps in service, regardless of age.

The purpose of the Single Assessment Process is to ensure that older people receive appropriate, effective and timely responses to their health and social care needs, and that professional resources are used effectively. The process should ensure that the scale and depth of the assessment is kept in proportion to the older person's needs; agencies do not duplicate each assessment; and professionals contribute to assessments in the most effective way.

There are four types of assessments:

- *Contact assessment*: this refers to the initial contact of the older person and the department agencies, where basic information is obtained, the nature of the problem established and wider issues might be explored.
- *Overview assessment*: this will be carried out if a more rounded assessment should be undertaken. It may be apparent immediately.
- *In depth/specialist assessment*: this offers a way of exploring specific problems in detail. For example, professionals should be able to confirm the presence, extent, cause and likely development of a health condition.
- *Comprehensive old age assessment/comprehensive assessment or comprehensive geriatric assessment*: these should be completed for people where the level of support and treatment likely to be offered is intensive or complex, including permanent admission to a care home, intermediate care services or intensive home care packages. This type of assessment can arise at other times.

All clients and carers should be provided with a copy of the assessment and the agreed care plan, which contains:

- a summary of assessed needs indicating the intensity, instability, predictability, and complexity of problems, the associated risks to independence, and the potential for rehabilitation;

- a note on whether or not the services user has agreed the care plan, and the reason where this was not possible;
- the objectives of providing help and anticipated outcomes for users;
- a summary of how services will impact on assessed need and associated risks;
- details on managing risk as appropriate; where it has been agreed that users will accept a certain degree of risk, this must be written in the care plan;
- details of what carers are willing to do, and related needs and support;
- a description of the level and frequency of the help that is to be provided, stating which agency is providing what service;
- a nursing plan, where appropriate;
- the level of Registered Nursing Care Contribution for nursing home admissions;
- the name of the person co-ordinating the care plan and their contact number;
- a contact number or office in case of emergencies and the contingency plan if things go wrong;
- monitoring arrangements and a date for review, usually after three months and then annually.

Where services are not being provided after the assessment the person should be given details of the decision made with reasons. A copy of the file held by the SSD can be obtained under the Data Protection Act 1998. Information can be withheld if it would breach confidentiality of any person other than the older person.

8.2 PROVISION OF SERVICES

Following assessment of an individual, the local authority 'having regard to the results of that assessment, shall then decide whether his needs call for the provision' by the authority of particular services (s.47(1) of the 1990 Act). It follows that there is no absolute duty to provide or arrange all the services that are assessed as being needed, it depends whether the individual's presenting needs meet the local authority's eligible needs criteria.

In *R* v. *Gloucestershire CC, ex parte Barry* [1997] 2 All ER 1, the House of Lords held that the authority must take the assessment into account but may also take into account what it can afford, is available or may be provided by other authorities. This is achieved by using eligibility criteria. It has since been held in *R* v. *East Sussex County Council, ex parte Tandy* [1998] 2 All ER 769 and *R* v. *Birmingham County Council, ex parte Mohammed* [1998] 1 CCLR 441 that when a duty to provide exists, resources are not to be taken into account but these cases do not relate to the same type of provision.

195

Lack of resources does not justify delaying assessment where there is clearly a need, or making no provision at all, but priority may be given to those with the greatest need.

8.2.1   Eligibility criteria: fair access to care services

Mandatory guidance has been issued in England to provide local authorities with a framework for determining eligibility for adult care services (LAC (2002) 13). It provides that authorities should make similar decisions in their area. It does not go as far as to say that different authorities should make identical decisions about eligibility or what services should be provided.

The basis of the criteria is to enable local authorities to prioritise eligible needs in terms of risks to independence. The framework for the authorities to follow is graded into four bands, based on the seriousness of the risk to independence if problems and issues are not addressed. They do not need to adopt all bands, as it depends on their own resources. Authorities should review their criteria at least annually. If there are any major changes, financial or otherwise, then the council may review criteria more frequently. Eligibility for an individual is determined by comparing the risks to their autonomy, health, safety, ability to manage daily routines and involvement in family and wider community life with the eligibility criteria. The local authority must balance the cost of the service with the merits in providing the service based on each case. The upper cost parameters should only ever be used as a guide. The local authority can choose how best to meet the need within its budget even if it means that the person is to be cared for in a care home rather than in their own home (*R* v. *Lancashire County Council, ex parte Ingham and Whalley*, unreported, 5 July 1995).

8.2.2   Waiting lists

A local authority should provide services promptly once it has agreed to do so. Where waiting is unavoidable, it should ensure alternative services are in place to meet the needs assessed. Community equipment such as pressure relief mattresses, commodes, equipment for daily living, minor adaptations, ancillary equipment for people with sensory impairments, communication aids, wheelchairs and telecare equipment should be provided within 21 days, with the aim that this will be reduced to seven days by 2004.

Delays can occur at the point of discharge from hospital, as there may be no suitable home for the patient to move to, social services may not have assessed the person or put arrangements in place for their move. The Community Care (Delayed Discharges etc.) Act 2003 applies to England and Wales and is fully in force from January 2004. For individuals who are the responsibility of an SSD, the Act introduces a financial incentive for local authorities to provide community care services for the individual and/or his or her carer that are needed for the individual's safe transfer from an NHS hospital to a more appropriate setting. Once notice is served by the hospital to the local authority, it will have a short period of time to assess the person and then arrange the service provision. If it fails to do this, the local authority must pay a daily sum to the hospital until the patient is discharged. Prior to the notice being served the patient and/or his or her carer should be consulted.

8.2.3   Withdrawal of services

Services cannot be withdrawn once provided until the person has been fully re-assessed, the results conclude that he or she no longer meets the eligibility criteria or the needs can be met in another way, and that withdrawal of the service will not put the person at serious physical risk. The person should also be advised of the complaints procedure to appeal the decision if they wish.

8.2.4   Who provides

The authority must not seek to provide all services itself, but make use of the voluntary and commercial sectors. Care services may be provided by health authorities, charities and private agencies as well as other local authorities (ss.21 and 26 of the 1948 Act), and may revolve round the care already being provided by family, friends and neighbours.

8.3   NON-RESIDENTIAL CARE SERVICES FOR OLDER PEOPLE

8.3.1   Health Services and Public Health Act 1968, s.45

A local authority may, with the approval of the Secretary of State, and to such an extent as he may direct, make arrangements for promotion of the welfare of old people. The purpose is to secure services to those still managing to cope in order to prevent or postpone deterioration and dependence. Possible services are described in Circular 19/71 and include provision of meals and recreation, facilities or assistance in travelling to services, visiting and advisory services and social work support, practical assistance in the home, including adaptations and/or wardens or warden services. No direction has yet been made, so this remains a power and not a duty.

8.3.2   National Health Service Act 1977, s.21, Sched. 8, para. 3(1)

Local authorities have a duty to provide (or arrange) under Sched. 8 para. 3(1) to the 1977 Act on a scale adequate for the needs of the area, home helps for households where help is required owing to the presence of a person who is 'aged'. The term is not defined and there is no case law to assist. For the provision that must be made and that which is authorised see LAC (93) 10.

8.4   NON-RESIDENTIAL CARE SERVICES FOR PEOPLE WITH DISABILITIES

8.4.1   Community care needs and disability

Specific services are available for disabled people of all ages under the statutes mentioned below and these should be considered in the context of community care. A person may have community care needs and also be a disabled person, in which event further services will be triggered under s.47(2) of the 1990 Act.

8.4.2   Disability defined

The 1970 Act defines 'disability' as being:

> substantially or permanently handicapped by illness, injury or congenital deformity or suffering from mental disorder of any description.

The 1986 Act uses a slightly different definition as found in the National Assistance Act 1948, s.29, as being:

> blind, deaf or dumb, and other persons who are substantially and permanently handicapped by illness, injury or congenital deformity or who are suffering from a mental disorder within the meaning of the Mental Health Act.

This is extended further in LAC (93) 10 as covering people who are 'hard of hearing or partially sighted'.

For definition of 'mental disorder' see Chapter 12 at 12.3.

8.4.3   Registers

The National Assistance Act 1948, s.29(4)(g) creates a duty on a local authority to keep a register of disabled persons in its area. (See LAC (93) 10, Appendix 4.)

Individuals can register with their local authority and may become eligible for various forms of help. Provision is made by the SSD and may depend upon economic constraints and the policy of the authority. Being on the register is optional and is not a condition precedent to receiving assistance under the legislation.

8.4.4   Types of services

National Assistance Act 1948, s.29(1) (LAC (93) 10)

Section 29 of the 1948 Act gives local authorities power to provide welfare services for disabled persons such as social work support and advice, facilities at centres for social rehabilitation and adjustment to disability, facilities for occupational activities, holiday homes, provision of free or subsidised travel for those who do not qualify for travel concessions where such concessions are available, assistance in finding suitable accommodation and/or contributions towards the cost of employing a warden on welfare functions or providing warden services in private housing.

National Health Service Act 1977, Sched. 8, para. 2(1) (LAC (93) 10)

SSDs may make provision for the prevention of illness and for the care and after-care of persons suffering from illness, including mental illness. In deciding what provision to make for a person living at home and receiving substantial care from another person, they must have regard to the ability of another person to continue to provide care as added by s.8(1) of the 1986 Act. Types of provision include night-sitting service, day centres, meals and social work support.

Chronically Sick and Disabled Persons Act 1970

Services for disabled persons are identified by s.2 of the 1970 Act, and include:

- practical assistance in the home;
- provision of, or assistance in obtaining, wireless, television, library or similar recreational facilities;
- provision of lectures, games, outings or other recreational facilities outside the home or assistance in taking advantage of educational facilities;
- provision of facilities for, or assistance in, travelling to and from home for the purpose of participating in services;
- assistance in arranging for the carrying out of any works of adaptation in the home or the provision of any additional facilities designed to secure greater safety, comfort or convenience;
- facilitating the taking of holidays, whether at holiday homes or otherwise and whether provided under arrangements made by the authority or otherwise;
- provision of meals whether in the home or elsewhere;
- provision of, or assistance in obtaining, a telephone and any special equipment necessary for its use.

8.4.5 Provision

Where a local authority is satisfied (in the case of a person ordinarily resident in its area) that it is necessary in order to meet the needs of that person to make arrangements to provide services under s.2(1) of the 1970 Act, it is the duty of the authority to do so. For more details of the term 'ordinarily resident' see Chapter 7 at 7.2.5. This does not mean that the authority must be satisfied beyond reasonable doubt, but merely that it must make up its mind in the specific case and this necessarily means making an assessment of need. See *Blyth* v. *Blyth* [1966] 1 All ER 524. It is as yet unclear how the Disability Discrimination Act 1995 affects community care.

Notable cases under s.2 of the 1970 Act include *R* v. *Powys County Council, ex parte Hambridge (No.1)* [1998] 1 FLR 643, which held that local authorities can charge for services under s.2 as the provision is made under s.29 of the 1948 Act.

In *R* v. *London Borough of Haringey, ex parte Norton* [1998] 1 CCLR 168 the court held that the local authority could not confine a person's needs to personal care needs but had to also consider their leisure and recreational needs.

For further information see Age Concern Fact Sheet 32, *Disability and Ageing: Your Right to Social Services*.

8.4.6 Mental Health Act 1983, s.117

A duty is imposed by the Mental Health Act 1983, s.117 on social services departments and health authorities to assess for and provide after-care services to those who leave hospital after ceasing to be detained (this applies only to those admitted under ss.3, 37, 47 and 48 of the 1983 Act). Services provided under this section (including residential and domiciliary care) may not be charged for: *R* v. *Manchester City Council, ex parte Stennett and others* [2002] 4 All ER 124. See also LAC (2000) 3: *Section 117 Aftercare Services* and the Local Government Ombudsman's Special Report on s.117 cases, July 2003 (www.lgo.org.uk/special-reports.htm).

8.4.7 Guardianship

Statutory guardianship under the Mental Health Act 1983, ss.7–10 should not be overlooked when considering the powers of the local authority, because a social worker will be involved. The purpose is to enable an adult to receive community care where this cannot be provided without the use of compulsory powers, but where it is used it must be part of the overall care and treatment plan.

See Chapter 12 at 12.3 (and also 'place of safety' orders) and the Mental Health Act Code of Practice at para. 13.

8.5 RESIDENTIAL CARE

Local authorities are under a duty by the National Assistance Act 1948, s.21(1)(a) to:

> provide residential accommodation for persons who, by reason of age, illness, disability or any other circumstances are in need of care and attention which is not otherwise available to them.

Section 26(1)(a)–(c) of the 1948 Act (as amended) allows for placement and funding in a private nursing home.

In deciding whether care and attention is otherwise available the local authority must disregard so much of the person's resources as may be specified in, or determined in accordance with, the National Assistance (Assessment of Resources) Regulations 1992 (as amended). However if the person is unable to make their own arrangements or does not have others who are able or willing to make arrangements for care, the local authority has a duty to do so on their behalf (LAC (98) 19). It must also disregard the value of the resident's home if the person is entering into a deferred payment agreement (LAC (2001) 25).

The authority has a duty to take reasonable steps to prevent or mitigate loss or damage to the movable property of a person admitted as a patient to hospital, or to Part III accommodation or removed to suitable premises under s.48 of the 1948 Act. This has in practice extended to finding a suitable home for a resident's pet.

The local authority is under a duty to provide accommodation on a continuing basis once the person's needs have been satisfied under s.21(1)(a). However, they could treat that duty as discharged if the person unreasonably refused to accept accommodation or persistently and unequivocally refused to observe reasonable requirements in relation to the accommodation (*R* v. *Royal Borough of Kensington and Chelsea, ex parte Kujtim* [1999] 4 All ER 161).

For the provision that must be made and that which is authorised, see LAC (93) 10.

Under s.47 of the 1948 Act, a magistrates' court may in certain circumstances authorise removal of persons to suitable premises for the purpose of securing necessary care and attention if they are:

(a) suffering from grave chronic disease, or being aged, infirm or physically incapacitated, living in unsanitary conditions; and
(b) unable to devote themselves, and not receiving from other persons, proper care and attention. This remedy is generally only available in extreme cases.

There is an *ex parte* emergency procedure under the National Assistance (Amendment) Act 1951, but *inter partes* applications are to be preferred.

8.6   COMPLAINTS PROCEDURE

8.6.1   Authorities

Relevant sources include:

- Local Authority Social Services Act 1970, s.7B (as inserted by s.50(1) of the 1990 Act);
- Local Authority Social Services (Complaints Procedure) Order 1990, SI 1990/2244;
- Complaints Procedure Directions 1990;
- *The Right to Complain: Practical Guidance on Complaints Procedures in Social Services Departments*, HMSO (1991).

8.6.2   Requirement

A local authority is obliged to establish a procedure for considering representations and complaints in relation to the discharge of, or failure to discharge, its social services functions in respect of persons for whom it has a power or duty to provide and whose needs (or possible needs) have come to its attention. It must comply with any directions of the Secretary of State as to the procedures to be adopted in considering representations and taking consequential action, publicise its complaints procedure (by leaflets, notices and presentations), include reference to the procedure in decisions on assessment or provision and give support and encouragement to the complainant at all stages.

Complaints may not be anonymous or unconnected with social services functions. Other available methods of complaint are not affected, but the authority cannot insist that they be used in preference to the statutory complaints procedure. It may be necessary to adopt the complaints procedure before being able to apply for judicial review, and the procedure itself is susceptible to judicial review.

8.6.3   Procedure

There are three co-ordinated stages in the complaints procedure:

- *The informal stage*: an attempt should have been made to resolve the problem informally.
- *The registration stage*: an explanation of the formal procedure is given and written representations invited which are then registered and responded to. Time limits apply for the response, which follows an investigation and must be notified to certain persons. It is important to be clear that a particular complaint has been registered.
- *The review stage*: if the previous stages have not resolved the complaint, the complainant can ask for it to be formally considered by a panel of the

authority (three people of whom at least one is independent and chairs the panel). There are time limits for this review.

The complainant is entitled to an informal oral hearing when he may be accompanied by a representative (not normally a solicitor though this may be justified in some cases). The recommendations of the panel are sent to all concerned.

8.6.4   Outcome

The authority is not bound to accept the recommendations but must take notice of them. It must notify the complainant and the person on whose behalf the representations were made in writing within 28 days of its decision with reasons, and the action it proposes to take. See *R* v. *Avon County Council, ex parte Hazell*, unreported, 5 July 1993.

8.7   INADEQUATE PROVISION OR FAILURE TO ACT

Problems are bound to arise when the authority responsible for assessing needs and providing services is also responsible for funding such provision. As a general proposition it seems that when deciding both whether an individual has a need and whether to provide services, the authority may take into account its own financial resources but not those of the individual. See *R* v. *Gloucestershire County Council, ex parte Barry* [1997] 2 All ER 1; *R* v. *Sefton MBC, ex parte Help the Aged* [1997] 1 CCLR 57 and *Robertson* v. *Fife Council* [2002] 68 BMLR 229. But see also the following cases, which seem to overrule the above cases: *R* v. *East Sussex County Council, ex parte Tandy* [1997] 3 WLR 884; *R* v. *Birmingham County Council, ex parte Taj Mohammed* [1998] 1 CCLR 441.

However, the problem may be outside the jurisdiction of the SSD (e.g. with the health or housing authority) so before challenging the decision, be sure as to which body owes the duty.

8.7.1   Checklist to secure adequate care provision

❏   Has an assessment of needs been requested (or the need for this arisen)?
❏   If so, what has been the response?
❏   If not, make the request (it cannot be refused)
❏   Has an assessment of needs been made?
❏   If so, on what statutory basis and what are the assessed needs (inspect the assessment)?

❑ If not, why not?

❑ Was the assessment properly made?

❑ Was it under the 1970 Act or the 1990 Act, or both?

❑ Did those who made the assessment listen to the elderly person and carer (and any advocate)?

❑ Was it a fair assessment of needs?

❑ If not, use the complaints procedure.

❑ Has a decision been made as to whether those needs should be provided for?

❑ If so, what is that decision?

❑ If not, why not?

❑ Has a decision been made not to provide for assessed needs?

❑ If so, what are the reasons for that decision?

❑ Does this reflect the authority's current criteria for determining when services should be provided?

❑ Has a decision been made as to provision for assessed needs?

❑ If so, what is that decision and will the provision meet those needs?

❑ If not, why not?

❑ What provision is actually being made to meet the assessed needs?

❑ Does this fulfil the decision to provide for assessed needs?

❑ If not, why not and what provision is available to meet these needs?

❑ Is any restriction or condition being imposed?

❑ If so, is it necessary?

❑ What purpose is it intended to fulfil?

❑ Can this purpose be fulfilled in some other way?

❑ Has an existing service been withdrawn or restricted?

❑ If so, is this the result of a re-assessment?

❑ If not, does it follow a decision or has it just happened?

❑ On what basis (if at all) can this be justified?

❑ Should the needs be re-assessed?

❑ If so, start from the first question again!

❑ If not, the existing provision should continue.

❑ Does this assessment/re-assessment suggest that the issues are primarily health care so that the responsibility should lie with the health authority? (See R v. North and East Devon Health Authority, ex parte Coughlan [1999] 2 CCLR 285.)

8.7.2 Remedies

In addition to the complaints procedure mentioned above, the following methods may be available for challenging the authority and enforcing its duties:

- reference to Local Government Ombudsman;
- judicial review;
- request to the Secretary of State to exercise default powers;
- civil action in damages for breach of statutory duty or negligence (see Chapter 5 at 5.3 and 5.4).

8.8 FUNDING

8.8.1 Local authority resources

Local authorities receive an annual allocation from central government for all services. Some allocation will be ring-fenced such as grants to provide carers respite care. Increasingly the NHS and social services are working in partnership and since the introduction of the Health Act 1999 can pool resources to fund services, particularly where there is an overlap between responsibilities.

8.8.2 Means-testing

Having made provision an authority can charge for the services provided and take civil proceedings to recover arrears, but cannot refuse or withdraw the service for non-payment. See Chapter 14 at 14.4 (residential care) and 14.3 (other services).

8.8.3 Insurance

Insurance packages may provide a solution for some people to long-term funding. There are many gaps in the insurance market and new, flexible schemes are being marketed. Advice will be needed on these, and they require similar consideration to that given to home income plans (see Chapter 18 at 18.7.7). Remember that transfers of capital made for tax purposes could have disadvantages if long-term care is then needed. Additionally the use of impaired lives policies for those entering residential care should not be overlooked.

CHAPTER 9

Care homes

Caroline Bielanska

9.1 LEGISLATION

9.1.1 Care Standards Act 2000

The growth of the private sector in the provision of residential and nursing care resulted in legislation to introduce safeguards and rationalise earlier legislation. Prior to 1 April 2002, the regulation of care homes fell under the remit of local authorities and health authorities. Many used widely differing regulatory standards and inspection methods, which resulted in unacceptable differences in standards of care across the country. The Care Standards Act 2000 was passed to set up, in England, the National Care Standards Commission (NCSC) and under the National Assembly for Wales through the Care Standards Inspectorate for Wales (CSIW) to regulate social care and private and voluntary health care services.

From 1 April 2002, the NCSC and the CSIW took responsibility for the registration and inspection of care homes and replaced the system of inspection by local authority and health authority inspection units.

The work of the NCSC is led by a non-executive board with a chair. On a day-to-day level, the work of the NCSC is directed by a team of 15 national and regional Directors, led by a Chief Executive. Like its counterpart in England the CSIW has national, regional and local offices. Details can be obtained from its websites (www.carestandards.org.uk and www.wales.gov.uk/subisocialpolicycarestandards/index.htm).

The role of the NCSC will change once the Health and Social Care (Community Health Standards) Act 2003 is in force. It will create the Commission for Social Care Inspection (CSCI) and the Commission for Healthcare Audit and Inspection (CHAI), bringing together work undertaken by the NCSC and other organisations.

The CSCI will bring together the work currently undertaken by the Social Services Inspectorate, the SSI/ Audit Commission joint review team and the social care functions of the NCSC. The CSCI will:

- carry out local inspections of all social care organisations (public, private, and voluntary) against national standards and publish reports;

- register services that meet national minimum standards;
- carry out inspections of local social service authorities;
- publish an annual report to Parliament on national progress on social care and an analysis of where resources have been spent;
- validate all published performance assessment statistics on social care;
- publish the star ratings for social services authorities.

CHAI will encompass all of the current and proposed work of the Commission for Health Improvement and the Mental Health Act Commission, the national NHS value for money work of the Audit Commission, and the independent health care work of the NCSC. The CHAI will:

- encourage improvement in the quality and effectiveness of care, and in the economy and efficiency of its provision;
- inspect the management, provision and quality of health care services and track where, and how well, public resources are being used;
- carry out investigations into serious service failures;
- report serious concerns about the quality of public services to the Secretary of State;
- publish annual performance ratings for all NHS organisations and produce annual reports to Parliament on the state of health care;
- collaborate with other relevant organisations, including the CSCI;
- carry out an independent review function for NHS complaints.

9.1.2 Regulations

Relevant regulations are:

- Care Home Regulations 2001, SI 2001/3965 and in Wales, Care Homes (Wales) Regulations 2002, SI 2002/324 (W37);
- National Care Standards Commission (Registration) Regulations 2001, SI 2001/3969;
- Care Standards Act 2000 (Commencement No. 9 (England) and Transitional and Savings Provisions) Order 2001, SI 2001/3852;
- Care Standards Act 2000 (Commencement No. 10 (England) and Transitional, Savings and Amendment Provisions) Order 2001, SI 2001/4150;
- Care Standards Act 2000 (Establishments and Agencies) (Miscellaneous Amendments) Regulations 2002, SI 2002/865;
- National Care Standards Commission (Fees and Frequency of Inspections) (Amendment) Regulations 2002, SI 2002/1505;
- National Care Standards Commission (Fees and Frequency of Inspections) Regulations 2003, SI 2003/1587;
- National Care Standards Commission (Registration) (Amendment) Regulations 2003, SI 2003/369;

- Care Homes (Adult Placement) (Amendment) Regulations 2003, SI 2003/1845;
- Registration of Social Care and Independent Healthcare (Fees) (Wales) Regulations 2002, SI 2002/921 (W 109);
- Registration of Social Care and Independent Health Care (Wales) Regulations 2002, SI 2002/919 (W 107);
- Care Standards Act 2000 (Commencement No. 8 (Wales) and Transitional, Savings and Consequential Provision) Order 2002, SI 2002/920 (W 108);
- Care Homes (Amendment) (Wales) Regulations 2003, SI 2003/947 (W 128);
- Care Homes (Wales) (Amendment No. 2) Regulations 2003, SI 2003/1004 (W 144).

9.2   TYPES OF CARE HOMES

Care homes still refer to themselves as residential, nursing, or mental nursing homes although the 2000 Act refers to all such homes as care homes, which have different conditions attached to their registration. A care home comes within the definition in s.3(1) if it provides accommodation with nursing or personal care for persons:

- who are or have been ill;
- who are or have had a mental disorder;
- who are disabled or infirm;
- who are or have been dependent on alcohol or drugs.

9.3   REGULATION

The introduction of national minimum standards for care homes for older people means that service providers now have a benchmark against which to measure the quality of their service. They can be obtained from the national, regional or local offices of the NCSC and CSIW as well as on their websites. The NCSC and CSIW should apply consistent standards across England and Wales, with private, voluntary and public sector services treated in the same way. Their role is to register, inspect, and deal with complaints, investigation and enforcement.

Older people as service users should see an improvement in the quality of care home services, which improve their protection. Users and their families should know exactly what they can expect from the care home, which provides safeguards and assurances for them.

9.3.1 Registration

The NCSC or the CSIW is the registration authority, responsible for formally approving and granting registration to persons or organisations providing or managing care homes. Applicants must provide various documentation and statements, be able to demonstrate that they are suitable to provide or manage the service, and the proposed service is suitable to meet the needs of those who will be using it. The registering authority looks at the fitness of person or persons applying, fitness of the premises and fitness of services and facilities. A criminal records check is undertaken on the person applying and the registered person will have to undertake such checks on all staff they employ.

Once registered the care home will receive a registration certificate, which must be displayed.

9.3.2 Refusal

Appeal is initially in writing but if this is not successful, within 28 days of the decision applicants can make a written and/or verbal appeal to the Care Standards Tribunal, which is an independent body outside the registering authority. For case decisions see the Tribunal's website (www.carestandards tribunal.gov.uk).

9.3.3 The registered person

Section 10(1) of the 2000 Act provides that any person who carries on or manages a care home must be registered. Failure to do so is a criminal offence. The principle is that each establishment should have a registered owner or proprietor. If the proprietor is not in day-to-day control of it, the regulations require the appointment of a manager who must also be registered by the registration authority (see s.22 of the 2000 Act).

9.3.4 Inspection

The NCSC or CSIW undertake inspections to assess the quality of care provided by all care homes. They use the national minimum standards and regulations as the basis for each inspection and assess to what extent service providers exceed, meet, or fail to meet each individual standard. They aim to work together with the registered person to identify problems and help them agree an action plan with a suitable timescale that will enable them to comply with the standards. New care homes are required to meet the national minimum standards as a prerequisite of registration.

9.3.5 Complaints investigation

The NCSC or CSIW have established a complaints procedure through which residents and family members can lodge complaints about the care home. It is expected that complaints, if appropriate, are made to the care home initially, through their internal complaints procedure. Otherwise complaints can be made to the local area office. For details of the local office check the telephone directory or their website (see 9.1.1).

The NCSC or CSIW investigate complaints and concerns raised and try to secure improvements where regulations and national minimum standards are not being met.

9.3.6 Enforcement

The 2000 Act gives extensive powers, which enable the NCSC or CSIW to take enforcement action against registered service providers that consistently fail to meet the level of service provision set out in the legislation. This could lead to prosecution and, ultimately, the cancellation of registration.

9.4 CHOOSING A HOME

9.4.1 Choice of care home

A care home may be run by:

- a company or an individual for profit;
- a charity or non-profit-making organisation ('voluntary homes');
- the social services department of a local authority ('Part III accommodation').

Many residents rely upon public funding in respect of the fees for accommodation but within resource constraints residents should be provided with their own choice of accommodation, which is suitable for their assessed needs and does not cost the local authority more than usual for the type of accommodation preferred. The care home must also agree to enter into a contract with the local authority. For assessment of need see Chapter 8 at 8.1 and for funding and means tests see Chapter 14 at 14.4. See Age Concern Fact Sheet 29, *Finding Residential and Nursing Home Accommodation.* Some organisations provide information about homes (see Appendix E).

9.4.2 Statement of purpose

Prospective residents must have the information they need to make an informed choice about where to live. Each home must produce a statement of purpose and other information materials (service users' guide) setting out its aims and objectives, the range of facilities and services it offers to residents and the terms and conditions on which it does so in its contract of occupancy with residents. In this way prospective residents can make a fully informed choice about whether or not the home is suitable and able to meet the individual's particular needs.

The statement of purpose must include:

- the name and address of the registered provider and of any registered manager;
- the relevant qualifications and experience of the registered provider and any registered manager;
- the number, relevant qualifications and experience of the staff working at the care home;
- the organisational structure of the care home;
- the age-range and sex of the service users for whom it is intended that accommodation should be provided;
- the range of needs that the care home is intended to meet;
- whether nursing is to be provided;
- any criteria used for admission to the care home, including the care home's policy and procedures (if any) for emergency admissions;
- the arrangements for service users to engage in social activities, hobbies and leisure interests;
- the arrangements made for consultation with service users about the operation of the care home;
- the fire precautions and associated emergency procedures in the care home;
- the arrangements made for service users to attend religious services of their choice;
- the arrangements made for contact between service users and their relatives, friends and representatives;
- the arrangements made for dealing with complaints;
- the arrangements made for dealing with reviews of the service user's plan;
- the number and size of rooms in the care home;
- details of any specific therapeutic techniques used in the care home and arrangements made for their supervision;
- the arrangements made for respecting the privacy and dignity of service users.

9.4.3   The service user's guide

The service user's guide should be written in plain English and made available in a language and/or format suitable for intended residents and includes:

- a brief description of the services provided;
- a description of the individual accommodation and communal space provided;

- relevant qualifications and experience of the registered provider, manager and staff;
- the number of places provided and any special needs or interests catered for;
- a copy of the most recent inspection report;
- a copy of the complaints procedure;
- service users' views of the home.

9.4.4 The contract

Each service user is provided with a statement of terms and conditions at the point of moving into the home (or contract if purchasing their care privately).
The statement of terms and conditions must include:

- room(s) to be occupied;
- overall care and services (including food) covered by fee;
- fees payable and by whom (service user, local or health authority, relative or another) (fees should be broken down into accommodation and board; personal care and nursing care);
- additional services (including food and equipment) to be paid for, over and above those included in the fees;
- rights and obligations of the service user and registered provider and who is liable if there is a breach of contract;
- terms and conditions of occupancy, including period of notice (e.g. short/long term intermediate care/respite).

9.4.5 What to expect

The minimum standards set out in detail what the resident should expect. The following paragraphs outline just some of the standards the resident can expect.

No older person should move into a care home without having had their health and personal care needs assessed and been assured that these can be met by the home. This may be undertaken as part of an assessment by the SSD and/or the NHS body or it may be conducted by the care home as part of their individual care plan. It should be reviewed periodically. The aim is that the older person and any representative know that the home they enter will meet their needs. To achieve this, prospective residents and their relatives and friends should have an opportunity to visit and assess the quality, facilities and suitability of the home prior to entering care.

Residents, where appropriate, can continue to be responsible for their own medication, and are protected by the home's policies and procedures for dealing with medicines.

Residents should be made to feel they are treated with respect and their right to privacy is upheld with particular regard to:

- personal care giving, including nursing, bathing, washing, using the toilet or commode;
- consultation with, and examination by, health and social care professionals;
- consultation with legal and financial advisers;
- maintaining social contacts with relatives and friends;
- entering bedrooms, toilets and bathrooms;
- following death.

Residents must:

- have easy access to a telephone for use in private and receive their mail unopened;
- wear their own clothes at all times;
- be addressed by all staff in the manner preferred by the resident;
- be given medial examinations and treatments in their own room;
- benefit from screening where they share a room with another to ensure their privacy is not compromised;
- be assured that at the time of their death, staff will treat them and their family with care, sensitivity and respect;
- live in a safe, comfortable bedroom with their own possessions (if they wish) around them;
- be able to maintain contact with family, friends, representatives and the local community as they wish.

Residents should find the lifestyle experienced in the home matches their expectations and preferences, and satisfies their social, cultural, religious and recreational interests and needs. The routines of daily living and activities made available must be flexible and varied to suit resident's expectations, preferences and capacities and residents should have the opportunity to exercise their choice in relation to:

- leisure and social activities and cultural interests;
- food, meals and mealtimes (they should receive a wholesome, appealing, balanced diet in pleasing surroundings at times convenient to them);
- routines of daily living;
- personal and social relationships;
- religious observance.

The registered manager should ensure that the resident controls their own money except where they do not wish to or they lack capacity. In that case, safeguards must be in place to protect the interests of the resident with written records of all transactions maintained. Where resident's money is handled, the manager must ensure that the personal allowances are not pooled with other residents and that appropriate records and receipts are kept.

9.5 CARE HOME CLOSURES

9.5.1 Reason for care home closures

Care homes since the late 1990s have been closing at an alarming rate. This has had an impact on choice of accommodation for both the self-funding client and for those funded by the state. The reasons for home closures are complex but it is a fact that local authorities that are the main contractors of care beds restrict the amount they will pay. There is now a distinction between homes that will not take local authority residents and charge a more realistic fee, and those that are tied into a local authority contract and are paid less for the bed. Some homes, however, charge one rate for self-funding clients and another rate for local authority funded residents.

9.5.2 Moving older residents

Bed occupancy is running at a high rate and so as demand exceeds supply in some areas, it restricts choice. In normal market conditions it would cause an increase in the charge for the bed and for this reason proprietors are increasingly asking residents to leave once their assets fall to be means-tested by the state, where the local authority will not pay a higher rate for the care bed. Moving an older and frail person, particularly if they have been in the care home for many years, may bring about their premature death. There have been a number of well-publicised cases of this happening. There is no guidance for social services on this type of situation but the NHS Executive issued Good Practice Guidance back in April 1998 on the procedure for transferring frail older NHS patients to other long stay settings under Health Service Circular 1998/048. This is available on the Department of Health website. See *R* v. *St Helens Council, ex parte Haggerty and others,* LTL 6.6.03.

9.5.3 Home for life?

Since the introduction of the NHS and Community Care Act 1990, there has been a big shift in care being provided by the independent sector. As a consequence there has been closure of a significant number of council-run homes. Although able to do this, there must be adequate consultation with residents (*R* v. *Wandsworth LBC, ex parte Beckwith* [1996] 1 All ER 504).

In *R* v. *North and East Devon Health Authority, ex parte Coughlan* [2000] 3 All ER 850, the Court of Appeal held that the health authority had made a promise to the resident that the home would be hers for life and this bound them. The decision to close the home constituted unfairness amounting to an abuse of power, which was in breach of Article 8 (the right to family life) of the European Convention on Human Rights. It has been followed in *R* v. *Camden BC, ex parte Bodimeade* [2002] 63 BMLR 154 and *R v Merton, Sutton and Wandsworth Health Authority, ex parte Perry and others* [2001] Lloyds Rep Med 73. The tide turned, however, in *R* v. *Brent, Kensington and Chelsea and Westminster Health NHS Trust, ex parte C, M, P and HM* [2002] Lloyds Rep Med 321, *Frank Cowl and others* v. *Plymouth City Council* [2002] 1 WLR 803, *R* v. *East Sussex County Council, ex parte Dudley and others*, LTL 16.4.03, where the homes did close as the facts were distinguished from the *Coughlan* case.

There is very little that one can practically do to stop a home closure of an independent home as they are not usually amenable to judicial review, as was highlighted in the cases of *Elizabeth Heather and others* v. *Leonard Cheshire Foundation and HM Attorney General* [2002] 2 All ER 936 and *R* v. *Servite Houses, Wandsworth LBC, ex parte Goldsmith and others* [2001] ACD 4. These cases are distinguished from *R* v. *Partnerships In Care Ltd, ex parte QBD* [2002] 1 WLR 2610 where the decision of the managers of a private psychiatric hospital to alter the care and treatment of a patient was an act of a public nature and was susceptible to judicial review.

CHAPTER 10

Provision of health care

Caroline Coats and Caroline Bielanska

10.1 THE NATIONAL HEALTH SERVICE

10.1.1 Legislation

Relevant statutes are:

- National Health Service Act 1977;
- National Health Service and Community Care Act 1990;
- National Health Service (Amendment) Act 1995;
- Health Authorities Act 1995;
- National Health Service (Primary Care) Act 1997;
- Health Act 1999;
- Health and Social Care Act 2001;
- NHS Reform and Healthcare Professions Act 2002;
- Health (Wales) Act 2003;
- Health and Social Care (Community Health Standards) Act 2003.

10.1.2 Reform

The National Health Service (NHS) was established in 1946 and reorganised in 1974. In 1989 a White Paper, *Working for Patients: The Health Service – Caring for the 1990s* set out two objectives:

- to give patients better health care and greater choice of the services available;
- to provide greater satisfaction and rewards for persons working in the NHS.

The consequent changes made by the National Health Service and Community Care Act 1990 were designed to produce a more efficient service that puts the patient first, reinforcing the main aim of the NHS which is to help people live longer and enjoy a better quality of life. Provision was made for the establishment of NHS Trusts and the financing of practices of medical practitioners. NHS structures have since undergone further changes.

The NHS Plan announced in July 2000 included the following, most of which have now been implemented:

- more staff;
- extra funding for intermediate care;
- rapid response teams to provide emergency care at home so preventing admission to hospital (established in only a few areas);
- integrated home care teams providing equipment, rehabilitation and recuperation facilities;
- incentives for joint working and pooling of resources by NHS and local councils building on the Health Act 1999;
- establishing Patient Advice and Liaison Service, Patients' Forums and Independent Complaints Advocacy Services;
- reduced waiting times;
- Care Direct Service to provide information and advice by telephone (0800 444 000) or by **www.caredirect.gov.uk**. The aim was that after the pilot study was finalised it would be phased in around England from 2003. This has not happened, although the website does give information to access local area websites.

10.1.3 Structure

The Secretary of State retains overall responsibility for the NHS in England and Wales. In addition to setting the strategic direction he has a number of other specific functions (e.g. under the Mental Health Act 1983) and may:

- provide any services which he considers appropriate for the purpose of discharging any of his statutory duties;
- do any other thing calculated to facilitate, or conducive or incidental to, the discharge of such duties.

The health services are to be free of charge unless the charges are expressly provided for by statute. The Department of Health (or National Assembly for Wales) is responsible for health service policy.

Strategic Health Authorities

Since April 2002 regional and district health authorities have merged and there are now 28 Strategic Health Authorities (StHAs). They are responsible for developing and implementing the health policy at local level for their area. They manage the performance of the Primary Care Trusts (PCTs) in their area and are a key link between the Department of Health and the NHS and ensure national priorities are integrated into local plans.

Primary Care Trusts

PCTs are responsible for the planning and provision of local hospital and family practitioner services. The Secretary of State may require them to exercise on his behalf such of his functions as are specified in directions. They:

- purchase hospital and community health services on behalf of local people;
- ensure there are enough GPs to provide services as well as securing the provision of other health services, including: hospitals, dentists, mental health care, walk-in centres, NHS Direct, population screening, patient transport (A&E) and pharmaceutical and optical services;
- are responsible for integrating health and social care so the two systems work together for patients.

The 303 PCTs in England will eventually control 75 per cent of the NHS budget to plan and commission health services for their local communities.

Special Health Authorities

These have particular functions such as the National Blood Authority and provide services for the whole population in England.

NHS Trusts

Hospital trusts usually offer a range of services to meet general health needs. Some trusts also act as regional or national centres of expertise for more specialised care, while some are attached to universities and help to train health professionals. Trusts can also provide services in the community such as through health centres, clinics or in people's homes. Other than in an emergency, hospital treatment is arranged by a referral through the GP. Appointments and treatment are free.

NHS Direct

Since March 1998, this service offers free 24-hour telephone assistance. Some GPs will use this as the initial out-of-hours service. The planning of it is managed locally through the Primary Care Trust.

Care Trusts

The Health Act 1999 created flexibility for the NHS and social care to work together to provide better integrated services. This is particularly important in regard to groups such as the elderly infirm, but is made difficult by the fact that health/local authority boundaries do not coincide.

A Care Trust is an NHS organisation to which local authorities can delegate health-related functions, in order to provide integrated health and social care to their local communities. Care Trusts were announced in the NHS Plan in July 2000. They are established on a voluntary basis and in partnership, where there is a joint agreement at a local level that this will be the best way to deliver better health and social care services.

Structure in Wales

The Welsh Assembly Government is responsible for policy direction and for allocating funds to the NHS in Wales.

From 1 April 2003 Local Health Boards (LHBs), similar to the English PCTs, hold three-quarters of the budget for the NHS in Wales so they can plan and pay for health services for people living in their area.

Each of the 22 LHBs has a decision-making board which is made up of local doctors, a nurse, other health professionals, members of the local council and voluntary organisations, and others to represent the voice of patients. They also have a small executive team to put the decisions into action and provide services for the public. LHBs plan and pay for most hospital and family health services with the exception of certain specialist services. These are the responsibility of the Health Commission Wales (Specialised Services).

The LHBs cover exactly the same areas as the 22 local authorities in Wales to allow much closer working between the NHS and the local councils with the aim to tackle long-term problems with health.

The National Public Health Service (see www.wales.nhsp.uk) gives advice and guidance to LHBs on a range of issues such as disease protection and control. The running of NHS Trust hospitals is as in England.

Patient representation

The Community Health Councils (CHCs) set up by statute in each health district were not involved in management but represented the interests of patients and advised on complaints in regard to hospital and community health services. They were phased out during 2003 in favour of:

- Patient Advice and Liaison Service;
- Patient Forums;
- Independent Complaints Advocacy Services.

Commission for Patient and Public Involvement in Health

The commission appoints staff to Patient Forums in each Primary Care Trust. They monitor and review local health services and make local recommendations. Each Forum has a non-executive director on the Trust board.

The commission sets standards and monitors the performance of Patient Forums and Independent Complaints Advocacy Services to ensure independence. They also carry out national reviews of services from the patients' perspective and report their findings to the Secretary of State.

10.1.4   Joint planning and funding

Joint Consultative Committees

Joint Consultative Committees are set up under the National Health Service Act 1977 to advise NHS bodies and their associated local authorities on the performance of their duty to co-operate with one another in order to secure and advance the health and welfare of the people of England and Wales, and on the planning and operation of services of common concern to those bodies. Joint care planning teams comprise officers of both bodies but specialist sub-groups may be set up.

Health Act 1999

Health bodies, such as Strategic Health Authorities, Primary Care Trusts, together with any health-related local authority service such as social services, housing, transport, leisure and library services, community and many acute services have power under the Health Act 1999 to engage in:

- pooled funds: each contribute agreed funds to a single pot, to be spent on agreed projects for designated services;
- lead commissioning: agree to delegate commissioning of a service to one lead organisation;
- integrated provision: their staff, resources and management structures work together to integrate the provision of a service from managerial level to the front line.

10.2   DELIVERY OF HEALTH CARE

10.2.1   NHS charters

Your Guide to the NHS, which replaced the Patient's Charter, is published by the Department of Health in a range of languages and is available at www.nhs.uk/nhsguide/nhs_guide.pdf or hard copies can be obtained by calling the Health Literature Line on 0800 555 777 or on written request from Your Guide to the NHS, PO Box 777, London SE1 6XH.

There are also local charters for long-term care called Better Care, Higher Standards, which explain what local authorities and health services can provide and how patients can get these services more easily. Copies are available by phoning local authorities or health authorities (and more information can be found at www.doh.gov.uk/longtermcare/index.htm).

National Service Frameworks

The frameworks set out expected standards covering a particular aspect of care provided by the NHS and social services, e.g. mental health services. The aim is to reduce variations in care and standards of treatment and care. The national service framework for older people states:

> NHS services will be provided, regardless of age, on the basis of clinical need alone. Social care services will not use age in their eligibility criteria or policies, to restrict access to available services.

10.2.2 Types

There are three types of health care provided under the NHS, though health care may also be purchased or arranged by the NHS privately:

- primary health care provided in the community by family doctors, dentists, opticians and others;
- secondary health care provided through hospitals and the ambulance services;
- tertiary health care provided through specialist hospitals, e.g. for cancer.

10.2.3 In the community

General practitioners

Family doctors (GPs) provide their services in medical practices to persons who register with them. Practices may offer a wider range of services with more emphasis on promotion of good health and prevention of disease. Practice nurses can undertake specialist training which allows them to prescribe certain medicines and other items, such as wound dressings. A new GP contract is in the process of being negotiated, which will allow GPs to take on new responsibilities where they have clinical specialist interest, such as dermatology. They would be able to carry out procedures in the practice rather than in hospital. Directories are produced of local GPs giving details of their practices which should produce an annual leaflet with details of the services provided.

Everyone has the right to be registered with a GP:

- the patient may approach a GP and ask to join his or her list of patients (but the GP is not obliged to accept a particular patient);
- the PCT will allocate a patient to a GP if he or she is unable to find one but there is then a risk of periodic transfer so the patient should seek to find their own GP;
- patients may change GP without giving reasons or getting permission.

Patients have the right to see a GP (not necessarily their own) at the surgery during surgery hours which should be displayed on a notice outside. The surgery should provide a telephone number for messages at all times. An appointment system may prevail except in an emergency. Home visits cannot be insisted upon and are at the doctor's discretion, but should be available to patients who genuinely need them.

Patients aged 75 and over must be offered an annual assessment and home visit to see how they are managing, but not necessarily at a time of year of their choice.

Patients away from home for up to three months can ask to be treated as a temporary patient by another GP and even if not accepted that GP must give any treatment immediately necessary.

Out-of-hours care may be managed by a deputising service or a co-operative. It may be that the GP's emergency telephone number will refer the caller to the NHS Direct who will then determine if the patient should go to hospital, give advice or make an appointment with the GP.

The NHS Plan envisages that by 2004:

- patients will be able to see a primary care professional within 24 hours;
- patients will be able to see a GP within 48 hours;
- on-the-spot booking system with choice of convenient times;
- referral from GP to out-patients reduced to three months;
- maximum wait for in-patient treatment of six months.

10.2.4 Dental care

Modernising NHS Dentistry sets out the government's plans for reform to dental practice. Patients may be accepted onto a dentist's NHS 'continuing care' list. All necessary treatment must be offered to continuing care patients under the NHS but private treatment can be arranged in addition or as an alternative. Registration usually lasts for 15 months which is renewed each time a new course of NHS treatment begins. In the event that the patient has difficulty finding a dentist they should phone NHS Direct who can give details.

223

10.2.5 Hospital care

Patients generally need to be referred to a hospital by a GP, but in an emergency an Accident and Emergency Department will provide treatment:

- there is no absolute right to choose the hospital or consultant, but a preference may be expressed to the GP;
- there is no right to a second opinion but patients can request one if in doubt;
- for hospital discharge see 10.5.

10.2.6 Private medical care

Medical care and treatment outside the NHS is provided under direct contracts between the provider and the patient. A private hospital may be set up as a commercial enterprise or a charity. There may be separate contracts with the private hospital, consultant, etc. Fees are charged which may be recovered as a civil debt and a matter of complaint may also be a breach of contract.

Health professionals involved are governed by the same professional bodies as those working in the NHS (some also work part-time for the NHS). The NHS can commission care in the private sector if the patient has been on a waiting list for an extended period of time.

The National Care Standards Commission is responsible for registering private hospitals and clinics.

Private medical insurance

The potential fees for private medical care may be covered by tailor-made insurance policies or schemes, providing a level of cover for an annual premium or subscription. Refer to the conditions of the particular policy or the rules of the scheme:

- not all forms of medical treatment are eligible for a claim;
- any additional cost of the treatment must be paid by the patient but cash benefits may be available for those who receive treatment under the NHS;
- there may be age restrictions on taking out a policy or joining a scheme.

10.3 INFORMATION

There is a general duty of confidentiality imposed upon health professionals at common law, so medical information concerning an older person may only be disclosed to third parties in certain defined circumstances. Older people may themselves wish to be told what the diagnosis of an illness is or to know what is held in their medical records. The obligations of an NHS body or medical practitioner in relation to the disclosure of information are dealt with in Chapter 2 and include:

- Data Protection Act 1998;
- Access to Health Records Act 1990;
- Access to Medical Reports Act 1988;
- Human Rights Act 1998;
- Health Service (Control of Patient Information) Regulations 2002, SI 2002/1438;
- NHS Confidentiality Code of Practice (July 2003).

10.3.1 Confidentiality

A doctor is under a general duty not to disclose information which he or she has gained in his or her professional capacity but there are the following potential exceptions to this general principle:

- disclosure with the patient's consent;
- disclosure in relation to the clinical management of a patient;
- disclosure to a close relative or another third party in the best interests of the patient;
- disclosure required by statute;
- disclosure in connection with judicial proceedings or in the public interest;
- disclosure for the purposes of medical audit, teaching and research.

A doctor who discloses confidential information about a patient must be prepared to justify this under one of the above heads.

Consent to disclosure

A doctor is free to disclose medical information with the consent of the patient but the consent should cover the extent of the information disclosed and the persons to whom it is disclosed:

- if the patient is incapable of giving consent the other exceptions must be considered, e.g. is the disclosure in the best interests of the patient;
- wherever possible questions of disclosure will be discussed with the patient in advance and express consent obtained or inferred.

Disclosure to other professionals

Medical information may only be disclosed to those directly involved in the care and treatment of the patient on a 'need to know' basis in relation to such care – other purposes will not suffice:

- all medically qualified staff share the duty of confidentiality;
- a doctor releasing information to non-medical professionals (e.g. social workers) must ensure that they too will treat it in confidence;
- information required for administrative purposes should be on a basis which does not identify the patient.

If a patient is particularly vulnerable disclosure of concerns about abuse to an appropriate source may be indicated.

Disclosure to others

Doctors may need to discuss with relatives or carers the nature of an illness and any treatment, and consent may often be presumed (unless expressly refused):

- if consent cannot be given the doctor must act in the patient's best interests;
- when it is undesirable, for medical reasons, to seek a patient's express consent, disclosure is essentially a matter of clinical judgement.

Public interest

It may be in the public interest for a doctor to disclose information about his patient where failure to disclose will expose the patient, or someone else, to a risk of death or serious harm, e.g.:

- where a doctor considers that the patient is no longer fit to drive (though he or she should advise the patient first and invite surrender of the licence);
- if it is apparent that a perpetrator of abuse to the patient is also abusing other vulnerable adults.

10.3.2   Withholding information

It is suggested that information may only be specifically withheld from the patient if disclosure would be likely to cause serious harm to the patient's physical or mental health.

NHS Code of Practice

In July 2003 the Department of Health published Confidentiality: NHS Code of Practice (similar Codes exist in Scotland and Wales). It provides:

- complaints about non-disclosure, delays in disclosure or charges for information should be made to the appropriate NHS manager;
- if complainants are dissatisfied with the response received they should write to the Chief Executive of the NHS body;

- those still dissatisfied may complain to the Health Service Commissioner (who has required a health body to establish the specific exemption relied upon in order to justify refusal to disclose information).

Caldicott guardians

The Caldicott review of personally identifiable information in 1997 recommended that 'guardians' of personal information be created to safeguard and govern the uses made of confidential information within NHS organisations. The Caldicott principles and processes provide a framework of standards for the management of confidentiality and access to personal information under the leadership of a Caldicott guardian. The Caldicott standard is extended into local authorities with social services responsibilities with the aim to provide a good foundation for joint working between health and social services.

The Caldicott principles are:

1. justify the purpose(s);
2. do not use patient-identifiable information unless it is absolutely necessary;
3. use the minimum necessary patient-identifiable information;
4. access to patient-identifiable information should be on a strict need-to-know basis;
5. everyone with access to patient-identifiable information should be aware of their responsibilities;
6. understand and comply with the law.

10.4   COMPLAINTS

A client may be dissatisfied about the delivery of health care and wish to complain. You should only pursue this on the request or with the consent of the actual patient and be careful about complaints made by other people (unless the patient lacks mental capacity and is dependent upon other people looking after his or her interests). Before pursuing a formal complaint it may be appropriate for the patient or someone on their behalf to discuss the problem with the professional involved and if not satisfied that this has been done you may wish to take the step yourself (it may be more appropriate to have the discussion with that person's manager).

The person or body to complain to depends upon the nature of the complaint and person complained about:

- many complaints relate to service failures (e.g. waiting times, poor hygiene in hospital wards) and these should be made to the service managers;

- help and advice should be available from the local Patient Advice and Liaison Service in regard to the different complaints procedures.

Distinguish cases where there is the possibility of legal redress (e.g. damages for negligent treatment) and consider:

- it may not be appropriate to delay matters by pursuing a complaint;
- if the complaint arises in the private sector it may amount to an action-able breach of contract;
- there is no legal justification for attempts to persuade complainants to waive legal rights before a complaint will be investigated;
- the purpose of a complaint is to resolve a problem, not to increase it.

10.4.1 Procedures

There used to be various procedures depending on which part of the NHS was involved, but a new NHS complaints system was introduced in April 1996. The Department of Health published, in April 2003, *NHS Complaints Reform: Making Things Right*, which describes its proposals to reform the NHS complaints procedure. It sets out a programme to improve management of the whole complaints system, subject to the Health and Social Care (Community Health and Standards) Act 2003.

Distinguish between oral and written complaints as an oral complaint will only be considered under formal procedures if the patient remains dissatis-fied or puts the complaint in writing, whereas written complaints are dealt with in accordance with national and local guidance and receive a written response.

A complaint may also be made to the professional body of the particular doctor, nurse or other health professional concerned.

It is usually necessary to exhaust all available procedures for dispute reso-lution before applying to the High Court for a judicial review and a similar approach is increasingly being adopted by Ombudsmen.

NHS complaints procedures

There are three stages in the procedure for complaints about the NHS:

- discuss the problem with the manager or professional concerned (the local resolution stage): this should be done within six months;
- a hearing before an independent review panel;
- reference to the Health Service Commissioner (the Ombudsman).

Hospital and Community Trust complaints

Complaints about service failures may be made to the service managers, whilst a more formal complaint is made to a specially appointed Complaints Manager whose name and location should be available in the hospital. A written reply will be received and if still not satisfied the patient may ask for an independent review by a panel. If this does not prove satisfactory then they can complain to the Health Service Commissioner (see the Hospital Complaints Procedure Act 1985 and directions made thereunder).

Family practitioner services

A complaint about family practitioner services (this includes a GP, dentist, pharmacist or optician but not complaints relating to clinical judgement or professional misconduct) should be made to the practice. An initial response should be received within two working days. The nominated officer should deal with the complaint under local resolution arrangements within two weeks. If it is not resolved the patient should be advised of their right to seek an independent review panel.

Clinical complaints

For clinical judgement complaints the matter should be discussed with the consultant for an explanation and possible resolution. Failing resolution the Complaints Manager of the Hospital Trust should consider whether:

- it is a complaint about diagnosis or treatment by a hospital doctor;
- every effort has been made to resolve it by explanation;
- it is a serious matter which cannot be dealt with by a different enquiry or disciplinary action and is unlikely to go to court.

The Complaints Manager may then make a reference to two independent consultants (of whom at least one comes from a different NHS body) who hold an independent review which the patient may attend with a representative.

Independent review panel

The request for review must be passed to the panel convenor (the Complaints Manager) of the local PCT or Hospital Trust (depending who and what the complaint is about) within 28 days. Within 20 days the convenor will decide whether to convene the panel by considering:

- a written statement from the patient;
- whether all opportunities to resolve the complaint have been explored;
- obtain external independent view of lay chair;
- take appropriate clinical advice.

The panel should convene within four weeks and complete its work within 12 weeks. It is normally comprised of three people. Legal representation is not allowed. A draft of the report is sent 14 days before issue. Following issue the patient is informed in writing of any action to be taken in consequence of the panel's decision and the right to take the case to the Health Service Ombudsman.

Professional misconduct

Professional misconduct complaints against GPs or hospital doctors are made to the General Medical Council and dealt with under established procedures. Sanctions range from a warning letter through suspension to removal from the Register. Complaints against nurses, dentists, pharmacists and other professional groups are made to the professional association concerned.

NHS discipline procedure

Discipline in respect of family health services practitioners is dealt with separately from complaints by special disciplinary committees of a different NHS body. They hear evidence, make findings of fact and recommend an appropriate penalty. Appeal lies to the Family Health Service Appeal Authority (FHSAA).

10.4.2 Health Service Commissioner

This Ombudsman investigates certain types of complaint about the NHS. There is a time limit of 12 months for a complaint and the matter must have been taken up with the appropriate NHS body first.

Types of complaint

Complaints can be investigated concerning:

- failure by an NHS body to provide a service which it has a duty to provide or in a service that is provided;
- maladministration connected with action taken by or on behalf of the NHS body, which includes failure to comply with a legal obligation and administrative action or inaction based on or influenced by improper considerations or conduct e.g. unjustifiable delay, incompetence, neglect, and failing to give proper advice or follow recognised procedures or take account of representations;
- complaints may relate to the attitude as well as actions of members of staff, e.g. discourtesy, harassment, bias or unfair discrimination.

Complaints cannot be investigated concerning matters before the courts or:

- about the general services provided by family practitioners because these relate to their contract with the FHSA to whom complaint should be made (complaints about the FHSA itself can be investigated, including how they handle complaints);
- within the clinical judgement complaints procedure (as distinct from the administration of that procedure).

Procedure

Only refer complaints which cannot be resolved with the NHS body, and send a letter outlining the complaint and enclosing copies of all relevant documents and correspondence:

- If the complaint is accepted, a letter with a summary of what is to be investigated is sent to the complainant and the NHS body. An officer may visit the complainant to discuss the matter and explain what happens.
- The investigation is conducted in private and will usually be informal so legal representation is seldom necessary. A solicitor may assist in presenting the complaint and help may be given with the costs.
- A written report is sent to the complainant and the NHS body and this may be published. If the complaint is upheld this report will state whether the NHS body has agreed to remedy any injustice or hardship caused, perhaps by offering an apology or agreeing to policy changes or new procedures.

A leaflet is available from the office of the Commissioner (addresses in Appendix E). For Ombudsmen generally see Chapter 5.

Human Rights Act 1998

Relevant articles in the European Convention on Human Rights are:

- Article 2: the right to life;
- Article 3: the right not to be subject to torture or degrading treatment or punishment;
- Article 5: the right to liberty and security of the person;
- Article 6: the right to a fair hearing by an independent and impartial tribunal;
- Article 8: the right to respect for family life, home and correspondence;
- Article 14: the right not to be discriminated against.

Remedy may be sought if any right is violated by a public body.

10.5 DISCHARGE FROM HOSPITAL

There is no right to stay in hospital indefinitely if hospital care is no longer required but discharge to a care home can be refused.

Patients may discharge themselves and leave hospital at any time unless detained under the Mental Health Act 1983 (see Chapter 12) or admitted under a JP's order for an infectious disease. An elderly patient whose mental capacity is impaired is likely to come under the care of a psycho-geriatrician so if a report is needed as to mental capacity refer to the consultant.

Before patients are discharged from hospital, proper arrangements must be made for their return home and for any continuing care that may be necessary. All local authorities and hospitals are required to have in place discharge procedures. See *Discharge from Hospital: Pathway, Process and Practice*, Department of Health (March 2003). Also useful are *Discharge from Hospital: A Matter of Choice* (2003) and *Discharge from Hospital: Getting it Right for People with Dementia* (2003), which are checklists on choice of accommodation and discharge planning.

The Better Care, Higher Standards Charter states:

- local housing, health and social services should work with the patient (and their carer) to make the necessary arrangements;
- a written care plan should be agreed prior to discharge.

Problems arise when it is proposed to discharge a patient from hospital who needs continuing nursing care, as there is a funding implication. There is no charge for services provided under the NHS although the individual will be means-tested for any local authority services. The Delayed Discharges (Continuing Care) Directions 2003 place a duty on the NHS to assess whether a person needs continuing NHS care before serving a notice to social services under the Community Care (Delayed Discharges etc.) Act 2003, that the patient may require community care services.

From April 2003 anyone requiring nursing care by a registered nurse should receive a multi-disciplinary assessment:

- Hospitals are not entitled to make a financial assessment of a patient. However from January 2004 they will be able to charge the local authority for every day that a patient (who is the responsibility of the local authority) remains in an acute hospital bed when they are ready to be discharged. Social services will have to assess for social care needs and then put in place services that meet those eligible assessed needs within a set period of time.
- There is no power to place people compulsorily in residential care or nursing homes against their wishes (except the National Assistance Act 1948, s.47), although they cannot occupy an NHS bed indefinitely.

There is now a single assessment process for health and social care for older people. See Chapter 8 for community care services and Chapter 14 for funding.

Continuing NHS health care

A special report into NHS funding of long-term care was issued in February 2003 with subsequent investigations reported in June 2003. It contains the results of investigations into long-term health care complaints. The report may be accessed at www.ombudsman.org.uk. For more on continuing NHS health care see Chapter 14.

Review of decision to discharge

If a patient believes they should not leave hospital they have the right to ask for a review of the decision. The person should remain as an in-patient during the review which should be carried out within two weeks. The NHS seeks the advice of an independent panel that will consider the case before making a recommendation. This procedure may be used to check that:

- the eligibility criteria have been properly applied to the patient;
- correct procedures have been followed in reaching the decision.

The panel's recommendation is advisory but it is generally expected to be followed. If rejected the reason must be given in writing.

This review procedure can also be used to challenge decisions on NHS continuing care funding and the registered nursing care contribution.

CHAPTER 11

Medical treatment

Julia Abrey

11.1 CONSENT TO TREATMENT

No medical treatment may be given to an adult patient without consent and treatment involving physical contact is a trespass to the person (a battery) in the absence of consent. Provision of basic nursing care may be excusable in the absence of consent (e.g. cleaning up a protesting patient) but intrusive medical treatment is not. Doctors cannot compel competent patients to accept treatment, however convinced they may be that it is in the patient's best interests. Special provision is made for patients who lack competence to make a decision about medical treatment. The Human Rights Act 1998 is likely to affect this area of the law.

11.1.1 The nature of consent

The onus is on the patient to prove that he did not consent (*Freeman* v. *Home Office* [1984] 2 WLR 130). Consent may be in writing (a signed form), verbal or implied by conduct (e.g. where a patient presents himself for treatment, but not where only a diagnosis is requested). The signature on a form is merely evidence which may be rebutted and the question is not whether the patient signed the consent form but whether he decided to have the treatment (see generally Chapter 1):

- Consent must be specific and valid, which means that the patient consents to the treatment actually given and does so voluntarily, i.e. consent is freely given and not under threat (e.g. to discharge or use compulsory powers).
- The information the patient receives is within the doctor's discretion but any questions should be answered; see *Sidaway* v. *Bethlem Royal Hospital Governors* [1985] 1 All ER 643. Failure to inform may nullify consent, but wrong information may give rise to an action in negligence if injury directly results, on the basis that the patient would not have consented if properly informed and damage resulted from the subsequent treatment.

- The patient must have capacity to consent (which should be continually re-assessed) and this is based on understanding in broad terms what he is consenting to, so the degree depends on the complexity of treatment. A patient's wishes in regard to treatment may be recorded in advance (e.g. in the form of a living will, see 11.4).
- The right of choice regarding treatment is not limited to decisions which others might regard as sensible but exists notwithstanding that the reasons for making the choice are rational, irrational, unknown or even non-existent: *Re T (An Adult) (Consent to Medical Treatment)* [1992] 2 FLR 458, CA.

See Chapter 12 at 12.7 of the Code of Practice under the Mental Health Act 1983, s.118(4) and the Department of Health's Good Practice in Consent Guidance (**www.doh.gov.uk/consent**).

11.1.2   Refusal of consent

A patient who remains competent to make a decision about continuing treatment may refuse it and then it cannot be given even if death will result. If a refusal to consent to life-saving treatment is to be legally binding the patient must have:

- capacity to make the decision and not have had his will overborne by the influence of a third party;
- understood in broad terms the nature and effect of the treatment;
- in refusing covered the actual situation in which the treatment is needed.

See the following cases: *Re T (An Adult) (Consent to Medical Treatment)* [1992] 2 FLR 458, CA; *Ms B v. An NHS Hospital Trust* [2002] All ER 449 (a seriously physically disabled patient with the mental capacity to make decisions about treatment, even when a consequence of such decision could be death, had the right to decide to refuse treatment); *R v. Dr M and others, ex parte N* [2003] 1 WLR 562 on what makes a treatment a medical necessity.

The treating doctor determines whether the criteria are fulfilled but his or her view of the reasonableness or rationality of the patient's decision may influence his or her approach.

11.2   INCOMPETENT PATIENTS

11.2.1   Competence

Competence is presumed unless the contrary is proved, and means that the patient has:

- sufficient understanding and intelligence to comprehend the nature, purpose and likely consequences of undergoing or refusing treatment: *Gillick* v. *West Norfolk and Wisbech AHA and another* [1986] 1 FLR 224, HL;
- the ability to communicate his decision in relation to the particular treatment.

Key points

- The ability to communicate can be impaired by mental or physical causes but the latter may often be overcome by imaginative techniques (see Chapter 2 at 2.1.1).
- A diagnosis of mental disorder does not by itself prevent a patient from consenting: a detained mental patient may obtain an injunction to prevent physical treatment: *Re C (Adult: Refusal of Medical Treatment)* [1994] 1 All ER 819.
- Short-term incompetence is of less significance than long-term because the minimum necessary treatment can be given until the patient can again express his wishes in regard to more drastic medical treatment.
- Whilst the decision of an incompetent person cannot validate treatment, withholding treatment from such a person may give rise to an action for breach of a duty of care.

There is no procedure whereby the personal power to consent to or refuse medical treatment may be delegated to others, either by the patient or the state, but see the draft Mental Incapacity Bill at **www.dca.gov.uk/menicap/meninc.pdf**.

11.2.2   Treatment without consent

Emergency treatment may be given to save the life of an unconscious patient, although there may be an exception where it is known that the patient would not wish to be treated because of religious or other beliefs.

Treatment without consent is also lawful in the case of an incompetent adult where it is considered by the doctor to be in the best interests of a patient. Best interests means necessary to save life, or prevent deterioration or ensure improvement in a patient's physical or mental health, but should not be restricted to purely medical interests. It is necessary to consider what the patient would have chosen taking into account all the evidence including any previously expressed wishes which may include signed documents, e.g. a living will.

A doctor must act in accordance with a practice accepted as proper by a responsible body of medical practitioners, skilled and experienced in the relevant speciality: see *Bolam* v. *Friern Barnet Hospital Management Committee* [1957] 2 All ER 118 and *F* v. *West Berkshire Health Authority* [1989] 2 All ER 545.

Treatment for a mental disorder (subject to safeguards) may be given to a patient detained under the treatment provisions of the Mental Health Act 1983 (see Chapter 12).

Next of kin

The next of kin (whether the lawful next of kin or those stated as such by the patient) do not have any legal right to consent or refuse consent on behalf of an adult patient:

- carers, home managers and social workers also do not have any legal status in regard to treatment decisions;
- there is no role for the 'nearest relative' similar to that for treatment under the Mental Health Act 1983.

If the treating doctor is to determine the patient's best interests he or she would need to consult with such persons and it may be prudent to have their approval.

11.2.3   Allowing the patient to die

Codes of medical ethics have never required the doctor to prolong life at any cost; caring for a patient as he dies in peace and dignity may be the last service a doctor can perform.

'Double effect'

Drugs given to relieve suffering may shorten the life of the patient – the principle of 'double effect' (the successful defence of Dr Bodkin Adams). A decision may need to be made to change from treatment for living to treatment for dying:

- administering a drug which will merely kill without first relieving suffering is murder (or attempted murder if there is no proof that it actually caused death).
- it is no defence that the patient pleaded to be put out of his misery, though juries are reluctant to convict doctors in this situation and it is also effective mitigation: *R* v. *Cox*, unreported, 18 September 1992.

Withholding or withdrawing treatment

Doctors may withhold or withdraw treatment which is not in the best interests of their patient without being in breach of duty or in breach of the criminal law, even if death is the inevitable consequence. There is no difference between withholding and withdrawing treatment: both are omissions rather than acts (*Airedale NHS Trust* v. *Bland* [1993] 2 WLR 316, HL).

11.2.4 Good medical practice

The interpretation of the law as to the extent to which the previously expressed wishes of an incompetent patient may or should be followed is difficult. The British Medical Association acknowledge that any patient may express views, orally or in writing, to his GP who will then be aware of them. Open sharing of views between patient, doctors and nurses, and also relatives and other carers (with the patient's consent where this is possible) should be encouraged and any conclusions should be noted on the patient's records. See DOH Guide to Consent (11.1.1) and the BMA Guidance on Withholding and Withdrawing Life-Prolonging Medical Treatment.

11.3 POWERS OF THE COURT

Where medical treatment is carried out without the consent of the patient or other justification there may be a reference to a court.

11.3.1 Damages

The court may award damages in various ways:

- for the tort of trespass to the person, or assault and battery, where there has been physical contact (e.g. an operation or injection); such a claim may be brought without proof of damage;
- on a claim in negligence based upon a breach of the duty of care and damages arising from that breach; if treatment without consent goes wrong, liability may be absolute as the patient does not need to prove further breach of the duty of care, though damages must still be proved;
- in the private sector, on a claim for breach of contract.

11.3.2 Injunctions and declarations

The High Court may also grant a declaration relating to the proposed treatment, if necessary supported by an injunction. The declaration procedure enables the court to declare as 'not unlawful' actions that no one (including the court) has jurisdiction to authorise or an injunction may be obtained to prevent specific treatment if a hospital refuses to give an undertaking not to carry out that treatment. See *F* v. *West Berkshire Health Authority* [1989] 2 All ER 545 and *Airedale NHS Trust* v. *Bland* [1993] 2 WLR 316, HL.

The court will not order a doctor to adopt a course of treatment which, in his or her clinical opinion, is not in the best interests of the patient but reference to another doctor may be appropriate.

An emergency order can be applied for from the High Court without the need to issue and serve the relevant applications and evidence in support but must comply with procedural requirements (and pay fees) as soon as possible after the urgent hearing.

11.3.3 Criminal liability

A prosecution of the doctor will be appropriate in certain circumstances (e.g. for murder if he or she administers a fatal injection without any other medical benefits, although this may be reduced to attempted murder if there is no proof that the injection actually caused the death).

11.4 LIVING WILLS

Incurably ill and incapacitated people may be kept alive for long periods by medical treatment which, if they remained competent to make a decision, they might refuse thereby enabling death from natural causes. Can the individual anticipate this situation by expressing wishes in advance or delegating the right to make decisions to someone else by making a living will? Terminology in this area is not yet settled and the terms 'living will' and 'advance directive' are often used in the same context.

11.4.1 Types

In general a living will is a document whereby a person seeks to provide for the basis on which health care decisions that affect him are made if he becomes incompetent and so unable to participate in such decisions. There are two types.

Advance directive or declaration

This is a requirement (or request) that certain treatment should, or should not, be given in certain situations if the individual is not competent to consent to or refuse treatment at the time – any presumption of consent may thus be rebutted:

- 'Best interests' are no longer restricted to 'best medical interests' and it is now good medical practice to take into account the properly expressed wishes of the patient if relevant to the particular treatment decision.
- Recent cases make it clear that an advance directive may be legally binding though much will depend on its terms. See *Airedale NHS Trust* v. *Bland* [1993] 2 WLR 316, HL and *Re C (Adult: Refusal of Medical Treatment)* [1994] 1 All ER 819.
- The 'directive' is an attempt by the patient to state what must (or must not) be done whereas the 'declaration' is merely an expression of wishes.

Whilst refusal may be effective, any such document can no more require treatment to be given than the patient could have done if competent. Most directives are of the refusal type.

Durable power of attorney

A durable power of attorney attempts to delegate the power to make decisions about treatment to another person in the event that the individual becomes unable to make those decisions (also known as a health care proxy or medical treatment attorney). Do not assume that relatives would necessarily wish to take the responsibility for these decisions for which they may be emotionally unprepared. There are at present no lawful procedures whereby the power to consent to or refuse treatment may be delegated and legislation would be necessary to introduce this: see the draft Mental Incapacity Bill at **www.dca.gov.uk/menicap/meninc.pdf**.

11.4.2 Implications

The concept of a living will applies to all kinds of medical treatment but it is mostly adopted for decisions relating to treatment that affects the preservation of life, invariably for refusal of treatment. The patients involved tend to be those who would die without treatment (e.g. on life support systems) or depend upon 24-hour care without which they would die (e.g. irreversible dementia).

The following benefits are claimed for advance directives:

- reassure patients as to loss of autonomy and alleviate fears as to prolonged pain or total incapacity;
- assist doctors with ethical dilemmas over treatment and create increased medical awareness;
- reduce stress and distress amongst relatives;
- reduce arbitrary medical decisions and discourage over-intrusive treatment;
- promote greater dialogue between doctors, patients and carers regarding end-of-life decisions. See BMA Statement on Advance Directives (1992).

11.4.3 Legality

A patient cannot require a doctor to take a positive step which would cause death and any document which directs this is invalid. Any person who encourages its preparation might commit an offence, but there is nothing illegal about a document relating to medical decisions within the powers of the individual. A distinction must be drawn between the following, and only the first is illegal:

- treatment intended to cause death or which will merely result in death without any beneficial effect;
- treatment to ease suffering which may accelerate an otherwise inevitable death;
- withholding or withdrawing treatment which may prevent or delay death.

There are two main ethical views:

- the sanctity (or mere existence) of life must be preserved at all times.
- people should be allowed to die if they so choose.

The doctrine of 'double effect' is well established; it may be necessary to change from 'treatment for living' to 'treatment for dying' and the patient should have some input in this decision.

The Department of Constitutional Affairs published a draft Mental Incapacity Bill in June 2003 (see **www.dca.gov.uk/menicap/meninc.pdf**). It makes wide-ranging proposals in the area of mental incapacity generally. The proposals include the replacement of Enduring Powers of Attorney with Lasting Powers of Attorney, the scope of such documents being widened to include health care as well as financial matters. The Bill also sets out a statutory scheme to recognise refusals directives.

11.4.4 Precedents

Living will precedents are available from the Terence Higgins Trust, the Alzheimer's Society and other charities. Remember that definitions about treatment that are too precise or too vague may give rise to later problems.

11.4.5 Practical problems

There are many practical problems in the use of these documents which may need to be discussed with the client, including:

- How do you make it sufficiently specific to cover a particular situation without being so general that it is of doubtful validity? Does the client wish to address specific situations only or use a standard form?
- How do you ensure that it is drawn to the attention of a doctor when needed?
- How may it be revoked or amended if wishes change, especially if several copies have been distributed?
- Should it be expressed to be of limited duration and then be renewed at intervals?
- What is the name and address of the person to be contacted about its validity?
- Where it is to be kept or who is to keep it?

242

The aim should be to ensure that a copy is produced in the event that a serious medical treatment decision has to be made when the client is incompetent, but such documents may be overlooked or ignored in major accident treatment. It is no use depositing the document with the client's GP if it merely remains in the file at the surgery when the client is admitted to hospital. One solution is to prepare several copies (or originals) and for the doctor, next of kin (or partner) and your office all to retain one, in the hope that a copy will be produced in the event of need.

CHAPTER 12

Mental health legislation

Joanna Sulek

12.1 LEGISLATION

Relevant statutes are:

- Mental Health Act 1983 (as amended);
- Mental Health (Hospital, Guardianship and Consent to Treatment) Regulations 1983, SI 1983/893, 1996, SI 1996/540 and 1998, SI 1998/2624;
- Human Rights Act 1998;
- Mental Health (After-care under Supervision) Regulations 1996, SI 1996/294;
- Mental Health (Patients in the Community) (Transfers from Scotland) Regulations 1996, SI 1996/295;
- Mental Health Act 1983 (Remedial) Order 2001, SI 2001/3712.

12.1.1 Rules

The following rules govern the procedure to be adopted by the courts and tribunals that deal with proceedings under the mental health legislation:

- Civil Procedure Rules 1998, SI 1998/3132 (as amended) (see County Court Rules, 1981, SI 1981/1687, Order 49 r. 12 which is reproduced in Sched. 2);
- Mental Health Review Tribunal Rules 1983, SI 1983/942, 1996, SI 1996/314 and 1998, SI 1998/1189;
- Court of Protection Rules 2001, SI 2001/824 (as amended).

12.1.2 Scope

The 1983 Act applies to persons suffering from a mental disorder (called patients) and provides for:

- Part II: compulsory admission to and detention in hospital, etc.;
- Part IV: medical treatment in hospital without consent;
- Part V: review by a tribunal of detention and treatment;

- Part II: guardianship in the community;
- Part VII: management of property by Court of Protection (see Chapter 4);
- Part III: special treatment in criminal proceedings (see Chapter 5).

Older people may suffer from mental disorder bringing them within the scope of the legislation and allowing assessment for compulsory admission and treatment in hospital or application to the Court of Protection. These disorders include Alzheimer's disease, depression and other forms of dementia.

12.2 GUIDANCE, CIRCULARS AND PRACTICE NOTES

Numerous documents provide guidance on the application of the legislation including:

- Code of Practice to the Mental Health Act;
- *Guidance on Supervised Discharge and Related Provisions* (HSG (96) 11);
- *Consent to Treatment* (DHSS No. DDL (84) 4; HC 1999/031, HC (90) 22);
- *The Care Programme Approach* (HC (90) 23/LASSL (90) 11);
- *Guidance on the Discharge of Mentally Disordered People and their Continuing Care in the Community* (HSG (94) 27/LASSL (94) 4);
- *Aftercare Services under the Mental Health Act 1983* (LAC (2000) 3);
- Mental Health Act Commission publications (see the Biennial Reports).

The following topics have been covered by practice notes:

- administration of clozapine;
- administration of medicine;
- Mental Health Act 1983, s.5(2) and transfers;
- Mental Health Act 1983, ss.17, 18;
- issues relating to the administration of the Mental Health Act 1983 in mental nursing homes registered to receive detained patients;
- treatment of anorexia nervosa under the Mental Health Act 1983;
- General Practitioners and the Mental Health Act 1983;
- responsible medical officers.

12.3 DEFINITIONS

Most definitions are found in Part I, s.1 of the 1983 Act:

- *Mental illness*: this term is not defined though it is more likely to afflict older people than other forms of mental disorder. These words 'should be construed in the way that ordinary sensible people would construe them': *W* v. *L* [1973] 3 All ER 884.

- *Mental disorder*: defined as 'mental illness, arrested or incomplete development of mind, psychopathic disorder and any other disorder or disability of mind' ('mentally disordered' is construed accordingly).
- *Severe mental impairment*: defined as 'a state of arrested or incomplete development of mind which includes severe impairment of intelligence and social functioning and is associated with abnormally aggressive or seriously irresponsible conduct on the part of the person concerned'. Mental impairment is the same as severe mental impairment but with 'significant' substituted for 'severe'.
- *Psychopathic disorder*: defined as 'a persistent disorder or disability of mind (whether or not including significant impairment of intelligence) which results in abnormally aggressive or seriously irresponsible conduct on the part of the person concerned'.
- *Medical treatment*: defined as including nursing and care, habilitation and rehabilitation under medical supervision (s.145(1)).

12.4   NEAREST RELATIVE

12.4.1   Powers and functions

The nearest relative is appointed under s.26 of the 1983 Act and has the following powers and functions in respect of the patient, namely to:

- request an assessment with a view to admission to hospital, or be informed about an application for admission for assessment;
- apply, or object to an application, for admission to hospital for treatment or for guardianship;
- be informed about discharge from section and be consulted about a supervised discharge application;
- request discharge to hospital managers and apply to a Mental Health Review Tribunal.

12.5   WHO IS THE NEAREST RELATIVE?

In relation to a patient the nearest relative will normally be the husband or wife, son or daughter, father or mother, brother or sister, grandparent, grandchild, uncle or aunt, nephew or niece. The elder of relatives in a class takes precedence and whole blood equates to half-blood but the former take precedence.

Living together as husband and wife for six months is sufficient. (This includes same sex partners: see *R* v. *Liverpool City Council and the Secretary of State, ex parte SSG* [2002] 5 CCLR 639). A relative who ordinarily resides with or cares for the patient will take precedence, and this may apply to a non-relative after five years.

Certain persons are excluded, namely a separated spouse, a person under 18 (unless a spouse) and a person not ordinarily resident in the United Kingdom.

A nearest relative may be displaced on application to the county court if he cannot be found, is incapable of acting, or objects unreasonably to an application for treatment or guardianship. The patient (who may have mental capacity) cannot nominate a nearest relative and has no status in court proceedings to displace the person nominated by law. This has been held to be incompatible with the European Convention on Human Rights (*JT* v. *United Kingdom* (Application 26494/95), *The Times*, 5 April 2000 and *R* v. *Secretary of State for Health, ex parte M*, *The Times*, 25 April 2003).

The nearest relative will not always be the next of kin and may be replaced.

12.6   APPROVED SOCIAL WORKERS

Approved social workers (ASWs) are appointed by social services authorities pursuant to s.114 of the 1983 Act and are approved as having appropriate competence to deal with persons suffering from mental disorder. They have various statutory duties and powers over persons believed to be suffering from a mental disorder. It can be an offence to obstruct them in the performance of their duties: see s.114, s.129 and DHSS Circular LAC 86/15.

12.7   CODE OF PRACTICE

Under s.118(4) of the 1983 Act, a Code of Practice has been prepared by the Department of Health and the Welsh Office (this role now comes under the Welsh Assembly). The Code offers guidance on how the Act should be implemented. It is updated periodically, most recently in 1999.

The Code is primarily aimed at the needs, rights and entitlements of mentally disordered persons who are detained but may be referred to as a good practice document for the care and management of informal patients. It deals with matters such as assessment prior to admission, admission to hospital or guardianship, treatment and care in hospital and leaving hospital.

The Code lays down the principles that patients should:

- receive respect for and consideration of individual qualities and diverse backgrounds (social, cultural, ethnic and religious);
- have their needs taken fully into account within the limits of available resources;

- receive any necessary treatment or care in the least controlled/segregated facilities compatible with ensuring their own health or safety or the safety of other people;
- be treated or cared for in a way that promotes self-determination and personal responsibility;
- be discharged from any order as soon as its application is no longer justified.

The Code does not have the same force as statute, but the Court of Appeal confirmed in 2003 that it must be followed unless departing from it can be justified in an individual case (see *R* v. *Mersey Care NHS Trust, ex parte Munjaz* and *R* v. *Airedale NHS Trust, ex parte S, The Times*, 25 July 2003).

12.8   ADMISSION TO HOSPITAL

12.8.1   General

Admissions may be on a voluntary, informal or compulsory basis. A voluntary admission is where the patient consents (and is capable of doing so) and admissions should be voluntary whenever possible. An informal admission arises where the patient is compliant but incapable of consenting. It relies upon the common law doctrine of necessity and is authorised under s.131(1) of the 1983 Act. The safeguards under the Act are not available: see *R* v. *Bournewood Community and Mental Health NHS Trust, ex parte L, The Times*, 30 June 1998, HL (see later for proposed law reforms).

A compulsory admission is pursuant to a statutory power, often referred to as being 'under section'. There are several statutory powers and various safeguards (see below).

12.8.2   Statutory powers

The different statutory powers are used in the following circumstances.

Section 2 for assessment

The patient is suffering from mental disorder of a nature or degree which warrants detention in hospital for assessment and it is in the interests of the patient's health or safety or for the protection of others:

- two medical recommendations are necessary;
- detention can be for up to 28 days but cannot be renewed;
- there is a right to apply to a Mental Health Review Tribunal.

Section 3 for treatment

The patient is suffering from a specific mental disorder and it is of a nature or degree which makes it appropriate to receive medical treatment in hospital and necessary for the health or safety of the patient or protection of others:

- two medical recommendations are required;
- detention can be for up to six months in the first instance, renewable for another six months and then one year at a time;
- there is a right to apply to a Mental Health Review Tribunal.

Section 4 for assessment in emergency

The patient is admitted on the grounds set out in s.2 but on the recommendation of one doctor in case of urgent necessity on a diagnosis of mental disorder:

- application is made by an ASW or nearest relative;
- detention can be for up to 72 hours but convertible to a s.2 detention on a second medical recommendation.

Section 5 for short-term detention for those already in mental hospitals

A hospital in-patient may be detained by the treating doctor or by a nurse for short periods in certain circumstances. Powers of compulsion are used infrequently in the treatment and care of older people.

12.8.3 Medical treatment

The 1983 Act contains powers for medical treatment to be given to a detained patient without his consent in certain closely defined circumstances, but apart from this normal common law principles apply (see Chapter 11):

- treatment for 'general medical or surgical' conditions cannot be given under the provisions of the Act but can be given under the common law;
- if the patient lacks capacity treatment not given under the Act can be given if it is in the patient's best interests.

Detention under the Act does not mean that a patient lacks capacity to consent to general medical treatment or that consent should not be sought.

Treatment for mental disorder

A patient who is detained under the treatment sections of the 1983 Act (i.e. ss.2, 3, 36, 37, 38, 46, 47 and 48) can be given 'medical treatment for a mental disorder' without his consent. If detained under the 'short-term' sections or subject to supervised discharge or guardianship, medical treatment cannot be given for a mental disorder without his consent.

There are 'safeguards' whereby particular treatments require the consent of the patient and/or a second medical opinion, with regular reviews of such treatment (see Part IV of the 1983 Act). There are special provisions for urgent treatment (see s.62).

12.8.4 Implications of detention

For the implications of admission under section refer to the books listed in Appendix F.

There is concern about the number of older people in NHS hospitals and nursing homes who do not have capacity to consent to admission or treatment but who are not formally detained. These patients do not have the 'safeguards' of the mental health legislation which include application to tribunal, attention of the Mental Health Act Commission, right to a second opinion about medication and regular renewal of their stay in hospital. Sectioning them under the Act is perceived as stigmatising and something that is best avoided.

Reform of the Mental Health Act 1983 is seen as necessary since it has been recognised that informal patients (of which there are many) do not have the safeguards provided under the Act to compulsory patients. Proposed legislation would address this anomaly (see the draft Mental Health Bill 2002).

12.9 COMMUNITY POWERS

12.9.1 Power to inspect

An ASW may enter and inspect premises in the area of the local social services authority in which a mentally disordered person is living if he has reasonable cause to believe that the patient is not under proper care (s.115). There is no power to force entry, restrain or remove the patient.

12.9.2 Removal to a place of safety

A constable has power to remove to a place of safety with a view to early examination, assessment and treatment a person believed to be suffering from a mental disorder who is:

- ill-treated, neglected or not kept under proper control or unable to care for himself and living alone (s.135); this must be under a warrant issued by a magistrate and the constable must be accompanied by an ASW and a registered medical practitioner;

- in a public place in immediate need of care or control and this is necessary in the interests of the person or the protection of others (s.136).

A magistrates' court has power to authorise removal of a person in need of care and attention to suitable premises (National Assistance Act 1948, s.47).

12.9.3 Statutory guardianship

A limited form of adult guardianship is available under s.8 of the 1983 Act. This is used far less frequently than detention in hospital, although its use has increased in recent years. It enables the establishment of an authoritative framework for working with a patient with a minimum of constraint to achieve as independent a life as possible within the community, but must be part of the patient's overall care and treatment plan (Code of Practice, para. 13.4).

A patient may be received into guardianship provided he suffers from one of the four specific categories of mental disorder and that both the following apply:

- this is of a nature or degree which warrants guardianship;
- it is necessary for the welfare of the patient or the protection of others.

Appointment

Guardianship initially lasts for six months but may be renewed for a further six months and thereafter annually. Application is made to the social services department by an ASW or the patient's nearest relative, in each case supported by two doctors. The nearest relative can object or subsequently discharge the patient. There is a right of appeal to a Mental Health Review Tribunal.

Who is appointed?

The guardian may be either the social services department or a private individual with the approval of the local authority, but a private guardian has duties which relate to notification of the local authority and appointment of a medical practitioner.

Powers

The guardian has very limited powers in respect of the patient but may require:

- that the patient resides at a specific place (but not with a specific person);

- that the patient attends at places and times specified for the purpose of medical treatment, occupation, education or training;
- access to the patient to be given at the patient's residence to any medical practitioner, ASW or other person specified.

The guardian has no power to detain the patient and cannot restrict his movements but can only insist that the patient ordinarily resides at the place specified and return the patient to that place if appropriate. He cannot authorise or require physical removal of an unwilling patient, or authorise medical treatment (the treatment provisions of the Act do not apply). He has no power over the money and property of the patient. However, the ability to use even limited powers when everyone else is powerless can be valuable and the guardian may adopt a dominant role (which may be all that is needed).

It is an offence to ill-treat or wilfully neglect a person subject to guardianship.

12.9.4 After-care

There is a specific duty on the health and social services authorities in co-operation with voluntary organisations to provide 'after-care services' for persons who have been detained under the treatment sections of the Act (s.117). It arises prior to the discharge if that can only take place when the arrangements are in hand and continues until the after-care authorities are satisfied that the person is no longer in need of such services.

The patient has a right to a community care assessment (see Chapter 8) and services provided under this section (including residential care) may not be charged for (*R* v. *Manchester City Council, ex parte Stennett and others* [2002] 4 All ER 124). See also the Local Government Ombudsmen's Special Report, *Advice and Guidance on the Funding of Aftercare under Section 117 of the Mental Health Act 1983* (available at www.lgo.org.uk/special-reports.htm).

Consideration may be given to guardianship if there is concern about risk of harm to the person or to others. A 'care plan' should be established in accordance with the Code of Practice and other guidance. This is often referred to as 'the Care Programme Approach' ('the CPA').

12.9.5 After-care under supervision

There may be discharge from hospital under supervision pursuant to provisions introduced in April 1996 (ss.25A to 25J of the 1983 Act inserted by the Mental Health (Patients in the Community) Act 1995).

Application

A supervision application may be made by the responsible medical officer caring for the patient in hospital. There are procedures that must be complied with and strict criteria as to the patients to whom this procedure may apply. The supervision order lasts for six months and is renewable for a period of six months and for periods of one year thereafter.

Implications

Supervision of after-care and monitoring of the care plan will be by a named supervisor (a community nurse, a social worker or other appropriate community worker). There is no power to treat the patient in the community without his consent, but the supervisor can as a last resort 'take and convey' the patient to hospital using force if necessary for the purposes of receiving treatment although the consent of the patient is then required for treatment to be given.

The responsible after-care bodies can impose requirements to ensure that after-care services are received by the patient, e.g. that:

- the patient resides at a specified place;
- the patient attends at a specified place and times for medical treatment, occupation, education or training;
- access be given by the patient at any place where the patient is residing to the supervisors, the RMO, ASW or other authorised person

See *Guidance on Supervised Discharge Related Provisions* (HSG (96) 11).

12.10   REVIEW AND APPEAL

12.10.1   Discharge

Detention or guardianship ceases if a written order for discharge is made (s.23). The order in respect of a hospital patient detained under s.2 or s.3 may be made by the responsible medical officer (RMO), the managers or nearest relative of the patient (and in respect of guardianship also by the responsible social services authority).

A nearest relative wishing to take the initiative must give at least 72 hours' notice in writing to the hospital managers. The RMO may within that time report to the managers that in his opinion the patient, if discharged, would be likely to act in a manner dangerous to himself or to some other person. If such report is made the discharge by the nearest relative will be of no effect but a similar order cannot be made within the next six months.

12.10.2   Mental Health Review Tribunal

A Mental Health Review Tribunal is an independent tribunal comprising a lawyer, psychiatrist and lay member, governed by the Council on Tribunals

and administered regionally by the Department of Health. Specific provisions and time limits are found in s.66 of the 1983 Act.

Reference to the tribunal

Under ss.16, 20, 25, 29 and 68 cases are referred to the tribunal by:

- patients detained under s.2 or s.3 or received into guardianship;
- hospital managers where a detained patient has not applied for a tribunal
  hearing within six months;
- the Secretary of State for a patient liable to be detained or subject to
  guardianship;
- a nearest relative where the patient demands discharge and the responsible
  medical officer bars this. A county court order directs that the functions of
  the nearest relative be carried out by an acting nearest relative.

The tribunal may discharge the patient, decline to do so, or may make
certain other orders (s.72).

Representation by lawyers is encouraged and is available free of charge
from lawyers experienced in these cases who have a public funded (legal aid)
contract with the Legal Services Commission. Contact the Professional
Competence Team, Education and Training Unit, Law Society, Ipsley Court,
Berrington Close, Redditch, Worcs B98 0TD; or visit the Community Legal
Service website at **www.justask.org.uk** (search under 'mental health' and
'specialist help').

12.10.3   Mental Health Act Commission

The Mental Health Act Commission is a Special Health Authority regulated
by the Mental Health Act Commission Regulations 1983, SI 1983/894, which
consists of a chairman, a vice-chairman, some 172 part-time Commissioners
and a Chief Executive.

The Commission publishes biennial reports of its work and protects the
interests of detained (i.e. compulsorily admitted) patients by:

- regularly visiting those hospitals and mental nursing homes with detained
  patients;
- reviewing their care and treatment, and investigating complaints made by
  them or on their behalf;
- appointing doctors to review treatment under Part IV of the 1983 Act;
- reviewing decisions to withhold postal packets.

It is a matter of concern that the Commission has no jurisdiction over
incompetent patients who are not compulsorily admitted (informal patients).

PART C

Finance and benefits

CHAPTER 13

Social security benefits

Jennifer Margrave

13.1 SOCIAL SECURITY SYSTEM

13.1.1 Sources of law

The relevant enabling statutory provisions are:

- Social Security Administration Act 1992;
- Social Security Contributions and Benefits Act 1992;
- Social Security (Incapacity for Work) Act 1994;
- Jobseekers Act 1995;
- Social Security Act 1998.

Regulations

Regulations are made under powers granted by the legislation, which provide detailed law as to entitlement to particular benefits, such as the Social Security (Widow's Benefit and Retirement Pensions) Regulations 1979, SI 1979/642 and the Income Support (General) Regulations 1987, SI 1987/1967. Some regulations specify procedure, in particular the Social Security (Claims and Payments) Regulations 1979, SI 1979/628 and 1987, SI 1987/1968, Social Security (Adjudication) Regulations 1995, SI 1995/1801, Social Security (Payments on Account, Overpayments and Recovery) Regulations 1988, SI 1988/664 and the Social Security (Decisions and Appeal) Regulations 1999, SI 1999/991.

Commissioners' decisions

Decisions of the Commissioners on appeal from tribunals are sources of law with significant decisions being published. The reference indicates the type of benefit, number of decision and year i.e. R(IS)1/98 is the first reported income support decision of 1998; an unreported income support decision might be referred to as CIS 13/98. Further appeals to the courts may be found in the law reports.

13.1.2 Administration

In 1991 the Benefits Agency took over the administration of most benefits from the DSS and the Contributions Agency took over NI contributions. Some benefits are dealt with at local offices but others in a single location (e.g. disability living allowance in Blackpool). Income support is handled by local offices but attendance allowance by regional centres.

In 1994 the War Pensions Agency took over the assessment of war pensions and the welfare service for war pensioners. This is now an Executive Agency called the Veterans Agency and is based at Blackpool.

In June 2001, the Department for Work and Pensions (DWP) was formed from the Department of Social Security and the former Department of Education and Employment as the government department responsible for state pensions and benefits. The Benefits Agency and Employment Service were replaced by the Pensions Service (PS) (which is responsible for pensions and benefits for older people) and the Disability and Carers Directorate (DCD).

A Customer Charter sets out the standards of service which all customers can reasonably expect from the Pensions Service, how customers can help the PS to help them and what they can do if things go wrong.

Significant changes in the decision-making and appeals process were made by the Social Security Act 1998 and regulations under the Act. Decisions on benefit claims are now made by the Secretary of State acting through authorised officers rather than by independent adjudication officers. Appeals are made to special tribunals (see 13.4).

13.1.3 Different countries

The same social security system covers Great Britain with some variations. A claimant living elsewhere in the European Union may qualify for benefits under the basic rules about going abroad or under EU rules but note that some benefits such as attendance allowance is not payable if a person in receipt of it moves *permanently* abroad.

13.1.4 Information

Practical information about benefits and claims is readily available: an invaluable series of free leaflets (available in other languages, Braille and large print) can be collected from local DWP offices and most post offices: GL23: *Social Security Benefit Rates*; MG1: *A Guide to Benefits*; RM1: *Retirement* and SD1: *Sick or disabled* (see **www.dwp.gov.uk/publications**) are a good starting point.

Advisers can keep up-to-date with welfare benefits information by joining the DWP's Publicity Register. The benefits of joining include a quarterly newsletter (*Touchbase*), a catalogue of leaflets, posters, and information: The Publicity Register, Freepost, NWW 1853, Manchester M2 9LU. Tel: 0845 602 4444, fax: 0870 241 2634, email: Publicity-Register@dwp.gsi.gov.uk.

For general benefit advice enquiries, contact the local DWP office by looking in the local telephone directory (Business Section) under 'Benefits Agency' or 'DWP'. In addition use the free Benefit Enquiry Line (BEL) for people with disabilities: 0800 88 22 00.

Rights membership of Child Poverty Action Group brings an annual selection of invaluable books and material: see address in Appendix E. There are now a number of informative Internet sites (with links to other sites), see Appendix E.

Reference may be also be made to the books mentioned in Appendix F, including:

- *Benefits Information Guide*, HMSO (revised annually);
- *Your Rights: A Guide to Money Benefits for Older People*, published annually by Age Concern (this is inexpensive and could be handed to clients);
- Age Concern Fact Sheets deal with particular benefits.

In the event of an appeal the relevant statutes, regulations and Commissioners' decisions should be referred to as the leaflets may have misled the client or matters of interpretation may arise. Up-to-date annotated statutory material is available at a moderate price (see Appendix F).

Similarly, when a dispute arises the leaflets issued by the DWP should not be treated as authoritative and reference should be made to the original statutory material and court or Commissioners' decisions.

13.2 TYPES OF BENEFITS

13.2.1 Weekly benefits

Weekly cash benefits are paid to meet different needs, but rates change yearly and the qualifying criteria are constantly amended. A claimant may not receive two overlapping benefits and it is important to claim the one that pays the highest rate.

Useful information can be found in:

- GL23: *Social Security Benefit Rates*;
- MG1: *A Guide to Benefits*;
- Age Concern Fact Sheet 18: *A Brief Guide to Money Benefits*;
- Help the Aged leaflets on pensions and benefits.

Contributory benefits

Contributory benefits depend upon NI contributions paid during a normal working life but people resident in Great Britain are entitled regardless of personal means. Most are taxable and all are taken into account when claiming means-tested benefits. Those claimable by an older person are:

- incapacity benefit (ICB) (formerly sickness benefit and invalidity benefit) is payable if working and up to age 70 for men and 65 for women. See leaflet SD1: *Sick or Disabled.*
- retirement pension, over 80s pension and widow's benefits. See Chapter 17 at 17.2 and: RM1: *Retirement*; NP46: *A Guide to Retirement Pensions*; NP45: *A Guide to Widow's Benefits*; Age Concern Fact Sheet 19: *The State Pension*; and Help the Aged leaflet on pensions.

Non-contributory benefits

There is no need to have paid NI contributions to qualify for non-contributory benefits and people resident in Great Britain are entitled regardless of personal means. There may be additions for dependants, but some benefits cannot overlap. Some are non-taxable and/or not taken into account for means-tested benefits. Many benefits awarded on disability are passports to other benefits and concessions.

See the following:

- HB5: *A Guide to Non-Contributory Benefits for Disabled People and their Carers*;
- SD1: *Sick or Disabled*;
- SD2: *Sick or Disabled and Unable to Work*;
- DS704: *Disability Living Allowance – You Could Benefit.*

Possible claims by an older person may be for the following:

- *Attendance allowance* (AA). This is available where disability begins at or after 65, and special rules and rates may apply for those terminally ill. There are two rates (higher rate for those needing supervision day and night) and it is tax free and non-contributory. See claim pack DS702: *Attendance Allowance.*
- *Disability living allowance* (DLA). This is available where disability begins before 65 but must be claimed before the 66th birthday and special rules may apply for those terminally ill. It is split into a care component at three levels and mobility component at two levels. See leaflets DLA1, DLA2.
- *Severe disablement allowance* (SDA). This is payable up to age 65 only and for those who do not satisfy contribution conditions for incapacity benefit. See leaflet SD1: *Sick or Disabled.*

- *Invalid care allowance* (ICA). This is paid to a carer in receipt of AA or DLA care component (upper rates) up to age 65 only and earning less than a specified sum (note the qualifying hours to obtain this benefit). It is taxable but provides class I NI contributions credits. See leaflet SD4: *Caring for Someone* and CAR2: *Important Information for Carers, Changes to Help Available*.
- *Industrial disablement benefit*. This is paid to those who became ill or disabled as a result of work for an employer. See leaflets GL27: *Compensation and Social Security Benefits* and SD6: *Ill or Disabled Because of a Disease or Deafness Caused by Work*.

In appropriate circumstances disability working allowance and guardians allowance (where a minor child is cared for) may also be claimable.

Means-tested benefits

These are weekly income supplements to which GB residents may be entitled whether or not they have paid NI contributions. They are assessed on the needs of a family living in the same household which includes the claimant and any partner with whom he or she is living 'as man and wife'. Either partner may claim and they may be non-taxable:

- pension credit brings the income up to a minimum level (see 13.2.2);
- family credit is only claimable by an older person if there is a dependent child. An award is made for a six-month period and the assessment rules are complex so not dealt with here.

See Age Concern Fact Sheet 16: *Income Related Benefits: Income and Capital*.

Winter fuel payment

A non-taxable winter fuel payment is paid to those receiving one or more qualifying benefits but each claimant is only entitled to one such payment. To qualify you have to be aged 60 or over and getting a social security benefit in the qualifying week (usually the third week in September).

13.2.2 Pension credit

Pension credit, introduced from 6 October 2003, is designed to provide pensioners with a minimum level of income but for the first time a new concept has been introduced; it will also reward those who have managed to save a little during their working life, up to a certain limit. There are two main parts: the guarantee credit and the savings credit.

It is designed to bring the claimant's income from all sources up to a certain figure, which is likely to change each year. Those over 65 will be credited with a small extra weekly sum. The calculation involves a complicated formula based on income and notional income from capital. Claimants in receipt of minimum income guarantee before October 2003 automatically receive pension credit. For the sake of clarification any references to means-tested benefit that was formerly income support or minimum income guarantee, and is now pension credit, will be referred to as 'PC'.

The government have set up a phone system (tel. 0800 99 1234) where application forms can be completed by officers and sent out to the applicant for checking and signing. Further information is available in:

- *Pension Credit: Pick it up. It's Yours*;
- PC025: *Pension Credit Support Pack* (which can be obtained by calling 0845 606 5065);
- Age Concern Fact Sheet 48: *Pension Credit*;
- Help the Aged publications.

13.2.3 The social fund

Lump sums are available to meet needs in accordance with directions given or guidance issued by the Secretary of State (refer to the *Social Fund Manual* for the policy). Regard must be had to a statutory list of factors and directions to be followed but the guidance is persuasive:

- means-testing is on the PC basis;
- payments are rationed on the basis of annual allocations for each office divided between loans and grants;
- review is by Social Fund Inspectors but there is no appeal to a tribunal.

Also see:

- GL18: *Help from the Social*;
- SB16: *A Guide to the Social Fund*;
- Age Concern Fact Sheet 48: *Pension Credit*.

If you receive this means tested benefit you may be able to access the following grants and loans.

Community care grants

Non-repayable discretionary grants are available to help people stay in the community rather than residential care and also to help people move out of institutional care into the community or to meet certain travel expenses. They are targeted at priority situations, groups and items. Any capital over £1,000 will reduce the amount if the claimant is over the age of 60.

Funeral payments may help with the cost of a funeral (also available to those receiving housing or council tax benefit).

Loans

Budgeting loans assist in meeting important intermittent expenses for which it is difficult for those receiving PC to budget. There are maximum and minimum amounts:

- the maximum takes into account any outstanding balance of previous loans;
- any capital over £1,000 will reduce the amount;
- it may not exceed £1,000 or the amount which the applicant can afford to repay;
- there is a list of items divided into high, medium and low priority.

Crisis loans assist a person in an emergency or following a disaster but may need to be the only means by which serious damage or risk to the health or safety of the claimant or a family member may be prevented. Various types of claimant are excluded, such as people in 'Part III accommodation' (see Chapter 8) and people in a nursing home or hospital. Any available resources will be taken into account including credit facilities.

Loans are interest free but recovery is normally by deduction from subsequent income support or other benefits of the applicant or a partner.

Cold weather payments

Payments are sent automatically to those on PC getting a pensioner or disability premium during periods of cold weather (as defined) and unlike the other grants and loans these are not discretionary.

13.3   PROCEDURE

13.3.1   Claims

A properly completed form (obtained from the local DWP office) must reach the appropriate DWP office in order for a claim to be validly made.

The claim may be amended or withdrawn before a decision is made but further information may be required in support of the claim. The claim may be treated as having been made on the date of receipt of a letter asking about the benefit if the form sent out in response is returned within a month. If the form is sent back because it is not properly completed but returned duly completed within a month, the claim is treated as made when first submitted.

Professional persons who claim benefits on behalf of elderly persons should make clear to the PS or DCD the capacity in which they act and the limit of their experience.

Backdating

Most benefits are paid from the date of claim and there are strict time limits on backdating. The maximum period for which any benefit can be backdated is three months and some benefits (e.g. retirement pension) will be automatically backdated this period. Others (e.g. PC) can only be backdated in prescribed circumstances (e.g. the claimant was caring for an invalid and could not obtain assistance from another person to make the claim). It may be possible to get round this but the rules have been tightened up. There are however special rules, which may apply (e.g. disability benefit claims for the terminally ill).

For agents and appointees generally see Chapter 4.

13.3.2 Decisions

The claim is now decided by the Secretary of State (in practice by his authorised representative). Payments of benefit are also controlled in certain ways:

- a claimant may not receive two overlapping benefits but receives the higher (Social Security (Overlapping Benefits) Regulations 1979, SI 1979/597);
- benefits providing for different purposes can be claimed simultaneously;
- changes in circumstances that may affect entitlement must be reported and a list will be found in the order book unless benefit is credited direct to an account, in which case the list is sent yearly;
- a claimant may have non-means-tested benefits such as attendance allowance reduced or withdrawn whilst in hospital but since April 2003 a person's retirement pension is not withdrawn after a period in hospital. See leaflet GL12: *Going into Hospital*.

Revision and supersession

The Secretary of State may revise a decision of his own initiative or on an application within one month of notification. A decision (whether or not on appeal) may be superseded by the Secretary of State of his own initiative or on an application outside the one-month period. In some circumstances this may be backdated to the original decision if this is advantageous to the claimant.

Suspension

The Secretary of State may suspend payment of benefit in certain circumstances (e.g. for failure to provide information or if an appeal is pending against a decision in a 'lead case').

13.3.3   Payment

Benefits have traditionally been paid weekly by order book or giro cheque and cashed at a post office, some in arrears and others in advance. This is being phased out and, as from April 2003 benefits can only be obtained via a bank account. Special arrangements have been made with the Post Office to ensure that those who wish to receive their payments in cash can still do so by way of either a bank account with the Post Office or a plastic card and pin number system. Payment may be direct into the account of the spouse or other person acting on behalf of the claimant, and this may be helpful to older people. Where practitioners are acting on behalf of a client the benefits should be paid direct into the client's bank account on a monthly basis, especially if the client is going into a care home.

See leaflet AC1: *Have Your Pension Paid Straight to Your Bank or Building Society Account.*

Delegation

There are procedures for authorising others to collect benefit:

- an agent may be nominated by the claimant using the form of authority printed on the allowance order slip – the agent accounts to the claimant;
- an appointee may be appointed when the claimant is unable to act through mental or physical disability – the agent collects and spends the benefit for the claimant.

Those acting as appointees should be advised of the personal liability that can attach to this role (see generally Chapter 4).

Overpayments

An overpayment of benefit may be recovered where any person whether fraudulently or otherwise misrepresents, or fails to disclose, any material fact and this results in the overpayment:

- the original decision (either to pay benefit or determining the amount of benefit) must first be revised;
- a misrepresentation can be wholly innocent and a failure to disclose may be the result of forgetfulness but knowledge of the material fact by the person who fails to disclose it must be established;

- the disclosure need not be in writing but must be made in such a manner that it is likely to be brought to the attention of the office handling the claim and if it appears that it has not been further disclosure may be required;
- the claimant is expected to have read the information in the back of the order book or in any leaflets forwarded with payment, and these may indicate the changes of circumstances which affect the benefit and should be disclosed;
- overpayment calculations tend to be complicated because of the need to take into account the claimant's position, as it would have been if the overpayment had not been made: the 'diminishing capital rule';
- overpayments may be recovered from the claimant (or the appointee) or the estate of a deceased claimant in cases of misrepresentation or failure to disclose.

Underpayments

Claimants are entitled to compensation if they are underpaid benefit of £50 or more resulting from clear and unambiguous error by the DWP and the delay in payment was more than 12 months:

- there is no leaflet or claim form, but the DSS 'now the DWP' Administrative Code instructs local offices to consider *ex gratia* payments in such cases (the onus is on the claimant to raise the issue with the office dealing with the claim);
- the benefit itself may also be backdated.

13.4   APPEALS

Appeals against a refusal of benefit or the amount awarded are dealt with by independent local tribunals with further appeal to the Social Security Commissioners on a point of law. Legal aid is not available but assistance and advice under Claim 10 may be available (previously 'Green Form'). Considering the amount of money that may be in issue it is surprising that solicitors are so seldom instructed in appeals. Many claimants deal with their own appeals and most representatives come from CABs or are welfare benefits advisers. A word of caution: advocacy is not enough and advisers need a detailed knowledge of the regulations and procedures as well as current Commissioners' decisions. All this is available from the books listed in Appendix F but membership of Child Poverty Action Group helps to keep one up to date. See leaflet NI260DMA: *A Guide to Dispute, Supersession and Appeals.*

13.4.1 Tribunals

Most readers will have been aware of the Independent Tribunal Service (ITS) and its range of tribunals including the Social Security Appeal Tribunal (SSAT), Disability Appeal Tribunal (DAT), Medical Appeal Tribunal (MAT), Vaccine Damage Tribunal (VDT) and Child Support Appeal Tribunal (CSAT). These have been replaced with effect from April 2000 by the Appeals Service (TAS) which consists of two separate bodies. The first is a tribunal with responsibility for the judicial functioning of appeals tribunals which is headed by a President and the second is an agency of the DWP headed by a Chief Executive with responsibility for the administration of appeals. The Chief Executive is accountable to the Secretary of State.

The new unified Appeals Service is organised (as previously) in regions under a regional chairman. District chairmen and panel members (some of whom including all full-time chairmen are legally qualified (LQPM)) are appointed by the Lord Chancellor. There are a number of differently constituted tribunals but each includes a LQPM and is attended by a full-time clerk. Some tribunals comprise only the LQPM rather than a chairman and two lay members. Many hearings are dealt with 'on paper' without the attendance of the appellant.

Procedure

An appeal is made to the local DWP office within one month of notification of the decision, but if this does not include a statement of reasons one may be requested within one month and the time limit is then six weeks. The time limit may be extended up to one year.

The procedure is then quite strict:

- the appeal must be in writing, signed by the appellant or an authorised representative, and state the grounds on which it is made;
- submissions will be sent out by the relevant DWP office with a form directing the appellant to opt for an oral or paper hearing;
- if the form is not returned within 14 days a clerk may strike out the appeal (it can be reinstated on request within one month if there are reasonable grounds);
- withdrawal of an appeal no longer requires leave or consent and there is power to strike out an appeal where it has no chance of success.

Appeals should be lodged in time if possible.

The hearing

If the appellant requests an oral hearing this takes place before a tribunal in the area in which the appellant resides:

269

- Fourteen days notice must be given to the appellant or representative (not both) and the tribunal can proceed in the absence of the appellant.
- Hearings are informal and should be attended by the appellant if possible. The procedure is in the chairman's discretion but the rules of natural justice apply. Expenses may be paid for attending (but not for legal representatives).
- The chairman must make a record of an oral hearing.
- Appellants should request an oral hearing and attend, especially where there is a dispute as to the facts.

The decision

The decision may be unanimous or by majority and a summary written decision is usually handed out at the end of the hearing:

- A full statement may be requested within one month of receiving the summary decision.
- The decision may be set aside at the discretion of a chairman if a relevant document was not received or a party or representative was not present or if the chairman or both parties consider that it is wrong (rather than have a hearing before the Commissioners).
- An application for leave to appeal to a Commissioner must be made within one month of receipt of a full statement (there is a discretion to extend this period to 13 months).

13.4.2   Social Security Commissioners

Commissioners hear appeals from tribunals on points of law only, but this includes cases where the decision was based on a mistaken interpretation of the law; inadequate reasons and/or findings of fact were recorded so that it is unclear how or why the decision was arrived at; the decision is not supported by any or any sufficient evidence and is therefore perverse, or there was a breach of the rules of natural justice.

The process normally takes many months and most appeals are dealt with on written representations. The appellant can ask for an oral hearing. This is not always granted but a written decision is ultimately sent to the parties. The Commissioners may make the final decision (if the tribunal determined all the material facts) or send the case back to a tribunal with directions as to how it should be dealt with.

13.4.3   Courts

There is a further right of appeal to the Court of Appeal and this will be on a question of law. Leave to appeal must be obtained from the Commissioner within three months or, if refused, from the Court of Appeal. After the

House of Lords the ultimate right of appeal is to the European Court of Human Rights but issues may be referred there at an earlier stage.

Legal aid is available for the first time at this stage, subject to means.

Judicial review

An application may be made to the High Court for judicial review but this will be refused if another remedy is available (e.g. the normal appeal process). Excessive delay by the DWP in carrying out its statutory duties may justify application. Some benefit decisions are taken by the Secretary of State without a right of appeal so there is scope for judicial review if he exercises his powers improperly.

European Court of Justice

Any issue of European Community law arising before a national court concerning questions of interpretation or validity can be referred to this court for a preliminary ruling (Article 177 of the EC Treaty). In social security matters, a reference can be made by the Appeals Service, a Commissioner or the courts.

13.5   NATIONAL INSURANCE CONTRIBUTIONS

National insurance contributions are intended to be paid during a normal working life so are not payable by those over pensionable age.

13.5.1   Types

There are different classes of contribution depending on the status of the individual and a series of leaflets dealing with contributions is available from the Benefits Agency:

- Class 1 earnings-related contributions are paid by both employers and employees in respect of anyone in employment;
- flat-rate Class 3 contributions can be paid voluntarily by those wishing to improve an incomplete record (within time limits);
- self-employed people pay flat-rate Class 2 contributions together with profit-related Class 4 contributions if their profits exceed a certain sum up to a defined maximum.

NI contributions are not paid beyond the age of 65 for a man and 60 for a woman.

13.5.2   Contributions record

Entitlement to certain benefits (including retirement pension) depends upon an adequate contributions record. This can be made up by credits rather than by actual payment of contributions. Either the claimant or spouse must have an adequate record but a man can only rely upon his wife's record if widowed or divorced. Those with an inadequate record should consider paying additional contributions before retirement.

Credits and protection

Credits are earned whilst a person is unemployed and registering for employment, off work sick or entitled to certain benefits paid during a working life e.g. severe disablement allowance.

Since 1978, home responsibilities protection provides some assistance with contribution conditions for periods when a person is unable to work because he or she is caring for someone. This might be a child or an elderly or disabled person. If receiving child benefit or income support, the necessary credits will be automatically recorded each year, otherwise form CF411 should be requested from the local DWP office at the end of each year to ensure that credits are given.

13.5.3   Pension forecasts

A comprehensive retirement pension forecast is available for those who have not yet drawn their pension and this indicates the effect of postponing the pension. Voluntary or late contributions can in some circumstances be paid in order to top up a pension contributions record. Application is by form BR19 to, RPFT, the Pension Service, Whitley Road, Newcastle-upon-Tyne, NE98 1BA.

CHAPTER 14

Local authority support

Caroline Coats

14.1 HOUSING BENEFIT

14.1.1 Sources of law

Relevant sources are:

- Social Security Act 1986;
- Social Security Contributions and Benefits Act 1992;
- Housing Benefit (General) Regulations 1987, SI 1987/1971.

14.1.2 Sources of information

See the following:

- leaflet RR2: *A Guide to Housing Benefit and Council Tax Benefit*;.
- Age Concern Fact Sheet 17: *Housing Benefit and Council Tax Benefit*;
- the books mentioned in Appendix F.

14.1.3 Purpose

Housing benefit helps people on low incomes to pay rent in respect of a dwelling, which they normally occupy. It includes hotels, hostels or lodgings and other residential accommodation in the United Kingdom whether furnished or unfurnished in the public or private sector but does not usually include residential care or nursing homes.

Housing benefit provides help with the cost of providing (but not owning) a home for those on low incomes.

14.1.4 Entitlement

Benefit may be claimed by people who are in full-time work or self-employed as well as those who are unemployed, sick or retired. The claimant must be the person who is legally liable to pay the rent (or treated as such). In order to prevent abuse certain claimants are treated as not liable, e.g. someone living with the person to whom the rent is paid where that person is a close relative or the agreement is not on a commercial basis. Individuals are excluded from claiming if they move into a registered care home.

Amount

The amount depends upon the amount of rent paid, the claimant's income (including that of a spouse or partner), and the number of people in the family and the age or disability of the claimant, partner or child. It is tax free, not dependent on NI contributions and paid in addition to other benefits:

- up to 100 per cent of the eligible rent can be allowed;
- claimants on income support or the guaranteed credit part of pension credit receive maximum benefit and others a proportion according to their income.

Assessment

Assessment is complicated. Income is compared with the statutory sum needed to live on (the applicable amount) calculated as for income support and the maximum benefit is reduced by any excess income. A deduction may be made for non-dependants living with the claimant:

- non-dependants are people who are not tenants and are over the age of 18 years;
- a person employed by a charitable or voluntary organisation as resident carer is not classed as a non-dependant;
- if a claimant is registered blind or receives attendance allowance or the highest or middle rate care component of disability living allowance then no non-dependant deductions will be made.

If a claimant receives attendance allowance or disability living allowance they are disregarded when assessing income.

A claimant may have up to £16,000 in capital:

- defined as for income support and certain income and capital is disregarded;
- from October 2003, income support for older people over 60 is replaced by pension credit; there are two parts: the guarantee credit and savings credit;
- the guarantee credit is disregarded as is the first £6,000 of the savings credit; any amount above that figure is deemed to generate £1 per week for every £500 or part thereof;

- for those on income support the first £3,000 is disregarded and above this there is notional income of £1 per £250 or part thereof;
- notional income and capital rules apply as for income support.

Eligible rent

There are restrictions upon the amount and nature of the rent that can be claimed and eligible rent cannot exceed any registered rent.

Rent may include a non-eligible element. Non-eligible services must be identified and the cost deducted from the charges made so as to identify the true rent:

- eligible charges include wardens and caretakers, removal of refuse, lifts, gardening and general management charges;
- non-eligible charges include water and sewerage charges, meals, fuel, laundry, leisure items, cleaning of personal rooms, transport, medical expenses, nursing or personal care, and other services not connected with the provision of accommodation.

The local authority may reduce the rent in certain circumstances by such amount as it considers appropriate having regard in particular to the cost of suitable alternative accommodation elsewhere:

- no deduction may be made if the claimant or a member of the family is over 60 unless suitable cheaper alternative accommodation is available and it is reasonable to expect the claimant to move;
- the rent may be referred to the Rent Officer for consideration but a claimant can request that a determination of rent be made prior to his entering into a tenancy agreement;
- certain claimants are protected for a period and claimants already receiving benefit prior to 1996 may not be affected unless they move home;
- there is some discretion to allow an increase in the maximum eligible rent when exceptional hardship can be established.

Rules for entitlement change at intervals and are being made progressively more stringent so up-to-date material should be relied upon.

Some of the service charges paid by housing benefit transferred to 'Supporting People' services in April 2003. For instance, local authorities now fund providers of supported accommodation for providing services to their residents.

14.1.5 Procedure

A claim form is submitted to the Housing and Council Tax Office of the local authority. Couples make a single claim but either partner may claim. There are time limits:

- the claim may be made up to 13 weeks in advance but may only be back-dated for a maximum of 52 weeks if there is good cause for a late claim;
- those away from home for a long period can still claim if they are intending to (and do) return within 52 weeks;
- claimants should be supplied with a written statement of their claim calculation within six weeks of a request.

Claims should be dealt with within 14 days. Those in receipt of income support or entitled to the guaranteed credit part of pension credit have a 'passported' claim.

Payment

Private tenants receive benefit by cheque or credit to a bank or building society account, but for council tenants the benefit simply reduces the rent. Benefit may be paid to the landlord where there are arrears. Overpayments may be recovered from the claimant (or the landlord) in certain circumstances.

Payment is made for a maximum period up to 60 weeks and will then have to be reclaimed.

Review and appeal

There may on request within one month be an administrative review of the decision followed by an appeal within one month thereafter to an independent tribunal.

14.2 COUNCIL TAX BENEFIT

14.2.1 Sources of law

Relevant sources are:

- Social Security Contributions and Benefits Act 1992;
- Council Tax Benefit (General) Regulations 1992, SI 1992/1814;
- Council Tax (Exempt Dwellings) Order 1992, SI 1992/558;
- Council Tax (Reductions for Disabilities) (Amendment) Regulations 1999, SI 1999/1004.

14.2.2 Sources of information

See the following:

- leaflet RR2: *A Guide to Housing Benefit and Council Tax Benefit*;
- Age Concern Fact Sheet 17: *Housing Benefit and Council Tax Benefit*;
- the books mentioned in Appendix F.

14.2.3 Nature

Council tax benefit helps people on low incomes and not more than £16,000 capital to pay council tax (see Chapter 6 at 6.4.1) whether they rent or own their home. Entitlement does not depend on NI contributions and benefit is tax free and allowed in addition to other benefits. It is paid by the Housing and Council Tax Office of the local authority to which claims must be made and can be claimed on the same form as housing benefit. A review can be requested within one month, and if necessary appealed to an independent tribunal within one month thereafter.

Council tax is payable on most residential dwellings and liability remains during temporary absences. Owners of care homes are usually liable rather than the residents. There are some exemptions:

- self-contained units occupied by a dependent relative, where the dependent relative is aged over 65; substantially and permanently disabled; severely mentally impaired;
- dwellings occupied by people who are severely mentally impaired;
- unoccupied dwellings due to hospital admission, entry into a care home, and where the former resident is receiving or providing personal care relating to old age, disablement or mental disorder.

Amount

Financial eligibility is broadly similar to that for housing benefit (see 14.1.4). A householder on income support or the guaranteed credit part of pension credit automatically has a 100 per cent rebate unless there are non-dependant deductions. If the property is in band F or higher, council tax benefit will be reduced. Payment is made in the form of a reduction in the bill.

Second adult rebate is available where another adult on a low income also lives in the home which can provide a rebate of up to 25 per cent for claimants even if they do not qualify for help based on their income and savings.

The disability reduction scheme applies if there are additional facilities for the use of a substantially and permanently disabled person. Council tax is reduced to that for the valuation band below. If the property is in band A then the bill is reduced by one-sixth.

A reduction of 25 per cent is given where there is only one adult resident and 50 per cent where there are none. A person is not a resident if they are:

- in a care home;
- resident in hospital;
- severely mentally impaired;
- a carer (in certain cases).

14.3 NON-RESIDENTIAL CARE FUNDING

14.3.1 Sources of law

Relevant soures are:

- Health and Social Services and Social Security Adjudications Act 1983 (HASSASSAA), s.17;
- Health and Social Care Act 2001, Part 4;
- Carers and Disabled Children Act 2000;
- Community Care (Delayed Discharges etc.) Act 2003;
- Community Care (Delayed Discharges etc.) Act (Qualifying Services) (England) Regulations 2003, SI 2003/1196;
- Community Care, Services for Carers and Children's Services (Direct Payments) (England) Regulations 2003, SI 2003/762;
- LAC (2001) 32: *Fairer Charging Policies for Home Care and Other Non-Residential Services*. There is similar guidance in Wales dated August 2002, April 2003 and September 2003.

14.3.2 Services

Local authorities are responsible for funding non-residential community care services assessed as needed by elderly people but may make whatever charges they think reasonable. For details of the types of services involved see Chapter 8 (e.g. home help, meals on wheels, day care). Local authorities are expected to make charges for these services but it is usually the person receiving the services who is charged. However, if services are provided to a carer under the Carers and Disabled Children Act 2000 the local authority can charge the carer.

Assessment for the need for the service is a separate process from the assessment of means to pay contributions. Failure to pay does not mean that the service can be withdrawn and the remedy for the local authority is an action in court to recover the debt.

14.3.3 Direct payments

It is now mandatory (previously discretionary) for local authorities to offer direct payments to those that qualify. Direct payments allow people to manage their own care services rather than rely on those provided by social services. Carers may receive direct payments for services.

The upper age limit for direct payments was abolished in 2000. A person will not qualify for direct payments if:

- on leave of absence from hospital under mental health legislation;
- conditionally discharged but subject to restrictions under criminal justice legislation;
- subject to guardianship or supervised discharge under mental health legislation;
- receiving any form of after-care under a compulsory court order;
- subject to a probation order or conditionally released on licence and required to undergo treatment for a mental health condition, drug or alcohol dependency.

The amount of the payment will not be more than it would cost social services to provide the service required. Any contribution to be paid is deducted from the payment. Direct payments cannot be used to pay:

- a spouse or partner living in the same house;
- a close relative or their spouse living in the same house;
- for residential accommodation for any period of more than four weeks in a 12-month period.

14.3.4 Charges

There is no national scheme and charges vary between authorities although mandatory guidance LAC (2001) 32 is aimed at reducing variations by providing a framework for all local authorities to follow. The maximum charge is the portion of the total cost of the service that is attributable to the particular service user.

The local authority should not put an arbitrary ceiling on what they will fund for care at home. It depends entirely on the service users assessed community care eligible needs. However, in practice there is often a ceiling on the amount of home care the local authority will provide, often set at the level where care in a home is the cheaper option. Local authorities must not fetter their discretion so must allow some flexibility for exceptional circumstances.

Authorities cannot charge more than it is reasonably practicable for the client to pay, so if the recipient states that he or she is unable to meet the charges the authority must consider this and reduce or waive them if appropriate. If the service user does not provide information as to personal means the full charge may be imposed for services but most authorities have hardship or exemption policies.

Charges made for services should not reduce the service user's income to below 'basic' levels of income support, plus a buffer of not less than 25 per cent, to safeguard the user's independence. In addition to this buffer, local authorities can choose to set a maximum percentage of disposable income over and above basic income support levels plus 25 per cent, which would be available to pay towards home care costs, leaving some income on which to live. Many authorities take state benefits into account when considering ability to pay, although any allowance for mobility cannot be assessed.

Where disability-related benefits are taken into account so too must disability-related expenditure, e.g. extra heating. National insurance, income tax, housing costs and council tax should be deducted from income.

If capital and income is taken into account then the limits should not be lower than those set for residential care.

Resources available to the local authority may be taken into account when setting their eligibility criteria, although charges should not be used as a way of avoiding the obligation to provide only on how they meet their duties *(R v. Gloucestershire County Council ex parte Barry)* [1997] 2 All ER 1 (HL)

A written statement of the amount to be paid and how to pay it is provided. Payments should not be made directly to the service provider. Information on notice periods, so that arrangements may be made to cover holiday periods, will also be provided.

Services with no charge

It is not policy to charge for social work support, occupational therapy, advice and assessments of need.

There is no power to charge for services provided pursuant to s.117 of the Mental Health Act 1983 (after-care services) where, following discharge from detention under one of the longer treatment sections of the Mental Health Act 1983 (usually s.3 or s.37), he or she requires care as a result of mental disorder. That section places a joint duty on the NHS body and local authorities to provide the services required free of charge, unless it is decided by both that the person is no longer in need of these by virtue of their mental disorder. See *R v. Manchester City Council, ex parte Stennett and others* [2002] 4 All ER 124.

Authorities cannot charge for community equipment services, which should be delivered within three weeks. This includes minor adaptations of £1,000 or less. Social services and health provide an integrated community equipment service under the National Service Framework for Older People.

Authorities cannot charge for intermediate care services – a programme of care for a limited period (up to six weeks) to assist a person to regain the ability to live at home.

(Only applicable to placements in care homes) there is no power to charge where his or her need is primarily a health care need. See *R* v. *North and East Devon Health Authority, ex parte Coughlan* (1999) 2 CCL Rep. 285 and 14.4.2.

14.3.5 Enforcement

Any charge levied 'may, without prejudice to any other method of recovery, be recovered summarily as a civil debt': HASSASSAA 1983, s.17(4). This means through the magistrates' courts (cf. council tax and see the Magistrates' Courts Act 1980, s.58(1)) although a far more appropriate course would be the use of the small claims system in the county courts.

Disputes as to charges should be dealt with under the social services complaints procedure and there is no separate appeal procedure, although decisions can be challenged by complaints procedure, Ombudsman or judicial review (see Chapter 8 at 8.6).

14.4 CARE HOME FUNDING

14.4.1 Sources of law

Relevant sources are:

- National Assistance Act 1948, s.22;
- NHS and Community Care Act 1990;
- Health and Social Care Act 2001;
- National Assistance (Assessment of Resources) Regulations 1992, SI 1992/2977 (as amended);
- National Assistance (Sums for Personal Requirements) Regulations 1996, SI 1996/391 (as amended);
- Charging for Residential Accommodation Guide (CRAG) comprising LAC (2001) 10, 11, 25, 29, LAC (2002) 11 and 15, LAC (2003) 8 and most recent LAC (2003) 23.

See Age Concern Fact Sheet 10: *Local Authority Charging Procedures for Residential and Nursing Home Care*.

14.4.2 Charges

Individuals who can afford to pay for a place in a care home may arrange this independently, though it is advisable to seek a 'needs' assessment prior to entering care in order to achieve continuity if local authority funding may be needed in future.

If met with a refusal to assess in advance, point out that the assessment of need for care provision does not depend upon the need for funding. It may also be wise to ensure that the particular home is willing to accommodate residents on local authority funding.

In regard to assessment of the need for residential care see Chapter 8.

Fully funded by the NHS

Where an NHS body arranges a place in a care home under a contractual arrangement the individual remains an NHS patient and no charge is made but social security benefits may be withdrawn or reduced.

To qualify for fully funded continuing NHS health care the individual must fall within the local Primary Care Trust's (PCT) or Health Board's (in Wales) eligibility criteria. The care needs must be primarily one of health. These are based on the nature, intensity, instability, unpredictability or complexity of health care needs or need for the use of routine health care equipment or the requirement for palliative care. Approximately 10 per cent of care home places are fully funded by the NHS.

The person will be the responsibility of social services (and therefore means-tested) if the nursing services provided are ancillary or incidental to the provision of accommodation and of a nature one would expect social services to provide. See *R* v. *North and East Devon Health Authority, ex parte Coughlan* [2000] 3 All ER 850.

It is useful to have a copy of the local eligibility criteria, as qualification in one area does not guarantee qualification in another, although since the special report on long-term care by the Health Service Ombudsman in February 2003 there is a move towards a more consistent system. Copies of local criteria are obtainable from the PCT, Health Board if in Wales or social services. The Patient Advice and Liaison Service should also be able to help.

Most eligibility criteria have now been reviewed in light of the *Coughlan* decision. If as a result of that decision it is thought that full funding should apply a review should be requested, particularly if local criteria have not yet been revised.

A review request should also be considered as health deteriorates. If hospital admission occurs due to failing health then review should take place as part of hospital discharge procedures. If care continues in the care home a review should be requested.

The NHS body responsible is determined by where the patient is ordinarily resident and will be responsible for funding care even though it may be received in another area.

NHS Registered Nursing Care Contribution

If staying in a care home providing nursing care the NHS pays for the cost of nursing care provided by a registered nurse. It covers care carried out by the registered nurse but not for care carried out by other care staff even where delegated by the registered nurse. Payment is made direct to the home by the PCT or Health Board in which the patient's GP is based.

The NHS body may continue to pay the nursing care contribution as a retainer during stays in hospital. Normally the NHS would not expect to pay for health care twice.

Nursing care by a registered nurse has been available in England since October 2001 for self-funding residents, and others since April 2003. The sum paid is based on the nursing needs of the resident and are assessed as: lower (£40); middle (£75); or higher (£120). These are figures for the year 2003/04.

In Wales, a single rate of £100 has been paid since December 2001 for self-funding residents. The local authority remains responsible for nursing care for existing council funded residents until April 2004.

This raises funding issues where residents cross the border. A protocol has been issued (see **www.doh.gov.uk/jointunit/nhsfundednursingcare/crossborder wales.htm**).

Should the NHS agree to pay more for registered nursing care a review should be requested for full funding. Continuing care assessments should be carried out before registered nursing care assessments. The assessment is reviewed after three months and then every 12-months. Assessments are handled by the nursing home co-ordinator and a review of assessment may be requested at any time.

Free nursing care also brings entitlement to free incontinence supplies in addition to the assessed entitlement. Specific needs should be included in the care plan.

Local authority

Those who enter a care home through an arrangement made by the local authority must pay or contribute to the cost, whether the authority provides or buys in the accommodation. Each authority must fix a standard weekly charge for its own homes which should represent the true economic cost of providing the accommodation. Many have a standard scale of fees geared to their eligibility criteria. Where the authority purchases a place from an independent home the weekly charge to the resident should represent the cost of the place to the authority. Residents must generally contribute in accordance with their resources up to the appropriate charge, but no one will be required to pay more.

The authority either pays the full fee to the home and collects the resident's contribution or pays its share whilst the resident and any third party pay the balance. A contract with the authority or the home should state what is included in the charge and what are extras (see Chapter 9).

If placed on a waiting list and alternative care arrangements are put in place in the meantime, contributions should not be any greater towards the alternative domiciliary or residential care than would be contributed for care required in the person's preferred care home.

Where care is required in a home providing nursing care the local authority will liaise with the NHS before making the arrangements. In an emergency they may arrange the placement and then refer to the NHS.

In cases where the local authority disagrees that care is required, or regarding the level of care, a copy of the needs assessment should be obtained and relevant medical evidence gathered.

Where a care home increases its fees above the rate paid by the local authority:

- ask for reassessment by social services that staying in the home is part of required needs and an assessment of the risk of any move;
- seek a third party to top up;
- ask social services to negotiate with the home to charge only what they will pay;
- move to another home.

Joint funding

The Health Act 1999 enables the NHS and local authority departments to pool budgets and jointly commission services. Since April 2000 funding has therefore passed between health and social services more easily.

Where the NHS partly funds a placement this may indicate that the case is borderline for qualification under local eligibility criteria. In those cases a review should be requested for full funding.

Deferred payments

Available in England since October 2001 and in Wales from April 2003 deferred payment agreements are operated by social services and funded by a grant from the Department of Health. Social services take a legal charge against the house instead of a contribution towards the cost of accommodation, so allowing the house to be retained. It delays payment until the property is sold. Such agreements:

- must be in writing;
- last from the day the agreement is entered into until 56 days after death or the property is sold, if earlier;
- charge interest from 56 days after death or the property is sold;
- cannot include legal expenses;
- cannot be terminated by social services.

Social services have discretion whether or not to agree to a deferred payments agreement. Reasons for a refusal should be put in writing. All of the following must apply in order to qualify:

- a property disregard does not apply;
- capital apart from the house is below the maximum prescribed limit;
- cost of care cannot be met in full from income;
- a desire not to sell the house or inability to sell quickly enough to pay the fees.

14.4.3 Means-testing

When the resident cannot afford the full charge an assessment is made of ability to pay and this is reviewed annually but a resident should ask for re-assessment at any time if this would be beneficial. Means-testing (similar to that for income support) applies to the provision or funding by local authorities of residential care, but provision by the NHS is free.

Points to note:

- The assessment relates to both income and capital and since April 1993 assessment has been brought largely into line with that for income support, though local authorities retain some discretion.
- The capital cut-off point in England is £19,500 but capital above £12,000 (2003–2004) will result in a tariff income (an attempt to apply a lower financial threshold before acknowledging need failed in *R* v. *Sefton Metropolitan Borough Council, ex parte Help the Aged* [1998] 1 CCLR 315 (CA)).
- Assessment relates only to the means of the resident (unlike for income support where spouses and partners are generally assessed together).
- There is no power to oblige a spouse/partner to take part but spouses are liable to maintain each other (National Assistance Act 1948, s.42) and court action may be taken against a liable relative (s.43).
- Since 1996 one-half of occupational and private pensions of the resident are re-routed back to the non-resident spouse.
- There is a minimum charge payable by all residents and the assessment determines what should be paid above this, but all residents retain a personal expenses allowance (revised annually) to be used by the resident for expenditure of personal choice such as stationery, personal toiletries, treats (e.g. sweets, drinks, cigarettes) and presents. The authority has a discretion to increase the amount, but it should not be used for top-up to provide more expensive accommodation. A variation may be considered to cover outgoings whilst selling the house. The allowance may be used for extra services at the care home that have not been contracted for.
- Local authorities should carry out a benefits check because they have an incentive to ensure that people in homes are receiving maximum state benefits. This should only be with the informed consent of the resident.

Once the amount to be paid by the resident is assessed, then unless agreed otherwise, this is paid to the local authority who in turn pay the full fee to the home.

Income

All income is required towards payment of the standard charge or contract rate for the accommodation except the personal expenses allowance and any disregarded income.

Usually this includes:

- state retirement pension and other benefits;
- occupational pensions (less 50 per cent for spouse);
- assumed tariff income from capital;
- trust income.

Temporary residents may be able to offset their other outgoings. Attendance allowance is also disregarded for temporary residents.

The same assessment rules as for income support apply for:

- income fully taken into account;
- income partially disregarded;
- income fully disregarded;
- capital treated as income;
- tariff income;
- trust income.

Notional income

Notional income is income that is not actually received, as follows:

- income paid to social services as a third party top-up;
- income paid to a third party for an item taken into account when the standard rate for the accommodation was fixed;
- income available if applied for;
- income due but not received;
- income deliberately deprived of to reduce or avoid charge.

Social services should only consider income that has been deliberately deprived if it would have normally been included in the financial assessment. Deliberate deprivation to reduce or avoid the charge does not have to be the main reason, only a significant reason for the deprivation. Where an income-producing asset is sold and thereby converted to a capital asset, any of the following may be taken into account:

- the former income;
- the difference between the former income and the tariff income;
- the increase in the tariff income.

Capital

All assets, including any overseas (which can be realised), are counted as capital. Tariff income is not applied to capital under £12,000 (for 2003/04). Up to £19,500 (for 2003/04) tariff income of £1 for every £250 is assumed. Capital over £19,500 is assessed as a completely self-funded placement. In Wales the threshold figures are £12,500 and £20,000 for 2003/04.

Disregards and valuations

These are as follows:

- The house is disregarded indefinitely where it is occupied by a spouse, a relative who is over 60, incapacitated or under 16, as is a child who the resident is liable to maintain or an estranged or divorced partner who has a dependent child.
- There is a discretionary power to disregard where occupation is by others.
- The value of the home is disregarded for the first 12 weeks of a permanent stay, after which a deferred payments agreement may be entered into or a legal charge applied against the property.
- If the home is jointly owned a nil valuation may be argued.
- Jointly owned assets (apart from the home) are treated as divided equally (subject to any expenses of sale and secured debts).
- The house is disregarded during the period it takes to sell it and a more suitable property found to live in.
- From 6 October 2003 a savings disregard applies to council supported residents aged 65 and over who are entitled to savings credit. Not all the credit is disregarded and depends on their income.

Most income support capital assessment rules apply.

Notional capital

Notional capital is assessed where an individual:

- deliberately deprives themselves of capital to reduce the amount of charge to pay;
- fail to apply for capital otherwise available;
- capital is paid by someone else to a third party on their behalf.

Deprivation of capital should only be considered where the capital would have been included in the financial assessment if possessed. The intention to reduce or avoid the charge is a subjective test. See *Yule* v. *South Lanarkshire Council* [2000] SLT 1249 (also on www.scotscourts.gov.uk/opinions).

In *Beeson* v. *Dorset County Council* [2002] HRLR 15 it was shown that the council misdirected itself in applying the subjective test but on appeal that its systems were not in breach of Article 6(1) of the European Convention on Human Rights ([2003] HRLR 345).

Where notional capital is assessed it should also be diminished by the difference in each payment made.

Interim arrangements

This is available in cases that would be self-funding but capital is not imme-diately available, for instance while a property is sold. Help with fees may be sought on an interim basis. During this period the charge will be based on income with the full fee being payable and backdated once the capital is avail-able. The value of the property is, however, disregarded for the first 12 weeks of a permanent stay in a care home.

Alternatively, consider a deferred payments scheme if the home is going to take a long time to sell.

14.4.4 Enforcement

The local authority is expressly empowered to recover sums due from the resi-dent as a civil debt through the magistrates' court (National Assistance Act 1948, s.56). This is 'without prejudice to any other enforcement procedures' so does not preclude a debt claim in the county court or bankruptcy proceedings.

First avoidance provision

Where a resident disposed of assets by way of gift or at an undervalue within six months before (or during) admission to residential accommodation knowingly and with the intention of avoiding charges for the accommodation then sums due may be recovered (Health and Social Services and Social Security Adjudications Act 1983, ss.21–24):

- liability may be imposed on a third party to whom assets have been trans-ferred, though only for any shortfall in the amount received from the resident and to the extent of the benefit accruing to that party;
- a legal charge can be imposed on a property of the resident (to the level of the resident's share) to secure arrears, with interest chargeable from the day after death: enforcement of the accruing debt is thus left to a later stage.

Second avoidance provision

Under the notional capital rules (see 14.4.3), the resident may be treated as possessing an asset which has been given away (or not obtained) for the purpose of avoiding assessment (National Assistance (Assessment of Resources) Regulations 1992, SI 1992/2977, reg.25).

If the authority can establish that the purpose of a gift was to avoid means-testing the asset may be treated as notional capital in the hands of the resident and a contribution assessed on it. Avoiding the charge need not be the main purpose but must have been a significant one. Any gift made immediately before (or after) admission to the home is vulnerable even if a further purpose can be established. There is no time limit but the longer it is since a gift was made the more difficult it will be to establish that the purpose was to avoid financial assessment. Notional capital is deemed to diminish over a period of time so that ultimately the resident will re-qualify for care costs (the diminishing capital rule).

There are two distinct procedures for taking into account the value of gifts and the six-month time limit so often relied upon only applies to one of these.

14.4.5 Recovery

The local authority is obliged to meet the continuing cost of care even if any assessed financial contribution is not paid. How can a contribution be enforced against an individual who no longer has assets, but has made a gift (e.g. of the home) more than six months before admission?

Recovery may be possible through three sets of proceedings but timing is difficult:

- judgment is obtained for the unpaid contributions;
- the individual is made bankrupt;
- application is made to set aside the gift (Insolvency Act 1986, ss.339–340).

Other provisions enable transactions at an undervalue to be set aside without time limit and without bankruptcy by a single application to the court if there was an intention to defraud creditors at the time of the transaction even if the transferor was then solvent. The court may then make orders to restore the position to what it would have been had the transaction not taken place (Insolvency Act 1986, ss.423–425).

It is sufficient if the purpose was to put the asset beyond the reach of a person who might at some time make a claim or otherwise prejudice the interests of such a person (*Midland Bank* v. *Wyatt* [1995] 1 FLR 697).

It may be sufficient for this to be a substantial rather than a dominant purpose (a finding of purpose sufficient for the gift to be treated as notional capital would also appear to justify the subsequent setting aside procedure).

A gift may be disregarded and set aside by a single application to the court.

Legal charge

Social services cannot force the sale of land. However, they may create a legal charge to cover any unpaid care costs. The amount of the debt will take into account the capital limits. Interest will only be charged from the date of death. Where property is jointly owned, a caution only may be registered, but consider the possibility of a nil value. If you disagree with the valuation of property the complaint will be heard by the complaints panel.

Challenge any attempt to pass on the cost of creating the charge.

Establishing the purpose

How is the authority to establish the purpose of a gift? It is for the resident to give information to the local authority from which they can conclude that the resident does not have funds from which he can pay the assessed charge. They have to look at what the resident's purpose was in making the disposal. If the resident cannot provide a reason the judge may conclude in the circumstances that it must have been made to avoid future care costs, although if a person makes the disposition when they were fit and healthy and had no reason to foresee the need to move into care then it would be unreasonable for the local authority to treat the gift as notional capital. There must therefore be a link established between the gift and the moving into care. Can the elderly resident or donee really give evidence and face cross-examination?

In the case of gifts of the home the Law Society advise that the donor should be advised of the implications on any possible future liability for care fees and this should be recorded in writing. The fact of advising in itself does not constitute intention. The file will normally be covered by legal professional privilege, but the court may order discovery if there is *prima facie* proof of fraud and also for public policy considerations (see *Royscott Spa Leasing* v. *Lovett* [1995] BCC 502 (CA); *Barclays Bank Plc* v. *Eustice* [1995] 4 All ER 511). If the court, within bankruptcy proceedings, considers that the purpose of the transaction may have been to avoid means-testing, disclosure of the solicitor's file may be required to ascertain whether this really was the case. If one of the marketed schemes has been used an inspection of the documents may reveal the source and thereby the motivation behind the transfer.

14.4.6 Liable relatives

Other provisions allow the local authority to recover the cost of residential care from a person 'liable to maintain' the resident (National Assistance Act 1948, ss.42 and 43). This includes a spouse but not unmarried couples. Liable relatives should not be asked to pay more than they can reasonably afford. There is no power to require the spouse to provide details of personal assets and income and the authority will seek to agree a reasonable amount taking into account all that spouse's circumstances so as not to cause financial hardship. Guidance suggests they should be left with income above means-tested benefit levels plus expense.

Payment cannot be enforced by the local authority but the remedy available is a complaint to the magistrates' court and the spouse may be ordered to pay such weekly or other sum as the court thinks appropriate. LAC (2002) 11 states this should be a last resort. A spouse making a maintenance payment as liable relative cannot also make a top-up payment for more expensive accommodation.

Top-ups

A third party may make up the difference in care costs. Social services need assurance that the ability to pay will continue for the likely duration of stay. Arrangements are made through social services and not with the care home provider. Where social services decide to place a person in more expensive accommodation a third party top-up should not be sought.

If the care home fees rise faster than the rise in the level social services pay then the difference may fall to the third party to pay. An increase in the resident's income will not necessarily reduce the third party contribution. Failure to pay may result in the resident having to move to other accommodation.

The resident may only pay if they have disregarded capital or income:

- during the 12-week property disregard (although the house cannot be used during this period and the person should not use below the minimum prescribed threshold);
- if a deferred payment agreement is in place.

14.4.7   Choice of care home

Within resource constraints residents are to be provided with their choice of home (preferred accommodation). The local authority should provide information about homes in its area but the choice is not restricted to these and homes in other areas may be chosen, though fees will usually only be met to the local level. The chosen home must appear to the authority to be suitable for the assessed needs and the cost should not exceed what it would normally expect to pay for these needs. Where no place is available at the price the local authority would usually expect to pay, it must pay a higher price if necessary. Choice cannot be restricted by the local authority to their own homes or those where they have block contracts.

Where a more expensive care home is chosen in another area this may be fully paid for by the local authority if it is shown to be part of assessed needs to be in the chosen area. There are protocols in place to deal with cross border placements.

Top-up of fees by non-liable relatives or others should be permitted so enabling more expensive accommodation to be provided. The local authority cannot expect third party top-ups as a matter of course and must be able to show that there are homes that could provide the service required within the cost paid by social services. See National Assistance Act 1948 (Choice of Accommodation) Directions 1992, National Assistance (Residential Accommodation) (Additional Payments and Assessment of Resources) (Amendment) (England) Regulations 2001, SI 2001/3441 and Circulars LAC (92) 27, LAC (93) 18 and LAC (2001) 29.

14.4.8 Temporary stays

Admission to a care home may be for respite care or convalescence. For stays of up to eight weeks the authority need not carry out a means test but may charge what is reasonable for the resident to pay and income support (or guaranteed credit part of pension credit) may include housing costs. For longer stays there must be a means test (as above) but the resident's home is disregarded if there is an intention to return and income support (or guaranteed credit part of pension credit) or housing benefit for housing costs is ignored. Intermediate care should be paid for by the NHS for up to six weeks.

A trial period in a care home is a temporary stay if it is because the need for permanent care is not ascertained. If it is to see if the particular home is suitable and return home is not an option then the trial period will still be as a permanent resident.

14.4.9 Entitlement to other benefits

Income support, guarantee credit, pension credit

If a resident entered a care home in the private sector after April 1993 subject to means they may be entitled to income support or guaranteed credit part of pension credit from 6 October 2003. The savings credit is in part disregarded. The local authority will meet the shortfall (if any) between income and care fees.

Attendance allowance

Attendance allowance, or the care component of disability living allowance, may continue whilst the resident is privately funding care but will cease after four weeks of receiving local authority financial support.

14.4.10   Practitioner's problems

When considering means-testing for services provided by local authorities and in particular admission to a care home, problem areas include:

- transfer of assets (see Chapter 19);
- liable relatives and means-testing of spouses;
- limited availability of occupational or personal pensions;
- choice of care home, home closures and shortfall in fees;
- run-down in resources and refusal of the local authority to assess in advance;
- presence of a non-relative or carer in a home belonging to the individual which is being assessed (the authority but not DWP has a discretion in this situation);
- local authority's available resources (there have been several appeal decisions concerning the implications of this).

CHAPTER 15

Other financial support

Caroline Coats

15.1 NATIONAL HEALTH SERVICE

Support for an individual who is ill, infirm or otherwise in need of medical or nursing services is available through NHS bodies and the provision of these services is considered in Chapter 10.

15.1.1 Charges

NHS health care is generally free but there are charges for some services such as prescriptions, dental treatment, sight tests and glasses, wigs and fabric supports, and fares to hospital. There is exemption from charges if:

- resident in a care home and in receipt of assistance with the fees from the local authority;
- a war disablement pensioner and the service is required because of war disability (contact the Veterans Agency);
- on a low income (apply on form AG1 or AG2 for sight tests).

Low income scheme

To qualify for full or partial remission from NHS charges (form HC1) a person must be over 60 and with capital of less than £12,000 (£19,000 if resident at a care home).

If a person's income is less than requirements they are exempt from NHS charges. If a person's income exceeds requirements, the amount of excess determines level of remission:

- help with hospital fares is reduced by amount of excess income;
- the cost of a sight test is reduced to the amount of excess income if lower;
- glasses/lenses voucher reduced by twice the amount of excess income;
- dental treatment charges and wig and fabric support costs that are higher than three times excess income are remitted;
- partial remission of prescription charges is not available.

A certificate is issued that lasts 12 months if aged 60 and over or living in a care home. If a charge is paid that could have been free or reduced, a refund may be obtained within three months (form HC5). If an item/service is received free or at reduced cost when full charge should have been made a maximum penalty of £100 can be issued.

Prescriptions

Help with the cost of prescriptions is possible by purchasing a pre-payment certificate lasting for four months or a year (form FP95). Free prescriptions are obtained by completing the declaration on the reverse of the prescription, if aged 60 or over or suffering from any of the following (form FP92A):

- continued physical disability meaning the person is housebound unless assisted;
- epilepsy, requiring continuous anti-convulsive therapy;
- diabetes;
- a permanent fistula needing continual surgical dressing or appliance.

Sight tests

To qualify for a free NHS sight test one of the following must apply:

- aged 60 or over;
- registered blind or partially sighted;
- have a complex lens prescription;
- suffer from diabetes or glaucoma;
- aged 40 or over and the parent, brother, sister or child of someone with glaucoma;
- a patient of the Hospital Eye Service.

Glasses

A voucher is available to buy or repair glasses if a person is a patient of the Hospital Eye Service needing frequent changes or complex lenses. A voucher is also available if:

- glasses or contact lenses are required for the first time or the old ones are worn out;
- given a different prescription than previously;
- glasses/lenses are lost or damaged because of illness.

Hospital services

No charge is made for NHS hospital services, whether or not as an in-patient, but social security benefits are affected whilst in hospital. This depends on the benefit and the length of stay. Means-tested benefits will be re-assessed. Usually there is no change for the first four weeks, but then invalid care allowance ceases and after six weeks severe disablement allowance and certain other benefits are reduced (the period before loss of benefits is extended to 13 weeks from October 2003). The mobility component of disability living allowance is the only benefit that survives a lengthy period in hospital.

A carer loses invalid care allowance after being in hospital for 12 weeks and sometimes earlier.

Benefits are reinstated during temporary absences but there are linking provisions for successive hospital stays. After one year in hospital the benefit paid to a patient is reduced to a weekly sum fixed annually:

- further benefits may be paid to any dependants;
- a personal expenses allowance is retained and when the patient is mentally incapacitated this may be collected by the hospital authorities and held in a special account.

It is not always easy to determine whether a claimant is in hospital. The question is: 'Is the individual receiving free in-patient treatment in a hospital or similar institution?'

15.1.2   Equipment

Certain items may be provided through the integrated community equipment service, such as:

- walking aids;
- artificial limbs;
- hearing aids;
- low vision aids;
- special footwear;
- incontinence pads.

Other items may be provided on prescription, such as:

- oxygen cylinders;
- diabetes equipment;
- elastic stockings;
- incontinence equipment.

15.1.3   Information

A series of leaflets is available free from DWP offices, Post Offices, and some family doctors:

- P11: *NHS Prescriptions*;
- AB11: *Help with NHS Costs*;
- D11: *NHS Dental Treatment*;
- G11: *NHS Sight Tests and Vouchers for Glasses*;
- NI9: *Going into Hospital*;
- H11: *NHS Hospital Travel Costs*.

15.2   GRANTS AND SUBSIDIES

15.2.1   Housing grants

Almost all housing grants are now payable at the discretion of the local authority, including renovation grants, and grants for works to common parts of a building and houses in multiple occupation. The Regulatory Reform (Housing Assistance) (England and Wales) Order 2002, SI 2002/1860, from July 2003, removed under the Housing, Construction and Regeneration Act 1996 provision that applied to renovation grants and home and repair assistance. The Order gives new powers to the local authority to improve living conditions in its area in the way it considers the most appropriate.

A grant is only likely to be mandatory when it is for defined works to make the dwelling suitable for a disabled occupier. For example, an application might be made to meet part or all of the cost of works needed to facilitate access to the dwelling, but the authority must be satisfied that the works are both:

- necessary and appropriate to meet the need;
- reasonable and practicable having regard to the age and condition of the dwelling.

Local housing authority assistance

The 2002 Order gives local housing authorities power to provide assistance for:

- repair, improvement and adaptation of housing;
- the demolition of living accommodation and assistance with rebuilding costs;
- the acquisition of new accommodation where the property has been either compulsorily or voluntarily purchased by the local authority or it considers it is not economic to adapt or improve the residence.

Policy on how the local housing authority uses its powers should be published and is available from it. The policy will set out such things as eligibility, conditions and the type of assistance that is available. This may be in any form and can include the giving of grants, loans, material and/or advice. There is no limit on the amount of help and can be in addition to a disabled facilities grant.

Disabled facilities grants

A person is treated as disabled if they are registered disabled with social services or suffering from:

- substantially impaired sight, hearing or speech;
- a mental disorder or impairment;
- substantial physical disablement.

Mandatory grants (maximum £25,000 in England or £30,000 in Wales) are awarded to provide facilities and adaptations to assist the disabled person to live independently and include:

- provision of disabled access;
- bedroom, toilet or bathroom;
- making property safe;
- food preparation facilities;
- adaptation to enable use of power and light;
- suitable heating;
- facilitation of free movement around the house.

The means test is applied to the disabled person and his or her spouse or partner. Decisions are given within six months and work should be completed within 12 months. Application is made to the housing department although it can also be made via the social services department, who having conducted a needs assessment, decide what adaptations are necessary and appropriate. If not eligible, but assessed by social services under the Chronically Sick and Disabled Persons Act 1970, s.2 as needing assistance with adaptations to the home, then social services may still be under a duty to make such arrangements (see Chapter 8).

Once eligible, the housing department cannot refuse to pay on the grounds of lack of funds (*R* v. *Birmingham City Council, ex parte Mohammed* [1998] 1 CCLR 441).

Home Energy Efficiency Scheme (Warm Front grants)

Grants are available to those aged 60 or over for insulation, draught-proofing and energy advice and those in receipt of most means-tested benefits are eligible. Contact: Energy Action Grants Agency, Eaga Partnership Ltd, Freepost NEA 12054, Newcastle upon Tyne, NE2 1BR, Tel: 0800 316 6011.

Community Care grants

Community Care grants may help with minor structural repairs, maintenance, internal decoration and refurbishment to enable the older person to remain in their home. See Chapter 13 at 13.2.3

15.2.2   Subsidies

Travel concessions

These include:

- Blue Badge parking: entitles the holder to parking concessions because they are blind or have severe walking difficulties. It allows parking near shops, public buildings and other places for extended periods without charge. It can be obtained from local authority social services departments.
- Disabled person's railcard: gives entitlement to one-third reduction in the cost of most train journeys. It can be obtained from train operators who may provide details of other assistance and concessions.
- Road tax exemption: qualification depends on receipt of higher rate mobility component disability living allowance or war pensioners mobility supplement. It can be obtained from the Vehicle Licensing Agency for one car used for the benefit of that person. It cannot be backdated.
- Motability: qualification depends on receipt of disability living allowance or war pensioners mobility supplement. The benefit is paid direct to Motability, a registered charity, who arrange concessionary rates for hire, purchase, adaptation, insurance and service costs of a suitable vehicle.
- Assistance may be provided for the cost of travel to hospital and a companion's travelling expenses where this is medically necessary.
- See generally Age Concern Fact Sheet 26: *Travel Information for Older People*.

Gas and electricity

Suppliers have codes of practice which should be referred to if problems arise and payment schemes include pre-payment, monthly budget and flexible payments. Consumers receiving income support or guaranteed credit part of pension credit may arrange direct payments.

Protection against disconnection is given to customers: customers of pensionable age will not be disconnected between 1 October and 31 March if they cannot pay. Licence conditions 12A (British Gas) and 19 (Public Electricity Companies) set out procedures to be followed.

See generally Age Concern Fact Sheet 1: *Help with Heating.*

Telephone

Help may be available from:

- the social services department of the local authority under the Chronically Sick and Disabled Persons Act 1970 (see Chapter 8 at 8.4);
- the Social Fund with a budgeting loan (see Chapter 13 at 13.2.3);
- DHSS Circular HSS (OS5A) 5/78: *Telephones for the Handicapped and Elderly*;
- British Telecom operate rebate schemes and a protected service scheme: see the BT guide for people who are disabled or elderly and the information pack available;
- contact DIEL (Advisory Committee on Telecommunications for Disabled and Elderly People), Export House, 50 Ludgate Hill, London EC4M 7JJ.

See Age Concern Fact Sheet 28: *Help with telephones.*

Television licence

Concessions are available to retired people of pensionable age who live in certain types of accommodation (residential care homes and some sheltered accommodation). Free licences are available for all those aged over 75 years (Wireless Telegraphy (Television Licence Fees) Regulations 1997, SI 1997/290). Contact the Concessionary Licensing Centre, TV Licensing, Barton House, Bond Street, Bristol BS19 1TL (Tel: 01272 230130).

See Age Concern Fact Sheet 3: *Television Licence Concessions.*

Water

Protection is afforded against disconnection in certain circumstances and it is unlawful to arrange automatic disconnection on non-payment.

Other

Private businesses are often willing to make home visits to provide their services and may offer discounted rates, e.g. hairdressers, chiropodists, chiropractors, beauticians, and therapists. However, many concessions for the elderly are little more than marketing tactics.

15.3 FAMILY AND CHARITIES

15.3.1 Family

Financial support may also be given to an older person by members of the family, normally on an informal basis without any legal commitment:

- care should be taken to ensure that support does not result in the reduction or loss of means-tested funding or increased charges for local authority services;
- informal carers should not neglect to claim all financial benefits that are available as of right either in respect of the person cared for or for themselves as carers.

In case means-testing applies it may be better to buy useful items and give these, rather than to make gifts of money. Another way may be to carry out tasks such as gardening or shopping.

15.3.2 Charities

Many charities, national and local, exist for the purpose of giving support to elderly or disabled people and this may include help with long-term care costs. They do not normally pay for services that should be paid for by the local authority.

Contact Charity Search (see Appendix E) and check with charities assisting the professions or the elderly.

Independent Living Fund

The Independent Living Fund was set up in 1988 to make payments to severely disabled people who needed to pay for care in order to continue living at home. In April 1993 it was replaced by:

- Independent Living (Extension) Fund which continues to make payments to those supported by the original Fund: no new applications are accepted;
- Independent Living (1993) Fund which deals with new applications but on a more restricted basis and only for those aged less than 66 years.

15.4 PRIVATE AND VOLUNTARY CARE AGENCIES

Social services may be able to provide details of private and voluntary care agencies in your area. Since April 2003, agencies are required to register with the National Care Standards Commission and adopt the minimum standards on domiciliary care.

The agency is obliged to provide to prospective users the Service User's Guide which includes:

- the aims and objectives of the agency;
- the nature of the services provided, including specialist services;
- people for whom the service is provided;
- an overview of the process for the delivery of care and support from initial referral, through needs and risk assessment and development of the service user plan, to review of the care and re-assessment of need;
- key contract terms and conditions;
- the complaints procedure;
- the quality assurance process;
- specific information on key policies and procedures: how to contact the local office of the National Care Standards Commission (NCSC), social services, health care authorities and the General Social Services Council (GSCC);
- hours of operation;
- details of insurance cover.

The care requirements of service users, their personal or family carers when appropriate, should be individually assessed before they are offered a personal domiciliary care service and a care plan written.

The contract between the service user and the service provider should specify the following, unless these appear in the Service User's Guide and care plan:

- name, address and telephone number of agency;
- contact number for out-of-hours and details of how to access the service;
- contact number for the office of regular care workers and their manager;
- areas of activity which home care or support workers will and will not undertake and the degree of flexibility in the provision of personal care;
- circumstances in which the service may be cancelled or withdrawn including temporary cancellation by the service user;
- fees payable for the service, and by whom;
- rights and responsibilities of both parties (including insurance) and liability if there is a breach of contract or any damage occurring in the home;
- arrangements for monitoring and review of needs and for updating the assessment and the individual service user plan;
- process for assuring the quality of the service, monitoring and supervision of staff;
- supplies and/or equipment to be made available by the service user and by the agency;
- respective responsibilities of the service user and of the agency in relation to health and safety matters and arrangements to cover holidays and sickness;

- keyholding and other arrangements agreed for entering or leaving the home.

When interviewing applicants it may help to have someone else present to assist and to take up references.

CHAPTER 16

Employment

Henry Scrope

16.1 INTRODUCTION

16.1.1 Main legislation

Relevant legislation includes:

- Employment Rights Act 1996;
- Employment Relations Act 1999;
- Trade Union and Labour Relations (Consolidation) Act 1992;
- anti-discrimination legislation, including EC Equal Treatment Framework Directive (2000/78/EC); Sex Discrimination Act 1975; Race Relations Act 1976; Disability Discrimination Act 1995;
- Working Time Regulations 1998, SI 1998/1833;
- Employment Act 2002;
- DTI consultation on 'proposals for outlawing age discrimination in employment and vocational training' (2003).

16.1.2 General

There are no legal restrictions in relation to older people working but their employment rights are reduced and there is at present no general protection against age discrimination.

The EC Equal Treatment Framework Directive (2000/78/EC) requires all EU Member States to outlaw all age discrimination in the employment field save where it is objectively justified by, at the very latest 2 December 2006. The British government has announced that it intends to introduce appropriate measures in Britain as from 1 October 2006. Accordingly in July 2003 the DTI issued a consultation document on the subject. This document entitled '*Equality and Diversity: Age Matters*' (74 pages) and a summary (10 pages) are both available on the DTI website (**www.dti.gov.uk/er/equality/age.htm**).

16.1.3   Employment or self-employment?

The common law, and most legislation, relating to employment only applies to those working under a 'contract of employment'. This should be distinguished from self-employment or a contract to provide services, but courts and tribunals look at the reality of the situation rather than the terminology applied. The courts have devised a number of tests of employment and no single one is determinative:

- the degree of control and of integration;
- whether someone is an entrepreneur in their own right;
- whether there is an obligation to provide work and be provided with work.

The definition is more extensive for some employment protection legislation. In particular anti-discrimination legislation extends to those who work under a contract to do personal work (Sex Discrimination Act 1975, s.82(1)).

16.1.4   Continuous employment

You must have worked for a minimum period to be able to claim for redundancy (two years) or unfair dismissal (one year) (see Employment Rights Act 1996, ss.155 and 135). There are no longer any requirements as to minimum hours of work. Where an older worker is employed on a casual basis and does not work in a particular week, this week might still count as a 'temporary cessation of work' in which event employment rights will be preserved (s.212).

16.1.5   Discrimination

All employees regardless of length of employment have a right not to be discriminated against on the grounds of sex, race, disability or trade union membership or activity during their employment:

- 'sex' includes 'sexual orientation' from December 2003 (Employment Equality (Sexual Orientation) Regulations 2003, SI 2003/1661);
- 'race' covers colour, race, ethnic or national origins and nationality (Race Relations Act 1976, s.3);
- 'disability' covers physical or mental impairment which is not a temporary condition (Disability Discrimination Act 1995, s.1 and Sched.1).

Until age discrimination is added to the list in October 2006, an older worker deprived of opportunities for employment, transfer, training or promotion could only bring an action if the discriminatory behaviour was based on the above grounds.

16.1.6 Remuneration

No employee can have a deduction made from his wages unless this has been agreed in writing (e.g. in the contract of employment) or under some statutory provision.

This does not apply to an overpayment of wages or expense. See Employment Rights Act 1996, s.13 (formerly Wages Act 1986). Employees are entitled to equal pay with those of the opposite sex (Equal Pay Act 1970).

16.2 COMMENCEMENT

16.2.1 Recruitment

Until (probably) October 2006, an employer can freely discriminate against older people when recruiting unless this is on the grounds of sex or marital status, race, disability or trade union membership. Thereafter age discrimination will be unlawful unless it can be objectively justified (for example, setting a maximum age for job applicants 'based on the training requirements of the post in question' might be objectively justified).

16.2.2 Contracts

Once appointed, or an offer is accepted, a contract comes into existence. The terms may be express (oral or in writing) or implied but cannot override certain terms implied by statute:

- there are statutory minimum provisions in regard to the notice period (Employment Rights Act 1996, s.86);
- equal pay between the sexes operates as a statutory implied term (Equal Pay Act 1970);
- there are rights relating to time off and union membership or activities.

16.2.3 Statement of terms of employment

There is no legal obligation for an employment contract itself to be in writing. However, it is a legal requirement that employers provide their employees with a 'written statement of particulars of employment' setting out specified basic terms (Employment Rights Act 1996, s.1):

- the main terms and conditions must be specified including the rate of remuneration and intervals at which it is paid, hours, holidays, sickness and sick pay;
- the period of notice and any terms relating to pensions must be included.

There is an example of a statute-compliant form of written particulars of employment on the DTI website (www.dti.gov.uk/er/individual/example-pl700a.htm).

The stated terms are not conclusive if the parties have behaved in a manner inconsistent with them. That behaviour is likely to be the best evidence relating to the relevant term. The terms of the contract may be deduced from custom or implication in so far as not specified. Terms may be implied because of long established custom and practice or simply because it is reasonable to do so.

There is no financial sanction on an employer for failure to provide written particulars of employment but this is due to change (Employment Act 2002, s.38, likely to be in effect by April 2004).

16.2.4   Part-timers

As from 1 July 2000 part-time employees have been entitled to all the same rights (pro rata) as full timers doing the same work (see the Part-time Workers (Prevention of Less Favourable Treatment) Regulations 2000, SI 2000/1551). There is no small employers exemption, none being permitted by the EC Part Time Work Directive 97/81/EC which the 2000 Regulations implement in the United Kingdom.

16.3   TERMINATION

Employment may be terminated by agreement, resignation of the employee (which may sometimes amount to 'constructive dismissal'), operation of law, notice from the employer, or expiry of a fixed term.

16.3.1   Notice

There are statutory minimum notice periods of one week after a month, two weeks after two years and thereafter one week per year up to a maximum of 12 weeks (Employment Rights Act 1996, s.86). The contract may stipulate for longer periods and there may be an implied term for reasonable notice which exceeds the statutory minimum. There may be instant dismissal (without notice) for gross misconduct, and the contract of employment may be frustrated, e.g. by sickness or injury.

16.3.2   Entitlement

Upon dismissal an employee is entitled to net salary and benefits for the entire notice period if termination is with immediate effect. The sum payable is subject to the duty to mitigate by finding other work which is usually more difficult for older workers. In some situations there may be a right to work during the period of notice. After two years' service the employee will be entitled to a written statement of reasons for the dismissal (Employment Rights Act 1996, s.92).

16.3.3 Wrongful dismissal

Damages may be claimed for any dismissal in breach of contract regardless of age, but an injunction to restrain such dismissal would be unusual. Either the courts or employment tribunal have jurisdiction but the tribunal cannot award more than £25,000.

16.3.4 Unfair dismissal

After one year's continuous employment an employee has a right not to be unfairly dismissed. Claims must be made within three months of 'the effective date of termination' (i.e. the date on which notice expires or if he is dismissed without notice 'the date on which the termination takes effect' or if he is on a fixed term contract the date on which the fixed term expires without being renewed).

A dismissal is 'unfair dismissal' unless the employer had a valid statutory reason and acted reasonably in treating that reason as justifying dismissal taking into account all the circumstances, including size and administrative resources (Employment Rights Act 1996, s.94). Valid reasons for dismissal generally relate to the employee's conduct, capability, redundancy or breach of an enactment although the law also allows for a rather vague 'some other substantial reason' to count as a valid reason. Some reasons for dismissal are automatically unfair, for example: dismissal on account of pregnancy, dismissal for asserting many statutory rights (such as the right to the minimum wage or to paid holidays) or dismissal for taking part in trade union activities (the complete list covers at least 25 separate reasons).

Fair dismissal

Dismissal may be fair where it relates to the capability of the employee for performing work of the kind he is employed to do, assessed by reference to skill, aptitude, health or any other physical or mental quality. Dismissal may also be fair on grounds of incapacity, e.g. due to prolonged sickness (provided this does not amount to disability discrimination) but full medical information should be obtained. Proper procedures must be followed before a dismissal for incompetence or sickness (it should be ascertained if there are reasons for this, both at work or outside work and monitoring is essential). If proper procedures are not followed a dismissal may be unfair just for that reason even if it was otherwise fair. In such a case compensation may be less that it might otherwise have been. New rules governing minimum standards for disciplinary procedures are due to come into force on 1 October 2004 (Employment Act 2002, Sched. 2).

A person who has reached 65 cannot normally bring an unfair dismissal claim as the law currently stands (there is an exception for employment where a normal retiring age is older than that for both men and women). This rule will be abolished from 1 October 2006 when age discrimination in employment is to become unlawful (the DTI issued a consultation document on this subject in July 2003, entitled *Equality and Diversity: Age Matters*). Attempts to circumvent the rule by claiming it is sex-discriminatory failed in October 2003 (*Secretary of State DTI* v. *Rutherford* (1) and Bentley (2) [2003] IRLR 858, EAT).

There are exceptions e.g. where dismissal relates to health and safety reasons, refusal of a shop worker to work on a Sunday or enforcement of a relevant statutory right.

Compensation for an employee dismissed before normal retiring age may take into account that employment should have continued beyond that age.

Awards

Unfair dismissal complaints are separate and different from wrongful dismissal complaints. Unfair dismissal is entirely a statutory creation and complaints can be heard only by employment tribunals, not by the courts. Wrongful dismissal refers to breach of contract and as noted above either the courts or employment tribunals have jurisdiction but a tribunal cannot award more than £25,000.

An unfairly dismissed employee can request re-employment or compensation. Compensation is normally composed of 'compensatory award' plus a set amount of 'basic award'.

Compensatory award is to compensate the employee for financial loss resulting from his unfair dismissal in so far as the employer is responsible for it, thus enabling tribunals to make reductions if an unfairly dismissed employee contributed to his dismissal by his conduct or if he unreasonably fails to try to mitigate his loss by looking for a new job. Basic award is calculated by a formula which takes into account weekly pay, age and length of service. Both types of award are subject to maximum limits, adjusted for inflation at 1 February each year. As from 1 February 2004 the maximum amount of compensatory award is £55,000 and the maximum weekly pay which can be taken into account in the basic award formula is £270 before tax (the absolute maximum basic award which the formula can currently produce is £8,100).

16.3.5   Redundancy

After two years continuous employment most employees have a right to a statutory redundancy payment if dismissed by reason of redundancy (commonly referred to as 'being made redundant'). Claims must be made within six months of 'the relevant date' (which is normally the date on which employment ended).

Dismissal is by reason of redundancy if the main reason for it is closure of the employing business either completely or at the place where the employee works, or a cessation or diminution in the need for employees to carry out work of a particular kind, either completely or at the place where the employee works (Employment Rights Act 1996, s.139).

Statutory redundancy pay is calculated in the same way as basic award in unfair dismissal cases (see above and Employment Rights Act 1996, s.162). There is an absolute upper age limit of 65 at date of dismissal for entitlement to statutory redundancy pay (Employment Rights Act 1996, s.156). The same considerations about changes to this age limit apply as in unfair dismissal cases (see above).

An employer can avoid a redundancy payment if he offers suitable alternative employment to the redundant employee (i.e. employment on the same or very similar terms and conditions without any significant loss of status; the new job should not require the employee to have more than a reasonable travelling distance). Unfair selection for redundancy may amount to unfair dismissal. Selection of older workers has been held to be an improper criterion and unfair. However, employers may seek to dismiss older staff on the basis that they are more expensive to employ or it is preferable to keep a younger person in a job. Care should be taken when volunteering for redundancy (e.g. for early retirement) because this could be interpreted as termination by agreement and not dismissal.

Until 1995 selection for redundancy 'in contravention of a customary arrangement or agreed procedure relating to redundancy' (e.g. last in, first out) made a redundancy dismissal automatically unfair. This is no longer so. Each case must now be decided on its merits (Deregulation and Contracting Out Act 1994, s.36).

16.4   RETIREMENT

16.4.1   Normal retiring age

This may be stipulated in the contract of employment or implied, and represents the age at which this class of employee can reasonably expect to be made to retire unless there is some special reason to apply a different age. If employees retire at a variety of ages there may be no normal retiring age and the maximum age will become 65. 'Normal retiring age' is not necessarily the same as 'pension age'.

The age stipulated in the contract may be varied where employees are regularly retired at some other age – the policy operated in practice or the employee's 'reasonable expectation' may apply. It is the employee's expectation at the date of dismissal rather than the date of recruitment which determines the retirement age.

As noted above EC law requires all EU Member States to outlaw age discrimination in employment by, at the very latest 2 December 2006 unless in particular cases it is objectively justified and the British government has announced that it will bring appropriate regulations into force on 1 October 2006.

16.4.2   Directorships

A director is not automatically disqualified by reason of age or mental incapacity, but those over 70 who wish to be appointed or continue to act as a director of a public company or its subsidiary have to be specially approved. A registered company may impose disqualification in its Articles of Association, and the terms of employment for an executive director may also provide for retirement.

Directors may be removed if they are not carrying out their duties properly. This can be carried out by shareholders in general meeting (whatever the Articles or any contracts say) without prejudice to the rights of the director to obtain compensation, but it is possible in a small company to make oneself irremovable by careful drafting of the Articles. Companies may include in their Articles grounds for removal based on becoming a patient under the Mental Health Act 1983.

16.4.3   Pensions

For rights to pensions see Chapter 17.

16.5   SELF-EMPLOYMENT

Self-employment may continue to any age and there may be tax incentives to retain a business (or a share in a business). Consider tax efficient schemes for handing on the business. For capital gains tax advantages on retirement and inheritance tax advantages in respect of business assets see Chapter 17.

16.5.1 Partnership

Partnership is the relationship which subsists between persons carrying on business with a view of profit (Partnership Act 1890, s.1). Partnership involves contracts between the partners and with persons dealing with them. In the absence of specific provision in the partnership agreement, there is no age limit to being a partner and subsequent mental incapacity does not cause immediate dissolution. Mental incapacity is a ground for asking the court to decree a dissolution: see Partnership Act 1890, s.35. If a partner is mentally incapable when purportedly entering a partnership he may still be bound if the other partner did not know of this. A person who allows himself to be represented as partner of an incapacitated individual could be liable to third parties (see Partnership Act 1890, s.14(1)).

16.5.2 Voluntary work

Those who engage in voluntary work must take care not to become personally involved in any contracts that are entered into on behalf of the organisation for which they work. The normal law of negligence will apply as regards any injury caused to any person or damage caused to property during the course of such work.

16.5.3 Committee member

Before becoming a committee member of an unincorporated society, club or association it is important to consider the rules or other constitution of the organisation and its financial state. The annual accounts should be examined. Committee members are jointly and severally liable for any liabilities incurred although they may usually seek indemnity from the assets of the organisation.

It is becoming increasingly desirable to form a limited liability company, usually incorporated by guarantee without a share capital, especially where there are employees or substantial contracts or risks may be involved. Committee members are, then, technically directors of the company. The directors can still be personally responsible if the company has traded whilst insolvent or they have acted imprudently or beyond the powers of the company. Insurance against directors' liability should be arranged by the company.

16.5.4 Club trustees

Club trustees should seek to limit their liability under any contracts to the amount of the club assets from time to time under their control, or exclude the right of any creditor to claim against them personally for any shortfall. Merely describing themselves as trustees does not limit liability. Trustees may also wish to obtain an indemnity from the individual club members or at least the members of the club management committee.

16.5.5   Charity trustees

Those who are charity trustees, whether in the capacity of ordinary trustees, committee members or directors, assume further responsibilities. Full particulars are available from the Charity Commissioners.

CHAPTER 17

Financial matters

Julia Abrey

17.1 INVESTMENT ADVICE

Reference should be made to the following chapters and also the books listed in Appendix F:

- Chapter 3 for the Practice Rules relating to investment business; for rules relating to the giving of financial advice, and for support in relation to financial services;
- Chapter 4 where the client is incapable of dealing with financial affairs.

Your Taxes and Savings 2003/04; a booklet for older people is published annually by Age Concern.

17.2 PENSIONS

Most elderly clients will be at the stage where they are drawing (or entitled to draw) such pensions as they have. However, do not overlook the tax advantages of making further pension contributions, when permitted, and the potential growth in a pension or pension fund, if the pension is deferred. There are tax incentives for individuals to provide for their own pensions:

- Income tax relief is given on contributions at the individual's highest rate.
- Pension funds are exempt from income tax and capital gains tax.
- Part of the pension can be taken as a tax-free lump sum.

17.2.1 State retirement pension

It is no longer necessary to have virtually retired from work before drawing the state pension. A taxable pension is paid on attaining state pensionable age (65 for men; 60 for women) but the claimant must have an adequate national insurance contributions record. An inadequate record means entitlement to a reduced pension or none at all. A claim can be based on the claimant's own contributions or on a spouse's or former spouse's record.

The state pension age is to be equalised at 65 years for both men and women, but this is to be phased in over 10 years from 2010 so will not affect anyone aged 50 or over in 1999.

Those living abroad should contact Pensions and Overseas Benefit Directorate (address in Appendix E).

For more information, see:

- PM2: *State Pensions: Your Guide*;
- PM3: *Occupational Pension: Your Guide*;
- PM4: *Personal Pension: Your Guide*;
- PM8: *Stakeholder Pension: Your Guide*;
- Age Concern Fact Sheet 19: *The State Pension*;
- Age Concern Fact Sheet 48: *Pension Credit*;
- For claims and payment relating to benefits see Chapter 13 at 13.2.

Amount

There are three components and the amount is affected by several factors but not by earnings:

- Basic pension: a weekly age addition is paid on reaching 80 years. If a pension is deferred it increases but only to age 70 (men) and 65 (women). Additions may be paid for dependants (e.g. a spouse) unless they receive some other benefits or have earnings above certain limits.
- Graduated pension based on contributions between April 1961 and 1975.
- Additional pension based on contributions after April 1978 until April 2002 (SERPS) and after this date the State Second Pension.

Over 80s pension

Those aged 80 or over can claim a pension even if they have not paid NI contributions, but there is a residence qualification.

Widow's and widower's benefits

A widow or widower who has reached pension age but does not qualify for their own full pension may use their spouse's contribution record to qualify for a full basic pension.

A widow or widower can inherit half of the spouse's graduated pension if both are over pension age at death

A widow aged over 60 may inherit all or part of her husband's additional pension and add it to her own pension (subject to a maximum sum). The amount of SERP's inherited depends on the age of her husband at death.

There are transitional rules for those that reach pension age between 6 October 2002 and 5 October 2010, so that after 6 October 2010, widows and widowers will only be able to inherit half of their spouse's SERPS. These rules apply to widowers if they are both over pension age when the wife dies. However, in some circumstances it may be possible for the husband to inherit his wife's SERPS if he is under pension age when she dies.

A widow or widower will only be able to inherit 50 per cent of their spouse's State Second Pension, regardless of when they were widowed. See leaflet SERPS L1.

Separation and divorce

It may be possible to rely upon a spouse or ex-spouse's contributions record:

- a separated wife can claim the married woman's retirement pension on the husband's record but only from the date that he draws his pension;
- following divorce either spouse may, on reaching pensionable age, use the spouse's record during the marriage (or from the start of working life to the divorce) to get a better pension than on their own record.

See leaflet CA10: *National Insurance for Divorcees*.

17.2.2 Occupational pensions

Occupational pensions are arranged by employers (e.g. company pension schemes) and may be contributory or non-contributory. A separate trust fund is set up and employees receive a booklet setting out the terms.

In general, benefits normally include:

- a pension at a specified age;
- a death benefit for those who die before retirement;
- a widow's (or widower's) pension.

There are Inland Revenue restrictions on:

- the maximum pension (two-thirds of final salary);
- the amount of the lump sum (one-and-a-half times salary);
- the size of any continuing pension following death.

Types of scheme

The available types of scheme include:

- final salary where pension is a proportion of salary for the last year (or average of last few years) and is based on years worked times a set fraction (e.g. 30/60ths); the pension may be contracted into or out of the State Second Pension;
- average earnings where pension is based upon average earnings over the period of participation with a set calculation being applied for the pension;

- flat rate pension which is based on the number of years employed;
- money purchase pension which depends upon the size of the employee's contribution to an investment fund and the growth in that fund; such pension may be contracted into the State Second Pension.

Additional voluntary contributions (AVCs)

AVCs are a way of saving for retirement through the pension scheme. Full tax relief is available on additional contributions (subject to limits) and free-standing AVCs can also be made to independent pension plans.

There is now more flexibility including early retirement or withdrawal, pre-served rights after two years in a scheme and transfer to another company scheme or to a personal pension.

17.2.3 Personal pensions

Self-employed people and employees may contribute to personal pensions:

- for employees this may be instead of the State Second Pension, Stake-holder Pension or an occupational scheme;
- there are revenue restrictions on contributions, retirement age and benefits;
- policies may be with-profit, unit-linked, deposit or non-profit;
- on retirement it may be worthwhile taking the maximum permitted lump sum and investing this in other ways.

Section 226 pension policies were available solely for the self-employed until July 1988 and those then in existence may continue but the revenue restrictions were slightly different from the new personal pensions.

An employee may switch from an employer's scheme to a personal pension but many have been encouraged to do so when this was not beneficial.

17.2.4 Stakeholder pensions

Stakeholder pensions are designed for people without access to employer-sponsored pension arrangements. Employers who are not exempt must designate and offer access to a stakeholder pension scheme. If any employees join the designated scheme, the employer must offer a payroll deduction facility to those who want it.

It is possible to invest up to £3,600 (including tax relief) in a stakeholder pension scheme each year. However, under certain circumstances the maximum level of pension contributions may be increased for people with earnings according to their age and earnings level.

Stakeholder pension schemes can be set up under a trust or can be set up by deed poll. Where the scheme is set up by deed poll, the manager of the scheme (the 'stakeholder manager') may enter into contracts with each member of the scheme or a person acting on their behalf. The stakeholder manager could be an insurance company, bank, or building society and must be authorised by the Financial Services Authority (FSA) to carry out stakeholder business.

17.3   TAXATION

17.3.1   Income tax

Allowances for elderly people

There are some allowances and reliefs in addition to those normally available:

- higher personal allowances are available at 65 and at 75 years but are progressively withdrawn once income reaches a certain level;
- a widow or widower may claim a bereavement allowance for the 52 weeks following the death of the spouse, subject to various conditions; the allowance will be paid at the full rate if the applicant is over the age of 55 when their spouse dies;
- a blind person's allowance may be available and any unused part may be transferred to the spouse;
- relief becomes available on gross rent (subject to a limit) from furnished rooms in the home: see IR87: *Letting and Your Home*.

Note the impact of self-assessment on the elderly client, particularly the dates for submission of a return and payments of tax.

Planning

Simple steps may reduce the annual tax bill for a married couple or assist with cash flow:

- obtain and complete a tax claim form R40 if in doubt at the end of the year or when the overpayment reaches £50;
- Ensure that any Notice of Coding for PAYE on pension income is correct: taxed income relief should be given if appropriate to secure the lower rate of tax on investment income (see P3 (2003): *Understanding Your Tax Code*);
- reduce or increase income if 'caught in the margin': higher allowances reduce proportionately if income is more than a certain sum and this means that a high effective rate of tax is paid until the allowance is lost;
- re-arrange investments so that income is received gross (without deduction of tax) where a repayment claim would otherwise be necessary; non-taxpayers can apply to receive gross interest on bank/building society accounts (form R85) (see IR110: *Bank and Building Society Interest: A Guide for Savers*).

319

- transfer investments between spouses to equalise income so that both gain the benefit of their personal allowances and the reduced rate band, any higher rate liability is minimised and neither party is caught in the margin as regards higher allowances;
- the Inland Revenue have stated that those in receipt of income of under £2,500 a year will not be required to complete a tax return for the year 2000 onwards;
- consider transferring allowances between husband and wife in appropriate cases – up to half of each allowance may be transferred;
- as dividend tax credits are now not repayable (1999/2000 onwards), consider a review of investments as a change to those which still attract a refundable tax credit (e.g. building society/gilt edged securities) may be beneficial but be aware of potential capital gains tax on any change.

Ensure that all eligible allowances have been claimed.

Information

Generally see Inland Revenue website (**www.inlandrevenue.gov.uk**). Keep an updated supply of the following free Inland Revenue leaflets and offer them to clients:

- IR121: *Income Tax and Pensions*;
- IR138: *Living or Retiring Abroad*;
- IR45: *What to Do About Tax When Someone Dies*;
- IR144: *Income Tax and Incapacity Benefit*;
- IR121: *Income Tax and Pensioners*;
- IR 170: *Blind Person's Allowance*;
- IR 2008: *ISAs, PEPs and TESSAs*;
- SA/BK4: *Self Assessment: A General Guide to Keeping Records*;
- SA/BK8: *Self Assessment: Your Guide*.

Also see Age Concern Fact Sheet 15: *Income Tax and Older People*.

17.3.2 Capital gains tax

The gain in the value of an asset during the taxpayer's ownership is taxed on disposal by way of a sale or gift (transfers between spouses are not treated as a disposal).

The expenses of acquiring, improving and disposing of the asset are deducted from the net sale proceeds or value to ascertain the gain:

- certain assets are exempt, e.g. an owner-occupied dwelling-house, but there is a restriction on the relief if the house is surrounded by a significant amount of land;

- there is presently rebasing to March 1982 which means that only gains or losses since that date are taken into account;
- there is a taper relief (formerly indexation allowance) whereby the effect of inflation is taken into account to reduce the actual gain (this may not increase or create a loss).

Retirement relief is available on disposals of business assets for those who retire after reaching a certain age (or earlier due to ill health). This is being phased out and replaced by a taper relief on business assets.

The net gains (after losses) of the taxpayer in the tax year are taxed at the taxpayer's highest rates of income tax for the year (top-slicing) but an annual exemption reduces or eliminates the taxable gain.

Independent taxation applies so each spouse has the benefit of the annual exemption; although the losses of one spouse cannot be set against the gains of the other.

CGT is payable on 31 January following the tax year of the disposal.

Information

See CGT1: *Capital Gains Tax: An Introduction*. There are also a number of useful help sheets listed in CGT1.

Planning

The following strategies may be adopted to reduce potential CGT bills (the first two being for married couples):

- ensure that realisations that produce gains are by the partner with the lower rate of tax;
- consider transferring assets into joint names before disposal to ensure utilisation of both persons' annual exemptions and/or lower rates of tax;
- review assets annually to consider disposals to use the annual exemption;
- dispose of assets that do not create a gain when cash is needed;
- realise losses prior to 5 April when a net taxable gain would arise;
- avoid making disposals that would produce a large gain shortly before death (all assets are re-valued on death but CGT is not then charged);
- ensure that wills and investments are neutral for CGT purposes.

Many older people contemplate moving abroad on retirement and the implications of a change of residence or domicile upon capital taxation in this country should be first considered.

17.3.3   Inheritance tax

The capital value of all net assets held at death above a threshold ('the nil rate band') (£255,000 in 2003/04) is taxed at a fixed rate (40 per cent):

- this includes lifetime gifts unless exempted (see Chapter 19 at 19.2.2);
- the capital value of trusts may be aggregated;
- certain types of asset are exempt or valued on a beneficial basis (e.g. business assets and agricultural property);
- assets passing on death to a spouse or a charity are also exempt.

Information

See IHT3: *Inheritance Tax: An Introduction*, which also lists various other useful help sheets.

Planning

Married couples may reduce potential IHT bills by ensuring that:

- they utilise the nil rate band on first death by leaving up to this sum to a non-exempt beneficiary (often the children) and the balance to the survivor either outright or in trust (but do make sure that the survivor will be adequately provided for); the nil rate band can also be held in a discretionary trust;
- a joint tenancy in the matrimonial home is severed with each spouse by will leaving his or her share as tenant in common to the children either outright or in trust (but be careful to consider occupation issues between the spouse and children).

Other possibilities include:

- making gifts within the annual exemption or the small gift exemption;
- making large gifts sooner rather than later to start the seven-year period running;
- reviewing income to see if regular gifts from surplus income could be made which are immediately exempt (IHTA 1984, s.21).

See Chapter 19 for more detail on making gifts.

Trusts for disabled beneficiaries

There are special dispensations in respect of CGT and IHT for certain trusts for the benefit of disabled beneficiaries:

- Taxation of Chargeable Gains Act 1992, s.3 and Sched.1, para.1;
- Inheritance Tax Act 1984, ss.3A(1) and (3) and 89.

On this topic generally refer to Chapter 20

CHAPTER 18

Housing

David Foster

Older clients normally occupy their homes as owners or as tenants. However, they may only have a licence to occupy. They may also share another person's home or allow another person to occupy or share their home. This chapter considers, in brief, the main issues which may arise in these contexts and where advice may be required and outlines some of the relevant law. Details of housing grants and subsidies is covered in Chapter 15 at 15.2 and issues on making a gift of the home in Chapter 19 at 19.3.4.

18.1 THE ELDERLY CLIENT IN HIS OR HER OWN HOME

18.1.1 Choice of home or location: practical issues

People do not automatically wish to move home on reaching retirement age, but it is a good time to take stock and think ahead. The starting point is whether the client is happy and comfortable in the present home and able to cope physically and financially. Then consider how long this situation is likely to continue: putting things off may reduce the options, but a move can seldom be reversed. It may be wise to anticipate future needs by applying to go on a council or registered social landlord (housing association) waiting list.

18.1.2 Contemplating moving checklist

> ❏ Will the client cope physically in the new home e.g. access, stairs, convenience of layout, garden, security?
> ❏ Will the client cope financially in the new home e.g. heating, maintenance and repairs?
> ❏ Is there room for all the client's personal possessions that are to be kept?
> ❏ Is the location suitable in terms of adequate facilities e.g. shops, transport, library, post office?

323

❏ Is the location suitable in terms of necessary services e.g. doctor, dentist, social services assistance?

❏ Is there enough to do in the area?

❏ Is it a safe and congenial environment at all times of the day and night?

❏ Will friends and acquaintances be lost who cannot be replaced?

❏ Can the client afford the costs of the move e.g. removals, estate agent, solicitor's fees, stamp duty?

❏ If moving nearer relatives is there a risk they will need to move?

❏ Is the move too hasty e.g. after a bereavement?

❏ In the case of a couple, would the survivor wish to remain in the new home?

18.2   OWNER-OCCUPATION

Always examine the implications as regards means-tested benefits when the sale or purchase of a dwelling for personal occupation is being considered. For more information and detail in this respect see Chapter 14.

18.2.1   Sole ownership

The sole owner may leave the home by will or it will pass to the next of kin on an intestacy. If the owner becomes mentally incapable and it is desired to dispose of the home or some interest in it, at present in the absence of a registered Enduring Power of Attorney (EPA) there is no alternative but to apply to the Court of Protection for the appointment of a receiver. However, practitioners in the light of the Mental Incapacity Bill will have to advise clients of anticipated changes. These will replace the EPA with the Lasting Power of Attorney (LPA), establish a new Court of Protection supported by the renamed Office of Public Guardian, which will have power to appoint 'deputies' as opposed to receivers. Transitional provisions will recognise validity of EPAs but the client will have to be advised of the limits of the EPA pending the introduction of LPAs. See generally Chapter 4.

18.2.2   Joint ownership

Often a home will be owned jointly by husband and wife or an unmarried couple. All jointly owned property is held by the owners on trust i.e. the joint owner will be a trustee or at least have an interest in the trust property.

Where a property is purchased or otherwise put in joint names it is important for there to be a precise statement as to how the beneficial interests are held, i.e. whether as joint tenants or tenants in common. Under a joint tenancy the survivor will automatically inherit on death. Under a tenancy in common the share as tenant in common may be left by will or pass under an intestacy and the precise shares should be agreed and recorded.

The statement is usually made in the appropriate section of the transfer deed placing an 'X' in the relevant box (a copy should be retained) or a separate deed of trust, but the statement to the Land Registry as to whether the survivor can give a valid receipt for capital money is not sufficient.

Upon a divorce (or judicial separation) the court may make a property adjustment between the parties, but in the case of unmarried joint owners there are no similar procedures and the courts can only give effect to the intention and contribution of the parties.

An equitable interest in a house or flat belonging to another may arise where a person makes a financial contribution towards the cost of buying the property or pays for or contributes towards the cost of extending or improving the property.

This is likely to be of particular significance where the incentive for the financial input was the prospect of living in or sharing the home and that expectation is not fulfilled. Ideally the expectations of the parties should be clarified and confirmed in a legal document before the arrangement is entered, although this seldom happens within families.

An elderly client who decides to contribute a substantial sum towards the cost of purchase or improvement of a home with the intention of residing there with a member of the family will need to decide whether to do so by way of shared ownership, loan or gift. Factors to take into account, depending on circumstances, are:

- a gift has potential inheritance tax advantages, but the money may not be recoverable if needed (if a gift is to be made the sooner this is done the better as regards both inheritance tax and means-testing);
- a loan or joint ownership creates vulnerability to means-testing if residential care is needed at a later date;
- a loan or joint ownership protects the elderly individual in the event that the relationship breaks down but may leave the other joint owner vulnerable to having to move house;
- testamentary provision may need to be changed to compensate for a gift.

If the money is spent on building a bungalow in the grounds or providing a self-contained flat it may be best for this to be conveyed into the name of the elderly client rather than establish joint ownership in the entire property, but in that event you must ensure that the deeds are properly split and independent legal advice would be indicated.

See the Law Society's Guidance on Gifts of Property at Appendix B and Chapter 19 at 19.3.4.

Disputes

Disputes relating to joint ownership of property may now be resolved under the Trusts of Land and Appointment of Trustees Act 1996. This overcomes various difficulties that arose under the Law of Property Act 1925, s.30, although previous case law may still be relevant.

Anyone who is a trustee or who has an interest in trust property may make an application to the court which is then required to have regard to the following matters in determining the application:

- the intention of the person or persons who created the trust;
- the purpose for which the property subject to the trust is held;
- the welfare of any minor who occupies or might reasonably be expected to occupy any property subject to the trust as his or her home;
- the interests of any secured creditor of any beneficiary.

18.2.3   Incapacity of joint owner

A trustee may not generally delegate his or her powers so must act personally in any sale or other transaction. There are exceptions to this.

Under s.25 of the Trustee Act 1925 a trustee can delegate his or her functions by a power of attorney. This can only be for limited periods and is subject to specific safeguards. Such a power cannot be an EPA. The amendments in the Trustee Delegation Act 1999, s.5 should be noted.

Under s.3(3) of the Enduring Powers of Attorney Act 1985 an attorney under an enduring power could exercise all or any of the functions vested in the donor as trustee. This was a last minute amendment to enable a jointly owned matrimonial home to be dealt with but its wider implications were not then appreciated. It was repealed with effect from 1 March 2000 (or 2001 for subsisting enduring powers) by the Trustee Delegation Act 1999, but note the transitional provisions in s.4.

Under the Trustee Delegation Act 1999 (following Law Commission recommendations to resolve the problem) an attorney can exercise a trustee function of the donor if it relates to land, or the capital proceeds or income from land, in which the donor had a beneficial interest. This applies to both general and enduring powers of attorney whenever made. An 'appropriate statement' made by the attorney at the time of a sale or within three months confirming that the donor had a beneficial interest in the property will be conclusive evidence (s.2). See Land Registry Practice Guide LRPG009. It will not be sufficient if the joint owner (e.g. spouse) is the sole attorney because a capital receipt by trustees needs two signatures (see s.7). In all other cases the provisions of s.25 of the 1925 Act (as amended) must be complied with.

Unless advantage is taken of the 1999 Act, if a joint legal owner of freehold property becomes incapable by reason of mental disorder of exercising his or her functions as a trustee, a new trustee may have to be appointed before the legal estate can be dealt with (see Chapter 4 at 4.9.5).

This is the current position. However, so far as concerns mental incapacity the Draft Mental Incapacity Bill (see Chapter 1 and 18.2.1) should be noted including the replacement of EPAs with wider Lasting Power of Attorney.

18.2.4 Mortgages

There is no age bar to taking on a loan secured by a mortgage or charge and many lenders have become willing to consider applications from those at or near retirement. An interest-only mortgage may be available from a bank or building society under a special scheme for those who need capital (see 18.7.7). Mortgage interest tax relief is no longer available.

For a cautionary tale where a mother charged her home as security for her son's borrowing and the same solicitors acted for both parties, see *Clark Boyce v. Mouat* [1993] 4 All ER 268, PC.

18.2.5 Possession proceedings

When monthly repayments under a mortgage fall into arrears, the lender may claim possession in the local county court and the possession order may be enforced by the bailiff under a warrant for possession.

Under the Administration of Justice Acts 1970 and 1973 the court may adjourn the possession proceedings or suspend any possession order if the arrears and future payments which will fall due are likely to be paid within a reasonable period. In determining the reasonable period the court should take as its starting point the full term of the mortgage: *Cheltenham & Gloucester Building Society v. Norgan* [1996] 1 WLR 343, CA.

The court may use the same powers if the borrower is attempting to sell the property to give the borrower a reasonable time to complete the sale. The existence of equity in the security will be a significant factor when the court is deciding whether to exercise its discretion in the borrower's favour.

Loans taken out for consumer purposes and secured on the borrower's home are covered by the Consumer Credit Act 1974 rather than the Administration of Justice Acts mentioned and the court has wider powers to give the borrower more time to pay.

18.2.6 Grants

Under the Housing Grants, Construction and Regeneration Act 1996 various discretionary grants may be applied for from local authorities.

Mandatory disabled facility grants can be applied for under the 1996 Act currently for up to £25,000 (in England) and £30,000 (in Wales), although there is discretion to make higher awards. For more information see Chapter 15.

18.3   LONG RESIDENTIAL LEASES

Many older clients own their homes under a long lease, in particular owners of flats, those who have a shared ownership lease and former council tenants or registered social landlord tenants who have exercised the right to buy or acquire a flat.

18.3.1   Relevant legislation

After examining the terms of the lease and establishing for how long it is to run and the identity of the landlord, the following legislation may need to be considered. In the event of disputes the Leasehold Valuation Tribunal may have jurisdiction rather than the county court or there may be concurrent jurisdiction.

- *Leasehold Reform Act 1967*: this gives leaseholders of houses the right to buy the freehold (and in some cases the right to extend the lease).
- *Landlord and Tenant Act 1987*: this contains the right of first refusal, the right to apply for a manager to be appointed, the right to apply for the terms of a lease to be varied and related matters.
- *Landlord and Tenant Act 1954, Part I*: this gives security of tenure to residential tenants who hold under long leases at low rents. This is achieved by extending the leases on expiry and providing for the creation of new statutory tenancies within the Rent Act at fair rents.
- *Leasehold Reform, Housing and Urban Development Act 1993*: this gives most owners of long leases of flats a right as one of a group of flat owners to acquire the freehold (collective enfranchisement) or as an individual flat owner to acquire a new lease. It also gives the right to have an audit of the management of the block carried out.
- *Housing Act 1996*: this extends the rights of long leaseholders in relation to service charges, bad management by freeholders and the right of first refusal including a new right to appoint a surveyor to advise on service charges. It also extends the enfranchisement and collective enfranchisement rights under the 1967 and 1993 Acts respectively.
- *Commonhold and Leasehold Reform Act 2002*: Part 1 of the Act introduces a new type of freehold ownership of buildings divided into flats – commonhold. Conversion of existing leasehold blocks into commonhold units will depend on the consent of every person with an interest in the land. Part 2 of the Act introduces the 'right to manage': the right to set up a company to manage without acquiring the freehold.

18.3.2 Shared ownership

Some councils and registered social landlords operate shared ownership schemes under which homes are part purchased and part rented on a long lease. There may be an option to purchase a greater share at a later date.

These schemes enable those with limited capital to enjoy the benefits of home ownership without borrowing, and investing available capital in this way may have advantages in regard to means-tested benefits, but increasing rents could become a problem.

Other arrangements for sheltered housing include:

- flexible tenure: option to buy, lease or share ownership;
- leasehold schemes for the elderly (LSE): buy at 70 per cent of the normal price and receive 70 per cent of value when you sell;
- loan-stock schemes: 'buy' housing by making an interest-free loan to the trust or charity;
- buying at a discount: usually involves selling at a discount;
- a 'life-share' in the property (or a part of it), usually organised through a finance company with the price depending on age, sex, marital status and the property value: there will be no return on death, but an annuity (or capital sum) may be paid to those who stop living in the property.

Ensure that the scheme is suitable for the client and that there are no restrictions which would inhibit resale. Most schemes are marketed for first-time buyers but some are designed for retired people.

18.3.3 Enfranchisement

Enfranchisement is a convenient word to describe the right to acquire the freehold. Long residential leaseholders have been given statutory rights. There is a distinction between houses and flats. The primary Act in respect of houses is the Leasehold Reform Act 1967 and that for flats the Leasehold Reform, Housing and Urban Development Act 1993.

In the case of houses, since 26 July 2002 the leaseholder has the right to acquire on fair terms the freehold or an extended lease where the following basic conditions are met:

- the original term of the lease must be at least 21 years;
- when giving notice exercising the right the leaseholder must have been the tenant of the house for the last two years.

In the case of flats, with effect from 1 November 1993 most long leaseholders paying a low rent in a predominantly residential building have the right to purchase collectively, at market value, the freehold of the building, where:

- at least two-thirds of the building is let on long leases.
- at least two-thirds of those leaseholders give notice of their wish to do so.

Since 26 July 2002 a condition that half of the leaseholders giving notice must be resident has been abolished. In addition most long leaseholders paying a low rent have the individual right to acquire an extended lease for a period of 90 years plus the outstanding period of the old lease.

18.4 TENANCIES

Some older clients will hold their properties under tenancies which are not long leases. Such tenants will be concerned about security of tenure, the amount of rent payable, succession to the tenancy and repairing obligations. The statutory rights in these areas vary according to the type of landlord and to some extent the date when the tenancy commenced.

The three main types of landlord are local authority type, registered social landlords and private landlords. Local authorities are accountable to the local electorate and registered social landlords to the Housing Corporation.

Government policy since 1979 has included:

- a shift from full protection of the tenant of the private landlord in terms of security of tenure and rent control to dependence on market forces: this is not retrospective so tenants do not lose any existing rights and should seek to retain earlier protected tenancies wherever possible;
- encouraging council tenants to purchase their properties through 'right to buy' legislation offering large discounts but then ultimately attempting to prevent the consequent haemorrhaging of public sector stock by substantially reducing the discount in some locations;
- encouraging privatisation of local authority housing by the transfer of council housing stock to registered social landlords: any tenant of a local authority whose home is so transferred ceases to be a secure tenant and becomes an assured tenant (with a preserved right to buy);
- increasing control of public sector tenant's behaviour by the introduction of probationary tenancies and extending landlord's powers to deal with anti-social behaviour.

18.4.1 Local authority type landlords

Tenants of a local authority, an urban development corporation, a housing action trust and certain other authorities will usually have the status of a secure tenant. The tenant (including most licensees) is a secure tenant provided the tenant condition is met. This condition is that the tenant resides in the dwelling as his only or principal home. (Problems arise where a tenant is absent from the dwelling for a significant period but absence for medical treatment should not affect rights as a secure tenant.)

The Housing Act 1985 (as amended) gives secure tenants long-term security of tenure and rights such as:

- the right to take in a lodger;
- the right to exchange tenancies;
- the right to buy.

However, local authorities now have the power to decide to grant probationary tenancies known as 'introductory tenancies' to all new tenants and this power is increasingly being exercised. For the first year of the tenancy the tenant in effect has no security of tenure. During this period, subject to the service of a written notice containing certain information including the reasons for bringing proceedings and the right to request an internal review, the landlord can recover possession for breaches of the tenancy agreement. After one year such tenancies automatically become secure.

A council tenant might be asked to consider a transfer to a private landlord (usually a registered social landlord) and the local authority and the relevant government department may be considering a large-scale voluntary transfer. Tenants must be consulted and are entitled to be balloted and vote on the proposed transfer. Following transfer, such a tenant ceases to be a secure tenant and becomes an assured tenant. If the transfer is to a registered social landlord the tenants in practice will be granted a tenancy agreement which contains terms which attempt in some areas to preserve the additional/ better rights given to secure tenants.

Notice to quit is not required to terminate a secure tenancy.

18.4.2 Registered social landlords

A tenancy of permanent accommodation granted by a registered social landlord after 14 January 1989 will usually be an assured tenancy. However, existing tenancies granted before that date remain secure tenancies (see 18.4.1).

In theory registered social landlords should follow Housing Corporation standards and guidance.

The Housing Act 1988 (as amended) gives assured tenants long term security of tenure. Assured tenants of registered social landlords may have the right to acquire their property under the Housing Act 1996. Registered social landlords cannot grant introductory tenancies. However, when letting temporary accommodation e.g. to homeless applicants to local authorities, in practice they grant assured shorthold tenancies and thus in effect are then more akin to private landlords (see 18.4.3).

Notice to quit is not required to terminate an assured tenancy.

18.4.3   Private landlords

Protected tenancies

Tenancies granted by private landlords before 15 January 1989 will generally be protected tenancies governed by the Rent Act 1977. Protected tenancies may be either contractual tenancies or statutory tenancies. Until the original tenancy agreement terminates they are contractual tenancies. After termination they become statutory tenancies. A contractual tenancy terminates on the expiry of a notice to quit or following the registration of a new fair rent by the rent officer and the service of a notice of increase by the landlord.

Protected tenancies represented the 'high water mark' for the protection of private tenants in a civilised society. The protected tenant generally has long term security of tenure. There is rent control through the regime of fair rents and registration by the rent officer. Succession rights are the most favourable. Consequently the elderly client still with a protected tenancy and faced with a landlord, for instance, wanting vacant possession may have a strong bargaining position.

Assured and assured shorthold tenancies

Tenancies granted by private landlords after 14 January 1989 will be either an assured tenancy or an assured shorthold tenancy under Part I of the Housing Act 1988. There are some exceptions. The most important are tenancies granted by resident landlords.

Before 28 February 1997 the landlord had to take the initiative and serve a notice in prescribed form before the tenancy started to create an assured shorthold tenancy. In addition the tenancy had to be for an initial fixed term of not less than six months. From 28 February 1997 the position was reversed by the Housing Act 1996. Consequently any new tenancies granted after that date are automatically assured shorthold tenancies unless notice is given that the tenancy is to be an assured tenancy. Registered social landlords usually do this but there is obviously no incentive for private landlords to do so.

A tenant who holds an assured tenancy and agrees with the same landlord to take a tenancy of a different dwelling will become an assured tenant under the new tenancy and not an assured shorthold tenant. The assured tenant generally has long term security of tenure. However, there is little rent control and market rather than fair rents. There are some succession rights.

The assured shorthold tenant has no long term security of tenure. However, there is little rent control and market rather than fair rents. There are no succession rights.

Where a long lease of a flat (or possibly a house) expires, until 14 January 1999 the tenant would have been entitled to a statutory tenancy under the

Rent Act 1977: see Landlord and Tenant Act 1954, Part I. After 14 January 1999 the occupying tenant will be entitled to an assured tenancy: see Local Government and Housing Act 1989.

18.4.4   Right to buy

Part V of the Housing Act 1985 gave the right to buy to secure tenants. This right was extended to tenants of some registered social landlords by the Housing Act 1996, s.16.

Local authority type tenants have the right to buy at a discount after two years. The tenant may nominate certain family co-residents to purchase jointly. A council tenant whose dwelling is transferred to a registered social landlord or private sector landlord has a 'preserved right to buy'. Certain types of property or tenancy may be excluded (sheltered housing and properties particularly suitable for older people and most housing provided by charitable bodies).

The discount depends upon the duration of the tenancy and can be up to 60 per cent for houses and 70 per cent for flats. However, the maximum discount varies depending on the location of the property. Up to 26 March 2003, the maximum discount in London was £38,000. From 27 March 2003 the maximum discount in London (except Greenwich London Borough Council) and for parts of the South East was further reduced. Part of the discount is repayable upon a sale within three years of purchase but not on death.

Section 17 of the Housing Act 1996 extended the right to buy – confusingly called the right to acquire – to assured tenants of housing associations and other registered social landlords. However, the dwelling must have been provided by public money and have remained in the social rented sector and have been built or acquired after 1 April 1997. Regulations cover the amount of discount.

There is no longer a right to a mortgage. Mortgages in practice can be obtained to cover the cost, possibly on an interest-only basis. If family members offer to underwrite the mortgage and repair costs, consider whether they will be able to do so and what will happen if they do not.

Whether to buy

It is not always advantageous for an elderly tenant to purchase. When comparing outgoings take into account that:

- the owner will be responsible for additional, uncertain outgoings (property insurance and repairing obligations);
- any service charges continue even though rent ceases;

- housing benefit will no longer be available (mortgage interest is covered by income support within limits).

18.4.5   Allocation

See the Housing Act 1996, Part VI (as amended by the Homelessness Act 2002) and the Code of Guidance *Allocation of Accommodation for Local Housing Authorities*.

From January 2003 there is a new statutory framework for the allocation of tenancies by a local authority. Allocation means the selection of a person to be a secure or introductory tenant, including an existing council tenant applying for a transfer, or the nomination of an applicant for the grant of a tenancy of permanent accommodation by a registered social landlord. Authorities have some discretion in the manner in which they allocate but this is now subject to a greater degree of central government control. In addition the applicant for housing in this context has a number of statutory rights.

Local housing authorities must have and publish an allocations scheme for determining priorities. They can only allocate accommodation in accordance with this scheme. Allocations may not be made to ineligible persons. A person may be ineligible and therefore disqualified because he or she:

(a)   is subject to immigration control;
(b)   falls within a prescribed class of person from abroad;
(c)   has been guilty of serious unacceptable behaviour in the opinion of the local authority.

Points (a) and (b) above do not apply to existing council tenants applying for a transfer.

If the person is disqualified then the local authority cannot allocate a tenancy to him or her. However, local authorities no longer have discretion to disqualify other groups of people. In determining priority between different applicants the local authority must give reasonable preference to a number of groups. The groups are now based on social need and include homeless people and are set out in the Housing Act 1996, s.167(2). The local authority may give additional preference to sub-groups within those groups, provided they can be identified as having urgent housing needs.

When deciding how to award preference within these groups the local authority may take into account:

- the financial resources open to an applicant to meet his or her housing costs;
- any behaviour of an applicant (or household member) which affects his or her suitability to be a tenant;
- any local connection between applicant and local authority's area.

However, the allocations scheme need not provide any preference at all for applicants who have been guilty of serious unacceptable behaviour. Subject to the reasonable preference groups mentioned, the allocations scheme may cover specific applicants or groups not within those groups. The government issues guidance to local authorities on allocation of accommodation. An applicant for an allocation of housing accommodation has the right to general information including likely priority and if an offer is likely to be made, how long before the offer. In addition there is the right to be informed of any decision about the facts of his or her case affecting the treatment of his or her application: s.167(4A) of the 1996 Act.

Reviewing or challenging the decision

An applicant has the right to request an internal review of any decision disqualifying him or her or reducing his or her priority for reasons of anti-social behaviour and any decision about the facts of his or her case affecting the treatment of the application. Decisions of local housing authorities on housing allocation or failure to comply with statutory duties in this area can be challenged by judicial review.

Registered social landlords in addition to nominations by local housing authorities allocate accommodation direct to applicants and have to deal with existing tenants applying for transfers. Under the Housing Act 1985, s.106 they too are required to publish their rules governing in effect their waiting list and transfer scheme and to supply details of the particulars which they have recorded as relevant to the application for accommodation.

Generally the courts have regarded housing associations/registered social landlords not as public bodies open to judicial review or having to act in a way compliant with the Human Rights Act 1998. However, following the case of *Poplar HARCA* v. *Donoghue* [2001] EWCA Civ 959 it is arguable that judicial review is available and Human Rights Act compliance is required when a function is being performed similar to that performed by a local housing authority.

18.4.6 Security of tenure

A court order is generally needed before a home is repossessed (see below for sanctions). In cases involving the discretionary grounds for possession either under the Rent Act 1977 (protected tenants) or the Housing Act 1985 (secure tenants) or the Housing Act 1988 (assured tenants) the court has a wide discretion to adjourn the proceedings or to suspend or postpone the possession order. However, when doing so the court may impose conditions. The court must impose conditions with respect to payment of rent and arrears unless this would cause exceptional hardship or would otherwise be unreasonable. In other cases possession orders against tenants must take effect not later than 14 days after the making of the order unless it would cause exceptional hardship, in which case the order can be postponed for up to six weeks (Housing Act 1980, s.89).

Secure tenancies

Security of tenure is achieved by the landlord only being able to obtain a possession order against the tenant on at least one of the 16 grounds set out in the 1985 Act. In addition to establishing the ground the landlord must also satisfy the court that is reasonable to make a possession order. On four of the grounds the landlord must also satisfy the court that suitable alternative accommodation is available at the date of the hearing.

Security may be affected by an assignment or sub-letting to the extent that this will often involve a breach of an express obligation of the tenancy which is covered in one of the grounds for possession

The landlord must serve a preliminary warning notice, known as a notice seeking possession, before starting possession proceedings, specifying the ground on which possession may be sought and the date (at least 28 days ahead) after which proceedings may start. However, in the case of alleged anti-social behaviour the latter period may be shortened or even the notice itself dispensed with.

Protected tenancies

The tenant has a fair degree of security of tenure. If the protected tenancy is a contractual tenancy the landlord must first terminate this by notice to quit before bringing possession proceedings.

Security of tenure is achieved by the landlord only being able to obtain a possession order where:

- the court is satisfied that it is reasonable to make a possession order and suitable alternative accommodation is available or will be so;
- the court is satisfied that it is reasonable to make a possession order and at least one of the first 10 grounds (called cases, discretionary grounds) set out in the Rent Act 1977 is proved;
- at least one of the 10 remaining cases (mandatory grounds) is proved.

Security may be affected by an assignment or sub-letting to the extent that this will often involve a breach of an express obligation of the tenancy which is covered in one of the discretionary grounds for possession. Where the claim for possession is based on suitable alternative accommodation being available, the court may direct that the new tenancy should be a protected rather than an assured tenancy. However, where there is statutory overcrowding or where a closing order or demolition order has been made the tenant cannot rely on the protection given by the Rent Act 1977. However, in the latter case the local authority has statutory duty to re-house the tenant under the Land Compensation Act 1973 which is more extensive than any duty owed under subsequent homelessness legislation.

See Rent Act 1977, s.98 and Sched. 15 for the grounds for obtaining possession.

Assured tenancies

The tenant has a lesser degree of security of tenure. Security of tenure is achieved by the landlord only being able to obtain a possession order against the tenant on the grounds set out in the 1988 Act. In addition to establishing the ground the landlord must also satisfy the court that it is reasonable to make a possession order in most cases. However, in respect of rent arrears there is a mandatory ground for possession open to the landlord for arrears exceeding eight weeks or two months depending on whether the tenancy is weekly or monthly.

The landlord must serve a preliminary warning notice, known as a notice of intention to seek possession, before starting possession proceedings, specifying the ground on which possession may be sought and the date (at least 28 days ahead) after which proceedings may start. However, in the case of alleged anti-social behaviour the latter period may be shortened or even the notice itself dispensed with.

See Housing Act 1988, Scheds 1 and 2 for grounds.

18.4.7   Unlawful eviction

All tenants and licensees apart from excluded tenants and licensees are given additional preliminary protection from eviction by the Protection from Eviction Act 1977 in two ways.

First, where a notice to quit is required to terminate the tenancy and in the case of a licence, at least four weeks' written notice in prescribed form is required. Notice to quit is required to terminate in particular protected tenancies which are contractual tenancies and non-secure council tenancies, e.g. where the tenant no longer occupies the property as his or her only or principal home.

Secondly, a court order is required before any eviction (s.3). Breach of this section is an actionable tort.

Excluded tenancies and licences are as follows:

- sharing with a resident landlord;
- sharing with a member of a resident landlord's family;
- temporary expedient to a trespasser;
- holiday accommodation;
- other than for money or money's worth;

- asylum-seekers;
- licence to occupy a public sector hostel.

In addition, under s.1 of the 1977 Act criminal offences are created where the landlord or any other person unlawfully evicts or harasses any residential occupier. Offences are investigated and prosecuted by local authorities rather than the police and the CPS.

An injunction can be sought from the local county court to prevent harassment or eviction. Damages can also be claimed for various torts but also for breach of covenant for quiet enjoyment. Under ss.27 and 28 of the Housing Act 1988 damages are available for the difference between the value of the property with and without a tenant. Claims for general, special, aggravated and exemplary damages can be considered.

18.4.8   Succession

Secure tenancy

The spouse of a deceased secure tenant, or another member of the family (including a cohabitee of the other sex), can qualify to succeed to a secure tenancy. Following the requirement not to discriminate under the European Convention and the Human Rights Act 1998 and a Court of Appeal decision in relation to protected tenancies under the Rent Act 1977, it is possible that a partner of a lesbian or homosexual couple could qualify to succeed as a spouse. In any event it appears such a partner would at least qualify to succeed as a member of the family following an earlier decision of the House of Lords in relation to the wording in the Rent Act 1977: *Fitzpatrick* v. *Sterling Housing Authority* [1999] 3 WLR 1113.

The property must have been the potential successor's principal or only home at the tenant's death. In addition a non-spouse must have lived there (or in other public sector accommodation) with the tenant for at least 12 months immediately prior to the death. There can be only one succession and where more than one person is qualified to succeed the spouse takes preference. If there is no spouse the potential successors may agree who succeeds. In the absence of agreement the landlord selects.

Protected tenancy

A protected tenancy may be succeeded to twice where the first successor is a spouse including a common law husband or wife. It may be succeeded to only once where the first successor is a member of the family. The spouse succeeds to a protected tenancy and must have been residing in the property immediately before the death. A member of the family only succeeds to an assured tenancy. The member of the family must have been residing with the deceased at the time of death and for the two years immediately before the death.

Following the requirement not to discriminate under the European Convention and the Human Rights Act 1998 and *Mendoza* v. *Ghaidan* [2002] EWCA Civ 133, CA, one surviving partner of a lesbian or homosexual couple succeeds as a spouse rather than a member of the family.

See the Rent Act 1977, s.2 and Sched. 1 (amended by the Housing Act 1988).

Assured tenancy

Succession rights to an assured tenancy are far more limited than those which apply to secure and protected tenancies. Only a spouse, which includes a common law husband or wife, may succeed and there can only be one succession. A joint tenant will automatically succeed to the tenancy but there can then be no further transmission. Another family member cannot succeed to the assured tenancy. Following the requirement not to discriminate under the European Convention and the Human Rights Act 1998 and the Court of Appeal decision in *Mendoza*, it is possible that one partner of a lesbian or homosexual couple could succeed as a spouse.

18.4.9 Assignment and sub-letting

The general position at common law is that a tenant may assign or sub-let a tenancy unless the tenancy agreement provides otherwise. This basic position may be altered by statute.

Section 19 of the Landlord and Tenant Act 1927 provides that there is an implied proviso in any term allowing assignment with the landlord's consent that such consent shall not be unreasonably withheld. However, the Housing Acts 1985 and 1988 change the position for secure and assured tenants respectively.

Secure tenancies

Assignment in general is prohibited unless:

- the assignment is made in a financial settlement following divorce;
- the assignment was to a person qualified to succeed (see above) although this need not be the person next entitled (this option could be used to ensure that a child rather than a spouse succeeds);
- there has been a mutual exchange with landlord's consent (Housing Act 1985, s.92).

Sub-letting of part requires written agreement of the landlord and failure to obtain agreement could be a ground for possession. But consent must not be unreasonably withheld and if so withheld is treated as given. There is a right to take in lodgers but if the tenant sub-lets the whole, the tenancy ceases to be secure and cannot subsequently become a secure tenancy.

Assured tenancies

It is an implied term of every assured tenancy which is a periodic tenancy that the tenant, except with the consent of the landlord, shall not assign or sub-let the whole or part. However, the landlord has an absolute discretion as to whether or not to give consent.

18.4.10   Rent control

Local authorities may make such reasonable charges as they determine. They are under a duty to review rents periodically and may alter rents generally in their locality or alter particular rents as circumstances allow. They have complete discretion as to the setting of rents but are influenced by government decisions as to the payment of subsidy to housing revenue accounts and must not act irrationally or in bad faith or take irrelevant factors into account. Before varying the rent of a secure tenancy they must secure the agreement of the tenant or serve a notice of variation.

A secure tenant of a registered social landlord has a 'housing association tenancy in accordance with the Rent Act 1977'. Either party can refer a proposed rent increase to a rent officer using the fair rent machinery of the 1977 Act and there is a further appeal to a Rent Assessment Committee.

A system of 'fair rents' applies to protected tenancies (notwithstanding any agreement to the contrary). Rent officers fix the rent with an appeal to a Rent Assessment Committee. The rent ignores the scarcity value of accommodation so is artificially low.

The rent for assured tenancies can be at market levels. Registered social landlords in practice set rents at affordable levels. Rent rises can be examined by the Rent Assessment Committee if they are above market levels but not if in accordance with rent review provisions in the original agreement.

The rent for assured shorthold tenancies can also be at market levels. A tenant has the right to refer the rent to a Rent Assessment Committee on the basis that the rent is artificially high but now only during the first six months of the tenancy.

Older people may be eligible for means-tested housing benefit to meet part or all of their rent. However, in the case of private landlords a rent stop may be applied restricting the amount of rent covered by housing benefit.

18.4.11   Service charges

Tenants of flats (including those of housing associations but not local authorities) have some statutory protection in respect of service charges:

- only reasonably incurred amounts are payable for services;
- any work must be carried out to a reasonable standard;
- a written summary of relevant costs may be required and accounts inspected.

See the Landlord and Tenant Act 1985 (and Housing Act 1985 for houses disposed of by the public sector).

18.4.12   Repairs and maintenance

A landlord is usually under an obligation to repair and maintain a dwelling which is let as such.

Contract: covenant to repair

In addition to any express term of the tenancy the landlord will normally be subject to a term implied by the Landlord and Tenant Act 1985, s.11. Section 11 applies to tenancies granted after 23 October 1961 for a term of less than seven years. Under this term the landlord is responsible for repairs to the structure and exterior of the dwelling and the installations for the supply of heating, hot water, gas, water and electricity.

On a tenancy of a flat granted after 14 January 1989, these repairing obligations extend to common parts of a building or other parts which are controlled by a landlord. The courts may imply similar obligations into older tenancy agreements in order to give business efficacy to them. However, a landlord is not liable for breach of an express or implied term to repair unless he had notice of the defect.

Tort

Liability may also arise in tort. This arises primarily under the Defective Premises Act 1972, s.4. The liability is similar to that under the Landlord and Tenant Act 1984, s.11 but restricted to damage to contents and/or personal injury. However, the notice requirement is less strict. The landlord must know or ought to have known about the relevant defect. Consequently failure to maintain reasonable arrangements for inspection when such defects would have come to light may result in liability.

Remedies

A number of different direct legal remedies are available to enforce repairing obligations:

- A tenant who suffers distress and inconvenience, injury or loss because of the landlord's failure to carry out repairs may seek compensation by a damages claim in the county court and/or apply for an order of specific performance or injunction including an interim injunction for urgent repairs in some circumstances.
- An aggrieved person (not necessarily a tenant) can bring a private prosecution in the magistrates' court under the Environmental Protection Act 1990, s.82 for an order to deal with a statutory nuisance – health risk. A 21-day statutory warning must first be given.
- Under the Housing Act 1985, s.606 a complaint can be made to a local magistrate who can then compel the local Environmental Health Department to inspect and report to the relevant council committee.
- A claim for judicial review may be possible against a local authority which is failing to exercise its statutory duties or to consider properly the exercise of its powers to deal in particular with unfitness, statutory nuisances and substantial disrepair in properties not in its own ownership.

Alternatively the local Environmental Health Department may be asked to take action.

The local authority may issue a repairs notice requiring the owner to carry out works in accordance with those specified in the notice and failure to do so is an offence (a right of appeal lies to the county court). Local authorities are required to take certain steps where a dwelling is unfit for human habitation (as defined in the Housing Act 1985, s.604). The local authority has power to carry out the works itself and charge the person responsible.

Local authority environmental health officers have general powers in relation to a property which is a statutory nuisance (as defined in the Environmental Protection Act 1990, s.79). The officer may serve a notice on the person responsible for the nuisance (e.g. the landlord or owner occupier) requiring the nuisance to be abated (appeal is to the magistrates' court within 21 days). If a notice is not complied with proceedings may be taken in the magistrates' court which can order the person responsible to abate the nuisance, impose a daily fine for as long as the nuisance continues and order compensation to anyone who has suffered injury or loss (such as a tenant).

18.5 LICENCES

18.5.1 Licence or tenancy?

The distinction between a licensee (e.g. a lodger) and a tenant is based upon control over the property and the degree of integration into the household (see *Street* v. *Mountford* [1985] 2 All ER 289).

An occupier who under the contractual arrangements has exclusive possession of a dwelling for a term and pays rent will usually be a tenant regardless of how he is described in the agreement. However, there will merely be a licence where there is a genuine service occupancy or there is no intention to create a legal relationship. In many situations the individual merely has a licence to occupy which may be:

- an exclusive licence where the accommodation is self-contained;
- a licence to occupy a private room where other essential facilities are shared;
- a licence to share a room and other facilities.

The distinction between a tenancy and a licence is important because only a tenant can have security of tenure and protection as to repair and maintenance.

18.5.2 Informal licence

When the individual is living with relatives or friends there will usually be merely an informal (or bare) licence to occupy a room or facilities, but:

- if regular payments are made there may be a contract and reasonable notice must then be given to terminate: this could include a contribution to household expenses;
- a 'licence coupled with an interest' may arise where the occupier contributes towards the cost of buying, altering or improving the home: someone who contributes towards the costs of acquiring a property will usually acquire an equitable interest in it.

If a court is asked to exclude an informal licensee from a property it may postpone any order to allow reasonable notice for alternative arrangements to be made, but if care services are being provided as well as the accommodation it may be difficult to ensure that these continue.

18.5.3 Contractual licence

When money is paid for the facility there will be a contract (e.g. a lodger or a room in a hotel or care home) and the terms should be complied with:

- the terms may have been published in advance (e.g. in an advertisement, letter or brochure) and will then be incorporated into the contract but some of the terms may need to be implied;
- a contract may arise even if the resident lacks mental capacity but any agreement should then be in simple terms and carefully explained to the resident (the contract will usually be entered into by the person managing his or her financial affairs, e.g. an attorney or receiver).

18.6   HOMELESS PERSONS

A homeless person or a person threatened with homelessness may apply to the local authority for accommodation. A person in inadequate accommodation may possibly be considered homeless if it is no longer reasonable for him or her to continue to occupy the existing home.

When exercising their functions under Part VII of the Housing Act 1996, local housing authorities are bound to have regard to *Homelessness: Code of Guidance for Local Authorities*. If such an application is made then the local authority must under the Housing Act 1996, s.184 make inquiries as to whether he or she is eligible for assistance and, if so, what legal duty (if any) is owed in relation to re-housing. Broadly a person is eligible for assistance unless a person from abroad within certain categories or an asylum seeker within recent years.

Priority need and unintentionally homeless

The local authority when making the inquiries mentioned must establish in particular whether the applicant has a priority need for accommodation and whether or not he or she is homeless intentionally. The categories of person in priority need are defined in s.189 of the 1996 Act and include a person who is vulnerable as a result of old age. This includes an applicant who has such a person living with him or her, or who might reasonably be expected to have such a person live with him or her. The Code suggests that authorities should consider whether old age is a factor which makes it hard for applicants to fend for themselves, and that all applications from people aged 60 or over should be considered carefully.

An act or omission that led to homelessness must have been deliberate. The Code provides that it should not be considered deliberate if the applicant was incapable of managing his or her affairs for example because of old age.

Not a priority need and intentionally homeless

If the local authority is satisfied that an applicant does not have a priority need and is not intentionally homeless, then it only owes a limited duty to give advice and assistance. In addition the local authority has the power to secure accommodation or to prevent the threatened homelessness.

Priority need but intentionally homeless

If the local authority is satisfied that an applicant became homeless intentionally but is in priority need, then it only owes a limited housing duty to secure accommodation to give the applicant a reasonable opportunity of securing accommodation him or herself. In addition there is a duty to provide advice and assistance in this context, but the local authority must first now assess the applicant's individual needs before giving such advice and assistance.

Duties for those with priority need and unintentionally homeless

While the local authority is making inquiries it has a legal duty to ensure that suitable temporary accommodation is available for the applicant pending the completion of the inquiries. Once the local authority has completed its inquiries and if it is satisfied that the applicant has both a priority need and did not become homeless intentionally, then it may refer the applicant to another local authority but only if there is a local connection with that other authority. In that event the local authority to which the applicant is referred completes the re-housing process and discharges the remaining legal duties owed in this respect.

Its remaining legal duty at that stage is to secure suitable accommodation for the applicant. This is the full re-housing duty. In practice this often will either be council or housing association accommodation. In the first case the tenancy would not be a secure council tenancy and in the second not an assured housing association tenancy. However, lodgings provided by householders may be suitable for some vulnerable applicants.

Termination of the duty

Such accommodation must be secured indefinitely until one of the following events occurs:

- the refusal of an offer of such suitable accommodation;
- ceasing to be eligible for assistance;
- becoming homeless intentionally from such accommodation;
- voluntarily ceasing to occupy such accommodation as an only or principal home;
- accepting an offer of permanent accommodation under the local authority's Allocation Scheme;
- refusing an offer of suitable permanent accommodation under the local authority's Allocation Scheme;

- accepting but not rejecting an offer of an assured shorthold tenancy from a private landlord.

Throughout the homelessness process, the homeless applicant may be allocated permanent council or housing association accommodation through the local authority's Allocations Scheme. The Allocations Scheme is the only route to permanent council accommodation. In that event the tenancy will be a secure or assured tenancy as appropriate.

Challenging the decision

A homeless applicant has a legal right under s.202 of the 1996 Act to challenge any of the following decisions made by the local authority by requesting a review within 21 days of being notified of the relevant decision:

- any decision on eligibility for assistance;
- any decision on what duty (if any) in relation to re-housing the local authority has towards the applicant;
- decisions concerning local connection referrals;
- decisions concerning the suitability of accommodation offered to the applicant.

There is also a statutory right of appeal to the county court in respect of the decision on review if this is adverse but only on a point of law and the appeal must be made within 21 days of notification on the adverse decision.

The only method of legal challenge of other decisions by the local authority in relation to a homelessness application is by an application to the Administrative Court for judicial review.

Alternatively, a person who is homeless may be entitled to accommodation being provided under the National Assistance Act 1948, s.21 if they are deemed to be in need of care and attention that is not otherwise available to them. See Chapter 8 at 8.5 and *R* v. *Bristol City Council, ex parte Alice Penfold* [1998] 1 CCLR 315.

18.7 SPECIAL SITUATIONS

18.7.1 Shared occupation

Either financial circumstances or care needs may dictate that an elderly individual shares a home. This could involve:

- moving into and sharing the home of a relative or friend;
- a relative or friend moving into the elderly individual's home;
- taking a lodger;

- employing a resident housekeeper or carer;
- living in the home of a paid carer.

Family arrangements

Arrangements within the family sometimes prove unsatisfactory to one side or the other so ensure that all relevant factors are considered before it is too late. Experience shows that there may be an unacceptable loss of independence and privacy by the elderly individual or of freedom and privacy for the sharing family.

The arrangement should be the choice of the elderly person rather than the family (though it may be suggested by the family) and hasty decisions should not be made following bereavement or any period of ill-health. Whilst a legal document cannot provide for personal relationships, a clear enforceable agreement is desirable if either party commits capital to the arrangement (see 18.2.2). It may be necessary to unscramble the financial arrangements in order to separate the personal relationships and it is better to discuss this before the parties are committed than after things have gone wrong – when the parties may not be talking anyway! If the arrangement does not work it is seldom possible for the previous situation to be restored.

Frequently shared occupation arises without any planning where a son or (more often) a daughter remains at home with parent(s). Often the parties rely on assumptions and fail to discuss their hopes and wishes, so you can perform a valuable service by encouraging them to do so in an open way in your presence. A mother may actually desire to move into a residential care home but not wish to leave her daughter alone, whilst the daughter may yearn for freedom yet not wish to desert her mother by putting her in a home.

Checklist for parties where family considering sharing arrangement

❑ How well they get on now and are likely to get on living in close proximity (taking into account the effect upon any marriage and the existence of children in the household)

❑ Whether the home is physically suitable and provides sufficient privacy

❑ The effect on state benefits and community care provision

❑ The implications of a decline in health and the need to provide care

Commercial arrangements

Where the arrangement is with a stranger for payment it is essential to identify the understandings and assumptions on which it is based, from both points of view, and these should be recorded in writing. A formal document is not necessary and may be off-putting, but an exchange of letters is a minimum requirement.

Taking a lodger may produce an additional income and, if the relationship works out, provide company. The notice period and weekly or other payment to be made should be confirmed in advance and also what it covers (e.g. meals, laundry, telephone). The effect of this income on state benefits should not be overlooked (similar principles apply if the client proposes to become a boarder). There are Inland Revenue concessions for income from letting one room.

If a housekeeper or carer is to live in, this will be an employment situation, but living in the home of a carer may be classed as being a boarder. In either event income tax, NI contributions and the effect on state benefits should be taken into account by both parties.

18.7.2 Sheltered housing

Housing restricted to and designed so as to be suitable for elderly people may be available and this is an option for those who want to live an independent life in their own home without all the responsibilities of home ownership. Most are apartments or bungalows, physical disabilities may be catered for and alarm systems are often installed.

Schemes include:

- purpose-built or converted housing without a warden;
- warden-assisted or warden-controlled housing;
- supportive housing where residents have their own room but use communal facilities and perhaps receive a cooked daily meal (e.g. Abbeyfield homes);
- housing with care (meals and care services are usually provided).

Tenure

The basis on which the property is held may be:

- freehold or long lease at a premium with service charge rent (enfranchisement may be possible for leasehold sheltered housing schemes);
- tenancy at a rent: those in the public sector will be secure or assured tenancies but private sector rent control may not apply if 'attendance' is included;
- shared ownership or shared equity arrangement;
- licensee only.

Checklist for sheltered housing when considering the lease/other contractual arrangement

---

❏ Check for any restrictions on occupation, resale or assignment (problems have arisen over disposal of some homes following death)

❏ Can younger carers live in?

❏ Check the effect of the owner or spouse becoming a Court of Protection patient

❏ Can the surviving spouse remain there (especially if younger)?

❏ Check what services are provided

❏ What are the warden's duties?

❏ Check the service charge liability

❏ Check whether there is a 'sinking fund' for property repairs

❏ Check the identity of the managers of the scheme

❏ Are they members of the Association of Retirement Housing Managers?

❏ Is there a residents association and is it recognised by the managers?

NHBC

Registered house builders selling sheltered housing must comply with the NHBC Sheltered Housing Code of Practice (1990):

- the Purchaser's Information Pack (PIP) contains useful information;
- legally binding management agreements are required to a specified standard.

Age Concern

Age Concern produces useful Fact Sheets in this area.

- 2: *Buying Retirement Housing*;
- 8: *Looking for Rented Housing*;
- 13: *Older Home Owners: Financial Help with Repairs and Adaptations*;
- 35: *Rights for Council and Housing Association Tenants*;
- 36: *Private Tenants Rights*.

18.7.3   Homes for disabled people

From 1980 the role of local authorities changed to that of strategic planner rather than direct provider. A duty is imposed on local housing authorities to consider the housing needs of their district and they must have particular regard for the special needs of chronically sick and disabled people: see the

349

Chronically Sick and Disabled Persons Act (CSDPA) 1970, s.3 and now the Housing Act 1985, s.8.

Adaptations

Frequently an overlapping responsibility for the provision of adaptations exists between the social services authority and the local housing authority.

The duty of the social services authority arises under CSDPA 1970, s.2(1)(e). This requires them to provide assistance in arranging for the carrying out of the works. This might be no more than finding a suitable builder or assistance with a grant application form.

Social services are under a duty to assess the needs of a disabled person for community care services, which would include assistance for adaptations. In this area unfortunately there is a national problem caused by the shortage of occupational therapists used in practice in the assessment process. This can result in delay. See Chapter 8.

The duty of the local housing authority arises under the Housing Grants, Construction and Regeneration Act 1996, Part I to provide disabled facilities grants subject to a means test (see also 18.2.4).

VAT

Building alterations are subject to VAT, but many alterations for people with disabilities are zero-rated.

18.7.4   Park homes

'Park homes' is a new name for mobile home parks. A fully-equipped caravan (or chalet designed so as to be classed as a caravan) may be purchased but a serviced site must be rented and security of tenure may be limited.

The Mobile Homes Act 1983 requires the park owner to enter into a legal agreement with each individual occupier dealing with rights and responsibilities regarding:

- increases in the site fees and any other charges that are made;
- the basis on which a caravan on a site may be sold or transferred (including commission charged and approval of the new occupier by the park owner);
- termination of the agreement.

References

The following may be useful:

- *Mobile Homes: A Guide to Residents and Site Owners*, Office of the Deputy Prime Minister (2003) (see www.odpm.gov.uk);
- Shelter, Leaflet 13: *Mobile Homes* (2003) and *Mobile Homes: An Occupier's Guide* (2nd edn, 1997);
- National Association of Park Home Residents.

18.7.5 Second homes and timeshare

Increased leisure may make second homes or timeshares attractive for those with the energy and sufficient capital, but it is necessary to take into account:

- the expenses involved, which will continue until disposal even if continuing use cannot be made of the property;
- the problems of management or maintenance, especially if other people must be relied upon due to a decline in mental capacity;
- the difficulty of disposing of the property (especially timeshare);
- the capital tied up in the investment (which may still be included in any means-testing for benefits or services);
- the capital gains tax implications.

18.7.6 Foreign properties

When purchasing a home (or second home) abroad you must encourage the client to consult a qualified lawyer practising in the country concerned (unless you have the expertise in your own firm), because if you fail to do so you could be liable if anything goes wrong. Each country has its own conveyancing procedures and the inheritance laws of the particular country may apply with surprising consequences.

The Law Society of England and Wales maintains a register of their members with recognised expertise in foreign jurisdictions.

Checklist for client before moving abroad

❏ Check pension and state benefits entitlement with the DWP.

❏ Check availability of health care and reciprocal arrangements.

❏ Check the income and capital taxes situation.

❏ Check ways to delegate powers, such as managing finances and affairs in the country of destination.

❏ Check the effect of a change of residence or domicile (e.g. on testamentary provision).

❏ Check the position if the person returns to the United Kingdom.

18.7.7 Equity Release

Older homeowners may wish to release income or capital from their home and as it is not suitable for everyone other options should be considered initially:

- An independent financial adviser may be able to advise if the older person's investments or assets could produce a better return.
- Check if the older person is entitled to any welfare benefits, particularly as not all are means-tested. See Chapter 13.
- If the older person is in debt they may need advice on managing the debt.
- It may be appropriate to downsize and release equity in this way.
- If the aim of the release is specifically to pay for repairs, improvements or adaptations, the Home Improvement Trust may assist. The not-for-profit company exists to help older homeowners release some of the equity tied up in their home, in order to fund such works. The Trust works closely with local home improvement agencies, sometimes called Care and Repair or Staying Put agencies.

Conditions

Conditions which must be satisfied to obtain an equity release vary from company to company but include:

- a minimum age, usually 60, although some schemes are open to those over 55 while others are only available to people over 80;
- a maximum amount to loan, for example 75 per cent of the property value;
- the applicant's home must be owned by them and worth at least £40,000;
- there is significant equity in the property;
- some providers may require a minimum amount of money to borrow.

Types of schemes

The home reversion scheme involves selling the whole or part of the home to a reversion company. The price will not be the same as if they sold the property on the open market. In return the owner receives either a cash lump sum or a monthly income. The older person can remain in the home rent-free or for a nominal monthly rent, for the rest of their life. When the property is eventually sold the reversion company receives the proceeds from the sale, depending on what proportion of the home was sold.

Home income plans, also known as a mortgage annuity scheme, enable the older person to receive a monthly income for life while still owning and living in the property. A mortgage loan is taken out against the home usually up to a maximum of 75 per cent of its value. The money is used to buy an annuity which pays a regular income each month for the older person's life. The interest payments on the loan are deducted from this income. Limited tax relief applies to plans taken out before 9 March 1999 but for new plans there is no such advantage.

Roll-up (mortgage) loans involve the older person taking out a loan against the value of their home. Either capital or monthly income (or both) are paid. No repayments are made until the house is eventually sold, where the interest is rolled up and added to the total loan. These schemes were a problem in the early 1990s when the housing market was depressed and many people ended up in negative equity. These schemes will have to be regulated by the Financial Services Authority from October 2004.

Interest only loans allow the older person to obtain a capital sum and they have to repay the interest from their assets. Some banks and building societies provide these types of loans.

Other considerations

Consideration needs to be given to the cost of entering the scheme, such as valuation and legal fees and the commission payable to the financial adviser. The client should also consider if they are likely to ever want to move and in what circumstances, as not all schemes allow the plan to be transferred. The older person remains responsible for the repair, insurance and usual outgoings as a homeowner and they need to be sure they can afford to take out the plan in the long term.

For more information see Age Concern Fact Sheet 12: *Raising Income or Capital from Your Home*.

PART D

Inheritance and death

CHAPTER 19

Gifts

Martin Terrell

A significant lifetime gift should be considered only when the money or asset involved is surplus to the client's present or anticipated requirements.

Concerns often arise when a gift is proposed, both as to the mental capacity of the client and whether there is undue influence, especially if the donee is pressing for the transaction to be completed. It is essential to ensure that the client is seen alone, except in the case of married couples where a joint approach may be appropriate (although not always in the case of second marriages). When assisting a client in making a gift, it is essential to establish, and carefully record, the reason for making the gift. It is surprising how often clients believe (or are led to believe) that a gift must be made to avoid inheritance tax or assessment for care costs. On closer examination, these concerns may be unnecessary. The client's estate may only be marginally over the inheritance tax threshold or a gift may give rise to a capital gains tax charge which the client does not want to pay. It may be impossible to avoid the liability because the gift would be caught by anti-avoidance measures. The client should be able to enjoy the benefits of his estate during his lifetime and the client's right to his own property includes the right not to make gifts as much as the right to make gifts.

If a solicitor is not satisfied that the client has capacity to make the gift or feels that undue influence has been brought to bear then he should obtain medical evidence addressing the client's capacity. If this is resisted or there is still pressure for the gift to be completed, then the solicitor must decline to act, while being aware of the consequent danger of financial abuse or fraud taking place.

For further details see:

- Chapter 1, for capacity to make lifetime gifts;
- Chapter 2, for taking instructions from elderly clients;
- Chapter 4, for gifts under an Enduring Power of Attorney or Part VII of the Mental Health Act 1983;
- Chapter 14, for the potential implications of means-testing for local authority services;

- Chapter 17, for tax planning issues;
- Appendix B: the Law Society's Gifts of Property Guidelines.

19.1 VALIDITY OF GIFT

19.1.1 Capacity of donor

A gift is only valid if the donor had capacity to make the gift at the time it was made: see *Re Beaney* [1978] 2 All ER 595 and Chapter 1 at 1.5.4. The level of capacity required depends on the nature of the gift relative to the value of the donor's estate. Clearly a lower degree of capacity is required if the donor is handing over a trinket compared to transferring a valuable property.

Undue influence and capacity

Not only must the donor have the requisite capacity, there must be no undue influence. Reported cases involving issues of capacity, such as *Re Beaney* referred to above, also involve questions of undue influence as it is unusual for an incapable donor to make a gift without some form of assistance, whether from the donee or other individual such as a solicitor.

The case of *Hammond* v. *Osborn* [2002] EWCA Civ 885 involved a gift of assets worth just under £300,000 by a retired teacher to a very helpful neighbour. Although the gift had been prompted by the donor, it would leave his estate significantly depleted and his liquid assets insufficient to meet the tax liability created by the gift. The Court of Appeal held that even though the donee was not guilty of any 'reprehensible conduct' the nature of the gift created a relationship of trust and confidence and therefore gave rise to a presumption of undue influence. The tax liability, the irrational nature of the gift, the lack of any form of independent or objective advice and the fact that the donor did not appreciate the scale of the gift together ensured that the presumption could not be rebutted.

19.1.2 Authority for the incapable donor

Where the donor is incapable of making a valid gift for himself, this may be done on his behalf by an attorney acting under an Enduring Power of Attorney (EPA). An attorney may make a gift on the donor's behalf when acting under an EPA pursuant to the Enduring Powers of Attorney Act 1985, s.3. Provided there are no restrictions in the power, such gifts may only be made to:

- provide for persons for whose needs 'the donor might have been expected to provide';

- persons 'related to or connected with the donor' where the gifts are of a seasonal or anniversary nature, of a reasonable value (having regard to all the circumstances and in particular the size of the estate) and are such that the donor might have been expected to make.

The donor's right to make such gifts depends on the circumstances. Provision for the needs of a grandchild has been allowed to include the payment of several years' school fees (*In re the Estate of Marjorie Langdon Cameron deceased* [1999] 2 All ER 924); the value of other lifetime gifts might for instance be made by reference to the inheritance tax allowances.

Without restriction by the donor

An attorney acting under a registered EPA, which has not been restricted by the donor, may make a gift on the donor's behalf on an application to the Court of Protection under the Enduring Powers of Attorney Act 1985, s.8(2) for the Court 'to authorise the attorney to act so as to benefit himself or other persons than the donor otherwise than in accordance with s.3'.

Restriction by the donor

An attorney acting under a registered EPA, which has been restricted by the donor, may make a gift on the donor's behalf. In this case a receiver may be appointed by the Court of Protection or any other person authorised under Court of Protection Rules 2001, SI 2001/824, r. 18, on an application to the Court of Protection under the Mental Health Act 1983, s.96(1)(d).

For applications to the Court of Protection generally, see 4.10.

19.1.3 Perfected gift

Make sure that the title to any gifted property is legally vested in the donee because a promise to make a gift is not enforceable and 'there is no equity to perfect an imperfect gift'. The donor must have done everything that he needs to do to effect the transfer but it does not matter that something remains to be done by a third party:

- chattels and cash are transferable by delivery if there is an intention to give: a signed letter is useful to confirm the intention and fix the date;
- a gift by cheque is not completed until the cheque is cleared;
- waiver of a debt must be by deed (unless there is consideration);
- a transfer of land or an interest in land must be by deed;
- in the case of securities it may be sufficient to hand over the certificates together with a signed transfer.

For tax purposes it is wise to encourage clients to record any large gifts, especially those relying on a tax exemption or which constitute a potentially exempt transfer for inheritance tax purposes.

19.1.4 Donatio mortis causa

An exception to the rule that a gift must be perfected applies where the donor:

- makes a gift in contemplation (not necessarily expectation) of death;
- delivers (or causes delivery of) the subject matter of the gift to the donee or transfers the means of getting at that subject matter; and
- intends that the gift was only to take effect on the donor's death.

Thus if a man on his deathbed tells his housekeeper that he wishes her to have some specific shares on his death and hands her the key to a safe containing the certificates, this may constitute a valid gift of those shares (provided there is proof of this). It now seems that even freehold property is capable of being the subject matter of such a gift (*Sen* v. *Headley* [1991] 2 All ER 636, CA).

19.2 TAXATION

A solicitor advising a client in respect of any lifetime gift should take account of the taxation consequences. Unless the solicitor clearly excludes tax advice from his retainer, which may well be appropriate where specialist advice is required, the solicitor could be negligent (*Hurlingham Estates* v. *Wilde and Partners* [1997] STC 627).

If the client is acting without advice and fails to take account of the tax consequences of a gift, this may be relevant in determining whether the client actually had capacity to make that gift, as in the case of *Hammond* v. *Osborn* referred to above.

19.2.1 Capital gains tax

A gift may be a chargeable transfer for CGT (see Chapter 17 generally), but in regard to gifts the following should be considered.

Hold-over relief

The donee takes the gifted property at the donor's acquisition value and there is no charge to tax on the transfer. Relief is not available if the transferee is not resident or ordinarily resident in United Kingdom. Hold-over relief now only applies:

- as between husband and wife (where there is no tax);
- on disposal of a business asset (including agricultural property);
- on transfers immediately chargeable to inheritance tax (e.g. transfers into and out of a discretionary trust).

Timing and payment

If a client intends to make a gift of an asset with a fluctuating value it is advantageous to do so when it has a relatively low value; appreciating assets should be given sooner rather than later. However, a client should also bear in mind the loss of the main residence exemption if gifting a property and the loss of the CGT uplift available to his assets on death.

There is a right to pay by instalments over 10 years for certain types of gift.

19.2.2   Inheritance tax

The value of lifetime gifts may be included in the estate of the donor (see Chapter 17 generally) but in respect of lifetime gifts the following should be considered.

A gift to a spouse is exempt from IHT (so is any inheritance by the spouse) but there are restrictions where one is not UK domiciled. Other things being equal, a transfer of assets to a spouse is useful to equalise the estates.

There are specific exemptions:

- small gifts (now £250 per donee) and normal, regular giving out of income;
- an annual exemption per donor (£3,000, or more on donee's marriage);
- payments for the maintenance of certain members of the family.

Certain gifts with no benefit reserved will be potentially exempt transfers (PETs) and become exempt if the donor survives seven years, with taper relief between three and seven years, but gifts must equal or exceed the nil rate band at the time the gift is made. For a gift to be a PET, it must be in favour of any of the following:

- an individual;
- a settlement with an interest in possession;
- an accumulation and maintenance settlement;
- a trust for a disabled person (see 17.3.3).

The primary liability for IHT on gifts falls on the donee but there is a secondary liability on the estate of the deceased donor. Any gift which is neither exempt nor a PET is a chargeable transfer liable to IHT immediately at one half of the rate applicable on death, taking into account all chargeable transfers during the past seven years. If the donor dies within seven years the full rate is charged, subject to taper relief and less any tax paid on lifetime gifts which is brought into account.

A gift between spouses does not usually involve any capital tax liability and may be beneficial in tax planning. However, any such planning should involve a careful consideration of both wills to ensure that it is clear where assets pass.

Practical points

- Do not overlook the reservation of benefit rule in regard to PETs. There are several schemes for giving a share in the home. Be alert to current Revenue practice.
- Consider arranging life assurance for the donee on the donor's life to cover the potential tax liability on a gift.
- Take care with timing (the nil rate band benefits earlier gifts first). If the client wishes to make a PET as well as create a discretionary trust, do the latter first to ensure that the annual exemption is used (and for other technical reasons).
- Establish the value of gifted property at the time and obtain a formal valuation.
- Obtain specialist tax advice from a colleague within your own firm or from another firm, an accountant or barrister. The cost of giving incorrect advice is much greater than the cost of taking such advice.

19.3   CHARITIES

Giving to charities is tax effective if made in the correct way and properly recorded.

19.3.1   Income tax

Under the Gift Aid scheme, tax paid on any donation to charity can be recovered by the charity provided the donor confirms that he is a taxpayer. The amount of tax recovered by the charity is the basic rate of tax applicable to the net donation grossed up at the basic rate. Thus a gift by the donor of £100 is grossed up to £128.21, allowing the charity to recover £28.21. There is no longer any limit on the amount that can be given in this way, although individual charities may not accept gifts below a certain amount in view of the administrative work involved.

A higher rate taxpayer can also recover the difference between the higher rate tax paid on his income and the basic rate tax recovered by the charity.

19.3.2   Reliefs from capital taxes

There is no CGT on the transfer of an asset to a charity either by way of gift or at an under-value and the charity will not pay CGT on a subsequent disposal. However, that relief only applies on a sale by the charity. If therefore a potential donor wants to sell an asset to make a gift to charity, he should consider transferring the asset to the charity before it can be sold.

A gift or legacy to a charity is exempt from IHT and the amount is not aggregated with the donor's estate. A beneficiary under a will may (possibly) be able to get the best of all worlds by:

- entering into a deed of variation in favour of a charity, thereby avoiding IHT on the amount transferred;
- also claiming income tax relief under Gift Aid on the same amount.

19.3.3   Bargain-bounty rule

A charity is in danger of losing its charitable status (and tax relief on gifts) if it repeatedly or on a substantial scale contracts in return for gifts to provide that which it would normally provide as part of its charitable activities:

- a charity cannot legally bind itself to provide a service for a particular person in return for a gift;
- nevertheless, having received a gift, the charity may have regard to the wishes of the donor (especially if more gifts may be made).

19.3.4   Gifts of the home

Advising the client checklist

Elderly people often contemplate transferring their home to their children even though they still intend to live there, and it may be a son or daughter who puts the idea into their heads and seeks to give instructions. Advisers should have detailed knowledge of the implications on the possible future liability to pay for care and the community care funding rules as the local authority may seek to disregard or set aside the gift.

The following matters should be considered before acting in such a transaction. They are not exhaustive and reference should be made to the Law Society's Guidance on the gifting of property in Appendix B.

> ❏   Who is the client? If it is the elderly person you must act in that person's best interests but if it is a son or daughter then the elderly person should be advised (and expected) to take independent legal advice to avoid conflict of interest issues.

❑ How well do you know the client? It may be necessary to spend some time with the client and talk about wider issues on their own before giving relevant advice to satisfy yourself as to capacity and undue influence issues.

❑ Has another solicitor previously acted for the client? If so, should you speak to that solicitor in case there are factors to be taken into account which are not apparent (and which the son or daughter seeks to avoid)?

❑ Does the client have the mental capacity to make the gift? (See Chapter 1 for tests of competence.)

❑ Why is the gift to be made and will the purpose be achieved?

❑ What other financial resources does the client have and can they afford to do so?

❑ Does the client understand the effect of the gift (that it passes ownership) and recognise and accept the vulnerability that the gift creates?

❑ What previous gifts have been made, how much and to whom?

❑ Do they understand the impact of the gift on their will or intestacy?

❑ Does the client actually want and intend to make a gift or expect that some rights or benefits will be reserved?

Reasons for making a transfer

There may be compelling reasons for the transfer by an elderly person of the home, or an interest in that home, to another member of the family or even an outsider. The legal title may not have been vested in the appropriate person in the first place, or the title may not reflect the true beneficial interests in the home. This may be the case where another person has:

• made substantial financial contributions to the home;
• provided care services over many years in reliance upon assurances that the home would become theirs after the death of the present owner.

In these (and other) situations it may be desirable to give effect to the transfer whilst the elderly owner can still make the decision so as to establish legal rights which all would wish to be acknowledged. This is of particular importance where the other person is already a joint occupier of the home.

Of most concern are gifts made to preserve the home for the next generation with vague assurances as to future occupation and provision of care if needed. Before the client decides to make the gift the factors to be taken into account should be explained on a benefits versus risks basis.

Potential benefits

These include:

- assumed certainty as to the future ownership of the property;
- saving of probate fees and administrative costs and (depending on the circumstances and asset) inheritance tax following death;
- minimising delays on incapacity or death;
- avoiding the stress of selling a property;
- avoidance of means-tested contributions towards the cost of residential or nursing home care or other services provided by the local authority;
- the release of income from maintaining the property (if the donee will meet these expenses);
- peace of mind where moral obligations are fulfilled.

Potential risks

These include:

- disputes within the family as to the validity of the gift;
- the value of the home may still be taken into account under means-testing rules (see Chapter 14 at 14.4.3); the donor could be deprived of funding even though lacking personal resources and without any redress against the donee; the home would not in any event be taken into account if still occupied by a partner or by a relative who is incapacitated or has attained 60 years;
- effect on capital gains tax liabilities: the owner-occupier exemption may be available for the gift but lost thereafter; there will be no revaluation of the home on the donor's death;
- effect on IHT liabilities: there could be a liability if the donee dies before the donor; there will be no saving whilst the donor continues to live in the home because of the 'reservation of benefit' rules (different schemes exist to mitigate this but the Revenue have challenged some of these);
- the donee may fail to support the donor or seek to release the value in the home by moving the donor prematurely into a care home; die without making any suitable provision for the donor; become ill, divorced or insolvent and unable to support the donor;
- the home may be put at risk or lost on the divorce of the donee; its use by the donee as security for a loan; the insolvency or bankruptcy of the donee.

Some of these pitfalls could be avoided by creating a tenancy or settlement of the home to secure the parent's right to continued occupation, but may not assist the usually desired benefit of avoiding a means-tested contribution towards the cost of care provision and may advertise the arrangement. Nevertheless the significance of proper legal documentation should not be overlooked in inter-generational arrangements.

CHAPTER 20

Testamentary dispositions and trusts

Amanda King-Jones

20.1 SUCCESSION

An individual may state by will who is to inherit any savings or assets owned at death and appoint executors to administer the estate. The Court of Protection may make a statutory will for a person who lacks testamentary capacity. In the absence of a will intestacy rules specify who is entitled to inherit and the order of priority for administrators. Such outcome may be changed in a number of ways:

- any beneficiary may disclaim a legacy;
- beneficiaries may enter into a deed of family arrangement and in effect re-write a will or the effects of intestacy;
- the court has power to provide for dependants under the Inheritance (Provision for Family and Dependants) Act 1975;
- foreign laws relating to foreign assets may override UK law and a UK will.
- a person who causes the death of another is usually prevented from benefiting from the death of his victim, whether under a will, intestacy or gift, although there is discretion in the case of manslaughter under the Forfeiture Act 1982.

20.1.1 Reasons for making a will: intestacy

It is very important to ensure the devolution of an elderly client's estate in a way that they wish, and not as the law decrees it under the intestacy rules (see 20.3). Where there is no valid will, an estate is administered according to the intestacy rules and this can lead to unexpected consequences. In many cases this will actually prejudice the surviving spouse, may distribute the estate to relatives who would not have been in the thoughts of the testator (e.g. brothers or sisters) or can create an unequal distribution between issue.

20.1.2 Reasons for making a will: other

These include:

- to include appropriate administrative powers;
- to take advantage of inheritance tax (IHT) planning through the use of the nil rate band on the death of first spouse to die;
- to appoint executors of the testator's choice to administer the estate and provide for substitution of executors;
- to protect assets and beneficiaries;
- to protect against potential claims under the Inheritance (Provision for Family and Dependants) Act 1975, particularly where insufficient provision would be made under the intestacy rules;
- to record funeral requests and arrangements;
- to protect against the future bankruptcy of a beneficiary;
- to protect against future financial claims on divorce;
- to overcome indecision of a testator as to how the estate is divided, giving executors guidance in a separate letter of wishes;
- to protect mentally/physically incapacitated beneficiaries and to preserve assets;
- to postpone the age of entitlement of beneficiaries.

These issues are addressed in more detail throughout the remainder of this Chapter and Chapter 21.

20.1.3 Foreign assets and domicile

It is very important to establish domicile of a deceased at the outset of taking instructions. This has an impact on:

- validity of the will;
- liability to IHT and other taxes (and particularly the application of the Inheritance Tax Act 1984, s.18 (spouse exemption));
- the acceptance of appointment of executor and trustees and the right to a grant to representation;
- succession to the estate and assets;
- deemed domicile provisions (Inheritance Tax Act 1984, s. 267) (a person may be domiciled outside the United Kingdom for other purposes but be deemed domiciled in the United Kingdom for IHT).

Many people assume if they own assets abroad these will not be taken into account for IHT on their death. If the client is domiciled in the United Kingdom (broadly, this is their home and where their assets are based) they will be liable for IHT on their worldwide assets.

Even assuming a UK will has been made it is advisable for there to be a will covering the assets in the foreign jurisdiction, particularly as many

European countries have laws which require particular proportions of an estate to go to certain 'reserved beneficiaries', generally the testator's children rather than their spouse. Whilst it may not be appropriate to determine domicile in advance of death, it is vital that the issues of evidence concerning domicile are addressed prior to death and should wherever possible be recorded including:

- nationality of the deceased (and if appropriate their surviving spouse) and where they were born;
- an outline of their education and employment history;
- the date they left the United Kingdom and set up their main home abroad;
- the dates of return to the United Kingdom;
- how long they stayed in the United Kingdom;
- the purpose of the stay;
- a statement as to why the deceased did not intend to remain in or return to the United Kingdom with details of the evidence to support this;
- details of citizenship and passports held by the testator during his or her lifetime.

20.1.4 The 'estate' and joint property

Schedules D4 (Joint Assets), D5 (Assets held in Trust), D6 (Pensions) and D9 (Life Assurance and Annuities) accompanying the IHT 200 Form raise pertinent and searching questions of personal representatives on the death of a testator. Provision of records by elderly clients in advance of death could save considerable time and costs if the information is available and in order.

Establishment of ownership is vital because it has an impact on:

- devolution of assets;
- the 'estate' available under Inheritance (Provision for Family and Dependants) Act 1975 claims;
- the burden of IHT and personal representatives' liability: they are liable to the extent of the 'estate' of the deceased and they are personally liable for the incorrect distribution of assets;
- intestacy;
- on the gross and net estate for probate;
- IHT;
- survivorship and commorientes.

The basic assumption is that the client's name on the title or other documentation is evidence of beneficial ownership, but if that is not to be treated as the correct ownership then further documentation must be in place. Declarations of trust must be made by deed or document to establish ownership as tenants in common or joint tenants, which in relation to land must be recorded by formal notice of severance and/or a restriction placed on the Land Registry title.

Assets that are not in sole or joint beneficial ownership, e.g. held as nominee, trustee, attorney, must be so documented. Assets written in trust particularly for tax planning purposes e.g. insurance proceeds, pension death benefits, must be recorded through proper documentation, normally in the form either of specially prepared declarations of trust or in standard printed forms produced by insurance companies. These need to be submitted to the insurance companies or placed with the will.

Any property or savings in joint names normally passes to the surviving joint owner(s) beneficially unless they are trustees, although land can be held in undivided shares (i.e. as tenants in common) which pass to the personal representatives on death.

20.1.5   Severance by will

It is well known that under the Law of Property Act 1925, s.36(2) the joint tenancy of a property can be severed. However, in the case of *Re Woolough, Perkins* v. *Borden* [2002] WTR 595 it was determined that it was possible for severance of the joint tenancy of a property to take place by will even though the wills were not sufficient to be mutual wills. It was held that the way in which the property was to be dealt with under the wills of each of the brother and sister was sufficient to infer that a severance of the joint tenancy of a property owned by the brother and sister had taken place on the execution of their wills. However, both wills contained an express reference to the property and both of them had given instructions to the same solicitors at the same time.

20.1.6   Professional risks

Solicitors may also be negligent if they do not advise on or prepare a notice of severance for a client where the terms of the will would make the devolution of the property go in the contrary direction intended if held one way or the other (*Carr-Glynn* v. *Frearson* [1998] 4 All ER 225).

20.1.7   Nominations

Certain assets may be disposed of on death by a written nomination which may be statutory or non-statutory but will be of no effect if the nominee dies first:

- these may include industrial and provident society accounts;
- pension schemes may also include provision for nominations;
- those for National Savings Certificates and National Savings Bank

accounts were discontinued in 1981 but any then in existence may still take effect.

20.2 WILLS

20.2.1 Testamentary capacity

When the will is made the testator must have testamentary capacity. This means that he must understand (see *Banks* v. *Goodfellow* (1870) 5 QB 549):

- the nature of the act and its effects, i.e. that he is giving his property to persons of his choice on his death;
- the extent of that property;
- the nature and extent of his obligations to relatives and others.

No disorder of the mind must bring about a disposal which would not otherwise have been made. Mere eccentricity or foolishness does not invalidate a will but fraud or undue influence may. See generally Chapter 1.

If capacity is in doubt a medical report must be obtained after outlining the legal test to be applied and if possible the doctor should witness the will.

20.2.2 Fees and confirmation of instructions

The cost of the will and any supplemental services should be discussed with the client at this stage in accordance with Rule 15 and Solicitors Costs Information and Client Care Code 1999. Remember that fees may possibly be claimed under the Legal Help scheme if the testator is within the income and capital limits, aged 70 or over, and can claim to be:

- blind (or partially sighted);
- deaf (or hard of hearing);
- without speech;
- suffering from a mental disorder,
- substantially and permanently handicapped by illness, injury or congenital deformity.

20.2.3 Taking instructions

You should obtain all necessary information (especially if you are to be an executor) and this generally comprises:

- personal and family details, including domicile and foreign assets; marital status; whether a cohabitee (same sex or heterosexual relationship); prospects or intentions; and issues involving second marriages and any possible claimants on the estate;

- the general nature and size of the estate including the extent of debts and liabilities (e.g. mortgages); personal chattels; jointly owned assets (joint tenants or tenants in common); life assurance provision and continuing pensions (and any nominations and declarations of trust); any business interests;
- any interests in a trust or settlement (or power of appointment);
- any substantial gifts made or to be made during lifetime;
- the persons for whom the client wishes to (or should) provide, including any cohabitee or dependent person and any particular problem situations (e.g. a mentally incapacitated beneficiary);
- any relevant special wishes: the importance to the client of tax planning; any beneficiary for whom provision is to be made in priority to all others;
- any changes that may occur before death in any of the foregoing matters.

It is sensible to use a detailed in-house questionnaire or the Law Society's Instruction Sheet to cover preliminary preparation. It may be helpful to ask the client to complete the Personal Assets Log (see 20.2.9).

At the same time as taking instructions the opportunity should be taken to consider whether the client also requires or needs:

- an Enduring Power of Attorney (see Chapter 4);
- a living will (see Chapter 11 at 11.4);
- assistance with tax affairs or investment or tax planning advice (IHT planning nil rate band, see Chapter 17).

20.2.4 Recording instructions

There is often a need for information about the circumstances in which a will was made. In accordance with the Law Society's Professional Purposes Committee Ruling of September 1959 there is an obligation on a solicitor who prepares testamentary instruments to state the circumstances relating to the preparation of these instruments. The Law Society's recommendation was considered by the Court of Appeal in *Larke* v. *Nugus* [2000] WTLR 1033 in an appeal from the decision of Browne Wilkinson J.

The Guide to the Professional Conduct of Solicitors, Law Society (8th edn, 1999) answers a frequently asked question on this topic in ch. 24, p. 450:

> 6. I drew up a will which is now in dispute. Can I disclose information concerning the making of the will other than to the personal representatives?
>
> Yes. To avoid unnecessary litigation, you should make a statement available concerning its execution to any person who is a party to probate proceedings or whom you believe has a reasonable claim under the will. If you are acting in the administration, you may need to consider the question of conflict.

A letter requesting this information has come to be known as a *Larke* v. *Nugus* letter. This type of letter may request some or all of the following information:

- How long you had known the deceased.
- Who introduced you to the deceased.
- The date you received instructions from the deceased.
- Contemporaneous notes of all meetings and telephone calls including an indication of where the meeting took place and who else was present at the meeting.
- How the instructions were expressed.
- What indication the deceased gave that he knew he was making a will.
- Whether the deceased exhibited any signs of confusion or loss of memory.
- Whether and to what extent earlier wills were discussed and what attempts were made to discuss departures from the deceased's earlier will-making pattern; what reasons the testator gave for making any such departures.
- How the provisions of the will were explained to the deceased.
- Who, apart from the attesting witnesses, were present at the execution of the will and where, when and how this took place.

20.2.5 Contents and form of will

A simple will may (and usually should) contain clauses dealing with:

- revocation of previous testamentary dispositions;
- appointment of executors (and guardians and trustees for any infant children);
- any specific legacies (of realty and of personalty) and pecuniary legacies;
- disposal of the residue of the estate;
- any wishes as to burial or cremation.

In less straightforward situations, especially where there are infant beneficiaries or continuing provision is intended, further clauses may need to deal with:

- the terms of any trust;
- any additional powers of the trustees;
- administrative provisions;
- survivorship provisions;
- gifts to charities.

20.2.6 Execution

A will must be in writing and the testator must sign or make his mark:

- The testator's signature need not be at the end of the will provided it was intended to give effect to the will.

- A person may sign on behalf and by the direction of the testator in his presence (Wills Act 1837, s.9 as substituted by the Administration of Justice Act 1982, s.17).
- The signature (or mark) must be witnessed by, or acknowledged to, two people present at the same time who sign as witnesses.
- An incomplete signature is only sufficient if the signatory is unable to finish for physical reasons and not because of a change of mind.
- A testator who cannot read needs to have known the contents of the will before signing and the attestation clause must make this clear. Include 'with knowledge of the contents thereof' in the attestation clause where the testator is blind or partially sighted. This is also desirable where the testator's signature appears doubtful.

You could be liable in a negligence claim to disappointed beneficiaries if you accept instructions for a will but delay in its preparation or fail to ensure that the will is valid. (See *White* v. *Jones* [1995] 2 WLR 187 and *Esterhuizen* v. *Allied Dunbar Assurance Plc* [1998] 2 FLR. 668.) In this case Longmore J. suggested that the process of signature and attestation of a will should be carried out in the following procedure:

1.   Invite the client to come into the solicitor's office to sign the will.
2.   If the client does not wish to, the solicitor should ask the client if he or she would like the solicitor to attend at home to get the will signed and witnessed.
3.   If the client says 'no' that is the end of the matter.

However, detailed written instructions on the process of signature and attestation of wills should always be provided to the client.

20.2.7   Revocation

A will may only be revoked by a testator, e.g. by a later will or physical destruction with intent to revoke. A will is revoked by subsequent marriage but not by supervening incapacity. The capacity required for revocation is the same as for execution of a will.

20.2.8   Mutual wills

In some situations the equitable doctrine of mutual wills may impose a trust on property to frustrate the effect of the revocation of a will.

If two (or more) people make complementary wills and agree not to revoke their wills without the others' consent and the first to die has kept to that agreement, the survivor's property will be subject to a trust on the terms of the mutual wills. There are three requirements which must all be satisfied for there to be valid mutual wills:

374

1.   the testators must agree to make their wills in agreed terms;
2.   they must agree not to amend them unilaterally;
3.   on the death of the first testator to die that person must have continued to have carried out the agreement: *Goodchild* v. *Goodchild* [1997] 3 All ER 63.

20.2.9   Precedents

Reference should be made to the published works listed in Appendix F.

20.3   INTESTACY

20.3.1   Legislation

See the Administration of Estates Act 1925 and Family Provision (Intestate Succession) Order 1993, SI 1993/2906.

20.3.2   Entitlement

On an intestacy a surviving spouse receives the following, but can make certain elections, including taking the matrimonial home at valuation as part of his or her share (or making up any shortfall):

*   all personal chattels (as defined);
*   a statutory legacy (with interest) which for deaths from 1 December 1993 is £125,000 when there is issue and £200,000 when there is no issue but there is a specified relative surviving;
*   when there is issue, a life interest in half the residue;
*   when there is no issue but there is a specified relative surviving, half the residue absolutely;
*   when there is no issue and there are no specified relatives surviving, the entire estate absolutely.

'Specified relatives' who may inherit apart from a spouse are a parent, brother or sister of the whole blood or the issue of such persons.

Issue receive all that the surviving spouse does not receive, and this is on the statutory trusts which means equally between those who attain 18 years or marry before then, with children of a deceased child taking that child's share on the same basis.

Others

If there is no surviving spouse or issue the estate goes to a surviving parent or brothers and sisters of the whole blood on the statutory trusts, whom failing to remoter relatives (and ultimately to the Crown, though *ex gratia* payments may then be made to persons whom the deceased would have been likely to benefit).

Only a spouse or blood relatives (or adopted persons) can benefit, and a cohabitee has no rights under an intestacy.

20.4 STATUTORY WILLS

Jurisdiction

The Court of Protection has jurisdiction to authorise the execution, for a patient who is mentally incapable of doing so, of a will making any provision which the patient could make if he were not mentally disordered (Mental Health Act 1983, s.96). This is particularly useful where wills may be out of date or may not carry out the intentions of a testator. For details of the procedure and considerations see Chapter 4 at 4.10.

20.5 INHERITANCE PROVISION

20.5.1 Claimants

Under the Inheritance (Provision for Family and Dependants) Act 1975, certain persons may apply to the court for financial provision out of the estate of a deceased person:

- a spouse of the deceased;
- a former spouse of the deceased who has not remarried, unless the claim is prevented by a court order made on the financial settlement following divorce;
- a child of the deceased, whether or not a dependant;
- any other person who was treated as a child of the family in relation to any marriage to which the deceased was a party; or immediately before the death was being maintained by the deceased, either wholly or partly, otherwise than for full valuable consideration.

20.5.2 Relevant matters

The application is made on the basis that the disposition of the deceased's estate effected by his will or the law relating to intestacy, or a combination of both, is not such as to make reasonable financial provision for the applicant. In deciding whether to make an order the court takes into account all the circumstances. When determining whether reasonable financial provision has been made the court must have regard to the following matters (s.3):

- the financial resources and financial needs which in the foreseeable future the applicant, any other applicant or any beneficiary of the estate has or is likely to have;
- any obligation and responsibilities which the deceased had towards any applicant or beneficiary;
- the size and nature of the net estate;
- any physical or mental disability of any applicant or beneficiary;
- any other matter, including the conduct of the applicant or any other person, which in the circumstances of the case the court may consider relevant;
- (on an application by a spouse or former spouse) the age of and contribution made by the applicant, and duration of the marriage (s.3(2));
- (on an application by a child or person treated as a child of the deceased) the manner in which the applicant was being (or might be expected to be) educated or trained and, if treated as a child, the extent to which the deceased had assumed responsibility for maintenance and whether any other person was liable;
- the standard of living enjoyed by the applicant during the lifetime of the deceased and the extent to which the deceased contributed to that standard.

It is not clear when and to what extent the financial resources of the applicant include any means-tested state benefits or support that could be received.

20.5.3 Objective test

The facts as known to the court and the claimant's circumstances at the date of the hearing are relevant, rather than those at the date of the will or the death.

The question is whether, in all the circumstances, the disposition of the deceased's estate makes reasonable financial provision for the applicant, not whether the deceased has acted reasonably in making no or only limited provision. The deceased's moral obligation, if any, may be a relevant factor, though again this must be balanced against all the other factors. The deceased's reasons and wishes comprise only part of the circumstances of the case and may be outweighed by other factors. A statement made by the deceased, whether or not in writing or signed, is admissible as evidence of any fact stated therein (Civil Evidence Act 1968, s.2).

20.5.4 Court's powers

The court may make an order in favour of the applicant for periodical payments, a lump sum, transfer of property or acquisition and transfer or settlement of property. It may also:

- treat a joint tenancy in any property as severed and the deceased's beneficial share as part of the net estate to such extent as appears just in all the circumstances;
- set aside dispositions made by the deceased within six years prior to the death with the intention of defeating an application for financial provision.

20.5.5 Procedure

An application must be made within six months from the date of the grant of representation to the estate, unless the court in its discretion gives leave to extend time.

Applications are made in the county court for the district in which the deceased resided at the date of death and there are criteria under the Courts and Legal Services Act 1990 for determining whether a case should be moved up to the High Court (Chancery Division or Family Division). Rules and Practice Directions set out the detailed procedure to be followed.

20.5.6 Tax implications

Where an order is made (including a consent order) the estate is treated for IHT purposes as if the deceased's property devolved subject to the provisions of the order (Inheritance Tax Act 1984, s.146). Unlike variations (see below) there is no time limit and an election is not required. If agreement is reached within two years this can be dealt with by a deed of variation rather than a consent order through the court.

20.5.7 Other claims

Consideration now also needs to be given to claims concerning proprietory estoppel. Where promises have been relied on to the detriment of someone, that person may be entitled to an interest in the property concerned although they may not be entitled to claim under the 1975 Act. *Gillet* v. *Holt* [2000] 2 All ER 289 set out prerequisites for a claim. The claimant succeeded in receiving a share of an estate. A promise had been made that a benefit in property would be received on a person's death and the claimant changed his situation and acted to his detriment based on that assurance or promise.

20.6 POST-DEATH TAX PLANNING

It is not too late to change the provisions of a will or the outcome of intestacy after the death. An individual beneficiary may disclaim a benefit or the beneficiaries may agree to vary the distribution of the estate, and the testator can even provide for this by leaving the estate (or part of it) on a short discretionary trust.

20.6.1 Variations and disclaimers

The Inheritance Tax Act 1984, s.142 provides that if, within two years of death, any dispositions are varied or benefits disclaimed, such variation or disclaimer is not a transfer of value and tax is charged as if the variation had been made by the deceased or the disclaimed benefit had never been conferred.

The variation or disclaimer:

- must be in writing;
- must not be made for any consideration in money or money's worth;
- must be entered into by the person 'whose interest is affected'. This can cause problems if there are owners whose interests are affected. If a beneficiary is mentally incapable, a Court of Protection order will be required to effect a variation which reduces or affects that beneficiary's interest under the will or intestacy. The same procedure is followed as for statutory wills (see 20.4);
- can be made even if the property involved has been distributed and the estate administered;
- may result in a repayment of IHT or additional IHT having to be paid.

There are differences between a variation and a disclaimer:

- a variation of the property can be given to anyone whereas a disclaimer is merely a refusal to accept the property and it passes to the next in line;
- receipt of a benefit prevents disclaimer but not a variation, and part disclaimer may not be allowed (but one of two gifts could be disclaimed);
- a variation will only be read back to the date of death if a written election is made in the instrument of variation, whereas this is automatic for a disclaimer;
- a variation is not retrospective for income tax purposes, whereas in the case of a disclaimer the beneficiary is deemed never to have had an interest.

The Inland Revenue Capital Taxes' Office has issued a leaflet IHT8 about instruments of variation and also an Instrument of Variation Checklist (IOV2).

20.6.2 Capital gains tax

Similar provisions exist in Taxation of Chargeable Gains Act 1992, s.62(6)–(10), whereby the variation or disclaimer need not be treated as a disposal. For capital gains tax (CGT) a separate election is made for a variation, but none is needed for a disclaimer.

20.6.3 Practical planning

Where a deceased spouse's estate passes entirely to the survivor, a variation may enable the nil rate band to be used, e.g. for the benefit of the children. The assets passing to the spouse and other beneficiaries may be redistributed so as to ensure that property with beneficial treatment (e.g. business and agricultural property) passes to the other beneficiaries.

If a valuable property becomes worth very little within two years of death, vary the will so that it passes to charity (the value at death is then exempt).

If a beneficiary dies within two years of the testator's death consider a variation (it can still be done) to achieve more advantageous overall IHT treatment: there are several possibilities.

20.6.4 Discretionary provision

Where flexibility is required, possibly for tax reasons, the testator may avoid the need for all beneficiaries to agree to a variation by giving a power of appointment to the executors or trustees and requiring them to exercise this within two years (see Inheritance Tax Act 1984, s.144):

- there should be a default trust at the end of the two-year period in case an appointment is not made;
- IHT is ultimately paid as if the will had provided for the outcome effected under the appointment;
- if there is an initial discretionary trust, IHT will be charged on the basis thereof on application for a grant;
- distributions made outside the two-year period will be subject to the normal IHT exit charge.
- there are no corresponding CGT provisions.

20.6.5 Precatory gifts

Where a testator expresses a wish that property bequeathed by the will be transferred by the legatee to other persons and the wish is complied with within two years of death, that disposition takes effect for IHT as if the property had been originally bequeathed to the transferee (see Inheritance Tax Act 1984, s.143). No particular formality is required.

20.7 DISABLED TRUSTS

An elderly testator may wish to make long term provision for a relative who is infirm or disabled. This commonly arises in the following situations, although the principles involved may be applied by anyone wishing to make financial provision for someone suffering from a disability:

- a parent seeks to make provision for a disabled son or daughter;
- a son or daughter seeks to make provision for an infirm parent;
- one spouse seeks to provide for the other who has become frail, infirm or mentally incapacitated;
- unmarried brothers or sisters or friends seek to provide for each other.

20.7.1 Key points

The beneficiary may be unable to handle his or her own financial affairs but quite apart from this there will often be:

- uncertainty as to what the needs of the beneficiary will be and the need to take into account the high cost of care and services and any provision under community care policies;
- uncertainty as to what provision will actually benefit the beneficiary due to the loss of Department of Work and Pensions (DWP) or local authority funding and means-testing in respect of the cost of services provided;
- a desire to provide tax-effective support by utilising normal tax planning principles and the tax concessions available in respect of disabled beneficiaries under trusts;
- concern about potential inheritance claims by (or on behalf of) the disabled beneficiary and others.

There is no simple solution and each case must de dealt with taking into account all the likely circumstances as best as these can be ascertained, including the wishes and priorities of the testator.

20.7.2 Care provision

The personal circumstances of the beneficiary will depend upon:

- the resources (both personal and financial) of the individual;
- the nature and degree of the disability or infirmity;
- availability of personal carers or care provision;
- outside funding available, whether from a trust or from the DWP or a local authority.

The beneficiary may, either at present or at some time in the future:

- be provided with a basic income and left to cope;
- live in his or her own home with some support;
- be cared for by another member of the family or friend;
- live in a supervised home or hostel with other disabled or infirm people;
- be looked after in a care home;
- be in need of full-time nursing care in hospital.

In many cases the testator is seeking to replace the care and support already being provided on a personal basis by financial support, and this will be for an uncertain period of time. Whatever the circumstances at the time when the provision is discussed, these are likely to change.

20.7.3 Funding and means tests

The financial resources available for the support of this beneficiary are likely to come from:

- personal income, including pensions, interests on savings and the return from any investments;
- personal capital resources, including savings and investments;
- the individual's home, if owned in full or in part;
- any trust provision available (including that now being contemplated);
- voluntary financial support from family and friends (or charities);
- support from society through the DWP, local authorities or NHS bodies.

Means tests are likely to be applied on a formal or informal basis as a pre-requisite to any support provided, and these may take into account the income and capital resources of the individual. Inflexible means tests regulate:

- pension credit from October 2003 paid by the DWP to those whose income from other sources is insufficient for their needs (see Chapter 13);
- housing benefit (to cover rent) paid by the local authority (see Chapter 15);
- housing or disabled facilities grants from local authorities (see Chapter 15);
- the cost of residential, day and domiciliary services provided or funded by the local authority (see Chapter 14).

Any financial provision that is made on a legal basis could result in reduction or withdrawal of a significant source of income, or a charge for services.

20.7.4 Objectives and strategy for financial provision

The testator is likely to have conflicting objectives:

- to provide for the disabled or infirm beneficiary to the extent necessary;
- to ensure that funds that are not needed pass ultimately to other beneficiaries;
- to avoid loss of other sources of funding but fill gaps in care provision;

Testators must decide their priorities as they often cannot achieve all objectives.

Trust provision may last for many years but the means-testing rules, circumstances of the beneficiary and services needed constantly change so flexibility is desirable in the provision made. The following are key points to have in mind:

- the terms of the trust will depend upon whether the beneficiary is likely to be self-reliant or dependent upon others, though many fall between these extremes;
- the beneficiary's own resources and all other sources of funding, actual and potential, should be taken into account;
- the means-tested rules and particularly those assets which are disregarded for assessment which include trust assets subject to certain conditions (see Chapter 14).

20.7.5   Options

The testator has the following options when seeking to make provision for a disabled or infirm beneficiary, and these may apply to the entire estate, a share thereof, or a specified sum set aside for the purpose.

Leaving money

Money may be left to:

- the beneficiary absolutely and ignoring means-testing implications;
- other relatives in the hope that they will support the disabled beneficiary on a voluntary basis (thereby avoiding means-testing);
- a charity on one of the special schemes available.

Creating a trust

A trust could be created:

- with the disabled beneficiary having a (protected) life interest;
- which is discretionary as regards income and/or capital and includes the disabled beneficiary;
- for charitable purposes (perhaps limited to charities with specific objectives);
- using a two-year discretionary trust to create a 'wait and see' period so that the changed needs of the beneficiary can be ascertained before the trustees choose between the above options.

If substantial funds are available a combination of money and trusts designed to fit the particular circumstances may be best.

20.7.6 Information required to create a trust

Before advising on the terms of a will or any trust provision you need to know in respect of the ultimate beneficiary:

- name and age;
- present capital and income and any changes that may arise;
- the nature and implications of any incapacity;
- present residence and extent of care, and any changes to be anticipated;
- present funding arrangements and any changes that may take place;
- any other financial provision that has been or may be made;
- help likely to be provided by charitable organisations or others.

You must determine and take into account the potential size of the fund available for this beneficiary (is it to be a share of the estate or a fixed sum?).

20.7.7 Practical points

Disabled trusts

Try to avoid identifying the trust fund too closely with the disabled beneficiary (to the extent that the testator will tolerate this). It may be better to:

- have a discretionary fund identifying many potential beneficiaries including this specific beneficiary;
- adopt a trust period other than the life of this beneficiary;
- ensure that the class of potential beneficiaries includes persons who may care for or support this beneficiary (the trustees can even be given a restricted power to enlarge the class).

Providing financial assistance to a carer often benefits the person cared for. If money can be paid to other people they may provide voluntary support (thereby avoiding means-testing issues).

Take care over the inclusion of any power to advance or appoint capital to the disabled beneficiary:

- restrict it to specific purposes;
- restrict it to specific situations.

Include adequate discretionary powers for the trustees, such as power to:

- invest in chattels and residential accommodation;
- make loans and permit occupation and use of trust assets (a power to appoint capital may not then be necessary);
- benefit those who may help the disabled beneficiary;
- benefit or support charities (they may help the disabled beneficiary);
- pay funeral expenses for the disabled beneficiary.

Tax dispensations are available under the provisions below in respect of certain trusts for the benefit of disabled persons, but utilising these may have adverse consequences in respect of means-tested support and benefits:

- Taxation of Chargeable Gains Act 1992, Sched. 1, para. 1;
- Inheritance Tax Act 1984, ss.3A(1)(3) and 89.

It may be a question of tax benefits or state benefits as the testator is seldom able to achieve the best of both worlds.

20.7.8 Challenges to the provision

An application may be made to the court under the Inheritance (Provision for Family and Dependants) Act 1975 by or on behalf of the dependent beneficiary on the ground that the will does not make reasonable provision:

- the court has wide powers to redistribute the estate;
- for the matters taken into account see 20.5.2;
- the financial resources of the potential beneficiary will be taken into account but the extent to which these include means-tested state benefits or local authority provision that would otherwise be available is not clear.

The question is not 'did the testator act reasonably?' but rather 'has reasonable financial provision been made for this person?'

20.8 DISCRETIONARY TRUSTS

These trusts are where trust income and capital are held at the discretion of the trustees amongst a class of beneficiaries. Income may be distributed or accumulated. Nil rate band discretionary trusts (see Chapter 17) are used for IHT planning. These trusts are used where the testator wishes to leave assets in favour of a number of beneficiaries, leaving the trustees to determine who should benefit.

20.9 INTEREST IN POSSESSION TRUST (OR LIFE INTEREST TRUST)

The trustees are directed to pay trust income to a particular beneficiary and then the capital to someone else. These are used, for example:

- to protect assets for children following a second marriage;
- to protect assets of a beneficiary whose assets may be vulnerable to claim by creditors, insolvency or divorce;
- for tax planning purposes.

20.10   ACCUMULATION AND MAINTENANCE TRUSTS

Three conditions imposed by the Inheritance Tax Act 1984, s.71 have to be complied with to qualify as an accumulation and maintenance trust. The basic form is a trust for a class of beneficiaries who have a common grand-parent giving the beneficiary a right to income and capital at 18 years old. Sometimes the beneficiary's age can be postponed to 25 years.

20.11   BARE TRUSTS

Bare trusts are included in wills, for example, where smaller legacies are gifted to minors but directed not to be paid to them until they reach 18. The money belongs to the minor but he or she cannot give a discharge until attaining the age of 18. Grandparents may also use bare trusts to settle smaller sums of money whilst control of the money is retained until the child reaches 18. The income and capital is treated as the child's own with the ability to use their personal income tax and CGT annual allowances

20.12   CHARITABLE TRUSTS

Charitable trusts might be created where a testator does not want to be com-mitted in advance to identifying specific charities or charitable objects or where they wish to leave their assets for the benefit of charitable causes gen-erally but with trustees of their choice making the determination which organisations should benefit.

20.13   LIFE POLICY AND DEATH BENEFIT TRUSTS

The proceeds of a life policy (death in service benefit or pension policy) may have been written in trust so that they do not form part of the deceased's estate and may not be subject to IHT. There are detailed rules relating to these (see Chapter 17) for IHT purposes under ss.3, 4 and 5 of the Inheritance Tax Act 1984. Careful consideration should be given to this at the time of taking out the policy but also when taking instructions for a will (see 20.2.3) to establish what will comprise the 'estate' of the testator to pass under the terms of the will (see also Chapter 17).

20.14   LETTERS OF WISHES, STATEMENT OR MEMORANDUM

Instead of revealing in the will their wishes and intentions in regard to the administration of their trust fund, testators should prepare and sign a suitable letter addressed to the trustees setting these out, which will reassure not only the testator but also the trustees when they consider the exercise of their powers in future years.

Unless the words in the will (or trust deed) direct the executors/trustees to take a particular action or refer to a letter already in existence, this type of letter is not a document incorporated in the will and is not legally binding.

These are vital papers giving testators opportunities to record and have in place their written record regarding:

- funeral arrangements and wishes, remembering that the executors of the will have legal authority over these, not the next of kin;
- requests for distribution of chattels (with timescale and mechanism for selection) enabling these to be dealt with by executors without large lists being made in the will or a testator having to make decisions on making the will and enabling the use of the Inheritance Tax Act 1984, s.143 (precatory trust);
- guidance to trustees of discretionary trusts (of nil rate or residue) which a testator might not otherwise be able to, or wish to, put on the face of a will, taking care not to fetter their discretion;
- guidance to the trustees for the advancement of capital or any other matters;
- reasons of a testator (if appropriate) as to why provision has or has not been made to seek to prevent claims on death for greater provision.

A letter of wishes should be signed and dated by the testator but not witnessed if it is not to be incorporated in the will. The basic rule of incorporation is that a document is deemed to be incorporated in a will (even though a document is not itself executed as a testamentary disposition) if:

- the document is in existence at the time of the will;
- the will refers to the document as an existing document;
- the reference in the will or other available evidence is sufficient to identify the document.

20.15   LIFETIME SETTLEMENTS OR BY WILL

It may be advantageous to establish the desired trusts under a lifetime settlement:

- the settlor's will (and that of a spouse) can leave money to the trustees and thus be kept simple;

- other people (e.g. grandparents of a disabled child or children of an infirm parent) can also leave money to the trustees of the settlement and avoid having to set out their own trusts;
- life insurance and pension benefits may be held on these trusts.

The administration costs of a settlement may make it an inadvisable option if the trust fund is too small, although a nominal sum may be settled initially in anticipation of substantial sums being added under the will of the settlor or other persons.

20.16 PRACTICAL POINTS

20.16.1 Information required to create a trust

Basic information required:

- trustees;
- beneficiaries;
- trustees' powers of appointment or advancement;
- default terms and beneficiaries;
- administrative powers;
- indemnity provisions;
- taxation considerations;
- restrictions on trustee powers;
- trust period;
- type of trust;
- trust fund.

20.16.2 Publications

On this topic generally, reference should be made to the published works in Appendix F.

CHAPTER 21

Death

Amanda King-Jones

21.1 REGISTRATION OF DEATH

Relevant legislation is:

- Births and Deaths Registration Act 1953;
- Registration of Births and Deaths Regulations 1987, SI 1987/2088.

21.1.1 Obligation to register

The death of every person dying in England or Wales must be registered by the Registrar of Births and Deaths for the district in which the death occurred. The address will be found in the local telephone directory or may be obtained from the hospital, doctor, police, local council or post office.

A registered medical practitioner (RMP) who has attended a person during his or her last illness is required to send to the Registrar a certificate stating to the best of his or her knowledge and belief the cause of death. Any qualified informant who has received such a certificate from the RMP must deliver it to the Registrar. Where death was in a hospital, the health authority may give the certificate to the Registrar direct but a qualified informant must still register the death.

21.1.2 The qualified informant

Where a person dies in a house, the persons under a duty to register are identified below (in descending order):

1. the nearest relative of the deceased person present at the death or in attendance during his or her last illness;
2. any other relative of the deceased residing or being in the sub-district where the death occurred;
3. a person present at the death or the occupier of the house if he or she knew of the happening of the death;
4. each inmate of the house who knew of the happening of the death or the person causing the disposal of the body.

Where a person dies elsewhere or a dead body is found and no information as to the place of death is available the persons who can register are either (in descending order):

1. any relative of the deceased with knowledge of any of the particulars required to be registered concerning the death;
2. any person present at the death;
3. any person finding or taking charge of the body;
4. any person causing the disposal of the body.

21.1.3 The obligation

The duty is to register within five days of the death or finding the body but if within that time written notice is given to the Registrar with the doctor's certificate the registration need not be completed until 14 days after the death or finding. When one qualified informant gives information and signs the register the others are discharged from their duty to do so. These obligations do not apply where an inquest is to be held.

It is an offence wilfully to give any false information upon registration.

21.1.4 Particulars to be supplied

The qualified informant must register the following particulars:

*   date and place of death;
*   name and surname, sex, maiden surname of a woman who has been married, date and place of birth, occupation and usual address of the deceased and name and occupation of any deceased spouse;
*   name and surname, qualification and usual address of the informant;
*   cause of death;
*   signature of the informant and date of the registration.

Other non-obligatory questions will be asked about date of birth of any surviving spouse, the NI number and any state benefits in payment, and the deceased's medical card should be handed in if it is available.

21.1.5 Death certificates

The Registrar issues a certificate as to registration of death (the death certificate) and duplicates may be requested for a fee, particularly as there is now Crown copyright in the certificates. The following are also issued:

*   a certificate for claiming any social security benefits (with a claim form);
*   a certificate for disposal by burial or cremation (the 'Green Form' which is required by the undertaker).

21.2   CORONERS AND INQUESTS

Relevant legislation is:

- Coroners Act 1988;
- Coroners Rules 1984, SI 1984/552.

21.2.1   Duty to report

There is a general duty to give information which may lead to the coroner having notice of circumstances requiring the holding of an inquest. It is normal practice for a RMP to report a death to the coroner where there is doubt or suspicion, and he or she may seek advice from the coroner about the certificate.

A Registrar of births and deaths must report a death to the coroner when (*inter alia*):

- he is unable to obtain a duly complete certificate of cause of death;
- the deceased was not attended during his or her last illness by a RMP;
- the deceased was not seen by the certifying RMP either after death or within 14 days before death;
- the cause of death appears to be unknown;
- he has reason to believe the death to have been unnatural or caused by violence or neglect or to have been attended by suspicious circumstances;
- it appears to have occurred during an operation or before recovery from the effect of anaesthetic;
- it appears from the contents of any medical certificate to have been due to industrial disease or industrial poisoning.

The coroner is a judicial officer and thereby immune from legal proceedings in respect of acts done and words spoken in the exercise of his judicial duty.

21.2.2   Role

The coroner for the district is under a duty to inquire into a death where the dead body of a person is lying within his jurisdiction and he is informed and there is reasonable cause to suspect that the person has died, such as:

- a violent or an unnatural death;
- a sudden death of which the cause is unknown;
- in prison or in such place or in such circumstances as to require an inquest in pursuance of any Act.

21.2.3 Post mortem examination

The inquiry by the coroner may include the cause of death and the coroner can direct that there be a *post mortem* examination and an inquest, but the inquiry may be:

- concluded without a *post mortem* or inquest where a doctor has completed a certificate and the coroner concludes that there is no reason for him to intervene;
- restricted to a *post mortem* where the coroner is of the opinion that this is sufficient in cases of sudden death where the cause was unknown.

Any person intending to remove a body out of the country must first give notice to the coroner within whose jurisdiction the body is and certain formalities must then be complied with (Removal of Bodies Regulations 1954, SI 1954/448).

The coroner will take possession of the body until any inquest is concluded but may release it for burial or cremation.

21.2.4 Inquests

The purpose of an inquest is to decide who the deceased was and how, when and where he or she came by his or her death. It must conclude with a verdict under five heads:

1. name of deceased;
2. injury or disease causing death;
3. time, place and circumstances of injury (where appropriate);
4. conclusion as to the death (there can be an open verdict);
5. particulars required by the Registration Acts.

The coroner decides where and when an inquest is to be held, and it must normally be held in public and be formally opened and closed. A jury (of at least seven people) is only required in certain circumstances, but the coroner has a discretion to summon a jury.

21.2.5 Evidence

Witnesses give evidence on oath but as it is an inquisitorial process it is for the coroner to decide which witnesses to summon. The coroner must examine anyone with knowledge of the facts whom he thinks it expedient to examine and anyone who wishes to give evidence. Medical witnesses may be called, including to express an opinion as to the cause of death. Certain classes of person (see the 1984 Rules) and any person who in the opinion of the coroner has a proper interest may also examine any witness either personally or by a solicitor, but legal aid is not available.

Strict laws of evidence do not apply, but the coroner takes notes of the evidence.

21.2.6 Powers

The coroner has power to:

- fine a person who will not attend or give evidence after being summoned;
- issue a warrant for the arrest of a witness who fails to attend after being served with a summons;
- commit a person for contempt in the face of the court (but not otherwise).

Upon conclusion the coroner completes a certificate and the death is registered without attendance by a qualified informant. The coroner may issue an order for burial or certificate for cremation without charge.

21.3 FUNERAL ARRANGEMENTS

21.3.1 Authority

Upon registering the death the Registrar gives the informant a disposal certificate and this must be handed to the person effecting the disposal of the body. The coroner authorises disposal when he is inquiring into the death. If after 14 days no notice as to the date, place and means of disposal of the body has reached the Registrar, he must make inquiry about this.

The court is reluctant to interfere on the application of a relative with the executors' decision as to funeral arrangements: see *Re Grandison (deceased)*, *The Times*, 10 July 1999. This may apply to those entitled to be administrators who will in any event be the next of kin.

21.3.2 Financial responsibility

The person who instructs the undertaker may become personally responsible for the cost but will normally be entitled to an indemnity from the estate. The deceased's bank may release funds to an undertaker direct before probate, on production of the death certificate and funeral account.

If the deceased leaves no money, arrangements will be made by those prepared to pay, but assistance may be available from public funds. A funeral expenses payment may be obtained from the Social Fund (see leaflet SFL2: *How the Social Fund Can Help You*):

- there is a time limit of three months;
- only an eligible person in receipt of means-tested benefits who takes responsibility for the costs of the funeral may claim;

- any savings of the claimant over £1,000 are taken into account and contributions from other sources will be off-set;
- only essential expenses (as defined) will be covered;
- the payment is refundable out of the estate of the deceased.

The local authority (usually Environmental Health Department) must arrange and pay for a funeral where the deceased has no relatives or friends willing to do so and has not made advance arrangements. The cost can be claimed from the estate, if there is one, or from any person liable to maintain the deceased.

The health authority will make the arrangements if the death was in a hospital.

Pre-paid funeral plans

Individuals may arrange directly with an undertaker or a plan provider for the payment of funeral costs in advance.

21.3.3   Funeral directors

It is not obligatory to use a funeral director, but there are two professional bodies that regulate their activities: the National Association of Funeral Directors (address in Appendix E) and the Society of Allied and Independent Funeral Directors. The former has a Code of Practice which members should follow and operates a complaints procedure. Quotes may be obtained and a basic funeral can be requested (see Age Concern Fact Sheet 27: *Arranging a Funeral*).

21.3.4   Burial or cremation?

The decision about disposal of the body is strictly that of the executors or, in the absence of a will, the next of kin who will be the potential administrators. Directions may be in or with the will and it is prudent to check in all cases. Although these are not legally binding they will invariably be followed where possible and will be compelling where there is disagreement between executors. It is wise to consult the next of kin (and tactful to consult any cohabitee) and professional executors will usually follow their wishes unless in conflict with the will or each other.

Always ascertain whether the deceased has already made arrangements: a grave space may have been reserved or there may be funeral insurance.

Burial

Everyone is entitled to be buried in the churchyard of the parish in which they die, if there is one and if there is still room. The permission of the local clergy is required elsewhere but grave space may have been bought in advance. There are also cemeteries owned by local authorities or privately, and widely varying fees are charged.

Cremation

Before a cremation takes place three statutory forms must be completed, these being by:

- the next of kin or other suitable person authorising the cremation;
- the doctor who attended the deceased in the last illness;
- another doctor who must also have seen the body.

Each doctor will charge a fee, but where a coroner issues the certificate there is no fee and no doctor's certificate, but the medical referee to the crematorium signs a document and a fee is charged.

21.3.5 Donations of body or organs

The executors can decide to donate the body for medical research and would usually follow any request of this nature in the will but are not obliged to do so. Organs can be removed soon after death if the deceased has indicated in writing a wish to be a donor (e.g. by carrying a donor card) or if no objections are raised by relatives when inquiries are made (see Human Tissue Act 1961).

21.3.6 Headstones and memorial stones

There may be regulations restricting the shape or style and wording of headstones. Advice should be sought from the incumbent or priest in charge of the parish where the burial or interment of ashes is to take place.

Law Society's Enduring Powers of Attorney Guidelines

Prepared by the Mental Health and Disability Committee (revised September 1999)

1. Introduction

1.1 The following guidelines are intended to assist solicitors in advising clients who wish to draw up an enduring power of attorney (EPA). They have been prepared by the Law Society's Mental Health and Disability Committee, after consultation with other Law Society committees and the Professional Ethics Division, in response to queries raised by practitioners.

1.2 Different considerations apply in relation to donors who make an EPA as a precautionary measure while they are still in the prime of life, and those who are of borderline mental capacity, where the EPA may need to be registered immediately. These guidelines set out general points for consideration, and their relevance will depend on the particular circumstances of individual cases.

1.3 The guidelines are based on the law in England and Wales. It should be noted that there is currently no internationally recognised form of EPA, and additional arrangements must be made for clients who have property in other jurisdictions.

2. Who is the client?

2.1 Where a solicitor is instructed to prepare an EPA, the donor is the client (The Law Society, *The Guide to the Professional Conduct of Solicitors* (8th edition, 1999) Principle 24.03, note 1).

   A solicitor must not accept instructions where he or she suspects that those instructions have been given by a client under duress or undue influence (*ibid.*, Principle 12.04).

   When asked to prepare an EPA on written instructions alone, a solicitor should always consider carefully whether these instructions are sufficient, or whether he or she should see the client to discuss them (*ibid.*, Principle 24.03, note 2).

2.2 Where instructions for the preparation of an EPA are received not from the client (i.e. the prospective donor), but from a third party purporting to represent that client, a solicitor should obtain written instructions from the client that he or she wishes the solicitor to act. In any case of doubt the solicitor should see the client alone or take other appropriate steps, both to confirm the instructions with the donor personally after offering appropriate advice, and also to ensure that the donor has the necessary capacity to make the power (see section 5

397

below). The solicitor must also advise the prospective donor without regard to the interests of the source from which he or she was introduced *(ibid.*, Principle 12.04 and Principle 24.03, note 2).

2.3 Once the EPA has been executed and comes into effect, instructions may be accepted from the attorney but the solicitor continues to owe his/her duties to the donor (*ibid.*, Principle 24.03, note 1). Before registration of the EPA, it may be advisable for the solicitor, where appropriate, to satisfy him/herself that the donor continues to have capacity and to confirm the instructions with the donor. See also the Practice Statement issued by Mrs A B Macfarlane, former Master of the Court of Protection, on 9 August 1995 (*The Law Society's Gazette,* 11 October 1995, p. 21 or The Law Society *Professional Standards Bulletin No. 15*, p. 53), which clarifies solicitors' duties in acting for patients or donors and sets out procedures for dealing with conflicts of interest.

The attorney is the statutory agent of the donor, just as in receivership proceedings the receiver is the statutory agent of the patient (*Re EG* [1914] 1 Ch 927, CA).

3. Capacity to make an EPA

3.1 The solicitor should be satisfied that, on the balance of probabilities, the donor has the mental capacity to make an EPA. Many EPAs are made when the donors are already losing capacity. Consequently they could be unaware of the implications of their actions and are more likely to be vulnerable to exploitation.

3.2 If there is any doubt about the donor's capacity, a medical opinion should be obtained. The solicitor should inform the doctor of the test of capacity laid down in *Re K, Re F* [1988] 1 All ER 358, 363 (see Appendix A attached, and *Assessment of Mental Capacity: Guidance for doctors and lawyers* issued by the Law Society and the British Medical Association (1995)). If the doctor is of the opinion that the donor has capacity, he or she should make a record to that effect and witness the donor's signature on the EPA (*Kenward v Adams* (1975) *Times*, 29 November).

4. Risk of abuse

4.1 The Master of the Court of Protection has estimated that financial abuse occurs in 10 to 15 per cent of cases of registered EPAs and even more often with unregistered powers (Denzil Lush, *Solicitors Journal*, 11 September 1998). When advising clients of the benefits of EPAs, the solicitor should also inform them of the risks of abuse, particularly the risk that the attorney could misuse the power. Throughout these guidelines, an attempt has been made to identify possible risk areas and to suggest ways of preventing abuse, which the solicitor should discuss with the donor. Written information for clients on both the benefits and risks of EPAs, whether in a brochure or correspondence, may also be helpful.

4.2 During the initial stages of advising a client, the solicitor should consider the following points:

(i) There may be circumstances when an EPA may not be appropriate, and a later application for receivership, with oversight of the Court of Protection, may be preferable. This may be advisable, for example:

- where there are indications of persistent family conflicts suggesting that an EPA may be contested; or

- where the assets are more substantial or complex than family members are accustomed to handle; or
- in cases where litigation may lead to a substantial award of damages for personal injury.

(ii) The solicitor should consider discouraging the use of an unregistered EPA as an ordinary power of attorney, particularly for vulnerable elderly clients. Instructions to this effect could be included in the instrument itself (see para. 5.3 below) or the donor could be advised to lodge the power with the solicitor, with strict instructions that it is not to be used until the donor becomes or is becoming incapable.

5. Taking instructions

The solicitor should take full and careful instructions from the donor, and ensure that the following matters, where applicable, are considered by the donor when giving instructions.

5.1 *Choice of attorney*

The choice of attorney is clearly a personal decision for the donor, but it is important for the solicitor to advise the donor of the various options available, and to stress the need for the attorney to be absolutely trustworthy, since on appointment the attorney's actions will be subject to little supervision or scrutiny (see section 4 above). The donor should be advised that the appointment of a sole attorney may provide greater opportunity for abuse and exploitation than appointing more than one attorney (see below).

The solicitor should ask questions about the donor's relationship with the proposed attorney and whether the attorney has the skills required to manage the donor's financial affairs. The donor should also consider the suitability of appointing a family member or someone independent of the family, or a combination of both.

More than one attorney

Where more than one attorney is to be appointed, they must be appointed to act either 'jointly' or 'jointly and severally' (Enduring Powers of Attorney Act 1985, s.11(1)).

One of these two alternatives must be chosen and the other crossed out. Failure to cross out one of these alternatives on the prescribed form makes the power invalid, and this is one of the commonest reasons for the Court of Protection or Public Trust Office refusing to register an EPA.

The differences between a 'joint' and 'joint and several' appointment should be explained to the donor:

- In addition to the explanatory information in the prescribed form to the effect that joint attorneys must all act together and cannot act separately, the donor should be advised that a joint appointment will terminate if any one of the attorneys disclaims, dies, or becomes bankrupt or mentally incapable. However, joint appointments may provide a safeguard against possible abuse, since each attorney will be able to oversee the actions of the other(s).
- Similarly, in addition to the explanatory information in the prescribed form to the effect that joint and several attorneys can all act together but can also

act separately if they wish, the donor should be advised that, where there is a joint and several appointment, the disclaimer, death, bankruptcy and incapacity of one attorney will not automatically terminate the power.

The donor may have to make difficult choices as to which family member(s) to appoint as his or her attorney. It is possible to allow some flexibility, as in the following examples:

(i)   The donor may wish to appoint a family member and a professional to act jointly and severally with, for example, the family member dealing with day-to-day matters, and the professional dealing with more complex affairs.

(ii) The donor may wish to appoint his or her spouse as attorney, with provision for their adult child(ren) to take over as attorney(s) should the spouse die or become incapacitated. One way to achieve this is for the donor to execute two EPAs: the first appointing the spouse as attorney, and the second appointing the child(ren) with a provision that it will only come into effect if the first power is terminated for any reason. Alternatively, the donor could appoint everyone to act jointly and severally, with an informal understanding that the children will not act while the spouse is able to do so.

(iii) The donor may wish to appoint his or her three adult children as attorneys to act jointly and severally, with a proviso that anything done under the power should be done by at least two of them. This could be achieved by careful wording of the EPA document or by an accompanying statement or letter of wishes, which although not directly enforceable, would provide a clear indication as to how the donor wishes the power to be operated.

5.2   *General or limited authority*

The donor must be clear whether the EPA is to be a general power, giving the attorney authority to manage all the donor's property and affairs, or whether the authority is to extend only to part of his or her property and affairs. Any restrictions to the power should be carefully drafted and should have regard to the provisions of the Enduring Powers of Attorney Act 1985 (see also paras 5.6 and 5.11 below).

The solicitor should also discuss with the donor what arrangements should be made for the management of those affairs which are not covered by the EPA. Donors should be advised that if they leave a 'gap', so that part of their affairs are not covered by the EPA, it may be necessary for the Court of Protection to intervene and appoint a receiver.

5.3   *When the power is to come into operation*

The donor must understand when the power is to come into operation. If nothing is said in the instrument, it will take effect immediately, and can be used as an ordinary power of attorney. The donor should be advised of the risk of abuse of an unregistered power, unless s/he is in a position to supervise and authorise use of the power.

If the donor does not want the power to take effect immediately and would prefer it to be held in abeyance until the onset of his or her incapacity, he or she must expressly say so in the EPA. The donor may also wish to include a specific condition that a statement from a doctor confirming lack of capacity must accompany the application to register the EPA.

In such circumstances, it may be preferable to state that the power will not come into operation until the need arises to apply to register the EPA, rather than state that it will not come into operation until it is registered. Pending completion of the registration formalities, the attorney has limited powers, and it may be better for the attorney to have these powers, rather than none at all.

5.4 *Gifts*

Section 3(5) of the Enduring Powers of Attorney Act 1985 gives the attorney limited authority to make gifts of the donor's money or property:

- The *recipient* of the gift must be either an individual who is related to or connected with the donor, or a charity to which the donor actually made gifts or might be expected to make gifts if s/he had capacity.
- The *timing* of the gift must occur within the prescribed parameters. A gift to charity can be made at any time of the year, but a gift to an individual must be of a seasonal nature, or made on the occasion of a birth or marriage, or on the anniversary of a birth or marriage.
- The *value* of the gift must be not unreasonable having regard to all the circumstances and in particular the size of the donor's estate.

The donor cannot confer wider authority on the attorney than that specified in section 3(5), but it is open to the donor to restrict or exclude the authority which would otherwise be available to the attorney under that subsection. This possibility should be specifically discussed with the donor, since improper gifting is the most widespread form of abuse in attorneyship. The donor may wish to specify in the power the circumstances in which the attorney may make gifts of money or property.

Section 3(5) applies to both registered and unregistered EPAs, but not to those which are in the course of being registered. Where an application to register the EPA has been made, the attorney cannot make *any* gifts of the donor's property until the power has been registered.

If the EPA is registered, the Court of Protection can authorise the attorney to act so as to benefit himself or others, otherwise than in accordance with section 3(5), provided that there are no restrictions in the EPA itself (Enduring Powers of Attorney Act 1985, s.8(2)(e)).

Solicitors must also take account of Principle 15.05 of the Guide to Professional Conduct (*op cit*, 1999) concerning gifts to solicitors.

5.5 *Delegation by the attorney*

It is a basic principle of the law of agency that a delegate cannot delegate his or her authority. Alternatively, this could be expressed as a duty on the part of an agent to perform his or her functions personally.

Like any other agent, an attorney acting under an EPA has an implied power to delegate any functions which are of a purely ministerial nature; which do not involve or require the exercise of any confidence or discretion; and which the donor would not expect the attorney to attend to personally.

Any wider power of delegation must be expressly provided for in the EPA itself: for example, transferring the donor's assets into a discretionary investment management scheme operated by a stockbroker or bank.

5.6 Investment business

Unless the power is restricted to exclude investments as defined by the Financial Services Act 1986, the attorney may need to consider the investment business implications of his/her appointment. A solicitor who is appointed attorney under an EPA is likely to be conducting investment business and if so, will need to be authorised under the Financial Services Act. In addition, the solicitor will need to consider whether the Solicitors' Investment Business Rules 1995 apply.

The Financial Services and Markets Bill due to come into effect in approximately mid-2000, is likely to change the definition of investment business and affect the need for authorisation. The detailed position, at the time of writing, is unclear and solicitors will need to keep this aspect under review.

5.7 Trusteeships held by the donor

The solicitor should ask whether the donor holds:

- any trusteeships; and
- any property jointly with others.

Section 3(3) of the Enduring Powers of Attorney Act 1985 has been repealed by the Trustee Delegation Act 1999 with effect from 1 January 2000. Section 4 of the 1999 Act contains detailed transitional provisions which affect existing EPAs, both registered and unregistered.

The general rule is that any trustee functions delegated to an attorney (whether under an ordinary power or an enduring power) must comply with the provisions of section 25 of the Trustee Act 1925, as amended by the 1999 Act.

However, section 1(1) of the 1999 Act provides an exception to this general rule. An attorney can exercise a trustee function of the donor if it relates to land, or the capital proceeds or income from land, in which the donor has a beneficial interest. This is, of course, subject to any provision to the contrary contained in the trust instrument or the power of attorney itself.

5.8 Solicitor-attorneys

Where a solicitor is appointed as attorney, or where it is intended that a particular solicitor will deal with the general management of the donor's affairs, it is recommended that the solicitor's current terms and conditions of business (including charging rates and the frequency of billing) be discussed with and approved by the donor at the time of granting the power.

Since the explanatory information on the prescribed form of EPA is ambiguous about the remuneration of professional attorneys, it is recommended that a professional charging clause be included in the power for the avoidance of doubt.

Where a solicitor is appointed sole attorney (or is reasonably likely to become the sole attorney), or where two or more solicitors in the same firm are appointed and there is no external attorney, the donor should be informed of the potential problems of accountability if he or she should become mentally incapacitated. If necessary, arrangements could be made for the solicitor's costs to be approved or audited by an independent third party in the event of the donor's incapacity.

In a number of cases solicitor-attorneys have disclaimed when it became apparent that the donor's assets were insufficient to make the attorneyship cost-effective. The Law Society's view is that, if solicitors intend to disclaim in such circumstances, they should not take on the attorneyship in the first place, or should warn the donor of this possibility at the time of making the power.

Further guidance is given in the Guide to Professional Conduct (*op. cit.*, Principle 24.03, notes 5,6,7). Solicitors are also reminded that any commission earned should be paid to the donor (see Annex 14G of the Guide to Professional Conduct).

5.9 *The donor's property and affairs*

It may be helpful for solicitors to record and retain information relating to the donor's property and affairs, even where they are not to be appointed as an attorney themselves. The Law Society's *Personal Assets Log*, which is sometimes used when taking will-drafting instructions, could be suitably adapted for this purpose. In addition, there are certain requirements under the Solicitors' Investment Business Rules where solicitors safeguard and administer documents of title to investments, e.g. share certificates.

5.10 *Notification of intention to register the EPA*

Solicitors should explain to the donor that the attorney has a duty to notify the donor in person, and at least three members of the donor's family, of his or her intention to register the EPA with the Public Trust Office if the attorney has reason to believe that the donor is, or is becoming mentally incapable.

It may be helpful to obtain a list of the names and addresses of the relatives at the time the EPA is granted. If the donor would like other members of the family, or friends or close associates to be notified in addition to those on the statutory list, details could be included in the EPA itself or in a separate letter.

In any event, solicitors should encourage donors to tell their family that they have made an EPA and perhaps explain why they have chosen the attorney(s). This may help to guard against the possibility of abuse by the attorney and may also reduce the risk of conflict between family members at a later stage.

5.11 *Disclosure of the donor's will*

Solicitors are under a duty to keep their clients' affairs confidential (The Law Society, *The Guide to the Professional Conduct of Solicitors* (8th edition, 1999) Principle 16.01). However, the attorney(s) may need to know about the contents of the donor's will in order to avoid acting contrary to the testamentary intentions of the donor (for example, by the sale of an asset specifically bequeathed, when other assets that fell into residue could be disposed of instead).

The question of disclosure of the donor's will should be discussed at the time of making the EPA, and instructions should be obtained as to whether disclosure is denied, or the circumstances in which it is permitted. For example, the donor may agree that the solicitor can disclose the contents of the will to the attorney, but only if the EPA is registered and the solicitor thinks that disclosure of the will is necessary or expedient for the proper performance of the attorney's functions.

Principle 24.03, note 4 of the Guide (*ibid.*) gives guidance where the EPA is registered and is silent on the subject of disclosure. Advice may also be sought from the Professional Ethics Division or from the Public Trust Office (see section 13 below).

The attorney also has a common law duty to keep the donor's affairs (including the contents of a will) confidential.

5.12 *Medical evidence*

It may be worth asking the donor to give advance consent in writing authorising the solicitor to contact the donor's GP or any other medical practitioner if the need for medical evidence should arise at a later date (for example, on registration of the power; or, after the power has been registered, to assess whether the donor has testamentary capacity).

5.13 *Safeguards against abuse*

Solicitors should discuss with the donor appropriate measures to safeguard against the power being misused or exploited. This could include notifying other family members of the existence of the power, and how the donor intends it to be used.

The solicitor could also consider offering an auditing service, by inserting a clause into the power requiring the attorney to produce to the solicitor, on a specified date each year, an account of his/her actions as attorney during the last 12 months. If the attorney failed to render a satisfactory account, the solicitor could apply for registration of the power to be cancelled on the grounds of the attorney's unsuitability. Again a charging procedure for this service must be agreed with the donor in advance.

6. Drawing up the EPA

6.1 *The prescribed form*

An EPA must be in the form prescribed by the Enduring Powers of Attorney (Prescribed Form) Regulations in force at the time of its execution by the donor. There have been three sets of regulations and the periods during which they have been in force are:

- 1986 Regulations   10 March 1986 to 30 June 1988
- 1987 Regulations   1 November 1987 to 30 July 1991
- 1990 Regulations   31 July 1991 onwards

Solicitors should ensure that existing EPAs are in the form prescribed on the date they were executed by the donors and that the form they are currently using is the one prescribed by the Enduring Powers of Attorney (Prescribed Form) Regulations 1990 (SI 1990 No. 1376).

6.2 Provided the prescribed form is used, it does not matter whether it is a printed form from a law stationers or whether it is transcribed onto a word-processor, although a law stationer's form is more easily recognisable by third parties. What is essential, however, is that there should be no unauthorised departure from the prescribed form. So, where the donor is to be offered an EPA which is not on a law stationer's form, the solicitor should be absolutely certain that the form complies with the prescribed form regulations. Use of inaccurate or incomplete word-processed forms are common reasons for refusal to register an EPA.

Part A ('About using this form') and the marginal notes must be included in the EPA because the Enduring Powers of Attorney Act requires the prescribed explanatory information to be incorporated in the instrument at the time of execution by the donor (s.2(1) and 2(2), and reg. 2(1) of the 1990 Regulations).

6.3 *Completing the form*

Solicitors should ensure that where alternatives are provided on the form (for example for 'joint' or 'joint and several' appointments, or to specify the extent of the authority granted), the required deletions are made by crossing out the options not chosen by the donor.

There is space on the prescribed form to provide details of two attorneys. Where it is intended to appoint three attorneys, the details of the third attorney may be included in the main document, fitted in to the space after the details of the second attorney.

Where more than three attorneys are to be appointed, details of the first two attorneys should be given in the main document, followed by the words 'and (see additional names on attached sheet)' and the details given on a sheet to be attached to the main document marked clearly 'Names of additional attorneys'.

6.4 About 10 per cent of EPAs are refused registration because of a defect in the form or the wording of the instrument. In some cases, registration may be possible after the filing of further evidence to overcome the defect. Solicitors who have assisted a donor in drawing up an EPA which is subsequently refused registration because of a defect that is material may be liable for the additional costs of receivership, since at that point the donor may not have the capacity to execute a new EPA.

7. Executing the power

7.1 An EPA must be executed by both the donor and the attorney(s). The donor must execute Part B of the prescribed form. The attorney must execute Part C. Where more than one attorney is appointed, each of them must complete a *separate* Part C, the additional sheets having been added and secured to the EPA document beforehand. One Part C cannot be 'shared' by more than one attorney.

The donor must execute the EPA before the attorney(s), because the attorney(s) cannot accept a power which has not yet been conferred. However, execution by the donor and attorney(s) need not take place simultaneously. There is no reason why execution by the attorney(s) should not occur at a later date, provided it happens before the donor loses capacity. It is often advisable for the attorney(s) to sign as soon as possible after the donor.

7.2 Execution by the donor and the attorney(s) must take place in the presence of a witness, but not necessarily the same witness, who must sign Part B or Part C of the prescribed form, as the case may be, and give his or her full name and address.

There are various restrictions as to who can act as a witness, and in particular:

- the donor and attorney must not witness each other's signature;
- one attorney cannot witness the signature of another attorney;
- the marginal notes to Part B of the prescribed form warn that it is not advisable for the donor's spouse to witness his or her signature – this is because of the rules of evidence relating to compellability; and
- at common law, a blind person cannot witness another person's signature.

7.3 If the donor or attorney is physically disabled and unable to sign, he or she may make a mark, and the attestation clause should be adapted to explain this. Alternatively, the donor or an attorney may authorise another person to sign the

EPA at his or her direction, in which case it must be signed by that person in the presence of two witnesses, as described in the marginal notes.

Although the Enduring Powers of Attorney (Prescribed Form) Regulations 1990 do not expressly state that, where someone executes the EPA at the direction of the donor or attorney, he or she must do so in the presence of the donor or attorney, it is essential that the power be executed in their presence in order to comply with section 1(3) of the Law of Property (Miscellaneous Provisions) Act 1989.

If the donor is blind, this should be stated in the attestation clause so that, if an application is made to register the EPA, the Public Trust Office can make enquiries as to how the donor was notified of the intention to register.

8. Copies of an EPA

8.1 The contents of an EPA can be proved by means of a certified copy. In order to comply with the provisions of section 3 of the Powers of Attorney Act 1971, a certificate should appear at the end of each page of the copy stating that it is a true and complete copy of the corresponding page of the original. The certificate must be signed by the donor, or a solicitor, or a notary public or a stockbroker.

9. Notification of intention to register the EPA

9.1 When it is necessary to give notice of the attorney's intention to register the power, the prescribed form of notice (Form EP1) must be used. The donor must be personally served with this notice, and the donor's relatives must be given notice by first class post.

It may be helpful, in the case of the relatives, to send the notice with an accompanying letter explaining the circumstances because, in the absence of such an explanation, there may be cause for concern. Giving an appropriate explanation and information at this stage may prevent the application from becoming contentious.

Although there is no statutory requirement to do so, a copy of the EPA could also be sent to the relatives, in view of the fact that one of the grounds on which they can object to registration is that the power purported to have been created by the instrument is not valid as an enduring power.

9.2 As stated above, the notice of intention to register (Form EP1) must be given to the donor personally. The notice need not be handed to the donor by the attorney. It can be given to the donor by an agent (perhaps a solicitor) acting on the attorney's behalf, and the name of the person who gives notice to the donor must be stated on Form EP2.

Many attorneys, both relatives and professionals, find it distressing to have to inform donors of the implications of their failing mental capacity. Schedule 1 to the Enduring Powers of Attorney Act 1985 makes provision for the attorney to apply to the Public Trustee for dispensation from the requirement to serve notice on anyone entitled to receive it, including the donor.

However, the Public Trustee is reluctant to grant such a dispensation because it is the donor's right, and the right of entitled relatives, to be informed and to have an opportunity to object to registration. A dispensation is only likely to be granted in relation to the donor where there is clear medical evidence to show that notification would be detrimental to the donor's health, and in the case of relatives, only in exceptional circumstances.

10. Statutory wills

10.1 An attorney cannot execute a will on the donor's behalf because the Wills Act 1837 requires a will to be signed by the testator personally or by someone in his or her presence and at his or her direction.

Where a person lacks testamentary capacity, the Court of Protection can order the execution of a statutory will on his or her behalf. The Court's will-making jurisdiction is conferred by the Mental Health Act 1983 – not the Enduring Powers of Attorney Act 1985 – but can be invoked where there is a registered EPA. An application for an order authorising the execution of a statutory will should be considered by solicitors where there is no will or where the existing will is no longer appropriate due to a change of circumstances. In statutory will proceedings, the Official Solicitor is usually asked to represent the testator.

10.2 The Court will require recent medical evidence showing that the donor:

- is incapable, by reason of mental disorder, of managing and administering his or her property and affairs. This evidence should be provided on Form CP3 because, in effect, the Court needs to be satisfied that the donor is a 'patient' for the purposes of the Mental Health Act; and
- is incapable of making a valid will for himself or herself.

The Court's procedure notes PN9 and PN9(A) explain the Court's requirements. Guidance on the relevant tests of capacity can be found in the Law Society/BMA publication *Assessment of Mental Capacity: Guidance for doctors and lawyers* (1995).

11. Support for attorneys

11.1 Section 4(5) of the Enduring Powers of Attorney Act 1985 provides that the attorney may, before making an application for the registration of the EPA, refer to the Court any question as to the validity of the power. However, such an application can only be made when the attorney has reason to believe that the donor is, or is becoming, mentally incapable. The Court will not determine any question as to the validity of an unregistered power in any other circumstances.

11.2 Under section 8 of the Act, the Court of Protection has various functions with respect to registered powers. However, the Court should not be seen as being available to 'hold the hand' of the attorney, who should in normal circumstances be able to act in the best interests of the donor, taking advice where necessary from a solicitor or other professional adviser. It should be noted that, although the Court may interpret the terms of an EPA or give directions as to its exercise, it does not have power to extend or amend the terms of the EPA as granted by the donor.

12. Where abuse is suspected

12.1 If solicitors suspect that an attorney may be misusing an EPA or acting dishonestly and the donor is unable to take action to protect him or herself, they should try to facilitate the remedies that the donor would have adopted if able to do so. In the first instance, the Public Trust Office should be notified and guidance sought from the Court of Protection as to how to proceed. This might include:

- an application to the Court of Protection under the Mental Health Act 1983 for an Order giving authority to take action to recover the donor's funds;

- an application to the Court for registration of the power to be cancelled on the grounds of the attorney's unsuitability and for receivership proceedings to be instituted;
- involvement of the police to investigate allegations of theft or fraud;
- where residential care or nursing homes are involved, using the local authority complaints procedure or involving the relevant registration authority.

13. Further advice

13.1 Solicitors may obtain confidential advice on matters relating to professional ethics from the Law Society's Professional Ethics Division (0870 606 2577) and on practice issues from the Practice Advice Service (0870 606 2522). The Mental Health and Disability Committee is also willing to consider written requests from solicitors for comments on complex cases.

Information and advice can also be obtained from the Customer Services Unit of the Public Trust Office (020 7664 7300).

APPENDIX A: CAPACITY TO MAKE AN ENDURING POWER OF ATTORNEY

A power of attorney signed by a person who lacks capacity is null and void, unless it can be proved that it was signed during a lucid interval. Shortly after the Enduring Powers of Attorney Act 1985 came into force, the Court of Protection received a considerable number of applications to register enduring powers which had only just been created. This raised a doubt as to whether the donors had been mentally capable when they signed the powers. The problem was resolved in the test cases *Re K, Re F* [1988] Ch 310, in which the judge discussed the capacity to create an enduring power.

Having stated that the test of capacity to create an enduring power of attorney was that the donor understood the nature and effect of the document, the judge in the case set out four pieces of information which any person creating an EPA should understand:

1. if such be the terms of the power, that the attorney will be able to assume complete authority over the donor's affairs;
2. if such be the terms of the power, that the attorney will be able to do anything with the donor's property which the donor could have done;
3. that the authority will continue if the donor should be or should become mentally incapable; and
4. that if he or she should be or become mentally incapable, the power will be irrevocable without confirmation by the Court of Protection.

It is worth noting that the donor need not have the capacity to do all the things which the attorney will be able to do under the power. The donor need only have capacity to create the EPA.

The implications of Re K, Re F

The judge in *Re K, Re F* also commented that if the donor is capable of signing an enduring power of attorney, but incapable of managing and administering his or her property and affairs, the attorney has an obligation to register the power with the Court of Protection straightaway. Arguably, the attorney also has a moral duty in such cases to forewarn the donor that registration is not merely possible, but is intended immediately.

The decision in *Re K, Re F* has been criticised for imposing too simple a test of capacity to create an enduring power. But the simplicity or complexity of the test depends largely on the questions asked by the person assessing the donor's capacity. For example, if the four pieces of basic relevant information described by the judge in *Re K, Re F* were mentioned to the donor and he or she was asked 'Do you understand this?' in such a way as to encourage an affirmative reply, the donor would probably pass the test with flying colours and, indeed, the test would be too simple. If, on the other hand, the assessor were specifically to ask the donor 'What will your attorney be able to do?' and 'What will happen if you become mentally incapable?' the test would be substantially harder. There is no direct judicial authority on the point, but it can be inferred from the decision in *Re Beaney (deceased)* [1978] 1 WLR 770, that questions susceptible to the answers 'Yes' or 'No' may be inadequate for the purpose of assessing capacity.

[Adapted from BMA/Law Society, *Assessment of Mental Capacity: Guidance for Doctors and Lawyers* (1995) BMA]

APPENDIX B: CHECKLIST OF DOS AND DON'TS FOR ENDURING POWERS OF ATTORNEY

In taking instructions

DO:

- Assess carefully the donor's capacity to make an EPA.
- Advise the donor fully on both the benefits and the risks.
- Discuss with the donor the suitability of the proposed attorney(s).
- Confirm instructions with the donor personally.
- Clarify and specify arrangements relating to:

  - disclosure of the donor's will;
  - dealing with investment business;
  - making gifts;
  - payment of professional charges.

DON'T:

- Forget that the donor is your client.
- Act on the unconfirmed instructions of third parties.
- Allow third parties to control your access to the donor.

In preparing the EPA

DO:

- Use the current prescribed form of EPA.
- Clarify when the power is to take effect.
- Ensure the power is executed by the donor while still competent.
- Ensure the power is signed by the attorney(s) after the donor has signed.
- Ensure the signatures of donor and attorney(s) are properly witnessed.
- Ensure the power is dated.

DON'T:

- Omit Part A of the form or any of the marginal notes.
- Fail to make the required deletions where alternatives are offered on the form.

- Include restrictions or instructions which are unclear or outside the scope of the Enduring Powers of Attorney Act 1985.

In applying for registration

DO:

- Notify the donor and the required relatives using Form EP1.
- Apply for registration within 10 days of the notification of the last person required to be notified.
- Enclose the original EPA with the application.
- Insert on form EP2 the dates on which the people concerned were notified and the date of the application for registration.
- Send the registration fee with the application.
- Send medical evidence in support of any application to dispense with the requirement to serve notice on the donor.

DON'T:

- Forget that Form EP1 must be given to the donor personally.
- Fail to comply with specified time-limits.

APPENDIX B

Law Society's Gifts of Property Guidelines

Gifts of Property: Implications for Future Liability to Pay for Long-Term Care

Prepared by the Mental Health and Disability Committee (revised March 2000)

1. Elderly people or those nearing retirement may seek advice from solicitors as to the advantages and disadvantages of transferring their home or other property to relatives, even though in some cases they still intend to live in the home. The solicitor's advice will of course vary, according to the individual circumstances of the client, their motivation for making such a gift, and what they are hoping to achieve by it.
2. The following guidelines are designed to assist solicitors, both to ensure that their clients fully understand the nature, effects, benefits, risks and foreseeable consequences of making such a gift, and also to clarify the solicitor's role and duty in relation to such transactions. In particular, consideration is given to the implications of making gifts of property on possible future liability for the payment of fees for residential or nursing home care. This area of law is still under review by the Government, so solicitors should be aware that the law may change.
3. Whilst these guidelines generally refer to the making of 'gifts' they apply with equal force to situations where the disposal of property at a significant undervalue is contemplated.

THE NEED FOR LEGAL ADVICE

4. The Law Society is aware of a number of non-solicitor legal advice services which are marketing schemes for elderly people to effect a gift of property with the intention of avoiding the value of that property being taken into account to pay for residential care. Some make unjustified claims as to the effectiveness of the schemes, or fail to take into account the individual circumstances of clients. Seldom do these schemes highlight the other risks involved in making a gift of the home to members of the family.
5. These guidelines are also intended to assist solicitors to stress the need for clients to obtain proper legal advice, and to highlight the risks of using unqualified advisers.

Who is the client?

6. The solicitor must first be clear as to who s/he is acting for, especially where relatives purport to be giving instructions on behalf of an elderly person. In most cases, it will be the elderly person who owns the home or property so if the solicitor is to act in a transfer the elderly person will be the client. This will be the

assumption for the purpose of these guidelines. It is important to recognise that there is an inevitable conflict of interest between the elderly person and anyone who stands to gain from the transaction, so the elderly person should receive independent advice (see also paras 30–31 below).

7.   The solicitor acting for the elderly person should see the client alone, to satisfy him/herself that the client is acting freely, to confirm the client's wishes and intentions, and to gauge the extent, if any, of family or other influence (see Principle 12.05 of *The Guide to the Professional Conduct of Solicitors* (1999)). It may be necessary to spend some time with the client, talking about wider issues, in order to evaluate these aspects, clarify the family circumstances, and assess whether the client has the mental capacity to make the gift (see Appendix A for details of the relevant test of capacity).

8.   If the client is not already known to the solicitor, it may also be advisable to check whether another solicitor has previously acted for the client, and if so, to seek the client's consent to contact that solicitor, in case there are factors to be taken into account which are not immediately apparent.

The client's understanding

9.   It is important to ensure that the client understands the nature of a gift, that this is what is intended and the long-term implications. Before making any such gift clients should in particular understand:

- that the money or property they intend to give away is theirs in the first place;
- why the gift is being made;
- whether it is a one-off, or part of a series of gifts;
- the extent of the gift in relation to the rest of their money and property;
- that they are making an outright gift rather than, say, a loan or acquiring a share in a business or property owned by the recipient;
- whether they expect to receive anything in return and, if so, how much, or on what terms (e.g. someone who is giving away their house might expect to be able to carry on living there rent free for the rest of their life: but who pays for the insurance and upkeep?);
- whether they intend the gift to take effect immediately, or at a later date – perhaps when they die, or go into residential care;
- that, if the gift is outright, they can't assume that the money or property would be returned to them on request;
- the effect that making the gift could have on their future standard of living;
- the effect that the gift could have on other members of the family who might have expected eventually to inherit a share of the money or property;
- the possibility that the recipient could die first, or become involved in divorce or bankruptcy proceedings, in which case the money or property given away could end up belonging to somebody else;
- that the donor and recipient could fall out and even become quite hostile to one another;
- whether they have already made gifts to the recipient or other people; and
- any other foreseeable consequences of making or not making the gift (some of which are considered below).

The client's objectives

10. The solicitor should establish why the gift of property is being contemplated, and whether the client's objectives will in fact be achieved by the making of the gift

or could be achieved in some other way. In establishing the client's objectives, the following matters may be relevant:

(i) If the objective is to ensure that a particular relative (e.g. a child) inherits the client's home rather than someone else, this can equally well be achieved by making a will.

(ii) If the objective is to avoid inheritance tax on the death of the client, a rough calculation should be made of the client's likely estate to assess the amount of tax which may be payable, and whether other tax saving measures could be considered. The client might not appreciate that the value of the property, together with the remainder of the estate, may not exceed the level at which inheritance tax becomes payable.

The client might also not be aware that if s/he intends to continue living in the home after giving it away, there may be no inheritance tax saving because of the 'reservation of benefit' rules. The consequence might also be to increase the liability to inheritance tax on the death of the relative to whom the gift has been made if s/he dies before the client. Again, other schemes to mitigate these vulnerabilities should be considered.

(iii) If the objective is to relieve the elderly client of the worry and responsibility of home ownership, other ways of achieving this should be discussed, such as making an enduring power of attorney.

(iv) If the client volunteers that a significant part of his/her objective is to try to avoid the value of the home being taken into account in various forms of means-testing, the implications and possible consequences should be explained to the client. These matters are considered in the following paragraphs in relation to liability to pay for long-term care. Alternative measures should also be discussed. The solicitor may also need to consider her/his own position (see paras 28–31 below).

Other reasons for transferring the home

11. There may, of course, be good reasons for transferring the home, or a share in the home, to a relative or another person quite apart from the desire to avoid means-testing. If such reasons exist the transfer should be effected sooner rather than later and it would be worthwhile reciting the reason in the transfer deed. For example:

(a) the home has not been vested in the appropriate names in the first place (e.g. it was funded in whole or in part by a son or daughter but vested in the name of the parent);

(b) a daughter has given up a well-paid job to live in the home and care for an infirm parent in the expectation of inheriting the home on the death of the parent;

(c) the parent has for some years been unable to meet the outgoings or pay for alterations or improvements to the home and these have been funded by a son in the expectation of inheriting the home on the death of the parent;

(d) the home comprises part of a family business (e.g. a farm) which would no longer be viable if the home was 'lost'.

12. If the home is already vested in the joint names of the infirm elderly person and another occupier, or can for justifiable reasons be transferred by the elderly person into joint names, the beneficial interest of the elderly person may, on a means assessment, have little value when subject to the continued rights of occupation of the co-owner.

Severance of a joint tenancy

13. If the home is vested in the joint names of an elderly couple it may be worth considering a severance of the joint tenancy with a view to preserving at least a one-half share for the family. Each spouse can then make a will leaving his or her one-half share to the children. This provides some protection in the event that a caring spouse dies before an infirm spouse but there may be vulnerability to a claim under the Inheritance (Provision for Family and Dependants) Act 1975. It is possible to take this step even after the infirm spouse has become mentally incapable.

IMPLICATIONS OF MAKING THE GIFT

14. A proper assessment of the implications of making a gift of the home, both for the client and for her/his relative(s) can best be achieved by listing the possible benefits and risks. These may include the following:

Possible benefits

- a saving of inheritance tax, probate fees and costs on the death of the client. Although in most cases the existence of a potential liability for inheritance tax will mean that a gift of the home by itself will not avoid vulnerability to means-testing, the high value of homes particularly in London may create this situation;
- avoiding the need to sell the home to pay for charges such as residential care or nursing home fees, thus securing the family's inheritance;
- avoiding the value of the home being taken into account in means-testing for other benefits or services.

Possible risks

- the value of the home may still be taken into account under the anti-avoidance measures in relation to means-testing (see paras 15–27);
- the capital gains tax owner-occupier exemption will apply to the gift, but may be lost thereafter and there will be no automatic uplift to the market value of the home on the client's death;
- the client may never need residential or nursing home care (it has been estimated that less than 6 per cent of people aged 75–85 need residential care), so the risks of giving away the home may outweigh any potential benefits to be achieved;
- if the client does eventually need residential or nursing home care but no longer has the resources to pay the fees him/herself because of the gift, the local authority may only pay for a basic level of care (e.g. a shared room in a home of its choice), so the client may be dependent on relatives to top up the fees if a better standard of care is desired;
- the relatives to whom the gift has been made may fail to keep their side of the understanding, whether deliberately or through no fault of their own. For example, they may:

  - fail to support the client (e.g. by not topping up residential care fees)
  - seek to move the client prematurely into residential care in order to occupy the home themselves or to sell it
  - die suddenly without making suitable provision for the client

- run into financial difficulties because of unemployment or divorce or become bankrupt and in consequence be unable to support the client;

- the home may be lost on the bankruptcy, divorce or death of the relative to whom it has been given, resulting in the client being made homeless if s/he is still living there;
- there may be no inheritance tax saving whilst the client continues to live in the home, yet there could be a liability for inheritance tax if the relative dies before the client;
- the relative to whom the home has been gifted may lose entitlement to benefits and/or services (e.g. social security benefits, legal aid) due to personal means-testing if not living in the home;
- the local authority may decide, having regard to the client's ownership of the notional capital value of the home, rather than the property itself (see paras 18–19 below), that s/he is not entitled to certain community care services, or even to be funded at all for residential care should this be needed.

Anti-avoidance measures

15. The client can be given no guarantees that there is a foolproof way of avoiding the value of the home being taken into account in means-testing, since the anti-avoidance measures in the law enable some gifts to be ignored by the authorities and even set aside by the court. Not only are these measures subject to change from time to time, but it is also unclear how far the authorities will go in order to pursue contributions they believe to be owing to them.

16. In most cases, the intention behind making the gift is the most important factor. Where the intention is clearly to create or increase entitlement to financial support from the local authority, measures can be taken to impose a charge on the asset given away in the hands of the recipients or even to recover the asset itself. However, it is necessary that the authority concerned believe that this was a 'significant' part of the client's intention in making the gift. Using one of the marketed schemes (see para. 4 above) which have been advertised specifically to help people to avoid local authority means-testing may make clear the client's intention.

CHARGES FOR RESIDENTIAL AND NURSING HOME CARE

17. At present, a major cause for concern among many older clients is the fear of having to sell their homes in order to pay for residential or nursing home care in the future, and they may wish to take steps to protect their families' inheritance. It is important that solicitors are familiar with the eligibility criteria for NHS funded nursing home care, the charging and funding arrangements by local authorities for residential and nursing home care (when applicable), when care must be provided free of charge and, if charges may be made, the means-testing rules which are summarised in Appendix B.

Implications of the 'notional capital' rule

18. Where the local authority believes that property has been given away by the client with the intention of creating or increasing entitlement to help with residential care home fees (or nursing home fees where these are payable), then it may decide that the client has 'notional capital' equivalent in value to that of the property given away. If that notional capital value exceeds the capital cut off (currently

£16,000, see Appendix B) the authority may decide that the client is not entitled to any assistance (or any continuing assistance) with the home care fees.

19. In such cases it would be the client who then had to take action if s/he wished to challenge the decision. This may involve the use of the local authority's complaints procedures, as well as the Ombudsman or a judicial review. These may all entail significant legal expense and anxiety for the client as the outcome could not be guaranteed. If a judicial review is necessary it would be the client who had to establish that the authority's decision was *Wednesbury* unreasonable (i.e. the burden of proof would be on the client).

Enforcing payment of fees (where charges may legally be made)

20. Having assessed someone as being in need of residential or nursing home care and then provided that care, the local authority cannot withdraw that provision simply because the resident does not pay assessed contributions. However, the authority can take steps to recover contributions, and in assessing ability to pay may take into account property that has been given away for the purpose of avoiding means-testing.

21. The enforcement provisions available to local authorities are as follows:

    (i)   taking proceedings in the magistrates' court to recover sums due as a civil debt (National Assistance Act 1948, s.56);

    (ii) imposing a charge on any property belonging to the resident, with interest chargeable from the day after death (HASSASSA Act 1983, ss.22 and 24);

    (iii) imposing a charge on property transferred by the resident within six months of going to residential care, or whilst in care, with the intention of avoiding contributions (HASSASSA Act 1983, s.21).

22. Once the debt for unpaid contributions reaches £750, insolvency proceedings could be taken to declare the resident bankrupt, whereupon transactions at an undervalue may be set aside within two years, or within five years if the person made bankrupt was insolvent at the time of the transaction, which is unlikely (Insolvency Act 1986, ss.339–341).

23. Under other provisions, a gift may be set aside without time limit and without bankruptcy, if the court is satisfied that the transfer was made for the purpose of putting assets beyond the reach of a potential creditor or otherwise prejudicing the creditor's interests (Insolvency Act 1986, ss.423–425). This provision is exceptionally wide, and the court has extensive powers to restore the position to that which it would have been had the gift not been made.

24. Although some local authorities have threatened to use insolvency proceedings, few have actually done so, perhaps because of lack of expertise or the prospect of bad publicity. However, with increasing pressures on local authority resources to provide community care services, there is no guarantee they will not do so in the future.

25. The burden of proof remains on the local authority to establish that the purpose behind the gift of the property was to avoid means-testing. But it may be difficult for the donor or his/her relatives to give evidence as to the donor's intentions, and if another purpose of the gift cannot be established or indicated the judge may conclude that it must have been to avoid means-testing.

26. The purpose of the gift will have been discussed in advance with the solicitor, and it would be prudent for the solicitor to retain evidence of the advice given in order to protect him/herself in the event of a subsequent family dispute or professional negligence claim. The file notes and correspondence will normally be covered by legal professional privilege or at least by the duty of confidentiality.

The court will not usually order discovery of a solicitor's file unless there is *prima facie* evidence of fraud, but has done so in similar circumstances on the basis of public policy considerations (*Barclays Bank plc* v. *Eustice* [1995] 1 **WLR** 1238). It is possible that a trustee in bankruptcy, or a local authority bringing proceedings under the Insolvency Act 1986, ss.423–425 may persuade the court to override privilege.

27. In *Yule* v. *South Lanarkshire Council* (1999) 1 CCL Rep 546 Lord Philip held that a local authority was entitled to take account of the value of an elderly woman's home transferred to her daughter over 18 months before the woman entered residential care. The court held that there was no time limit on local authorities when deciding whether a person had deprived themselves of assets for the purposes of avoiding residential care fees.

THE SOLICITOR'S DUTY

28. The solicitor's role is more than just drawing up and registering the necessary deeds and documents to effect the making of the gift. S/he has a duty to ensure that the client fully understands the nature, effect, benefits, risks and foreseeable consequences of making the gift. The solicitor has no obligation to advise the client on the wisdom or morality of the transaction, unless the client specifically requests this.

29. The Professional Ethics Division of the Law Society has advised that the solicitor should follow his/her client's instructions, provided that by doing so, the solicitor will not be involved in a breach of the law or a breach of the principles of professional conduct. Reference is made to Principle 12.02 of *The Guide to the Professional Conduct of Solicitors* (1999), which indicates when instructions must be refused. Solicitors will want to satisfy themselves in each individual case that no breach of the law is involved in the proposed transaction. Having advised the client as to the implications and possible consequences of making the gift, the decision whether or not to proceed remains with the client.

30. Solicitors must also be aware of the possible conflict of interest, or significant risk of such a conflict, between the donor and recipient of a gift. While there is no general rule of law that a solicitor should never act for both parties in a transaction where their interests might conflict, Principle 15.01 of *The Guide to the Professional Conduct of Solicitors* states: 'A solicitor or firm of solicitors should not accept instructions to act for two or more clients where there is a conflict or a significant risk of a conflict between the interests of the clients'. Given the potentially vulnerable position of an elderly client, the solicitor will have to consider carefully whether he can act for the donor and the recipient or whether there is an actual or significant risk of conflict. If the solicitor has initially advised the donor alone as to all the implications of the gift and is satisfied that there is no undue influence and that the donor has capacity, the solicitor may be able to act for both clients in the conveyancing.

31. If the solicitor is asked to act for both parties, the solicitor should make them both aware of the possibility of a conflict of interest and advise one of them to consider taking independent advice. S/he should also explain that as a result of any conflict of interest, a solicitor acting by agreement for both parties may be unable to disclose all that s/he knows to each of them or to give advice to one of them which conflicts with the interests of the other and may have to cease acting for both. Both parties must be content to proceed on this basis, be competent to do so and give their consent in writing. However, if any doubt remains, the solicitor would be advised not to act for both parties.

417

Further reading

[In addition to the relevant books referred to in Appendix F].

Age Concern Fact Sheets available from Age Concern England, FREEPOST, (SWB 30375), Ashburton, Devon TQ13 7ZZ. Tel: 0800 00 99 66:

- No. 10   *Local authority charging procedures for residential and nursing home care*
- No. 11   *Financial support for people in residential and nursing home accommodation prior to 1 April 1993*
- No. 38   *Treatment of the former home as capital for people in residential and nursing home care*
- No. 39   *Paying for care in a residential or nursing home if you have a partner*
- No. 40   *Transfer of assets and paying for care in a residential or nursing home*

APPENDIX A

Capacity to make a gift

The relevant test of capacity to make a gift is set out in the judgment in *Re Beaney (Deceased)* [1978] 1 WLR 770. In that case a 64-year-old widow with three grown up children owned and lived in a three-bedroom semi-detached house. Her elder daughter lived with her. In May 1973, a few days after being admitted to hospital suffering from advanced dementia, the widow signed a deed of gift transferring the house to her elder daughter. The widow died intestate the following year, and her son and younger daughter applied successfully to the court for a declaration that the transfer of the house was void and of no effect because their mother was mentally incapable of making such a gift. The judge in the case set out the following criteria for capacity to make a lifetime gift:

> 'The degree or extent of understanding required in respect of any instrument is relative to the particular transaction which it is to effect. ... Thus, at one extreme, if the subject matter and value of a gift are trivial in relation to the donor's other assets, a low degree of understanding will suffice. But, at the other, if its effect is to dispose of the donor's only asset of value and thus, for practical purposes, to pre-empt the devolution of his estate under [the donor's] will or ... intestacy, then the degree of understanding required is as high as that required for a will, and the donor must understand the claims of all potential donees and the extent of the property to be disposed of.'

It is arguable that, when someone makes a substantial gift, a further point should be considered, namely, the effect that disposing of the asset could have on the donor for the rest of his or her life.

[Adapted from British Medical Association/Law Society, *Assessment of Mental Capacity: Guidance for Doctors and Lawyers* (1995) BMA.]

APPENDIX B

Paying for residential and nursing home care

Charges

Individuals who can afford to pay for a place in a residential care or nursing home may arrange this independently, though it is advisable to seek a 'needs' assessment prior to entering residential or nursing care in order to achieve continuity if local authority funding may be needed in future:

- if met with a refusal to assess in advance, point out that the assessment of need for care provision does not depend upon the need for funding;
- it may also be wise to ensure that the particular home is willing to accommodate residents on local authority funding.

Local authority

Those who enter such a home through an arrangement made by the local authority must pay or contribute to the cost, whether the authority provides or buys in the accommodation:

- each authority must fix a standard weekly charge for its own homes which should represent the true economic cost of providing the accommodation – many have a standard scale of fees geared to their eligibility criteria;
- where the authority purchases a place from an independent home the weekly charge to the resident should represent the cost of the place to the authority;
- residents must generally contribute in accordance with their resources up to the appropriate charge, but no one will be required to pay more;
- the authority either:

  – pays the full fee to the home and collects the resident's contribution, or
  – pays its share whilst the resident and any third party pay the balance;

- a contract with the authority or the home should state what is included in the charge and what are extras.

Health authority

Where a health authority arranges a place in a nursing home under a contractual arrangement the individual remains an NHS patient and no charge is made but social security benefits may be withdrawn or reduced.

It is important to ascertain whether a move from hospital to a private nursing home also involves a transfer of responsibility from the health authority to social services.

Means-testing

When the resident cannot afford the full charge an assessment is made of ability to pay and this is reviewed annually but a resident should ask for re-assessment at any time if this would be beneficial:

- the assessment relates to both income and capital:

  – since April 1993 assessment has been brought largely into line with that for income support, though local authorities retain some discretion;
  – the capital cut-off point is £16,000 but capital above £10,000 will result in a tariff income (an attempt to apply a lower financial threshold before acknowledging need failed in *R* v. *Sefton Metropolitan Borough Council, ex parte Help the Aged* (1997) 1 CCL Rep 57, CA;
  – *notional capital* and *notional income* rules apply as for income support;

- assessment relates only to the means of the resident (unlike for income support where spouses and partners are generally assessed together):

  – there is no power to oblige a spouse/partner to take part *but* spouses are liable to maintain each other (National Assistance Act 1948, s.42) and court action may be taken against a liable relative (s.43)

- jointly owned property may be deemed to be owned in equal shares (but query whether it has a value if a home is occupied by the joint owner);
- since 1996 one-half of occupational and private pensions of the resident are re-routed back to the non-resident spouse;

- the value of the resident's home is disregarded during a temporary stay or:

- if occupied by a spouse/partner, or a relative who is aged 60 or over or incapacitated;
- if occupied by someone else and the local authority exercises its discretion;

- there is a minimum charge payable by all residents and the assessment determines what should be paid above this, but all residents retain a personal expenses allowance (revised annually):

- to be used by the resident for expenditure of personal choice such as stationery, personal toiletries, treats (e.g. sweets, drinks, cigarettes) and presents;
- the authority has a discretion to increase the amount, but it should not be used for top-up to provide more expensive accommodation;

- authorities should carry out a benefits check because they have an incentive to ensure that people in homes are receiving maximum state benefits:

- this should only be with the informed consent of the resident;
- income support will include a *residential allowance* (not for local authority homes).

Power to charge?

In two main situations no charges may be made for the care of an individual:

- where, following discharge from detention under one of the longer treatment sections of the Mental Health Act 1983 (usually s.3 or s.37), he or she requires residential or nursing home care as a result of mental disorder:

- no charge may be made for care as this is deemed 'aftercare' service provision under Mental Health Act 1983, s.117;
- that section places a joint duty on the health and local authorities to provide the services required free of charge, unless it is decided by both that the person is no longer in need of these by virtue of their mental disorder;

- (only applicable to placements in nursing homes) where his or her need is primarily a health care need:

- the health authority must fund the entire cost of the placement and the local authority has no power to purchase such care and pass the costs to the client;
- the only exception is where the nursing care is 'merely ancillary or incidental to the provision of the accommodation' in a nursing home. This will depend on the level and type of care. Most nursing homes placements will be the responsibility of the NHS because a client will not be placed there unless their primary need is for nursing care, i.e. health care.

See *R* v. *North and East Devon Health Authority ex parte Coughlan* (1999) 2 CCL Rep 285; *R* v. *London Borough of Richmond ex parte Watson* (1999) 2 CCL Rep 402.

Regulations and guidance

National Assistance (Assessment of Resources) Regulations 1992 *as amended.*
Circular LAC (99)9 *'Charging for Residential Accommodation Guide' (CRAG)* (copies
available from the Department of Health, PO Box 777, London SE1 6XH;
Fax: 01623 724 524; e-mail: doh@prologistics).

[The above Appendix is adapted from Chapter 19 of this Handbook.]

BBA Guidance on Enduring Power of Attorney and Receivership

FOREWORD

Disabled people are important customers in the financial services sector. Consequently, the Disability Rights Commission welcomes this guidance which addresses the particular needs of customers who use third parties in order to access banking services.

The British Bankers' Association instigated this work after the Disability Rights Commission identified specific difficulties for customers who are not mentally capable of managing or administering their property or affairs and who were disadvantaged as a result of their attorneys being unable to access the best rates of interest offered on internet savings accounts.

Working with the British Bankers' Association, and a number of banks, it became apparent that many bank branch and call centre staff were unclear how to respond when contacted by a person representing such customers.

This guidance sets out how banks can help this specific customer base, ensuring a speedy and helpful response to their queries and requests. I am confident that the British Bankers' Association, the Public Guardianship Officer together with other Government departments and the Disability Rights Commission will continue to work in partnership looking into the question of how banks may operate where there is not an Enduring Power of Attorney or Court of Protection Order.

In the meantime I commend this guidance to members of the British Bankers' Association, and urge banks to refer to it.

Bert Massie
Chairman
Disability Rights Commission

BBA GUIDANCE ON ENDURING POWER OF ATTORNEY AND RECEIVERSHIP

This guidance was drafted by the British Bankers' Association (BBA) in conjunction with the Public Guardianship Officer (PGO) and Disability Rights Commission (DRC) and suggests how banks should deal with:

- People who are appointed as attorneys using an Enduring Power of Attorney (EPA)
- Receivers appointed by the Court of Protection

Please note that:

This guidance does not apply in Scotland or Northern Ireland, where the legal situation is different.

Since we started drafting the guidance the Government has published (June 2003) their draft mental incapacity bill. If enacted (at time of writing there is no Parliamentary time for the bill) this may change the position and we would therefore look to amend the guidance.

We have also identified particular difficulties for customers on low incomes or in receipt of benefit payments who do not have an EPA or a Court of Protection Order. We are talking to Government departments and other interested parties about the desirability of using an 'appointee' to operate an account on behalf of a mentally incapacitated customer if sufficient evidence of mental incapacity can be provided, and the appointee can satisfy the Benefits Agency and bank identification checks. We expect to issue further guidance shortly.

The PGO is keen to ensure that all EPAs are registered at the appropriate time. They intend to raise awareness amongst legal and financial professionals later this year and consider that banks can play a major role in this, by encouraging their staff to tell attorneys that the EPA must be registered if the donor is, or is becoming, mentally incapable.

CONTENTS

- Introduction and general principles
- Enduring Power of Attorney (EPA):

    - Registering an EPA and treatment of accounts during registration period
    - The Disability Discrimination Act and treatment of accounts following registration of an EPA

- Receivership
- Further Information
- Appendices

    1. Specimen Short Order
    2. Specimen Receivership Order of the Court of Protection

Introduction and general principles

A number of instances have been brought to our attention where banks have apparently not treated an attorney appointed under a registered Enduring Power of Attorney (EPA) or a receiver appointed by the Court of Protection (an office of the Supreme Court) in the way that was expected.

The BBA's disability working party and legal advisory panel have, in conjunction with the Public Guardianship Office (PGO) which is the administrative office of the Court, and the Disability Rights Commission (DRC), drawn up this guidance to assist banks in dealing with these customers. Its aim is to ensure that mentally incapacitated customers represented by attorneys and receivers acting on their behalf, are not discriminated against and that bank staff are clear as to their responsibilities.

What is the correct procedure for managing banking for mentally incapacitated customers?

- Where customers, or close family members or friends, approach bank staff to enquire what to do when customers are losing mental capacity, they should be informed that it is possible to prepare an EPA, *providing the customer is still suf-ficiently mentally capable at the time.*

- Where close family members or friends approach bank staff to enquire what to do *when customers have already lost mental capacity* and where there is no EPA in place, they need to be told where they can go for advice. They will need to make an application to the Court of Protection for a 'receiver' to be appointed to manage the customer's financial affairs. To do this they should contact the PGO for further information on the application process. The PGO also produces book-lets on EPAs and receivership (see the 'further information' section at the end of this guidance). Enquirers should also be advised to seek legal advice if they are unsure about their options.

The DRC strongly recommends that banks should act on the principle that attorneys (appointed when mentally incapacitated customers are acting through a registered EPA) *and* receivers *should* have the same equal access to services as the customer would have had. This includes offering credit[1] or particular savings facilities.

Banks need robust procedures in place to provide multi-channel access for people who are appointed to manage the financial affairs of mentally incapacitated people using a registered EPA and for receivers appointed by the Court of Protection. All customers should receive a speedy response to their queries from a member of staff fully familiar with the current policies, practices and procedures. Therefore, bank branch staff and those dealing with enquiries via direct channels such as telephone and internet need to know the options available to people seeking to open and operate accounts on behalf of mentally incapacitated customers. If customer-facing staff do not have this expert knowledge, quick and direct access to a specialist team should be made available. Banks may need to update guidance issued to staff and may need to schedule dedicated staff training.

Neither attorneys nor receivers may delegate their powers – unless delegation is permitted by the terms of the EPA – without the prior agreement of the Court of Protection.

Enduring Power of Attorney (EPA)

An EPA is a legal document enabling a person (the donor) to appoint one or more persons (the attorney/s) to manage their financial affairs and property for them either immediately or when they are no longer mentally capable. The donor must be men-tally capable when they sign the document, but it can come into effect when they choose. The attorney must register the EPA if they think the donor is or is becoming mentally incapable. It would be good practice for bank staff to encourage attorneys to register the EPA in such circumstances.

Anyone can create an EPA provided they have sufficient mental capacity at the time of creation. They are often used by people with Alzheimer's and progressive neu-rological disorders that predominantly affect older people (although it is important to note that their use is not limited exclusively to these groups).

Use of EPAs is increasing. Whilst there are no figures for how many EPAs are in existence, the PGO, which records all registered EPAs, advises that over 13,000 were registered last year and that this number is growing. In addition, with an ageing pop-ulation, increased wealth and more public awareness of EPAs, this number will cer-tainly rise.

The Enduring Power of Attorney Act 1985 introduced this new form of Power of Attorney that was capable of surviving the donor's mental incapacity. An ordinary Power of Attorney ceases to have effect when the donor ceases to have mental ca-pacity and is unable to manage their affairs.

Treatment of an account during registration of an EPA

When the donor is, or is becoming, mentally incapacitated, the EPA must be registered with the Court of Protection. This involves sending the PGO the EPA together with a registration form (available from the PGO – contact details at the end of this guidance). It also involves notifying any relatives of the intention to register. The PGO will then ensure that the EPA can be registered and providing no objections to registration are received, will return the EPA to the attorney, stamped by the Court of Protection. From that point onwards the attorney will have the power to manage the donor's financial affairs.

The Lord Chancellor's Department's guidance for legal practitioners[2] makes this clear:

> 'Once the EPA is registered, the attorney can take over the handling of the donor's property and affairs as specified by the donor in the EPA document. The donor can no longer make financial decisions for themselves unless this has been agreed in advance, although it will always be good practice for the attorney to consult with and involve the donor so far as possible.

If the EPA is already held (but has not been registered) and the donor becomes mentally incapacitated, it should be suspended as a general authority to act until such time as it is registered with the Court of Protection, or the Court of Protection appoints a receiver. While this is happening, the attorney has limited powers to maintain the donor and prevent loss to their money and property. As a result, the attorney may provide instructions for funds to be made available for 'necessaries'.[3] Banks should, therefore, be aware that where they have evidence that the donor has lost capacity, they should not take instructions from the attorney until the EPA has been registered, except for the purposes of maintaining the donor, and/or preventing loss to their money and property.

Banks should, therefore, seek to put in place arrangements so that the account cannot be operated except for the limited purposes mentioned above. Banks may otherwise be liable for any misuse of the account, as they would not be able to rely on the statutory protection given to third parties dealing with attorneys. However, this protection would apply where the bank was not aware that the EPA was being used in circumstances when it should have been registered.

The Disability Discrimination Act and treatment of accounts following registration of an EPA

If the donor has sufficient mental capacity they should not be deprived of their right to manage their own affairs having executed an EPA. There are many cases where customers execute EPAs in anticipation of the need for someone else to operate their account in the future but, whilst they are still mentally capable, do not want to give up control of the account.

Since the registered EPA effectively hands lawful authority to manage the financial and personal affairs of the mentally incapacitated person to the attorney of the EPA, the donor should be excluded from issuing instructions to banks during 'periods of lucidity'. The only exception to this is where the Court of Protection has determined that the EPA should be set aside because the donor has satisfied the court that they can resume management of their financial and personal affairs.

In practice, therefore, if the donor has made an EPA that has subsequently been registered, or had a receiver appointed by the Court of Protection, they cannot regain control of their own affairs without the agreement of the Court of Protection. If they recover the capacity to manage their own affairs, they must apply to the Court of

Protection for an order to revoke the EPA or to remove the receivership. The Court will require medical evidence that the person no longer has a mental disorder or any other condition that affects their capacity to manage their own affairs.

The Disability Rights Commission acknowledges that since the Court of Protection does not monitor the operation of the account by the attorney (as the PGO does in cases where a receiver has been appointed), there is a justification for additional personal terms being imposed upon the attorney to assign to them liability for misuse, on the grounds that such treatment is necessary for the bank to be able to provide services to the disabled person.[4] (Although they also advise that in their opinion the use of the same justification to prevent access to services would not be lawfully justifiable under the DDA.) In other words, banks can, for example, require an attorney to sign an indemnity.

As we have seen, the DRC strongly recommends that in cases involving mentally incapacitated customers, banks should allow attorneys and receivers the same access to services as they would have allowed the original customer if they were not mentally incapacitated. The principal problem that has arisen regarding banking is where the attorney has sought to open an account for the donor, usually in order to obtain a higher rate of interest on the donor's funds. Many accounts with higher interest rates are offered via direct channels, such as internet and telephone banking. In seeking to open such accounts attorneys have experienced difficulties because of banks' strict identification and 'Know Your Customer' rules, which are set by law to comply with requirements on money laundering.

Banks need to follow the spirit as well as the letter of the Disability Discrimination Act. The Act requires 'reasonable adjustments' to prevent their services being impossible or unreasonably difficult for people with disabilities to use.[5] Banks must, therefore, devise procedures that allow attorneys to open and then access accounts, whilst fulfilling 'Know Your Customer' identity requirements. The main issue seems to be that by supplying a security password for internet or telephone banking to the attorney, the bank is in breach of its own terms and conditions on the account. Similarly, if the customer (whilst still mentally capable) passes security information to the attorney, they are likely to be in breach of the terms and conditions of both their account and the Banking Code.[6] Banks have dealt with this in different ways, for example:

- Taking up references on both the attorney and the donor.
- Requiring an indemnity from the attorney.
- Adopting a waiver procedure where they will waive security requirements so that the customer can give the details to the attorney, but only when they accept that by signing the waiver form they are responsible for the attorney's acts.

The DRC's clear view is that preventing access to direct banking services in respect of registered EPA-managed accounts would constitute unlawful disability discrimination under the DDA. So as well as dealing with security issues some banks have put in place a manual workaround to the IT problems surrounding this situation. For example, the account is opened manually and operated through access to specialist teams who are aware of the precise circumstances of the EPA-managed account. The DRC is content with this until such time as the IT problems can be surmounted.

A further issue that has arisen regards the monitoring of registered EPA accounts. The law does not currently stipulate mandatory monitoring of an EPA by the Court of Protection following registration (although the donor can now include a specification in the EPA that an annual account must be presented to the PGO as a safeguard against potential misuse of their funds). Therefore, whilst the Court's role does not include monitoring of the use of the EPA, it may call on an attorney to present accounts at any time or, on the instruction of the donor, may cancel an EPA if these are not satisfactory. The PGO will also follow up any complaints received from third parties regarding the operation of an EPA – including those from banks and other institutions. If these accounts are misused the liability is the attorney's; the bank has no responsibility for monitoring the account beyond its normal obligations in respect of abuse. (So if, for example, the bank was given clear evidence that an account was being misused the bank would be negligent if it did not investigate.)

Although a bank has no duty to monitor the way an attorney operates an account, in cases where the attorney has a restricted authority, there is greater risk the bank might be liable, especially if it permits the use of an account in circumstances that fall outside the terms of the EPA or a subsequent Court Order. In such cases, the PGO also acknowledges that it is not unreasonable for the bank to seek an indemnity from the attorney, given the practical difficulties of monitoring accounts.

Receivership

Where an EPA has not been made and a person is no longer mentally able to handle their own financial affairs, the Court of Protection can appoint a 'receiver' to manage day-to-day finances.

Receivers can be either relatives or friends – 'lay' – or professional such as solicitors or local authority officers. Potential lay receivers apply to the Court to take on the role of receiver. Receiverships are issued where it is considered in the interests of the mentally incapacitated person for this to happen and where assets are shown to be in excess of £16,000. If assets are below £16,000, and if there is no property to be sold, a 'Short Order' may be issued.

The Short Order is an official document of the Court of Protection and will bear its seal. The terms of a Short Order will vary, but it will probably authorise the applicant to receive some or all of the mentally incapacitated person's fund that are held in bank or building society accounts.

Before receivership is granted, the applicant will undergo a basic assessment to find out how suitable they are to be a receiver. In addition, the applicant will be required to take out a security bond to cover any potential financial loss to the mentally incapacitated person.

On appointment, the PGO advises receivers to open a bank account in their name as receiver for the mentally incapacitated client, by taking the court's Receivership Order to the bank or building society where the person's account is held. The PGO reports that in the past branch staff have not always recognised this form. The precise terms of orders vary but they usually authorise the receiver to receive interest, income and benefits on the person's behalf, receive the balance on an account and close an account and transfer the money to an account in Court. Receivers are advised that they should not run an overdraft on the receivership bank account or any account holding money belonging to the mentally incapacitated person without the PGO's agreement, nor can they enter into any other kind of borrowing. Each year the receiver has to provide an account of how they have dealt with the client's money.

Bank branch staff need, therefore, to be familiar with the Short Order and Receivership Order of the Court of Protection both of which carry the Court of Protection's seal (specimen orders are attached at appendices 1 and 2). Staff should also know how to check with their legal department quickly and easily that the Order submitted by a customer when they wish to set up a receivership account is genuine. Some banks deal with these accounts centrally if they consider customers will receive better service this way.

The bank will still need to be satisfied as to the identity of the receiver, who would probably be subject to the usual Know Your Customer procedures. A sensible approach may be for banks to include the receivership order in the list of accepted identification documents for verifying ID or address for account opening.

Before opening a new account or redesignating an existing account into the name of a receiver for the customer, the bank needs to study the Order to establish exactly what powers the receiver has been granted under the terms of the Order.

There is no need for banks to monitor receivership accounts as this is the role of the PGO, and the bank will not be liable if the receiver is not acting properly.

Further information

The PGO produces booklets on EPAs and receivership. These are available from their Customer Services telephone line: 0845 330 2900 or on the their website www.guardianship.gov.uk. This also contains other useful information such as the receivership application pack and EPA registration forms. Banks may well wish to provide links from their own websites to this information.

Other useful sources of information are:

The Disability Rights Commission has been in discussion with a number of banks on the issues relating particularly to Enduring Powers of Attorney and direct banking channels. These are summarised on their website at www.drc-gb.org

Other useful information can be found on the following websites:
www.ageconcern.org.uk
www.alzheimers.org.uk
www.learningdisabilities.org.uk
www.mencap.org.uk
www.guardianship.gov.uk
www.actaps.com
www.caringmatters.dial.pipex.com

Endnotes

1 Though the existing Consumer Credit Act does not allow for attorneys or receivers to sign consumer credit agreements.
2 'Making Decisions: Helping People Who Have Difficulty Deciding For Themselves: A Guide For Legal Practitioners' Lord Chancellor's Department, May 2003.
3 The PGO refers to 'necessaries' as things relating to the maintenance of the donor and any family member they provide for, for example: food, clothing, paying bills/rent/mortgage, organising urgent repairs to the house.
4 See section 20(4)(d) of the DDA 1995.
5 DDA s.21(l).
6 Do not allow anyone else to use your card, PIN, password or other security information. (Paragraph 12.4 of the Banking Code, March 2003 edition.)

APPENDICES

Appendix 1 – Specimen Short Order

01 (SO)

COURT OF PROTECTION   No. SO/[Number]

SHORT ORDER DATED THE [date]

This document is not valid unless it bears the impressed seal of the Court of Protection (in the bottom right hand corner) on all pages

IN THE MATTER OF [Name]

UPON THE APPLICATION OF [Name] (hereinafter called 'The Applicant') of [Address]

AND THE COURT having considered medical evidence IT IS DIRECTED as follows:

1. The Applicant is authorised in the name and on behalf of the said [Client Name] to receive and give a discharge for:

   - the occupational pension to which the said [Client Name] is entitled including any arrears from [Pension Company]
   - the sum of £[Sum] or other the amount standing to the credit of the said [Client Name] on [Type of Account] Account No. [Number] at [Name of Bank] Bank PLC (Building Society)
   - the sum of £[Sum] or other the amount standing to the credit of the said [Client Name] on [Type of Account] Account No. [Number] at [Name of Bank] Bank PLC (Building Society)
   - the sum of £[Sum] under the control of [Name of Person (position)/Company] belonging to the said [Client Name]
   - the sum of £[Sum] or other the amount payable in respect of Policy (Policies) No(s) [Number] taken out by the said [Client Name] on the life of [Name of whose life it is on] deceased with the [Name of Company]

2. The Applicant is authorised to deal with the sums received pursuant to paragraph 1 hereof as follows:

   - to pay the fee (if any) to Dr [Name of Doctor] in respect of providing the medical evidence
   - to pay £[Sum] plus (including) VAT to [Name of Solicitors] Solicitors in respect of their costs in the matter/A detailed assessment of the costs of [Name of Solicitors] incident and consequent upon this application being carried out on the indemnity basis and the said [Name of Solicitors] are to apply to the Court for directions as to payment of the certified amount thereof
   - to pay £70.00 to the Public Guardianship Office (to retain the sum of £70.00) in respect of the Commencement Fee

     – to pay the amount due for the maintenance of the said [Client Name] (including any arrears)
     – to pay the debts of the said [Client Name]
     – to pay the funeral expenses of [Name of deceased] deceased
     – to apply the balance for the general benefit of the said [Client Name]

- to remit the balance to the Building Society or Bank of the Applicant's choice for the credit of a High Interest Account to be opened in the sole name of the said [Client Name]

3. The Applicant is further authorised in the name and on behalf of the said [Client Name]:

   (i)   to receive and give a discharge for the interest due and due to accrue on the said Account which is to be applied for the benefit of the said [Client Name]
   (ii) to withdraw such sums as may from time to time be required from the said Account which are to be applied for the benefit of the said [Client Name]
   (iii) to remit such sums as may from time to time become surplus to the requirements of the said [Client Name] for the credit of the said Account

The passbook relating to the said Account (when opened) is to be held by the Applicant for safe custody.

The Applicant is further authorised in the name and on behalf of the said [Client Name] to keep on foot out of the income of the said [Client Name] premiums payable in respect of Policy/Policies Nos. [Number] with the [Name of Company]

The Applicant is further authorised in the name and on behalf of the said [Client Name] to determine the tenancy of [Address] upon the best terms that can be obtained

The Applicant is further authorised in the name and on behalf of the said [Client Name] to sell or otherwise dispose of the furniture and household effects belonging to the said [Client Name] (other than any items desired to retain) and to apply any proceeds received for the benefit of the said [Client Name]

The Applicant is further authorised to receive and give a discharge for any Premium Bond prize not exceeding £100 to which the said [Client Name] is entitled and to apply the same for the benefit of the said [Client Name]

The Applicant is further authorised to complete such documents as may be required for the assessment of the said liability to pay income tax or to recover any sums due by way of over payment of income tax and to receive and give discharge for any sums which subsequently become payable to the said [Client Name] which are to be applied for the benefit of the said [Client Name]

The Will of the said [Client Name] (and codicil) may be retained for safe custody by Messrs [Name of Solicitors] (solicitors of [Address]) (the solicitors in the matter) but is to be held by them subject (during the lifetime of the patient) to the directions of the Court.

Requested by:
Ref: SO/

Appendix 2 – Specimen Receivership Order

COURT OF PROTECTION   No. XXXXXXXX

FIRST GENERAL ORDER DATED THE XXTH MONTH 200X

This document is not valid unless it bears the impressed seal of the Court of Protection (in the bottom right hand corner) on all pages

IN THE MATTER OF [CLIENT FULL NAME] (hereinafter referred to as 'the Patient')

UPON THE APPLICATION OF [Receiver Full Name] of [Receiver Address] the [Relationship to] the Patient

AND the court having considered medical evidence IT IS ORDERED as follows:

1. The said [Receiver Name] is appointed Receiver in this matter with such powers only as are conferred by this Order or by any subsequent order certificate or direction

2. As from the date hereof so much as may be necessary not exceeding the net income of the Patient is allowed for the maintenance and general benefit of the Patient and for such other purposes as the Court may from time to time direct and insofar as the net income of the Patient may be insufficient for those purposes the Receiver is to apply to the Court for resort to capital

3. The Receiver is authorised in the name and on behalf of the Patient to give any necessary notices of withdrawal and to receive and give a discharge for:

    (a) all social security benefits pensions rents annuities dividends and interest (being so far as holdings on the Bank of England Register are concerned the interest standing in the sole name of the Patient) and any other income (including arrears) of whatever nature and form whatever source to which the Patient is entitled

    (b) the sum of [£amount] other the amount standing to the credit of the Patient and [Receiver name] on joint Current Account No. XXXXXXXX at the [Bank Name] of the [Bank branch] and the said [Receiver Name] is at liberty to transfer the remaining half share into his/her sole name for his/her own use and benefit

4. The Receiver is to deal with any money under her control belonging to the Patient and any specified sums received under this Order as follows:

    (a) to pay the fixed amount of costs hereinafter mentioned

    (b) to apply the balance as a supplement to the Patient's income

5. The Receiver is to account to the Court as and when required and the first of such accounts covering the period to a date one year from the date of this Order is to be submitted within one month from the end of such period

6. The Receiver is authorised in the name and on behalf of the Patient to [insert details] and sign any necessary documents and to lodge the proceeds into Court as hereinafter provided

7. The Receiver is authorised in the name and on behalf of the Patient to [insert details] and sign any necessary documents and to lodge the proceeds into Court as hereinafter provided

8. The Will of the Patient (and codicil) may be retained for safe custody by [insert details] the solicitors in the matter but is to be held by them subject (during the lifetime of the Patient) to the directions of the Court

9. Any securities and documents of the title belonging to the Patient and any jewellery not required for the Patient's own use are to be deposited in the name of the Patient with the Bank at which the Receiver maintains the Receivership Bank account and are to remain so deposited subject (during the lifetime of the Patient) to the directions of the Court

10. The costs of this application are fixed at the sum of £XXX.XX plus VAT and disbursements

11. The lodgements may be made and the fund is to be dealt with as provided in the Lodgement and Payment Schedule and for that purpose the Receiver is authorised in the name and on behalf of the Patient to give any necessary notices of withdrawal.

If you would like the Court to reconsider any of the terms in this Order, then you must ask for a review within 14 days of the Order being entered.

COP Rules 2001, rr.54–55

FIRST LODGEMENT

Lodgement and Payment Schedule

COURT OF PROTECTION **Order date the XXth Month 2003**

Ledger Credit: [Patient Name] – XXXXXXXX

[I. – LODGMENT]

Particulars of Funds to be lodged to the account of the Accountant-General of the Supreme Court	Person to make the Lodgement.	Amounts	
		Money	Securities
		£ p	£ p
Cash representing [insert details]	[insert details]		
Cash representing [insert details]	[insert details]		

APPENDIX D

About Solicitors for the Elderly

Solicitors for the Elderly (SFE) is a unique organisation as membership is open to all lawyers who have established a set level of experience in advising on the legal issues which affect the older client, their family and carer. This criteria reflects the differing specialities of the lawyers who advise their clients in this area, such as solicitors, barristers and legal executives. Membership of SFE ensures that clients and referrers know that the lawyer they see or recommend is specialised and will work to SFE's code of practice.

Objectives of SFE

1. To develop expertise in areas of public and private law relevant to our clients' needs and where there is at present a skills shortage. These include:

    * consent, capacity and substituted decision-making;
    * financial planning, including retirement and long-term care;
    * housing and community care issues;
    * dealing with abuse

2. To continue to exercise the expertise which members of this group will have in the more traditional legal services which older people require, e.g. wills, trusts and probate, Court of Protection, enduring powers of attorney, property matters and litigation.
3. To promote best practice by means of high quality training and the dissemination of information and know-how.
4. To facilitate networking and the building of constructive relationships with statutory voluntary agencies, charities, housing and social care providers, the financial services sector and other interested organisations or individuals.

Membership benefits

* Access to the membership pages of **www.solicitorsfortheelderly.com**.
* Working with charities and voluntary organisations to gain recognition of SFE and to facilitate referral of work to our members.
* Organising a National Conference tailor-made to the needs of our members, qualifying for CPD and reasonably priced.
* Periodical newsletter.
* Raising SFE profile by the production of press releases and contributing to relevant journals, speaking at conferences and other media-related activities.
* Representing SFE at a number of Department of Constitutional Affairs Forums to improve working practice, such as at the Court of Protection.

- Sending news by email of any important issues arising.
- Responding to Government papers and raising issues with relevant bodies which affect clients.

SFE website

Members can access:

- the database of our members;
- profile of members;
- the diary of what SFE has planned both regionally and centrally;
- resource section;
- discussion forums to raise current problems and solutions;
- news on current developments;
- links to relevant web sites;
- free site to recruit staff;
- area to purchase SFE publications, such as our general leaflet and the copy of other leaflets to use for marketing purposes;
- SFE newsletter.

Regional groups

Regional groups provide a vital role within the organisation, which include:

- running training courses locally (qualifying for CPD);
- networking at local level with other lawyers and charities;
- raising the SFE profile through the media;
- developing expertise on a regional basis.

Joining the SFE

To obtain an application form to join SFE please visit our website or write to:

The Administrator
Solicitors for the Elderly
PO Box 110
Colwyn Bay
Wales
LL29 9YJ

APPENDIX E

Contacts

PROFESSIONAL BODIES

The Bar Council
3 Bedford Row
London WC1R 4DB
Tel: 020 7242 0082
www.barcouncil.org.uk

The Law Society

113 Chancery Lane
London WC2A 1PL
Tel: 020 7242 1222
    0870 606 2511 (Library enquiries)
    020 7320 5801 (Probate Section)
    0870 606 2522 (Practice Advice
         Service)
    0870 606 2555 (Practising
         Certificate)
    0870 606 2577 (Professional Ethics
         enquiries)
Fax: 020 7831 0344
DX: 56 Lond/Chancery Ln
www.lawsociety.org.uk
www.solicitors-online.com
www.lawgazette.co.uk
www.guide-on-line.lawsociety.org.uk

Office for the Supervision of Solicitors

Victoria Court
8 Dormer Place
Royal Leamington Spa
Warwickshire CV32 5AE
Tel: 01926 820082
Fax: 01926 431435
DX: 292320 Leamington Spa 4

National Association of Funeral Directors

618 Warwick Road
Solihull
West Midlands B91 1AA
Tel: 0845 230 1343
Fax: 0121 711 1351

Society of Allied and Independent Funeral Directors

3 Bullfields
Sawbridgeworth
Herts CM21 9DB
Tel: 0845 2306777
Fax: 01279 726300
www.saif.org.uk

Solicitors for the Elderly

PO Box 110
Colwyn Bay LL29 9YJ
Tel: 01492 517717
Fax: 01492 517717
www.solicitorsfortheelderly.com

Society of Pension Consultants

St Bartholomew House
92 Fleet Street
London EC4Y 1DG
Tel: 020 7353 1688
Fax: 020 7353 9296
www.spc.uk.com

Society of Trust and Estate Practitioners (STEP)

26 Dover Street
London W14 4LY
Tel: 0207 763 7152
www.step.org

GOVERNMENT

Administrative Court
Administrative Court Office
Royal Courts of Justice
Strand
London WC2A 2LL
Tel: 020 7947 6205
Fax: 020 7947 7845

Care Direct

Tel: 0800 444 000 (freephone)
www.caredirect.gov.uk

Care Standards Inspectorate for Wales (CSIW)

Heol Billingsley
Parc Nantgarw
Nantgarw
Nr Cardiff CF15 7QZ
www.wales.gov.uk/
subisocialpolicycarestandards/

Care Standards Tribunal

18 Pocock Street
London SE1 0BW
Tel: 020 7960 0660
Fax: 020 7960 0661
www.carestandardstribunal.gov.uk

Court of Protection

Archway Tower
2 Junction Road
London N19 5SZ
Tel: 020 7664 7000
Fax: 020 7664 7168
DX: 114750 Archway 2 London

Department of Health

PO Box 777
London SE1 6XH
Tel: 0800 555 777 (Health Literature Line)
Tel: 0845 4647 (NHS Direct)
Tel: 020 7210 4850 (Public Enquiry Line)
www.doh.gov.uk
www.nhs.uk
www.nhsdirect.nhs.uk

Department for Work and Pensions

Correspondence Unit
Room 540
The Adelphi
1–11 John Adam Street
London WC2N 6HT
Tel: 020 7712 2171
Tel: 0800 882200 (Benefit Enquiry Line for People with Disabilities)
Fax: 020 7712 2386

Department of Work and Pensions: Disability Unit

Level 6
Adelphi building
John Adam Street
London WC2N 6HT
Tel: 0800 882200 (Benefit Enquiry Line for People with Disabilities)
www.disability.gov.uk

Department of Work and Pensions: Pensions Service

Tel: 0845 300 1084 (New State Pension Claims)
Tel: 0800 028 1111 (New Minimum Income Guarantee Claims)
Tel: 0800 99 1234 (Pension Credit Enquiries)
Tel: 0845 301 3011 (Pensions Directly into Bank Accounts)
www.thepensionservice.gov.uk

Department of Work and Pensions: Publicity Register

Freepost NWW 1853
Manchester M2 9LV
Tel: 0845 602 4444
Fax: 0870 241 2634

Disability Rights Commission (DRC)

DRC Helpline
Freepost MID02164
Stratford upon Avon CV37 9BR
Tel: 08457 622 633
www.drc-gb.org

Energy Action Grants Agency

Customer Services Manager
Eaga Partnership Ltd
Freepost NEA 12054
Newcastle upon Tyne NE2 1BR
Tel: 0800 316 6011
Fax: 0191 247 3801

Financial Services Authority

25 The North Colonnade
Canary Wharf
London E14 5HS
Tel: 020 7066 1000
Fax: 020 7676 1099
www.fsa.gov.uk

Independent Living Funds

PO Box 7325
Nottingham
NG2 4ZT
Tel: 0845 601 8815
Fax: 0115 945 0948
www.ilf.org.uk

Information Commissioner

Wycliffe House
Water Lane
Wilmslow
Cheshire
SK9 5AF
Tel: 01625 545 740
www.dataprotection.gov.uk

Inland Revenue (Capital Taxes)

Capital Taxes Office
Ferrers House
PO Box 38
Castle Meadow Road
Nottingham NG2 1BB
Tel: 0845 234 1000
Fax: 0845 234 1010
DX: 701201 Nottingham 4
www.inlandrevenue.gov.uk

Law Commission

Conquest House
37–38 John Street
Theobalds Road
London WC1N 2BQ
Tel: 020 7453 1220
Fax: 020 7453 1297
www.lawcom.gov.uk

The Legal Services Commission

85 Gray's Inn Road
London WC1X 8TX
Tel: 020 7759 0000
www.legalservices.gov.uk

Mental Health Act Commission

Maid Marian House
56 Houndsgate
Nottingham NG1 6BG
Tel: 0115 943 7100
Fax: 0115 943 7101
www.mhac.trent.nhs.uk

Mobility Advice and Vehicle Information Service (MAVIS)

Department of Transport
Macadam Avenue
Old Wokingham Road
Crowthorne
Berkshire RG45 6XD
Tel: 01344 661 000
Fax: 01344 661 066
www.dft.gov.uk

439

National Care Standards Commission (NCSC)

St Nicholas Building
St Nicholas Street
Newcastle upon Tyne NE1 1NB
Tel: 0191 233 3600
Fax: 0191 233 3569
www.carestandards.org.uk

Official Solicitor of the Supreme Court

81 Chancery Lane
London
WC2A 1DD
Tel: 020 7911 7127
Fax: 020 7911 7105
DX: 0012 London/Chancery Lane
www.offsol.demon.co.uk

Ombudsman

Financial Ombudsman Service
South Quay Plaza
183 Marsh Wall
London E14 9SR
Tel: 020 7964 1000 (switchboard)
www.financial-ombudsman.org.uk

Health Service Commissioner for England
13th Floor
Millbank Tower
Millbank
London SW1P 4QP
Tel: 020 7217 4051
Minicom: 020 7217 4066

Health Service Commissioner for Wales
5th Floor
Capital Tower
Greyfriars Road
Cardiff CF1 3AG
Tel: 029 2039 4621

Local Government Ombudsman

Millbank Tower
Millbank
London SW1P 4QP
Tel: 020 7217 4620
Fax: 020 7217 4621
www.lgo.org.uk

Beverley House
17 Shipton Road
York YO30 5FZ
Tel: 01904 380200
Fax: 01904 380269

The Oaks No 2
Westwood Way
Westwood Business Park
Coventry CV4 8JB
Tel: 024 7682 0000
Fax: 024 7682 0001

Office of the Legal Services Ombudsman

3rd Floor
Sunlight House
Quay Street
Manchester M3 3JZ
Tel: 0845 601 0794
Fax: 0161 832 5446
DX: 18569 Manchester 7

The Pensions Ombudsman

11 Belgrave Road
London SW1V 1RB
Tel: 020 7834 9144
Fax: 020 7821 0065
www.pensions-ombudsman.org.uk

Pensions Advisory Service (OPAS)

11 Belgrave Road
London SW1V 1RB
Fax: 020 7233 8016
www.opas.org.uk

Public Guardianship Office (PGO)

Archway Tower
2 Junction Road
London N19 5SZ
Tel: 020 7664 7000
Fax: 020 7664 7168
DX: 114750 Archway 2 London
www.guardianship.gov.uk

Royal Courts of Justice

The Strand
London WC2R 1PL
Tel: 020 7936 6000
DX: 44450 Strand WC2

Social Services Inspectorate HQ

Richmond House
79 Whitehall
London
SW1A 2NS
Tel: 020 7210 5484

Supreme Court Costs Office (Court of Protection Section)

Cliffords Inn
Fetter Lane
London
EC4A 1DQ

Treasury Solicitor

Queen Anne's Chambers
28 Broadway
London
SW1H 9JS
Tel: 020 7210 3000

TV Licensing – Concessionary Licensing Centre

Barton House
Bond Street
Bristol
BS19 1TL
Tel: 01272 230130

ACCOMMODATION AND CARE

The Abbeyfield Society
Abbeyfield House
53 Victoria Street
St Albans
Hertfordshire AL1 3UW
Tel: 01727 857 536
Fax: 01727 846 168
www.abbeyfield.com

The Brendoncare Foundation

The Old Malthouse
Victoria Road
Winchester
Hampshire SO23 7DU
Tel: 01962 852133
Fax: 01962 851506
www.brendoncare.org.uk

British Association of Services for the Elderly (BASE)

(Membership, Accounts and Training in England)
119 Hassell Street
Newcastle-under-Lyme
Staffs ST5 1AX
Tel: 01782 661033
Fax: 01782 661033
www.base.org.uk

British Association of Services for the Elderly – Wales (BASE Cymru)

Cardiff Meeting House
43 Charles Street
Cardiff CF10 4GB
Tel: 02920 384545
Fax: 02920 239245

British Nursing Association

The Colonnades
Beaconsfield Close
Hatfield
Hertfordshire AL10 8YD
Tel: 0800 581 691
www.bna.co.uk

Carers UK

20/25 Glasshouse Yard
London EC1A 4JT
Tel: 020 7490 8818
Fax: 020 7490 8824
www.carersonline.org.uk

Crossroads Association

10 Regent Place
Rugby
Warwickshire CV21 2PN
Tel: 0845 450 0350
Fax: 01788 565 498
www.crossroads.org.uk

Elderly Accommodation Council (EAC)

Third Floor
89 Albert Embankment
London SE1 7PT
Tel: 020 7820 1343
Fax: 020 7820 3970
www.housingcare.org

Hospice Information

St Christopher's Hospice
51–59 Lawrie Park Road
Sydenham
London
SE26 6DZ
Tel: 0870 903 3903
www.hospiceinformation.info

Housing Corporation

Maple House
149 Tottenham Court Road
London
W1T 7BN
Tel: 020 7393 2000
Fax: 020 7393 2111
www.housingcorp.gov.uk

The National Association of Park Home Residents (NAPHR)

38B Abergele Road
Colwyn Bay
North Wales
LL29 7PA
Tel: 01492 535 677
Fax: 01492 535 677
www.naphr.co.uk

National Care Homes Association

45–49 Leather Lane
London
EC1N 7TJ
Tel: 020 7831 7090
Fax: 020 7831 7040
www.ncha.gb.com

National House Building Council (NHBC)

Buildmark House
Chiltern Avenue
Amersham
Buckinghamshire HP6 5AP
Tel: 01494 753 363 (non-claims)
Tel: 0870 241 4329 (claims)
www.nhbc.co.uk

Nursing Homes Fees Agency

St Leonard's House
Mill Street
Eynsham
Oxford OX29 4JX
Tel: 01865 733000
Fax: 01865 733001
www.nhfa.co.uk

Registered Nursing Home Association

15 Highfield Road
Edgbaston
Birmingham B15 3DU
Tel: 0121 454 2511
Tel: 0800 074 0194
Fax: 0121 454 0932
www.rnha.co.uk

The Relatives and Residents Association

5 Tavistock Place
London WC1A 9SN
Tel: 020 7916 6055
Fax: 020 7916 6093

COUNSELLING AND ADVICE

Action on Elder Abuse

Astral House
1268 London Road
London SW16 4ER
Tel: 020 8765 7000
Fax: 020 8679 4074
www.elderabuse.org.uk

Age Concern (England)

Astral House
1268 London Road
London SW16 4ER
Tel: 0800 009 966
www.ace.org.uk

Age Concern (Wales)

1 Cathedral Road
Cardiff CF11 9SD
Tel: 029 2037 1566
Fax: 029 2039 9562
www.accymru.org.uk

442

Alzheimer's Society

Gordon House
10 Greencoat Place
London SW1P 1PH
Tel: 020 7306 0606
Fax: 020 7306 0808
www.alzheimers.org.uk

Arthritis Care

Helplines
18 Stephenson Way
London NW1 2HD
Tel: 080 8800 4050
www.arthritiscare.org.uk

The Arthritis Research Campaign

Copeman House
St Mary's Court
St Mary's Gate
Chesterfield
Derbyshire S41 7TD
Tel: 0870 850 5000
Fax: 01246 558 007
www.arc.org.uk

British Heart Foundation

17 Fitzhardinge Street
London W1H 6DH
Tel: 020 7935 0185
Tel: 08450 70 80 70
www.bhf.org.uk

British Medical Association

BMA House
Tavistock Square
London WC1H 9JP
Tel: 020 7387 4499
Fax: 020 7383 6400
www.bma.org.uk

British Red Cross Society

UK Office
9 Grosvenor Crescent
London SW1X 7EJ
Tel: 020 7235 5454
Fax: 020 7245 6315
www.redcross.org.uk

Centre for Policy on Ageing

19–23 Ironmonger Row
London EC1V 3QP
Tel: 020 7553 6500
Fax: 020 7553 6501
www.cpa.org.uk

Child Poverty Action Group (CPAG)

94 White Lion Street
London N1 9PF
Tel: 020 7837 7979
Tel: 0800 99 1234 / 0845 606 5065
(Pension Credit Support)
Fax: 020 7837 6414
www.cpag.org.uk

Citizens' Advice (National Association of Citizens' Advice Bureaux)

Myddelton House
115–123 Pentonville Road
London N1 9LZ
www.citizensadvice.org.uk

Contact the Elderly

15 Henrietta Street
London WC2E 8QG
Tel: 0800 716 543
Fax: 020 7379 5781
www.contact-the-elderly.org

Counsel and Care for the Elderly

Twyman House
16 Bonny Street
London NW1 9PG
Tel: 0845 300 7585 (advice)
Tel: 020 7241 8555 (admin)
Fax: 020 7267 6877
www.counselandcare.org.uk

CRUSE – Bereavement Care

Cruse House
126 Sheen Road
Richmond
Surrey TW9 1UR
Tel: 020 8939 9530
Tel: 0870 167 1677
Fax: 020 8940 7638
www.crusebereavementcare.org.uk

443

Disablement Information and Advice Lines (Dial UK)

St Catherine's
Tickhill Road
Doncaster
South Yorkshire DN4 8QN
Tel: 01302 310 123
Fax: 01302 310 404
www.dialuk.org.uk

DIEL (Telecommunications for the disabled & elderly)

50 Ludgate Hill
London EC4M 7JJ
Tel: 020 7634 8773
Fax: 020 7634 8924

Disability Alliance

Universal House
88–94 Wentworth Street
London E1 7SA
Tel: 020 7247 8776
Fax: 020 7247 8765
www.disabilityalliance.org

Disabled Living Foundation

380–384 Harrow Road
London W9 2HU
Tel: 020 7289 6111 (switchboard)
Tel: 0845 130 9177 (Helpline)
www.dlf.org.uk

Employers Forum for Disability

Nutmeg House
60 Gainsford Street
London SE1 2NY
Tel: 020 7403 3020
Fax: 020 7403 0404

Family Health Service Appeal Authority (FHSAA)

30 Victoria Avenue
Harrogate HG1 5PR
Tel: 01423 530280
Fax: 01423 522034

Help the Aged England

207–221 Pentonville Road
London N1 9UZ
Tel: 020 7278 1114
Fax: 020 7278 1116
www.helptheaged.org.uk

Help the Aged Wales

12 Cathedral Rd
Cardiff CF11 9LJ
Tel: 02920 346 550
Fax: 02920 390 898

Macmillan Cancer Relief

89 Albert Embankment
London SE1 7UQ
Tel: 0808 808 0121
www.macmillan.org.uk

MIND (National Association for Mental Health)

15–19 Broadway
London E15 4BQ
Tel: 020 8519 2122
Fax: 020 8522 1725
www.mind.org.uk

MIND Cymru

3rd Floor
Quebec House
Castlebridge
5–19 Cowbridge Road East
Cardiff CF11 9AB
Tel: 029 2039 5123
Fax: 029 2040 2041

Motability

Goodman House
Station Approach
Harlow
Essex CM20 2ET
Tel: 01279 635 666
Fax: 01279 632 000
www.motability.co.uk

Multiple Sclerosis (MS) Society

MS National Centre
372 Edgware Road
Staples Corner
London NW2 6ND
Tel: 020 8438 0700
www.mssociety.org.uk

National Association of Widows

National Office
48 Queens Road
Coventry CV1 3EH
Tel: 024 7663 4848

National Council of Voluntary Organisations (NCVO)

Regent's Wharf
8 All Saints Street
London N1 9RL
Tel: 020 7713 6161 (general)
Tel: 0800 2798 798 (Helpdesk)
www.ncvo-vol.org.uk

Parkinson's Disease Society

215 Vauxhall Bridge Road
London SW1V 1EJ
Tel: 020 7931 8080
Fax: 020 7233 9908
www.parkinsons.org.uk

Patients Association

PO Box 935
Harrow
Middlesex HA1 3YJ
Tel: 020 8423 9111
Tel: 08456 084455
Fax: 020 8423 9119
www.patients-association.com

Royal Association for Disability and Rehabilitation (RADAR)

12 City Forum
250 City Road
London EC1V 8AF
Tel: 020 7250 3222
Fax 020 7250 0212
www.radar.org.uk

Royal National Institute for the Blind (RNIB)

105 Judd Street
London WC1H 9NE
Tel: 020 7388 1266
Tel: 0845 766 9999 (Helpline)
Fax: 020 7388 2034
www.rnib.org.uk

Royal National Institute for Deaf People (RNID)

19–23 Featherstone Street
London EC1Y 8SL
Tel: 020 7296 8000
Fax: 020 7296 8199
www.rnid.org.uk

Royal United Kingdom Beneficent Association (RUKBA)

6 Avonmore Road
London W14 8RL
Tel: 020 7605 4200
Fax: 020 7605 4201
www.rukba.org.uk

RNID Sound Advantage

1 Metro Way
Welbeck Way
Peterborough PE2 7UH
Tel: 01733 232607
Fax: 01733 361161

Shelter (National Campaign for Homeless People)

88 Old Street
London EC1V 9HU
Tel: 0808 800 4444
Fax: 020 7505 2030
www.shelter.org.uk

The Stroke Association

240 City Road
London EC1Y 8JJ
Tel: 0207 5660 3000
Fax: 0207 490 2686
www.stroke.org.uk

Terence Higgins Trust

National Office
52–54 Grays Inn Road
London WC1X 8JU
Tel: 020 7831 0330
Fax: 020 7242 0121

Veterans Agency

Veterans Agency
Norcross
Blackpool FY5 3WP
Tel: 0800 1692277
Fax: 01253 330561

OTHER USEFUL WEBSITES

Note: preface all (except those marked *) with '**www.**'

Legal research

British and Irish Legal Information Institute (**bailii.org/databases.html#ew**)
Bills before Parliament (**parliament.uk/bills/bills.cfm**)
The Court Service (**www.courtservice.gov.uk**)
Delia Venables' Legal Resources (**venables.co.uk**)
HMSO Acts of Parliament and Statutory Instruments (**legislation.hmso.gov.uk**)
ICLR Law Reports (**lawreports.co.uk**)
Justis (**justis.com**)
Smith Bernal's Casetrack (**casetrack.com**)
United Kingdom Parliament World Wide Web Service
(**parliament.the-stationery-office.co.uk**)

General

Age Concern Institute of Gerontology
(**kcl.ac.uk/kis/schools/life_sciences/health/gerontology/**)
A–Z Care Homes Guide (**carehome.co.uk**)
Bettercaring (**bettercaring.co.uk**)
British Association of Domiciliary Care (**badco.org**)
Caring Decisions (**caringmatters.dial.pipex.com**)
Department of Health – Caring About Carers (**carers.gov.uk**)
Elderly Client Adviser (**ecadviser.com**)
Nursing Older People, RCN Publications (**nursingolderpeople.co.uk**)
Patient UK (**patient.co.uk**)
The Princess Royal Trust for Carers (**carers.org/**)
Retail Price Index (full table) (**devon.gov.uk/dris/economic/retprice.html**)
Royal Commission on Long Term Care for the Elderly, Final Report, March 1999
(**royal-commission-elderly.gov.uk**)
Safe Home Income Plans (SHIP) (**ship-ltd.org/**)
Seniors Network (**seniorsnetwork.co.uk**)
Social Care Institute for Excellence Electronic Library for Social Care (**elsc.org.uk**)
UKcare.net (**ukcare.net**)

APPENDIX F

Further reading

LAW BOOKS AND JOURNALS

Community care law

Clements, L. (2004) *Community Care and the Law*, 3rd edn, Legal Action Group.
Gordon, R. and Mackintosh, N. (1997) *Community Care Assessments*, Sweet & Maxwell.
Jones, R. (looseleaf) *Encyclopaedia of Social Services and Child Care Law*, Sweet & Maxwell.
Mandelstam, M. (2004) *Community Care Practice and the Law*, 3rd edn, Jessica Kingsley Publishers.
Pearl, D. and Hershman, D. (2002) *Care Standards Legislation Handbook*, Jordan Publishing.
Richards, M. (2001) *Long Term Care for Older People: Law and Financial Planning*, Jordan Publishing.
Ridout, P. (2003) *Care Standards: A Practical Guide*, Jordan Publishing.

Disability

Disability Alliance (2003) *Disability Rights Handbook*, 28th edn, Disability Alliance.
Doyle, J. (2003) *Disability Discrimination: Law and practice*, 4th edn, Jordan Publishing.
Cooper, J. (2000) *The Law, Rights and Disability*, Jessica Kingsley Publishing.

Financial management

Aldridge, T. (2000) *Powers of Attorney*, 9th edn, Sweet & Maxwell.
Lush, D. (2001) *Cretney and Lush on Enduring Powers of Attorney*, 5th edn, Jordan Publishing.
Lush, D. (looseleaf) *Heywood & Massey: Court Protection Practice*, 13th edn, Sweet & Maxwell.
Terrell, M. (2003) *A Practitioner's Guide to the Court of Protection*, 2nd edn, LexisNexis UK.
Thurston, J. (2003) *A Practitioner's Guide to Powers of Attorney*, 5th edn, LexisNexis UK.

Health and medical care law

Freeman, M. and Lewis, A. (2000) *Law and Medicine*, Oxford University Press.
Harper, R. S. and Butler-Sloss, E. (1999) *Medical Treatment and the Law: The Protection of Adults and Minors in the Family Division*, Jordan Publishing.

Kennedy, I. and Grubb, A. (2000) *Kennedy and Grubb: Medical Law*, 3rd edn, LexisNexis UK.
Mason, J. K. et al (2002) *Mason and McCall Smith: Law and Medical Ethics*, 6th edn, LexisNexis UK.
McHale, J. and Fox, M. (2003) *Health Care Law: Text and Materials*, Sweet & Maxwell.
Montgomery, J. (2002) *Health Care Law*, reissued 2nd edn, Oxford University Press.

Housing

Arden, A. and Hunter, C. (2002) *Manual of Housing Law*, 7th edn, Sweet & Maxwell.
Arden, A. and Hunter, C. (2003) *Homelessness and Allocations: A Guide to the Housing Act 1996 Parts VI and VII*, Legal Action Group.
Baker, C., Carter, B. and Hunter, C. (2001) *Housing and Human Rights Law*, Legal Action Group.
Madge, N. (2003) *Housing Law Casebook*, Legal Action Group.

Inheritance

Ross, S. (2000) *Inheritance Act Claims: Law and Practice,* Sweet & Maxwell.
Thurston, J. (2001) *A Practitioner's Guide to Inheritance Claims*, LexisNexis UK.
Wright, C. E. et al (looseleaf) *Butterworths Wills, Probate and Administration Service*, LexisNexis UK.

Journals

- British Geriatrics Society (bi-monthly) *Age and Ageing*, Oxford University Press.
- Ark Group (bi-monthly*) Elderly Client Adviser*, Ark Group Publishing.
- Lyon, C. M. and Goddard, J. (monthly) *Journal of Social Welfare and Family Law*, Taylor and Francis Group.
- Harris, N. and Wikeley, N. (quarterly) *Journal of Social Security Law*, Sweet & Maxwell.

Law and the elderly

Ashton, G. R. (looseleaf) *Butterworths Older Client Law Service*, LexisNexis UK.
Ashton, G. R. (1995) *Elderly People and the Law*, Gordon R Ashton, LexisNexis UK.
Endicott, D. and Jones, A. (2002) *Brighouse's Precedents of Wills*, 13th edn, Sweet & Maxwell.
Kessler, J. (2002) *Drafting Trusts and Will Trusts*, 6th edn, Sweet & Maxwell.
Lush, D. and Clarke, H. (2004) *Elderly Clients: A Precedent Manual*, 2nd edn, Jordan Publishing.
Sherrin, C. H et al (2002) *Williams on Wills*, 8th edn, LexisNexis UK.
Smart, J. (2003) *A Practitioner's Guide to Drafting Trusts*, LexisNexis UK.
Taylor, M. and MacDonald, A. (1995) *The Law and Elderly People*, Sweet & Maxwell.
Walker, R. (looseleaf) *Encyclopaedia of Forms and Precedents*, LexisNexis UK (vol.42(1) Wills and Administration).
Whitehouse, C. (2000) *Finance and Law for the Older Client*, LexisNexis UK.
Withers (looseleaf) *Practical Trust Precedents*, Sweet & Maxwell.
Withers (looseleaf) *Practical Will Precedents*, Sweet & Maxwell.

Law Society Publishing

Books and packs published by the Law Society are available through all good legal bookshops and direct from Marston Book Services (Tel. 01235 465 656).

Adam, L. (2001) *Marketing Your Law Firm.*
BMA and Law Society (1995) *Assessment of Mental Capacity: Guidance for doctors and lawyers*, BMJ Books.
Boutall, T. and Blackburn, B. (2001) *Solicitor's Guide to Good Management*, 2nd edn.
Bown-Wilson, D. and Courtney, G. (2002) *Marketing, Management and Motivation.*
Camp, P. (2002) *Solicitors and Financial Services*, 3rd edn.
King, L. (2002) *Probate Practitioner's Handbook*, 4th edn.
Law Society (1991) *Personal Assets Log*, pack of 25 forms.
Law Society (1993) *Your Will: Client Questionnaire*, pack of 25 leaflets.
Law Society (1999) *The Guide to the Professional Conduct of Solicitors*, 8th edn [see also: **www.guide-on-line.lawsociety.org.uk** for updates].
Law Society (2004) *Lexcel Practice Excellence Kit*, 3rd edn.
Law Society (2001) *Solicitors Accounts Manual*, 8th edn.
Law Society (2002) *Family Law Protocol.*
Ling, V. and Pugh, S. (2003) *Understanding Legal Aid: A Practical Guide to Public Funding.*
Moore, M. (2001) *Quality Management for Law Firms.*
Otterburn, A. (2002) *Profitability and Law Firm Management.*
Owston, P. and McCall, S. (2003) *Making a Success of Legal Aid.*
Scrope, H. and Barnett, D. (2002) *Employment Law Handbook.*
Silverman, F. (2003) *Conveyancing Handbook*, 10th edn.
Smith, M. (2002) *Setting Up and Managing a Small Practice*, 2nd edn.
Stewart, H. (2003) *Excellent Client Service.*
Taylor, C. and Postgate, D. (2000) *Advising Mentally Disordered Offenders.*
Webb, N. (2003) *Internet Marketing: Strategies for Law Firms.*

Mental health law

Jones, R. (2002) *Mental Health Act Manual*, 8th edn, Sweet & Maxwell.
Hale, B. (1996) *Mental Health Law*, 4th edn, Sweet & Maxwell.
Bartlett, P. and Sandland, R. (2003) *Mental Health Law: Policy and Practice*, Oxford University Press.
Eldergill, A. (1997) *Mental Health Review Tribunals: Law and Practice*, Sweet & Maxwell.

State benefits

Bonner, D., Hooker, I. and White, R. (2002) *Social Security Legislation 2002: Volume I Non Means Tested Benefits*, Sweet & Maxwell.
Ennals, S. (2003) *Tolley's State and Social Security Benefits: A Practical Guide*, 3rd edn, LexisNexis UK.
Ennals, S. and Self, R. (looseleaf) *Tolley's Social Security and State Benefits*, LexisNexis UK.
Knipe, R. and Tonge, K. (looseleaf) *Butterworths Welfare Law* Smith, LexisNexis UK.
Puttick, K. (2003) *Welfare Benefits 2003*, EMIS Professional Publishing.
Rowland, M. and White, R. (2002) *Social Security Legislation 2002: Volume III Administration, Adjudication and the European Dimension*, Sweet & Maxwell.
Wikeley, N. J. (2002) *Wikeley, Ogus & Barendt: The Law of Social Security*, 5th edn, LexisNexis UK.

Wood, P., Wikeley, N., Paynter, R. and Bonner, D. (2002) *Social Security Legislation 2002: Volume II Income Support, Jobseeker's Allowance, Tax Credits and the Social Fund*, Sweet & Maxwell.

GOVERNMENT PUBLICATIONS

Department of Constitutional Affairs

The Department of Constitutional Affairs has a series of booklets which are available to view on **www.dca.gov.uk/family/mi/**.

- A guide for legal practitioners.
- A guide for social care professionals.
- A guide for healthcare professionals.
- A guide for family and friends.
- Planning ahead – a guide for people who wish to prepare for possible future incapacity.
- A guide for people with learning disabilities.

Department of Health circulars

- DHSS Circular 12/70: The Chronically Sick and Disabled Persons Act 1970.
- DHSS Circular 19/71: Welfare of the elderly: implementation of s.45 of the Health Services and Public Health Act 1968.
- LAC (87) 7: Health and Social Services and Social Adjudications Act 1983: implementation of ss.17, 19 and 20.
- LAC (87) 6: Disabled Persons (Services Consultation and Representation) Act 1986: implementation of ss.4, 8(1), 9 and 10.
- LAC (88) 2: Disabled Persons (Services Consultation and Representation) Act 1986: implementation of ss.5 and 6.
- LAC (93) 7: Ordinary residence.
- LAC (98) 19: Community Care (Residential Accommodation) Act 1998 (mandatory).
- LAC (98) 25: Modernising mental health services – safe, sound and supportive.
- LAC (99) 3: The national service framework for mental health.
- LAC (2000) 3: After-care under the Mental Health Act 1983: s.117 after-care services.
- LAC (2000) 7: 'No secrets' guidance on developing multi-agency policies and procedures to protect vulnerable adults from abuse (mandatory).
- LAC (2001) 1: Intermediate care.
- LAC (2001) 6: Better care, higher standards.
- LAC (2001) 12: National service framework for older people (mandatory).
- LAC (2001) 13: Community equipment services.
- LAC (2001) 18: Continuing care: NHS and local councils' responsibilities.
- LAC (2001) 26: Guidance on free nursing care in nursing homes.
- LAC (2001) 32: Fairer charging policies for home care and other non-residential social services – guidance for councils with social services responsibilities (mandatory).
- LAC (2002) 1: Guidance on the single assessment process for older people (mandatory).
- LAC (2002) 13: Fair access to care services: guidance on eligibility criteria for adult social care (mandatory).
- LAC (2003) 3: After-care services under the Mental Health Act 1983.

- LAC (2003) 7: Guidance on NHS funded nursing care.
- LAC (2003) 14: Changes to local authorities charging regime for community equipment and intermediate care services.
- LAC (2003) 21: Community Care (Delayed Discharges etc) Act 2003 – guidance for implementation.
- Circular CI (92) 34: Social Services Inspectorate implementing caring for people: assessment (from the Chief Inspector dated 14 December 1992 and known as 'the Laming letter' and later clarification).
- HSC 1998/048: Transfer of frail older NHS patients to other long stay settings.
- HSC 1998/220: Standards of NHS hospital care for older people.

Department of Health circulars – Welsh

The following circulars are available from **www.wales.gov.uk**

- 19/00: Charges for residential accommodation.
- 26/00: 'Fully equipped': the provision of equipment to older or disabled people by the NHS and social services in England and Wales (Audit Commission report).
- 27/00: In safe hands: guidance and developing multi-agency policies and procedures to protect vulnerable adults from abuse.
- 03/01: Charges for residential accommodation – CRAG amendment.
- 11/01 and 11a/01: Charges for residential accommodation – CRAG amendment.
- 34/01: Paying for NHS funded care in nursing homes.
- 05/02 and 05a/02: Community care: six weeks support at home for vulnerable people guidance.
- 09/02 and 09a/02: Health and social care for adults: creating a unified and fair system for assessing and managing care.
- 14/02: CRAG amendments.
- 28/02 and 17/03: Fairer charging policies for home care and other non- residential social services.
- 43/02:Intermediate care.
- 10/03: Review of standards and regulations for small care homes for older people in Wales.
- 12/03: NHS funded nursing care in care homes providing nursing: Supplementary Guidance 2003–4.
- 19/03: Charges for residential accommodation – CRAG amendment.
- 21/03: Charges for residential accommodation.
- 24/03: Domiciliary care: implementation of regulations and national minimum standards.

Department of Health directions

- Complaints procedure directions 1990.
- LAC (92) 27: National Assistance Act 1948 (Choice of Accommodation) Directions.
- LAC (93) 10: Secretary of State's approvals and directions for arrangements from 1 April 1993 made under schedule 8 to the National Health Service Act 1977 and ss.21 and 29 of the National Assistance Act 1948.
- LAC (92) 27: National Assistance Act 1948 (Choice of Accommodation) Directions.
- LAC (93) 10: Secretary of State's approvals and directions for arrangements from 1 April 1993 made under schedule 8 to the National Health Service Act 1977 and ss.21 and 29 of the National Assistance Act 1948.

Department of Health general guidance

- Community Care in the Next Decade and Beyond: Policy Guidance (HMSO 1990).
- Care Management and Assessment: Managers' Guide (HMSO 1991).
- Care Management and Assessment: Practitioners' Guide (HMSO 1991).
- Care Management and Assessment: Summary of Practice Guidance (HMSO 1991).
- Getting the Message Across: a Guide to Developing and Communicating Policies, Principles and Procedures on Assessment (HMSO 1991).
- Carers (Recognition and Services) Act 1995 Policy Guidance (HMSO 1995).
- Supporting People – Policy into Practice (DETR Jan 2001).
- Guide to Integrating Community Equipment Services (March 2001).
- NHS Funded Nursing Care Practice Guide and Workbook (August 2001).
- Fair Access to Care Services Policy and Practice Guidance.
- 25 July 2002: Care management for older people with serious mental health problems.
- Fairer Charging for Home Care and other non-residential social services: Policy and Practice guidance – August 2002.
- Discharge from Hospital: Pathway, Process and Practice (Jan 2003).

Department of Work and Pensions publications

The following publications are all available online at www.dwp.gov.uk/resourcecentre/

- A Guide to benefits (MG1)
- A guide to dispute, supersession and appeal (NI260 DMA)
- A guide to housing benefit and council tax benefit (RR2)
- A guide to incapacity benefit (IB1)
- A guide to income support (IS20)
- A guide to non-contributory benefits for disabled people and their carers (HB5)
- A guide to retirement pensions (NP46)
- A guide to the social fund (SB16)
- A guide to widow's benefits (NP45)
- A helping hand for benefits (GL21)
- Caring for someone? (SD4)
- Compensation and social security benefits (GL27)
- Decision-makers guide
- Decisions of the commissioner
- Going into hospital? (GL12)
- Help from the social fund (GL18)
- Help if you live in a residential care home or nursing home (GL15)
- Help with your council tax (GL17)
- Help with your rent (GL16)
- Incapacity benefit (IB203)
- Index of housing benefit and council tax benefit circulars
- Long term ill or disabled? (SD3)
- Minimum income guarantee (for people aged 60 or over) (MIG1L)
- Neligan's digest
- Pension credit – Pick it up it's yours (PC1L)
- Pensioners' guide – England and Wales (PG1)
- Retirement – A guide to benefits for people who are retiring or have retired (RM1)
- Sick and unable to work (SD2)

- Sick or disabled (SD1)
- Social fund guide
- Social security benefit rates (GL23)
- The law relating to child support
- The law relating to social security
- The law relating to war pensions
- The personal capability assessment (IB214)
- What to do after a death in England and Wales (D49)
- Widowed? (GL14)
- Your guide to winter fuel payments 2003

Disability Rights Commission Codes of practice

The following codes of practice are available to view and download from www.drc.gov.uk

- Code of practice for the elimination of discrimination in the field of employment against disabled persons or persons who have had a disability.
- Code of practice: duties of trade organisations to their disabled members and applicants.
- Code of practice (revised): rights of access – goods, facilities, services and premises.

DTI

Current consultations from the DTI are available from **www.dti.gov.uk/er/inform** and previous consultations from **www.dti.gov.uk/er/archive.htm**.

- DTI (2003) Consultation: 'Proposals for Outlawing Age Discrimination in Employment and Vocational Training'.
- DTI (2003) Consultation: 'Equality and Diversity: Age Matters'.

Home Office circulars on mentally disordered offenders

- Home Office Circular 66/90 Provision for Mentally Disordered Offenders.
- Home Office Circular 12/95 Mentally Disordered Offenders – Inter-agency Working.
- Home Office Circular 59/90 Cautioning of Offenders.

Inland Revenue publications

Available to view and download **from www.inlandrevenue.gov.uk**

- Bank and building society interest – A guide for savers (IR110)
- Blind person's allowance (IR170)
- Capital gains tax: An introduction (CGT1)
- Claim pack for incapacity benefit (SSP01)
- Income tax and incapacity benefit IR 144:
- Income tax and pensioners (IR121)
- Inheritance tax: An introduction (IHT3)
- ISAs, PEPs, and TESSAs (IR2008)
- Letting and your home (IR87)
- Living or retiring abroad (IR138)
- Living or retiring abroad? A guide to UK tax on your UK income and pension (IR138)

- Married couple's allowance (FS1 (MCA))
- PAYE Understanding your tax code (P3)
- Personal pension schemes (including stakeholder pension schemes) – A guide for members of tax approved schemes (IR3)
- Self assessment – Your guide (SA/BK8)
- Self assessment: A general guide to keeping records (SA/BK4)
- What to do about tax when someone dies (IR45)

Law Commission

The Law Commission's Report 'Mental Incapacity' (no.231, 1995) is available to view on **www.lawcom.gov.uk**.

National Audit Office

National Audit Office (1999) *Protecting the Financial Welfare of People with Mental Incapacity*, TSO.

Pensions Service publications

Available to view and download from **www.thepensionservice.gov.uk**

- State pensions – Your guide (PM2)
- Occupational pensions – Your guide (PM3)
- Personal pensions – Your guide (PM4)
- Stakeholder pensions – Your guide (PM8)
- State pensions for parents and carers (PM9)
- Pension credit – Pick it up it's yours (PC1L) (PC1L Wales)
- A guide to pension credit (PC10S)
- Your guide to winter fuel payments 2003 (English)
- Your guide to winter fuel payments 2003 (Welsh)
- Direct payment giving it to you straight (DPL1)
- Have your pension paid directly into your account (AC1)
- A guide to state pensions (NP46)

Public Guardianship Office publications

Available to view and download from **www.publictrust.gov.uk**

- Charter standards
- Enduring powers of attorney
- Making an application
- Medical certificate (form)
- Notification letter (form)
- Reaching out (newsletter)
- Receiver's declaration (form)
- Receiver's handbook
- Statement of client's assets and income (form)

OTHER PUBLICATIONS

Age Concern publications

Finance

Managing Debt: A Guide for Older People, Yvonne Gallacher and Jim Gray (2002).
Pensions Handbook 2003: Planning Ahead to Boost Retirement Income, Sue Ward (2002).
Using Your Home as Capital 2003/2004: A Guide to Raising Cash From the Value of Your Home, David McGrath and Cecil Hinton (2003).
Your Rights 2003/2004: A Guide to Money Benefits for Older People, Sally West (2003).
Your Taxes and Savings: A Guide for Older People, Paul Lewis (2002).

Dementia care

Caring for Someone who has Dementia, Jane Brotchie (1998).
Dementia Care: A handbook for residential and day care, 2nd edn, Alan Chapman, Donna Gilmour, Iain McIntosh (2001).
Introducing Dementia: The Essential Facts and Issues of Care, David Sutcliffe (2001).
Promoting Mobility for People with Dementia: A Problem Solving Approach, Rosemary Oddy (1998).

Home and professional care

An Introductory Guide to Community Care, Alan Goodenough (2001).
CareFully: A Handbook for Home Care Assistants, 2nd edn, Lesley Bell (1999).
Counselling and Older People: An Introductory Guide, Verena Tschudin (1999).
Culture, Religion and Patient Care in a Multi-Ethnic Society: A Handbook for Professionals, Alix Henley, Judith Schott (1999).
Home Care: The Business of Caring, Linda How and Lesley Bell (1996).
Money at Home: The Home Care Worker's Guide to Handling Other People's Finances and Belongings, Pauline Thompson (2003).
Moving on From Community Care: The Treatment, Care and Support of Older People in England, Lorna Easterbrook (2003).
Nutritional Care for Older People: A Guide to Good Practice, June Copeman (1999).
Resident's Money: A Guide to Good Practice in Care Homes (1996).
Staying Sane: Managing the Stress of Caring, Tanya Arroba and Lesley Bell (2001).
Their Rights: Advance Directives and Living Wills Explored, Kevin Kendrick and Simon Robinson (2002).
Working with Family Carers: A Guide to Good Practice, Jacqui Wood and Phil Watson (2000).

Health

Better Health in Retirement, Dr Anne Roberts (2001).
Caring for Someone with Cancer, Toni Battison (2002).
Know Your Medicines, 3rd edn, Pat Blair (1997).
Nutritional Care for Older People: A Guide to Good Practice, June Copeman (1999).

Housing

A Buyer's Guide to Retirement Housing: Revised edition, National Council for Housing and Planning and Age Concern (2001).
Housing Options for Older People, Louise Russell (2000).

Policy

Elder Abuse: Critical Issues in Policy and Practice, Phil Slater and Mervyn Eastman (1999).

Age Concern Factsheets

Age Concern England Factsheets are designed to provide practical information for those who wish to help themselves; and a guide for those whose work helps older people. To request individual printed Factsheets, please call the Information Line free on 0800 00 99 66 (7 am–7 pm). A Factsheet subscription service is also available by calling 0870 500 99 66. An asterisk (*) denotes that a Scottish version is also supplied by Age Concern Scotland. All Factsheets are available for viewing and downloading at www.ace.org.uk.

1. Help with heating*
2. Buying retirement housing*
3. Television licence concessions
5. Dental care and older people
6. Finding help at home
7. Making a will*
8. Looking for rented housing*
9. Noise and neighbour nuisance – what you can do*
10. Local authority charging procedures for care homes*
12. Raising income or capital from your home
13. Older home owners: financial help with repairs and adaptations*
14. Dealing with someone's estate*
15. Income tax and older people
17. Housing benefit and council tax benefit
18. A brief guide to money benefits
19. The state pension
20. Continuing NHS health care, 'free' nursing care and intermediate care
21. The council tax and older people
22. Legal arrangement for managing financial affairs*
23. Help with continence
24. Direct Payments from social services
25. Income support (minimum income guarantee) and the social fund.
26. Travel information for older people
27. Arranging a funeral*
28. Information about telephones
29. Funding care home accommodation
30. Leisure and learning
31. Older workers
32. Disability and ageing: your rights to social services*
33. Crime prevention for older people
34. Attendance allowance and disability living allowance
35. Rights for council and housing association tenants*
36. Private tenants rights*
37. Hospital discharge arrangements*
38. Treatment of the former home as capital for people in care homes
39. Paying for care in a care home if you have a partner
40. Transfer of assets and paying for care in a care home
41. Local authority assessment for community care services*
42. Disability equipment and how to get it
43. Obtaining and paying for legal advice*
44. NHS services and older people
45. Fitness for later life
46. Paying for care and support at home
47. Care home closures
48. Pension credit from October 2003

Age Concern Information Sheets

The following Information Sheets are available for viewing and downloading at www.ace.org.uk.

- LC1 – Retiring abroad
- LC2 – Information for older people moving to the UK
- LC3 – The benefits of being an older person: Rights and concessions
- LC4 – How to get information and advice about your investments
- LC5 – Living wills: Advance directives
- LC6 – Holidays for older people
- LC12 – Paying for long-term care and long-term care insurance
- LC13 – Attendance allowance in care homes
- LC14 – The pension credit – questions and answers
- LC15 – Carer's allowance (formerly invalid care allowance (ICA))
- LC16 – Changes to pension and benefit payments
- LC18 – Instructions for my next-of-kin and executors upon my death
- LC20 – Help with health costs for older people
- LC21 – Basic guide to attendance allowance and disability allowance

Child Poverty Action Group publications

- *Welfare Benefits and Tax Credits Handbook 2003/2004*, 5th edn (2003).
- *Council Tax Handbook*, 5th edn (2002).
- *Debt Advice Handbook*, 5th edn (2002).
- *Paying for Care Handbook*, 4th edn (2003).
- *Welfare Rights Bulletin* (bi-monthly).

Help the Aged Information Sheets and Advice Leaflets

The following leaflets can be viewed or downloaded from the Info Point section of the website **www.helptheaged.org.uk**:

Attendance allowance
Beating the blues
Benevolent societies
Bereavement
Bereavement benefits
Better hearing
Better sight
Bladder and bowel weakness
Buying goods and services at home
Can you claim it?
Check your tax
Claiming disability benefits
Community care
Coming out of hospital
Council tax 2003–2004
Equipment for daily living
Equity release plans
Fight the flu
Fire
Fitter feet

Gardening
Going into hospital
Health and ageing
Health benefits
Healthy bones
Healthy eating
Help in your home
Holidays
Home repairs and improvements
Housing matters
Hypothermia
Individual savings accounts
Keep out the cold
Keeping mobile
Leisure ideas
Living alone safely
Managing your savings
Managing your medicines
Neighbours
Oral health

Paying for residential care
Paying for residential care: problems
Pension credit
Pets
Pre-paid funeral plans
Questions on pensions
Residential care

Safety in your home
Security in your home
Sheltered housing
Shingles
The older population
Thinking about money
Welfare benefits for carers

Law Society client leaflets

The Law Society *Customer Guides* are written in plain English and give guidance on dealing with legal issues. They are also available in Arabic, Bengali, Greek, Gujarati, Hindi, Punjabi, Somali, Turkish, Urdu, Vietnamese, and Welsh.

- Client's Charter
- Buying a home
- Renting a property
- Renting a home
- Making a will
- Getting a divorce
- Problems at work
- Setting up in business
- Making a personal injury claim
- Financial matters for the elderly
- Setting up home with your partner
- Using a solicitor

The leaflets may be viewed and downloaded from **www.lawsociety.org.uk**. Orders and enquiries to:

Email law.society@alphamail.co.uk
Fax 01444 871355
Post Data Department, Alpha Mail Ltd, 18 Victoria Way, Burgess Hill, West Sussex RH15 9NF.

Law Society website

The following materials can all be viewed on the Law Society's website at **www.lawsociety. org.uk**.

- *The Disability Discrimination Act 1995: An Essential Guide for Solicitors* (2001).
- *Enduring Powers of Attorney: Guidelines for Solicitors* (1999).
- *Gifts of Property: Implications for Future Liability to Pay for Long-Term Care* (1995).
- '"Proceeds of Crime Act 2002" – it's here and now!' (*Gazette* article, April 2003).
- Money Laundering Warning Card (September 2002).
- Money Laundering Legislation Guidance Pack (February 2002).
- 'Solicitors as gatekeepers' (letter, February 2002).
- *Software Solutions.*
- *Complaints in Probate Matters.*
- *Keeping Clients – A Client Care Guide for Solicitors.*
- *General Notes for Guidance – Example of Client Care Letters.*
- *Handling Complaints Effectively.*

MIND publications

Available to view and download from **www.mind.org.uk**.

- Legal briefing: Advance directives.
- Legal briefing: Aftercare and charging.
- Legal briefing: Clinical negligence.
- Legal briefing: Confidentiality and data protection.
- Legal briefing: Disability Discrimination Act.
- Legal briefing: Rights and powers of the nearest relative.
- Legal briefing: The Human Rights Act 1998.
- Legal Support for black patients (II) – from Diverse Minds magazine article.
- Legal FAQs.
- Mental Health Act 1983 – an outline guide.
- Mind Rights Guide 1: Civil admission to hospital.
- Mind Rights Guide 3: Consent to treatment.
- Mind Rights Guide 4: Discharge from hospital.

Index

461

Understanding Legal Aid

A Practical Guide to Public Funding

Vicky Ling and
Simon Pugh

This is a quick reference guide to the various types of public funding available and the context in which they operate. The emphasis is on the practical implementation of the schemes and wherever possible tactical advice and checklists are provided.

- covers both civil and criminal legal aid schemes
- providing useful insights into other services performed by the Legal Services Commission, such as the Community Legal Service and Public Defender Service
- includes cross-references to official sources of information for other areas.

Written by a leading consultant and a specialist practitioner, *Understanding Legal Aid* is an easily comprehensible guide to undertaking publicly funded work, applicable equally to solicitors, the not-for-profit sector and the Bar.

Available from Marston Book Services:
Tel. 01235 465 656

1 85328 895 0
256 pages
£29.95
2003

The Law Society